A History of Education in Modern Russia

The Bloomsbury History of Modern Russia Series

Series Editors: *Jonathan D. Smele (Queen Mary, University of London, UK) and Michael Melancon (Auburn University, USA)*

This ambitious and unique series offers readers the latest views on aspects of the modern history of what has been and remains one of the most powerful and important countries in the world. In a series of books aimed at students, leading academics and experts from across the world portray, in a thematic manner, a broad variety of aspects of the Russian experience, over extended periods of time, from the reign of Peter the Great in the early eighteenth century to the Putin era at the beginning of the twenty-first.

Published:

Peasants in Russia from Serfdom to Stalin: Accommodation, Survival, Resistance, Boris B. Gorshkov (2018)

Crime and Punishment in Russia: A Comparative History from Peter the Great to Vladimir Putin, Jonathan Daly (2018)

Marx and Russia: The Fate of a Doctrine, James D. White (2018)

A Modern History of Russian Childhood, Elizabeth White (2020)

Marriage, Household and Home in Modern Russia: From Peter the Great to Vladimir Putin, Barbara Alpern Engel (2021)

A History of Education in Modern Russia, Wayne Dowler (2021)

Forthcoming:

Russian Populism: A History, Christopher Ely (2021)

A History of Education in Modern Russia

Aims, Ways, Outcomes

Wayne Dowler

BLOOMSBURY ACADEMIC
LONDON • NEW YORK • OXFORD • NEW DELHI • SYDNEY

BLOOMSBURY ACADEMIC
Bloomsbury Publishing Plc
50 Bedford Square, London, WC1B 3DP, UK
1385 Broadway, New York, NY 10018, USA
29 Earlsfort Terrace, Dublin 2, Ireland

BLOOMSBURY, BLOOMSBURY ACADEMIC and the Diana logo are trademarks of
Bloomsbury Publishing Plc

First published in Great Britain 2022
Paperback edition published in 2023

Copyright © Wayne Dowler, 2022

Wayne Dowler has asserted their right under the Copyright, Designs and Patents Act, 1988, to be identified as Author of this work.

Series design by Sandra Friesen.
Cover image: © Nikolaj Petrovic Bogdanov-Bel'skij, *Study from Life*, circa 1903 (1965). (Photo © The Print Collector/Getty Images)

All rights reserved. No part of this publication may be reproduced or transmitted in any form or by any means, electronic or mechanical, including photocopying, recording, or any information storage or retrieval system, without prior permission in writing from the publishers.

Bloomsbury Publishing Plc does not have any control over, or responsibility for, any third-party websites referred to or in this book. All internet addresses given in this book were correct at the time of going to press. The author and publisher regret any inconvenience caused if addresses have changed or sites have ceased to exist, but can accept no responsibility for any such changes.

Every effort has been made to trace copyright holders and to obtain their permissions for the use of copyright material. The publisher apologizes for any errors or omissions and would be grateful if notified of any corrections that should be incorporated in future reprints or editions of this book

A catalogue record for this book is available from the British Library.

A catalog record for this book is available from the Library of Congress.

ISBN: HB: 978-1-3501-0132-6
PB: 978-1-3502-4520-4
ePDF: 978-1-3501-0133-3
eBook: 978-1-3501-0134-0

The Bloomsbury History of Modern Russia Series

Typeset by Newgen KnowledgeWorks Pvt. Ltd., Chennai, India

To find out more about our authors and books visit www.bloomsbury.com and sign up for our newsletters.

Contents

List of Figures	vii
Preface	ix
Introduction	1
1 Facing West: Peter the Great and His Successors	5
2 Roots of the System: Catherine the Great	23
3 Refining the System: Alexander I and Nicholas I	37
4 Engaging the Public: Alexander II	63
5 Reasserting Authority: Alexander III and Nicholas II	87
6 From Revolution to Revolution: The Duma Period	103
7 Schooling for Socialism: Revolution to Cultural Revolution	123
8 Retrenchment: Stalin to Chernenko	143
9 Ends and Beginnings: Gorbachev to Putin	171
Conclusion	199
Glossary	203
Notes	207
Bibliography	221
Index	231

Figures

2.1	Russian language lesson of Catherine the Great	24
3.1	Pupils of the Smolny Institute of Noble Maidens in the canteen, 1889	59
4.1	An elementary class in 1905	67
4.2	Institutions of education for women	83
5.1	Nikolaj Petrovic Bogdanov-Bel'skij, "Study from Life," *c.* 1903	92
5.2	Types of elementary schools in the early twentieth century	97
6.1	The general education system *c.* 1914	109
8.1	Students listening to their teacher tell a story	146
8.2	Russian teacher holding a book	161
9.1	The education system of the Russian Federation in 2018	190

Preface

In 2018, 63 percent of Russians between the ages of 25 and 34 held tertiary degrees. The comparable figure among the countries of the Organization of Economic Cooperation and Development was 44 percent. Compared to its neighbors and competitors in Western Europe, Russia came late to formal schooling. From the beginning in the early eighteenth century, the state, driven by the need for technological knowledge and a better educated elite for military and administrative service in an expanding empire, took the initiative in promoting education. The need to catch up to its competitors among the great powers led to extensive borrowing from western models of schooling. Nobility and clergy adopted separate educational models while the vast peasant population clung to the religious culture of the past, alienating the social estates and undermining cultural cohesion. Progress was slow. Revenues in the vast empire were limited, and education was rarely a priority. Underfunding of schools was and remains chronic. By the end of the eighteenth century tensions arose between the need for a better educated public to advance the interests of the state and fears among the rulers and elites that education nurtured opposition and threatened the political and social status quo. An enduring pattern of reform followed by partial retrenchment emerged. The nineteenth century witnessed two major state-initiated reforms of education. But what the state could promote the state could impede. Retreat followed reform, but retreat was never total. Only at the beginning of the twentieth century did the state commit to universal primary education. The victorious Communist Party of the Soviet Union pursued that goal after the revolutions of 1917. An important feature of the story of education in Russia and the Soviet Union has been the emphasis placed on the education of girls and women. As early as the reign of Catherine the Great, the state promoted education for foundling boys and girls as well as for girls of the middle and upper social estates. In the 1860s women among the social elite and men among the intelligentsia fought together to create higher education for women. Soviet educators insisted on equality of the sexes in opportunities for education.

This work outlines the story of education in modern Russia from its painful beginnings to its present-day successes. It is a vast topic with many facets and supported by an extensive literature in many languages. I have delved deeply into that literature. In a relatively short work, it is impossible to acknowledge fully the many sources consulted. The endnotes acknowledge the sources of quotations and statistics. Where I have relied extensively on one or two authors in a section, I have noted my indebtedness. I have chosen not to fill the pages with tables of statistics. The extant numbers are often unreliable and contradictory from source to source. Instead, I have used statistics, often rounded, to point to trends and tendencies.

Rather than provide an extensive list of those who have contributed to the making of this book, I offer a blanket thank you. I am indebted and grateful to you all.

Introduction

Education has been integral to modernization in the West since the early seventeenth century. As Russia engaged more closely with its Western neighbors, it encountered technologies, techniques, and tactics that it needed to acquire to defend its interests. As early as the 1640s the tsars were importing experts from the West in leading military and technical roles. At the beginning of the eighteenth century, while continuing to draw on Western experts, Peter the Great also employed foreigners to train a cadre of native Russians capable of assuming roles in the administration and economy of the empire. From these beginnings, schooling was born in Russia. Russia's commitment to education posed questions similar to those faced by other nations. What is the purpose of education? Whom should it serve? What is the appropriate balance between the cultivation of individual personality and larger public and economic goals? Who should control and who should finance learning? What methods of instruction best suit the character and the historical and cultural experience of the population?

Russia's late start in formalizing education and the pressing need to compete with the West dictated extensive borrowing from Western models. Borrowing, however, was complicated by the many differences between the Russian Empire and Western nations. These differences reshaped the Western models of education on which the Russian state drew. Even in the reign of Peter the Great, Russia was a vast territory marked by ethnic, linguistic, and religious diversity. The empire grew further in the eighteenth and early nineteenth centuries. The Soviet Union incorporated even greater diversity, and the Russian Federation of today is the largest and among the most diverse polities in the world. Russia was an autocracy until 1917 that countered size, diversity, and limited state revenues with administrative centralization. Power in the Soviet Union was also centralized through Communist Party control. Education did not escape the centralizing proclivities of the state.

Imperial Russian society was divided into legal social estates: the nobility, the clergy, merchants and townsmen, and peasants, each with defined obligations to the state. A major divide lay between those who paid the poll (head) tax and those who did not. Only the clergy, nobles, some great merchants until 1807, when the tax was reimposed on them, and honorary citizens (eminent artisans, artists, scientists, and other professionals), a rank created in 1832, were exempt from the tax. The tax was phased out in the mid-1880s. The responsibility for paying the tax and other dues fell on the group. Departures from the group left those who remained with a heavier tax burden; understandably leaving was often resisted, impeding social mobility. For a few, education did provide a path to higher status. Social mobility, however, remained arduous throughout the Imperial period, especially for the peasantry. All social estates owed service in one or another form to the state. The Russian nobility had a long tradition of state service. They were highly diverse, scattered around the empire, ranging from the few with thousands of serfs to the many provincial gentry on tiny estates with a handful of male serfs. The latter were the great majority. A significant segment of the nobility were detached from the land. They owed their rank to their service to the state. Roughly half of the peasant population was enserfed until 1861; the rest lived on state or crown lands. Peasant society was for the most part communal. The commune served as a survival mechanism against the vicissitudes of nature and the encroachments of officialdom. The Russian economy until well into the twentieth century rested heavily on agriculture. The small internal market limited the growth of commerce and industry and the role of urban populations.

Education plays a dual role in most countries. It serves to develop intellect and disseminate knowledge among the populace but is also a tool for moral upbringing, the assimilation of shared values, and promotion of allegiance to the nation and responsible citizenship. The Russian language distinguishes between these functions. *Obrazovanie* refers to academic learning, *vospitanie* to moral upbringing, and *obuchenie* to instruction or training. Vospitanie has played a major role in Russian education. Its content has varied from the Enlightenment goal of "the new man" to the Orthodox Church's Law of God and on to communist morality and the new Soviet Man. The line between upbringing and indoctrination is fine; there is room for disagreement as to when it is crossed. Readers are invited to compare Russian practices over the years with those of their own nation before judging the former.

This book tells the story of education in Russia from the time of Peter the Great. Learning and teaching have proceeded, and still proceed, beyond classrooms. This is a history of education in Russia within the confines of organized schools and the nursery. Space constraints limit its scope largely to Russian schools. Only state language and schooling policies toward the many non-Russians of the country are considered here. Each chapter is organized around the regime's aims for education, the many ways in which learning was delivered, and the outcomes of schooling policies and practices, including their reception by the public. In each case I have tried to give some sense of how individuals experienced schooling. Chapter 1 traces the beginnings of formal schooling in Russia in the first half of the eighteenth century and the cultural changes among the social and political elites that education fostered. Chapter 2 treats the beginnings of a system of education under Catherine the Great and the seeds of the future education of Russian women.

The subject of Chapter 3 is the major education reform of Alexander I in the early nineteenth century that attempted and largely failed to create a ladder system of education from elementary to tertiary levels under a newly founded Ministry of National Enlightenment and outlines the restructuring of education by Alexander's brother Nicholas I to accord with the functions within the state of each of the social estates. The reign of Nicholas was marked by the growth of an intelligentsia that grew critical of the regime and its educational practices. From that time the aims of education were increasingly in dispute.

Chapter 4 embraces the Great Reforms carried out by Alexander II: the emancipation of the serfs, the reform of the judicial system, the institution of limited local self-government, the reorganization of the military, and a major reform of education. The early years of Alexander's reign were distinguished by openness and public discussion. The principles of pedagogy were widely and hotly debated. The second half of his reign witnessed a retreat from the principles of the earlier reforms. After a protracted campaign, higher courses for women were opened. Alexander's assassination in 1881 inaugurated the accession of his son Alexander III. His reign and the early years of the reign of Nicholas II are the subject of Chapter 5. These were years of retreat and repression in schooling, especially in the universities. They also witnessed a determined push by progressives through the *zemstvos* (institutions of rural governance) and *dumas* (municipal governments) to advance elementary education among the populace. The divide between the regime and the progressive public sharply widened, culminating in the revolution of 1905. Chapter 6 details the development of educational policies and practices in the interlude of semi-parliamentary government in Russia between the revolution of 1905 and the beginning of the First World War. After a struggle between the new Duma (parliament) and the state, a compromise was reached that saw elementary education make rapid advances.

The pressures of the First World War crushed the old regime in 1917. After a brief interlude in which Russia was ruled by a Provisional Government, a revolution in November brought the Bolsheviks to power. Chapter 7 explores the radical experiments in education conducted by the new communist regime and the problems that its reforms encountered. Experimentation culminated in the "cultural revolution" of the late 1920s that threatened the very existence of schools. Stalin's conservative reordering of education in the 1930s and the efforts of his successors to shape education to perpetuate communist rule in the postwar years form the subject of Chapter 8. The failure of the planned economy to meet the needs of a modernizing society rendered the content of schooling in Soviet Russia increasingly irrelevant to the country's needs. Chapter 9 exams the effort by Mikhail Gorbachev to rescue the communist order, including its system of education. It traces the collapse of the Soviet Union in 1991 that precipitated a fresh round of educational reforms that sought to decentralize and democratize the school system. Those efforts experienced many of the obstacles that had thwarted earlier reforms. Under the presidency of Vladimir Putin, education has been recentralized and again subordinated to the interests of the state.

1

Facing West: Peter the Great and His Successors

The Legacy of Muscovy

Peter the Great has popularly been credited, through force of his mind and will, with raising Russia out of the Asian stagnation of Muscovy into a dynamic Westernizing empire. As is often the case with great leaders, as Peter surely was, the reality was more complex. Muscovy was far from stagnant. The two centuries preceding the coronation of the boy Peter in 1682 had witnessed momentous changes. The princes of Moscow had consolidated the Russian lands under their rule by the end of the sixteenth century. In the early seventeenth century, the newly established Romanov dynasty emerged with autocratic powers that were soon to be enshrined in a comprehensive law code, the *Ulozhenie* of 1649. The conquest of the Kazan' Khanate in the mid-sixteenth century, penetration into Siberia, and the annexation of Ukraine laid the foundations of the future Russian empire. Through natural increase and territorial expansion, the population grew rapidly. Growth further accelerated in the eighteenth century, creating new burdens of administration. As ties of trade with Western Europe grew, so did tensions with neighbors to the west and south. In the seventeenth century, Russia fought wars with Poland, Sweden, and the Ottoman Empire. Trade and the need to outfit the Russian army for wars against militarily sophisticated states brought many Westerners to Russia in the guise of merchants, technical experts, officers, and mercenaries. A large population of West Europeans accumulated in the Foreign Quarter of Moscow by the end of the century.

The Foreign Quarter with its Protestant churches and secular ways provided one counterpoint to traditional Muscovite culture. During the reigns of Peter's father, Tsar Alexis, and of his son, Feodor, a court culture emerged that mingled new religious thinking with a secular interest in poetry, theater, and the reading of Polish and Latin books by an aristocracy increasingly receptive to new Western cultural influences. The tsar hired foreign tutors for his sons; several boyars followed suit. The young Peter grew up in that more worldly court culture and eagerly embraced the practical skills and techniques of the Westerners that he cultivated in the Foreign Quarter. The new religious thinking of the court was sparked by the influx from the 1640s of Orthodox Church clerics from Ukraine. From the late sixteenth century, the Orthodox Church in Ukraine had engaged in a theological struggle with the Jesuits and adherents of the

Uniate Church, which retained the Slavonic liturgy but recognized the authority of the Pope. Orthodox Brotherhoods formed to defend their faith; they operated parochial schools that provided the tool of literacy to Orthodox believers better to equip them to combat the proselytizing of Catholics and Uniates. Borrowing from their rivals, many Orthodox clerics temporarily converted to Catholicism or joined the Uniates in order to study in the schools of the West. The Kiev Latin Academy, founded in the 1630s by the Orthodox, modeled its curriculum on that of the Jesuit Latin grammar schools. Clerics trained at the academy came to Russia in numbers, especially after the annexation of Ukraine by Russia in 1654. Many of them engaged at first in correcting the translations into Slavonic of religious texts from Greek. The reform of the texts that altered the traditional liturgy of Muscovy precipitated a schism in the Russian Orthodox Church in the 1660s. Tsar Alexis ultimately supported the reformers against the so-called Old Believers while at the same time asserting the primacy of the state over the Church. The reformers blamed the schism on the ignorance of an illiterate flock and on a clergy ill-equipped to explain the faith. The new religious thinking at the court and among the Church hierarchy enabled the establishment of the Slavic-Greek-Latin Academy in Moscow in 1685. Its charter affirmed that "it is through wisdom that we distinguish between good and evil in civil and in spiritual matters."[1]

The historian Paul Bushkovitch rightly observed that Peter accelerated "a vehicle that was already moving swiftly, not starting with a slow moving cart."[2] The vehicle, however, was loaded with baggage that exercised a powerful influence on education in Imperial Russia. There were teaching and learning in pre-Petrine Russia but no formal schools. In some Petrine documents the word *shkola* (school) referred to a place to teach and not to a structured institution of learning. Teachers were private individuals, often priests, but also so-called masters of literacy, who taught individuals or small groups for money. The model was that of master and apprentice and not teacher and pupil. Muscovite Orthodox culture was oriented toward the rewards of the afterlife. The ability to read Church Slavonic, the language of religious texts, in order better to understand the path to salvation was seen as a practical skill like carpentry or masonry. In monasteries, learning to read began with a primer (*azbuka*), followed by study of the breviary and later of the Psalter. Much was simply memorized, and most reading was of religious texts. Private teachers used the same method. There was also some highly practical secular learning. During the seventeenth century, government departments increasingly hired literacy masters to teach employees to read and write chancery Russian. All the new ideas and changing mentalities within the Church leadership and among the elites challenged the traditional homogeneous culture of Muscovy. Once the shared culture of all social estates, traditional culture became primarily the culture of the peasantry. For the next century and a half, the state took almost no interest in educating its peasant population.[3]

State Schooling

Peter envisaged a school "from which people could go forth into church service, civilian service, and ready to wage war, to practice engineering and medical art."[4] In practice,

Peter tied education closely to service to the state. The emperor was profoundly influenced by German cameralism. He relied heavily on German personnel in the army, navy, and state offices. The college system of state administration that he established in 1717 was based on German and Swedish models. Each college (government department) had a Russian president and a German vice president. A cameralist state, usually led by a benevolent autocrat, assigned to itself the leading role in securing the welfare of the citizens through central management of the economy and competent state administration. Cameralists equated the welfare of the public with the welfare of the state. Peter rested his legitimacy as ruler less on the claims of heredity or divine right and more on utilitarian service to the general good. Cameralism subordinated individuals to the group to which they belonged and assigned roles in governance and the economy to each group. Central to Peter's vision was the service state. Under Peter, the existing estate structure was legally formalized. The estate structure emerged as critical to the history of education in modern Russia. There were four estates: noble, clergy, urban, and peasant. Each was defined by its duty to state and society. The Table of Ranks of 1722 assigned state service to the nobility. The nobility was not, however, a closed estate. There were fourteen ranks on the Table of Ranks across the military and civilian sectors of state service. Ranks fourteen to seven conferred on the holder personal nobility; the sixth rank and above conferred hereditary nobility. Rank was at least in part tied to educational attainment. The Table of Ranks introduced an element of merit into promotion in state service, although muted in Peter's punitive regime. Some well-educated commoners did advance in state service. The tradition of peasant communalism served only to reinforce the suppression of individualism characteristic of cameralist societies.

Important as cameralism was to Peter's vision, the historian Richard Wortman has identified a new narrative in Petrine Russia that transcended utilitarian borrowings from the West. It portrayed the monarch and the ruling elite as "foreigners or like foreigners," rendered distinct from ordinary Russians by their Western appearance, learning, and manners. *The Honorable Mirror of Youth*, a book of etiquette issued in 1717, detailed standards of polite behavior and the art of genteel conversation, conducted not in Russian but in a foreign language. Court ritual and art emphasized the foreign nature of Russia's rulers. The new title of Imperator (Emperor) signified a ruler-conqueror who conferred progress and civilization on Russians. While utility remained a leitmotif of Peter's reign, the elevation of his wife Catherine to empress and her stylish and extravagant court tied service to refinement and good taste in the Western manner. The narrative associated Catherine and subsequent empresses with the goddess Minerva and women as symbols of civilization and progress.[5] Following Peter's reign, Western sophistication among the nobility emerged as meritorious and justified in their eyes their advancement and position.

Peter regularly played an active personal role in the planning and implementation of major reform projects. That was not the case, especially in the early years of his reign, with regard to schooling. His conception of education leaned heavily on tradition. The emperor's writings contain few thoughts on the organization of schools, their curricula, or the nature of teaching. The occasional references he made suggest that he thought of schools in the traditional way, as workshops in which an individual master trained apprentices. However, his enthusiasm for learning, which he understood primarily as the mastery of practical skills and technology, created a favorable climate for so-called projectors to propose projects that simultaneously created a job for the projector, enhanced the authority and influence of the projects' sponsors in the state, and promised a public benefit.[6] The harsh realities of the Great Northern War with Sweden and a related war with the Ottoman Empire from 1700 to 1713 placed the priority of government on the needs of the military and the war economy. From 1699 to 1716, Peter sanctioned projects for the founding of schools of artillery, mathematics and navigation, medicine, and engineering. They were organized in the traditional manner: a master or in some cases masters who trained apprentices. Reading of Slavonic was required for admission. Students who arrived without it had first to learn it through study of the primer, breviary, and Psalter in the traditional way before entering the school. Mathematics at the Naval Academy was taught in Slavonic. The state made no effort to control what was taught or how. There were no formal classes, set curriculum, enrollment cycles, or standard evaluations of students, the markers of the modern school.

The state provided meager funding for the schools and in some years none at all. Schools functioned under the auspices of various government departments and were rarely seen as budget priorities by department directors. Founders had to scramble for resources. The evolution of the School of Mathematics and Navigation opened in 1701 in Moscow exemplifies the role played by individuals in the gradual formalization of educational institutions. Among many experts that Peter brought to Russia from abroad was Henry Farquharson, a navigation expert. As in the case of many of his hires, Peter had no particular role for him in mind and assigned him no duties on his arrival in Russia. A. A. Kurbatov, who had already engineered several projects and gained Peter's favor, worked in the Armory. He proposed the foundation of a navigation school, first under the auspices of the Armory and later within the Admiralty. The master in the new school was Leonti Magnitskii, a mathematician. Farquharson became a teacher. The school had a preparatory division to teach Russian and basic arithmetic and a higher division for the study of naval skills. Students came from a wide variety of social backgrounds and received a subsidy for their upkeep. They progressed through a series of subjects beginning with arithmetic and culminating in geography and spherical navigation. The subjects were taught one at a time. When the school passed from the Armory to the Admiralty, supervision became stricter: reports on attendance were required; Magnitskii was ordered to offer both morning and afternoon classes; two senior students were assigned to assist with student discipline. More importantly for the future of the school, the roles of Magnitskii and Farquharson were delineated. Magnitskii taught the early subjects in the curriculum and Farquharson the higher subjects.

In 1715 another projector, the French adventurer Joseph de Saint-Hilaire, proposed the establishment of a Naval Academy under the Navy Office. The proposal envisaged a recognizably modern school with rules of administration, a set curriculum, clearly defined duties of school officials, and structured supervision of students. Peter accepted the proposal, and the Academy opened in October 1715. Half of the students of the School of Mathematics and Navigation in Moscow transferred to the Naval Academy, as did Farquharson. The rest remained in Moscow under the direction of Magnitskii. To supplement enrollments, Peter, as he would often do, ordered all the sons over the age of 10 from the most prominent noble families of the country to attend the Academy. Few did so. Saint-Hilaire was soon ousted as director. On his departure, much of the order and rules that he had authored were abandoned, suggesting Peter's indifference to regulation in education.[7] Other schools similarly struggled to survive and attain a solid footing. In addition to the schools mentioned earlier, mining schools opened in Olonets in 1716 and Ekaterinburg in 1721. Although students in all schools were of mixed social origins, the great majority, especially in the schools of the two capitals, were from the nobility. Most of the teachers were foreigners who rarely spoke Russian and taught in their native languages. The schools were chronically underfinanced, often lacked purpose-built facilities, and were poorly equipped. Teachers were paid sporadically and stipends promised to students frequently failed to materialize. Discipline in the schools was harsh; beatings were common. For all their faults, these school/workshops produced a first generation of specialists in a variety of technical disciplines.

With the running down of the Great Northern War from 1713, Peter devoted more time to domestic reform. Perhaps with the aim of providing a better prepared cohort of students to enter the specialist schools, the emperor decreed in 1714 the creation of cipher schools. Admiralty officials charged with implementing the decree complained of its lack of clear direction and detail. Teachers were to be despatched to various part of the empire to teach the children of nobles. In reality the schools were open to children of all free estates. There was no prohibition on the attendance of girls, although few were present. Peter tasked the Admiralty with supervising the schools and supplying the teachers. Teachers in turn were charged with engaging local notables to support the schools and attracting their children into them.[8] The schools were to be located in diocesan centers and towns with monasteries and provide instruction to children aged 10–15 in grammar, arithmetic, and basic geometry. Graduates were to receive a diploma without which they would be forbidden to marry. The admiralty despatched forty-seven teachers to the schools, but half of them soon returned to the capital for lack of students. Between 1714 and 1716 only twelve schools opened; by 1720 there were twenty. The schools won little public support. The nobility avoided them and were soon exempted from compulsory attendance. The sons of the clergy attended the diocesan schools of the Orthodox Church; merchants preferred to keep their children in the family business rather than set them on the path to state service through schooling. They too were soon exempted from attendance.

The scarcity of teachers and students and the high dropout rates of those who did attend resulted in the merger of the cipher schools with the garrison schools in 1744. An army reform of 1705 legally recognized a new cohort of young people called "soldiers' children," that is, the children of army recruits. From 1716, these children received a basic education in garrison schools. Attendance was compulsory. Entering them at age 6 or 7, pupils studied reading, writing, and arithmetic in the lower grades and geometry, fortification, and other military skills in the upper classes. They graduated at age 15 and entered the army ranks. In 1721 some fifty garrison schools with 4,000 students existed. By 1765, 9,000 students attended 108 schools.[9]

An early initiative in vocational training was the "Russian" schools decreed in 1717. The Admiralty operated the schools in centers with a naval presence with the aim of creating a body of capable artisans. Most students were the children of local workers. They learned basic literacy and arithmetic and received training in practical skills such as drafting and construction techniques. Instruction was in vernacular Russian. Stipends provided books, food and lodgings, and even appropriate clothing for pupils in need. Entering at age 5, students remained until they were 15. Russian schools operated in thirteen cities but were chronically handicapped by a lack of mathematics teachers. Nevertheless, hundreds of children acquired basic literacy in these schools. That said, these and other schools in Petrine Russia were unhappy places. Religious texts remained the foundation of literacy. All subjects were taught through drill. Memorization with little or no understanding of the material studied was the norm. The traditional Muscovite notions of child-rearing, based on the biblical nostrum of "spare the rod, spoil the child," prevailed. Discipline was brutal; runaways were common. Lack of funds made physical conditions in the schools nearly intolerable; outbreaks of deadly contagious diseases were chronic. Parents were often reluctant to send their children to school, preferring home education if they could afford it or often none at all if they could not.

With the more utilitarian needs of the state addressed, Peter turned his mind to the larger question of attaining for Russia some of the accoutrements of Western culture. The first public library opened in St. Petersburg in 1714. Most of the books in it had been confiscated from libraries in the recently conquered Baltic provinces. In the same year the emperor purchased the collection of a Dutch anatomist that formed the basis of his St. Petersburg Kunstkamer that opened to the public in 1719. Common in Western Europe, these were collections of natural curiosities that later evolved into museums of anthropology. In the wake of his meeting in Paris with French academicians in 1717, Peter determined to invest his hopes for the spread of higher education in Russia in the creation of a Russian Academy of Sciences. His principal adviser on matters of education was the German cameralist thinker Christian Wolff. Wolff was skeptical of the plan. He urged the emperor first to establish a university in which foreign professors could train Russians for future membership in an academy. With an eye to Russia's image among the cultured nations of Europe, Peter opted to establish an academy of sciences with a university and secondary school attached.

The plan submitted to the Senate for approval in 1724 was ambitious. It envisaged three areas of academic concentration: (1) mathematics and the sciences that rested on mathematics (astronomy, geography, and navigation); (2) physics, including anatomy, chemistry, and botany; and (3) humanities, consisting of antiquities, rhetoric, ancient and modern history, law, politics, and economics. The attached university boasted faculties of law, medicine, and philosophy. The gymnasium (secondary school) was preparatory to admission to the university. Students in the first two grades studied Latin, Greek, German, and French and in the upper grades history, basic mathematics, and geography, as well as the four languages of the early grades. The curriculum did not include Russian language, literature, history, or geography. Most of the teachers were German as was the language of instruction.[10]

The academy opened in 1726, a year after Peter's death. At first it was handsomely funded and equipped. It drew a capable membership of foreign scholars, many from Germany. Leonard Euler, the Swiss mathematician, was an especially distinguished recruit. The dominance of foreigners soon became, however, a source of conflict with the few Russian academicians, an irritation that persisted well into the middle of the century. If the research mission of the academy began well, its teaching mission floundered. Since there were scarcely any students in Russia with a secondary education, the first students of the university came from abroad. When it opened there were eight students. In 1731 there were none. A fresh start was made in 1732 when twelve students were drafted from the Slavic-Greek-Latin Academy, but enrollments remained negligible. The gymnasium, whose purpose was to prepare students for the university, enrolled 120 students in 1726. The numbers fell to 58 in 1727 and to 26 a year later. The students came from the poorer levels of society; many were soldiers' children. Teachers were difficult to recruit, and turnover among them was high. To bolster the flagging enrollments, the Slavic-Greek-Latin Academy seconded twenty students to the gymnasium in 1735. Among them was Mikhail Lomonosov, destined to become one of Russia's greatest scientists and educators. By the time of Peter's death in 1725, there were about two thousand students in various secular schools, and a few hundred in specialist technical schools. In 1724 the Naval Academy had 394 students.[11]

Peter was succeeded on the throne by his wife Catherine I. Catherine was committed to preserving Peter's Westernizing legacy. A number of prominent men, the so-called Learned Guard, strongly supported Peter's agenda for Russia, particularly the goal of spreading general education. Among them was Feofan Prokopovich, whom Peter had appointed as rector of the Kievan Academy. He linked education to state interests and advocated learning in the Russian language instead of in the foreign languages in which it was routinely conducted. Vasilii Tatishchev, a state official and historian, called for the establishment of schools within monasteries in every province to teach secular as well as religious subjects. Ivan Pososhkov, an advocate of mercantilist economics, supported compulsory schooling for peasant children for three or four years. He believed that literate peasants were of greater value to landlords than illiterates. Prince Antioch Kantemir, a poet, satirized those who opposed education, such as clerics who viewed it as heresy and nobles who dismissed it as a waste of effort. All deplored the level of resistance to education in society and called for state coercion to advance learning.[12] The Learned Guard remained influential during the 1730s.

Catherine died in 1727 and was followed by Peter II, Peter the Great's grandson through his first wife Evdokia. The young Peter was a traditionalist, as had been his father, Peter's son Alexei. He decided to move the capital from St. Petersburg back to Moscow, the traditional heart of Muscovy. Fate, however, intervened. Peter II died on his planned wedding day. He was succeeded by Anna, Duchess of Courland. She was the daughter of Peter the Great's half-brother, Ivan. A cabal of boyar aristocrats, led by members of the powerful Dolgorukii and Golitsyn clans, persuaded Anna to agree to conditions that would impose limits on her autocratic powers. At first, Anna agreed but on arriving in Moscow learned that the vast majority of lesser nobles strongly opposed the scheming of the cabal, preferring autocratic to aristocratic rule. She tore up the agreement and assumed autocratic authority.

Most of the educational institutions established in the reign of Anna met narrow military and technical needs and were patterned on the Petrine workshop model. The exception was the Nobles' Land Cadet Corps. Many among the nobility had long chafed against Peter's expectation that they should attend school with commoners and enter the army as privates. In 1731 the government bowed to the pressures and established the Nobles' Land Cadet Corps, the first functioning, recognizably modern, state school in Russia. A charter defined its purpose, organizational structure, and teaching principles as well as setting out regulations on student life and formal methods of assessment, all hallmarks of organized schools. Anna had brought several Baltic Germans from Courland to lead her administration. Field Marshall Count von Münnich, appointed as the corps' director general, modeled the new school on the Berlin Cadet Corps. He staffed the corps with a number of officers who had taught in the Berlin school. The Nobles' Land Cadet Corps provided a means by which the sons of the noble elite could attain commissions as officers without passing through the ranks as ordinary soldiers as Peter had required. The corps admitted only sons of nobles and commissioned officers. It opened in 1732 with two hundred students aged 13–18 from among the sons of the Russian and Baltic nobility. It is notable that the status or wealth of parents of cadets played a secondary role in the rank on the Table of Ranks that they received on graduation. Instead, prior exposure to Western subjects and cultural attainment was a leading criterion, a measure of the cultural capital and presumed merit conferred by familiarity with Western ways. By 1762, some 2,500 nobles had enrolled and about 1,700 had graduated as commissioned officers.

The Nobles' Land Cadet Corps trained not only officers but also future civil servants. Beyond that purpose, the avowed goal of the school was to create in Russia a "true" nobility on the model of Western aristocracies. Students were housed in the Menshikov Palace in St. Petersburg, effectively secluded from outside influences and closely supervised. They were expected to internalize the values of discipline, restraint, and order thought to be the mark of nobility. The regimen was strict, beginning at 4:45 in the morning. Classes ended at 6:00 in the evening. Most of the instruction was conducted in German and later in French. The teaching staff was mostly foreign. The curriculum embraced a wide range of military subjects, including artillery, fencing, fortification, riding, and field tactics, but also provided a broad general education. Subjects included arithmetic, drawing, geography, geometry, physics, Russian language and literature, Greek and Roman history, modern and classical languages, jurisprudence, music, and dancing. Such an encyclopedic curriculum gave the students only a superficial grasp of any single subject. In fact, deep academic achievement was frowned upon by a nobility devoted to the refined manners and aristocratic comportment that distinguished them from other Russians. The reality of daily life in the Cadet Corps was far from the ideal set out in the regulations. Students brought serf servants with them to tend to their whims. Dogs fouled rooms and corridors. Breaches of discipline were common.[13]

There were wide wealth differences within the Russian nobility. The Cadet Corps catered to a small minority. A series of decrees in 1736–7 mandated that all nobles acquire an education suitable for military or civil service. Now at age 7 the sons of nobles were required to register with the Master of Heraldry in St. Petersburg or with the local provincial governor. At age 12 and again at ages 16 and 20 they were subjected to tests set by the state. Sons with noble fathers who owned a hundred or more male serfs as well as boys who had already begun to learn arithmetic and geometry at home by age 12 could continue their schooling at home. All the rest had to enrol in one of a choice of state schools. Failure to meet the state's educational standards resulted in summary enlistment in the navy as common sailors without right of promotion. The draconian threats for noncompliance had little effect on behavior. Many failed to register and remained at home. Noncompliance reached such levels that mass amnesties were periodically issued. Most miscreants were permitted to enter the army as privates.[14]

The decrees of 1736–7 permitted candidates to list their preferred school. Wealth and the preferences expressed were closely correlated. Those who opted for the Nobles' Land Cadet Corps or the Guards, Peter the Great's special regiments, were by far the better off. Only a handful of those who applied for the Cadet Corps came from families with fewer than fifty male serfs. Sons of families with fewer than fifty male serfs (two-thirds of whom had fewer than twenty male serfs) overwhelmingly chose to enter the army directly as privates. The artillery and engineering schools appealed to nobles of moderate means, and the poorest who chose a school over the army went to garrison schools. Those who preferred home education until age 20 were generally wealthier than those who chose technical schools but poorer than Cadet Corps applicants. The choices were dictated by family wealth, father's rank, influential connections, and early exposure to Western ideas. Those who were best connected grasped the cultural capital inherent in Western culture. They perpetuated their family dominance by pursuing it.

Anna died in 1740 after naming her grandnephew Ivan VI, a 2-month-old baby, as her heir under the regency of his mother. During Anna's reign, resentment against the predominance of foreigners in government had grown among Russians. The new regime of the little Ivan promised more of the same. The regent appointed Germans in leading roles. A complex of conspiracies ended in late 1741 with the imprisonment of baby Ivan and the installation of the daughter of Peter the Great as Empress Elizabeth. Several of the Germans in high office were exiled and Russians put in their place. While many of the educational institutions founded under the new empress addressed narrow utilitarian needs as in the past, Elizabeth cloaked herself in the mantle of defender of science and promoter of civic virtue. In that guise she issued a new charter in 1747 for the Academy of Sciences, enabled the founding of the University of Moscow in 1755, and established an Academy of Arts at the university in 1758.

The Academy of Sciences needed special attention. Tensions between the foreign academicians who predominated in it and the handful of Russian academicians had disrupted the work of the academy and tarnished its image abroad. A rift had emerged between those who saw the academy as a body of pure theoretical research and others who believed its mission included the provision of practical solutions to the nation's needs. In 1746 Elizabeth moved to Russianize the administration of the academy with the appointment of Kiril Razumovskii as president. The appointment had little effect as day-to-day operations remained under the control of the academy's German secretary. The new charter of 1747 separated academicians from professors in the academy's university and excluded the humanities from the academy while retaining them in the university. The charter repositioned the academy as a scientific department of the state, tasked with addressing the practical problems faced by government departments. The charter gave precedence to the teaching of science in the academy's university over the study of languages. It called for the admission to the university of thirty stipendiary students each year, young men of all ranks, who were knowledgeable in Latin, the language of science. Enrollments languished, however; by 1783 there were two students and only three in 1796.[15]

The most distinguished Russian member of the Academy of Sciences was Mikhail Lomonosov. Born a commoner in a northern village near the mouth of the Dvina River on the White Sea, Lomonosov was exposed in his youth to Western influences through the presence of the traders and agents of the London-based Muscovy trading company in the region. In 1730 at age 20, he enrolled in the Slavic-Greek-Latin Academy where he learned Latin. After five years of study, his teachers sent him to the Academy of Sciences. There he was a rare Russian among the predominantly German students. After a year, the Academy sent him to the University of Marburg and then on to Freiburg. He returned to Russia in 1741. By 1745 he had become a full member of the academy and a professor of chemistry. A brilliant experimenter in several scientific fields, a man of literature, and a poet, Lomonosov was also an ardent advocate of education and of Russian as a language of learning. With the support of Ivan Shuvalov, an educated aristocrat with influence at the court of Elizabeth, Lomonosov persuaded the empress to establish the University of Moscow in 1755. The university opened with faculties of law, medicine, and philosophy. Students from all social estates were accepted; even a few serfs enrolled with their landlords' consent. Commoners, on entering the university, were accorded personal nobility and permitted to wear a sword. In order to entice members of the nobility to attend, the years of study in the university were counted toward the noble's seniority in state service, an important element of promotion up the Table of Ranks. Despite such inducements, the university struggled for enrollments. The few who chose to study there seldom completed the full program. In its early days the university was a lax place of study with a surfeit of drunken professors. Cheating was common and abetted by teachers. D. I. Fonvizin, who became one of Russia's first playwrights, recalled that on the evening before his class faced an oral examination in Latin by a university board, his instructor assembled the students. He was wearing a kaftan with five buttons on it and a vest with four buttons. The five buttons he told them were the five Latin declensions and the four were the four conjugations. During the examination he rested his finger on the button that corresponded to the declension or conjugation about which the examiners were asking. Fonvizin hastened to add that such practices were now a thing of the past.[16]

Unlike the gymnasium of the Academy of Sciences, where nobles and commoners studied together, the new university in Moscow offered a separate gymnasium for each of the two groups. Graduates from the gymnasiums could either go on to study in the university or enter state service. Those who were university-bound took Latin, history, genealogy, rhetoric, prosody, and translation; those destined for state service studied French or German instead of Latin. Students in both schools were required to study Russian language, arithmetic, geometry, geography, and some basic science. Music, painting, and catechism were optional. In the gymnasiums as in other institutions, the breadth of the curriculum assured superficial learning. The gymnasiums were relatively popular. In 1758 about a hundred students attended the two gymnasiums of the university; in 1764 there were 289. Kazan' acquired a gymnasium in 1758 where arithmetic, geometry, fortification, history, geography, and Latin were taught. Gymnasiums subsequently opened in five other provincial cities. All gymnasiums offered financial support. Students of noble origin received annual stipends of eighteen roubles in the lower grades and twenty-five roubles as seniors; commoners received ten and fifteen roubles, respectively. Commoners significantly outnumbered nobles among students. Lack of resources often resulted in the two groups sharing a classroom. In 1787 a total of more than one thousand students were enrolled in all gymnasiums. Tellingly, only the gymnasium of the Academy of Sciences, where nobles were compelled to study with commoners, floundered. Lomonosov briefly gave it life by establishing a "Russian school" within it that offered several subjects in Russian. When he died in 1765, the academy again allowed the gymnasium to languish.

The establishment of the Nobles' Land Cadet Corps in 1731 had drawn the better-prepared and wealthier nobles away from other schools. The Naval Academy had especially suffered. The navy, therefore, proposed a corps of its own to provide better housing and a program that instilled in its students the social skills and manners for which the Nobles' Land Cadet Corps was known. In 1752 a decree abolished the Naval Academy and the Moscow School of Navigation and established the Naval Cadet Corps on the model of the Nobles' Land Cadet Corps. The charter initially provided no guidance on teaching, discipline, or organization of the school, but subsequent regulations established a more fixed regimen. Peter's artillery and engineering schools were amalgamated in 1758 into the Artillery and Engineering Cadet Corps. The Corps of Pages founded in 1759 to train pages and chamber pages for court service was later to evolve into an elite school for the training of officers for the Guards regiments. Elizabeth's preference for Russians in government office had little effect on the language of study in schools, where German, French, and Latin predominated.

Church Schooling

Before the eighteenth century, Russian priests received no formal education or religious training. The little learning that they possessed was basic literacy in Church Slavonic acquired from another priest or literate layman. New challenges from religious sectarians and the incorporation of cultural influences from the West created a need for a better educated clergy. An early response was the Slavic-Greek-Latin Academy in Moscow. Modeled on the classical schools of the Jesuits, the academy shaped the future course of clerical education in Russia. By 1725 the academy had three schools, Slavonic/Russian, Greek, and Latin; the latter predominated. Students took the same progression of courses that culminated in the upper years in philosophy and theology. Few students, however, reached the final levels. Students came from a variety of backgrounds. A third were sons of clergy or soldiers; the rest came from families of officials, peasants, and a few nobles. From 1729, peasants were excluded.[17] In 1725 the Moscow Academy had 505 students and its parent in Kiev 654 students.[18]

The Church did not escape Peter's push for administrative centralization in his realm. When the Patriarch of the Church died in 1700, Peter refused to allow the selection of a replacement. In 1721 he established a new body to administer the Orthodox Church, the Holy Synod, a board of clergymen headed by a government-appointed layman. The reform was partly motivated by Peter's wish to enroll the Church in his project to educate his subjects. The instrument of reform was the Ecclesiastical Regulation of 1721 that brought sweeping changes to the Church, including its role in education. The Ecclesiastical Regulation required every diocese to establish a seminary to be funded by a levy on Church lands. The order required the sons of clergy to attend them. In addition, townsmen and artisans were urged to send their sons to the schools, and nobles could attend them at the discretion of the emperor.[19]

The regulation envisioned a partnership between church and state. The state saw a well-educated clergy as a tool for the conversion of the religious minorities of the empire and the eradication of popular superstition. Religious education would foster decency and civilization within the public and provide stability in the state and loyalty to established authority. Above all, Peter need educated personnel for a wide variety of secular occupations. The Church hierarchy believed that educated parish priests would better deliver "true" Orthodoxy to parishioners through an informed presentation of the liturgy. Reformist church hierarchs wanted to improve the quality of church leaders through higher education and study abroad and to train a body of scholars equivalent to those in rival confessions.[20] The likely author of the Ecclesiastical Regulation, Feofan Prokopovich, envisaged the creation of an ecclesiastical academy in St. Petersburg with a curriculum that included grammar, geography, history, arithmetic, logic, dialectics, rhetoric, poetics, physics, metaphysics, and theology. Teaching would be in Latin, the language of the classics of Christianity and of science. The projected academy did not materialize until much later. The project, however, pointed to the desire of the hierarchy to raise the status of the Orthodox faith both abroad and at home by training an educated and socially sophisticated clerical estate to a level commensurate with the educated ranks of the nobility. Social graces, French, and German entered the course of study at the Moscow and Kiev Academies and later at some seminaries.

Instead of focusing on the training of priests and deacons for their parochial duties, the Church decided that its schools should provide all males born into the clerical estate with a narrowly classical education. These seminaries were modeled on the Latin grammar school in the form that it had arrived to Moscow from Kiev in the late seventeenth century. Until 1760, the full seminary program provided a preparatory school and elementary school, a school for advanced Latin, and a school of philosophy and theology. Students in the preparatory school studied reading and writing in Slavonic, church singing, and catechism. The elementary school focused on the teaching of Latin. It had four grades, with one grade of basic reading and writing in Latin followed by three years of intensive Latin grammar. Many pupils stumbled at this hurdle and either repeated or left. A few of the better students went on to a year of poesy, that is, the study of the rules of versification in Latin while ignoring their own language. Before 1760, the final two years were dedicated to rhetoric or the writing of Latin prose with limited composition in Russian. By the 1760s, more emphasis was placed on philosophy and theology. Only a tiny number of students attended at the highest level. Those who did learned Aristotle's logic and the works of Thomas Aquinas. Oddly, the curriculum had little to do with Orthodoxy. The injunction of the Ecclesiastical Regulation to teach arithmetic, geometry, geography, and history was equally ignored, a reflection of the Church's reluctance to prepare clergy for secular work.[21]

The seminaries were slow to open. Those that did were elementary schools and only gradually evolved into full seminaries. Empress Anna ordered that all church schools be transformed into seminaries, but growth remained slow until after 1740 when more schools opened. Expansion was hindered by the lack of teachers of Latin, the basis of the curriculum, and the reluctance or inability of bishops to fund them. Priests refused to send their sons. Many regarded the schools as unnecessary. Priests' sons continued to be educated at home, and a high proportion of them attained sufficient literacy to qualify for ordination without attending school. Students who attended remained through the lower grades but left before reaching the advanced classes. Only in or near the capitals did the seminaries attract much support.

The Ecclesiastical Regulation outlined a harsh, almost military, regimen in the seminaries. It specified practically every detail of daily life. Pupils entered around age 10 (a few at 6 or 7) and were not permitted to see their families. Seminary authorities had unrestricted disciplinary powers, which they regularly exercised. Beatings were commonplace. Seniors, appointed as "commanders," tormented juniors. Chronic underfunding resulted in freezing, unsanitary conditions, and at times near starvation. Hunger drove seminarians into the streets to rummage for discarded food. Townsmen often regarded them as unruly ruffians; nobles despised them as potential rivals for state positions. Some students were unfit for schooling but remained at their desks. Teachers were in short supply. Those who taught were poorly qualified, especially in the provinces. Learning was by rote memory with no attempt to test student comprehension of the material. Parents, understandably, were often reluctant to subject their sons to such misery. Flight from the schools was common. One seminary reported that 31 percent of its students in 1750 had run away. Some preferred the discipline of the army to the suffering they endured in school.[22]

The Ecclesiastical Regulation had opened the seminaries to all social classes except the serfs. Sons of priests were compelled to attend, but those of townsmen and nobles could enter if they wished. By mid-century, however, the student body at the seminaries consisted almost entirely of the sons of clergy. By then the clergy was essentially a closed caste characterized by a form of education that ill-prepared them for parish duties and separated them from the worldview of the peasantry and the cosmopolitanism of the nobility. Increasingly the seminaries turned out more and more students beyond the available places for ordained clergy in the parishes, a problem that only grew in subsequent years.

Private Schooling

The old tradition of private religious instruction continued in the eighteenth century, especially among townsmen and the clergy. Their children learned to read church literature. Only rarely did their studies include the first four functions of arithmetic. M. V. Danilov, who became a major in the artillery, began his education with the sexton of his village church at age 7 along with his two cousins. Studies began early in the morning and entailed many long sessions sitting at a desk. Learning was by rote; he frequently forgot by the evening what he had learned in the morning. His poor memory resulted in frequent canings. He recalled that "I thought then that it was inevitable to suffer punishment while learning."[23]

By the beginning of the eighteenth century, a new, more secular form of private education began to flourish alongside the traditional ways. The first private schools in Muscovy were opened by foreigners for the children of foreigners. A few Russians were drawn to them. When, however, Peter the Great made schooling compulsory for advancement in state service and linked rank in service to social status, the opportunities for private educators blossomed. The existing state-supported educational institutions accommodated few students. Most of them were poorly funded and often lacked capable instructors. State schools opened then closed for want of students or teachers. Discipline in the schools was harsh and material conditions wanting. Peter's legislation requiring the sons of the nobility to register and attend state schools was often ignored. Nobles balked at sending their sons to study with commoners as Peter decreed. The reluctance of the nobility to study with their inferiors forced the government in 1737 to permit private home education. Many noble boys received a home education, often from a priest if poor or from a hired tutor if well off.

Peter highly valued the acquisition of foreign languages, especially German, which he saw as the language of commerce and practical learning. It was the language of instruction in most of his schools. Although Peter preferred German in the conduct of diplomacy, French soon emerged as the language not only of diplomacy but also of the cultural sophistication that was the sign of nobility. German remained popular among merchants as the language of commerce. Demand for tutors in both French and German was high. To meet demand, aspiring teachers flooded in from the West. Many were refugees from authorities in their home countries. Often arriving to work as servants, they soon sought positions as private tutors or schoolteachers. Class and regional accents that were far from the speech coveted by the educated elite were common among them. One enterprising Finn taught his native language to his charges who believed that they were learning French. None of the early tutors had pedagogical training or any experience in language instruction. The worst of them used brutal methods on their students; others provided minimal instruction.[24]

Foreigners also opened private schools. There were four in St. Petersburg by 1711. Some offered academic study. A Jesuit school in Moscow from 1701 provided instruction in Latin, mathematics, German, and military science. The German School in Moscow taught at the secondary level of a gymnasium. The curriculum claimed to include geography, philosophy, ethics, politics, Latin rhetoric and poetics, Greek, Hebrew, Chaldean, French, German, Swedish, dancing, riding, and dressage. It closed in 1715. A school in Novgorod provided instruction in Latin, Greek, French, mathematics, and ethics. As earlier, many of the students in these schools were foreigners, but a few Russians attended.[25] Native Russians also operated private schools. The Metropolitan of Rostov, Dmitrii, ran a school open to all social estates that taught Russian, Greek, and Latin to some two hundred students. Feofan Prokopovich opened schools in Novgorod and St. Petersburg for orphans and children of the poor. They learned French and German, Latin, rhetoric, logic, Roman history, geography, drawing, and music.[26] The historian V. N. Tatishchev established schools in Siberian industrial enterprises that offered a broad curriculum. From 1740, *pensions* offering instruction in French, dancing, music, and etiquette proliferated. By 1757 there were nine pensions in St. Petersburg and a few also appeared in provincial towns.[27]

All private schools and home tutors in the first half of the century operated beyond state control and regulation. Schools were organized in multiple ways, had no set curriculum or methods of instruction, and required no special training for teachers in the subjects taught. The lack of regulation and the predominance of often unqualified foreigners in Russian schooling alarmed the government of Empress Elizabeth. The efforts during her reign to Russianize the administration and teaching in state educational institutions were accompanied by an attempt to regulate teaching in private schools and home education, often by foreigners. Elizabeth was especially critical of homeschooling. In 1757 a regulation required that foreigners who wished to establish a private school had to apply for permission and demonstrate their fitness for the role. Foreign teachers in private schools were now to be tested for competence in the subjects they proposed to teach. The regulation extended to foreign tutors in noble and merchant homes. They too were ordered to pass a test administered by the Academy of Sciences or Moscow University. Those who employed tutors who had not been certified were subject to a fine and the tutor to expulsion from the country. The regulation had little effect. Distance prevented many from traveling to one of the capitals to take the test; those who knew that they would fail avoided testing. Demand remained high and the risk of fines low.[28]

Another form of education was study abroad. The practice of sending youths abroad to learn particular skills began as early as the sixteenth century. Peter sent young men abroad to study military techniques and industrial processes. Others were despatched to learn languages, business practices, and art and architecture. Students were unsupervised and received meager state stipends that often left them in penury. Many lacked the language skills needed for foreign study. Early bad experiences led to better practices. Supervisors were sent to assist students and monitor their progress. By the 1750s a few noble families sent their sons abroad to study in German universities. A. R. Vorontsov, the scion of a great family, went at age 17 to study at the Light Cavalry School in Versailles, a military school for the wellborn. He found his studies there "useful."[29]

Vocational education had its roots in the early eighteenth century, largely through private initiative. Nikita Demidov founded a mining and metallurgy school in the Urals in 1702. In 1758 the school was admitting students from a large region. More than a hundred students in that year studied religion, reading, arithmetic, and the skills related to the mining industry. Other owners of factories and works followed Demidov's example.[30] By the 1740s several landlords were educating serf children to become future administrators of their estates. Others sent serfs to train as musicians or artists. The Kurakin family operated six schools for serfs. In its multiple forms, private education provided more Russians with learning than did the state. Private schools outnumbered state schools and enrolled more students. State policies in the eighteenth century often hindered the spread of education. The influence of the Church narrowed the scope of educational activity. The scope of education was further narrowed by its linkage to state service. The elite took little interest in an education not leading to service to the state. Strict social control excluded whole groups from formal schooling.

Outcomes

The effort initiated by Peter the Great and pursued by his successors to force Western education on some of his subjects from above had limited success. Nevertheless, policies and patterns established in the early eighteenth century left enduring marks on education in Russia for the future. Deeply influenced by cameralism, which entrusted to the state the leading role in advancing the public good, Peter saw education as the business of the state. Education was the servant of the administrative, economic, and military needs of government, which Peter associated with the public good. Science was government science. Education was preparation for state service. Peter conceived of his schools as open to all social estates except the serfs. Commoners and nobles were expected to study together. Although the Table of Ranks opened a narrow window for social mobility and status through merit, the linkage to state service limited the uses and scope of education. Students saw just enough education to get on in state service as sufficient. Limited resources and a lack of trained personnel prevented the state control over schooling that Peter envisaged. Subsequent regimes, however, gradually imposed it.

After Peter's death, the commitment to social commonality of schooling, while not repudiated, was gradually subverted. Differences in education began to define social divisions. The nobility accepted a Western education as a valuable social asset, but on their own terms, not those of the state. The wealthier nobles turned to private education or to a few elite educational institutions like the Nobles' Land Cadet Corps to separate themselves from socially open schools. The cultural gap between an aristocratic elite, largely in the capitals, and a poorer provincial gentry grew. The latter petitioned regularly for more state-supported schools exclusively for their estate. The nobility stubbornly rejected academic education. They opted for a broad but superficial education and valued social graces and manners above learning. The ideal of aristocratic exclusivity drove the elite to speak French to one another and bad Russian to their servants.

The commonality of learning in the seminaries envisaged by the Ecclesiastical Regulation also withered within a few decades. By 1750 the seminaries had become almost the exclusive preserve of the clergy. Education in the seminaries that was based on the model of the classical school had little in common with the curriculum preferred by the nobility. The growing surplus of priests' sons beyond the available places for priests, deacons, and sextons available in parishes, the obstacles to moving upward socially, and the loss of status associated with entering the poll-tax paying estates left many sons of the clergy with few viable options. The state periodically skimmed off a few of the best seminarians to teach in state schools, to fill places in institutions of higher education, or to take lower administrative postings. The education provided by the seminary did little to prepare priests and deacons for their parochial duties and alienated them from the culture of their parishioners. In spite of small inroads of Western know-how, the peasantry remained culturally tied to the Muscovite past. The relative homogeneity of culture that characterized pre-Petrine Russia was severely ruptured by the Petrine revolution and survived largely among the peasantry.

A growing social group in the eighteenth century were the *raznochintsy* (people of various ranks). They were the sons of clergy who had avoided the seminary, soldiers' sons, and those of artisans who got their initial education in garrison schools. Some of them went on to acquire an education in a variety of practical specializations. Their education separated them from their original estate and usually from their family as well. They lived as best they could in occupations requiring a measure of education. Alienated from class as they were and still few in numbers, they would in the future play an important role in opposition to the autocratic order.

The education of women was much talked about by progressive thinkers as early as the reign of Peter the Great. Peter himself envisaged a school for women modeled on the French school St. Cyr. The plan remained on paper as did an elaborate plan proposed by F. S. Saltykov to create schools for girls from ages 6 to 15 in monasteries. There they would learn Russian grammar, foreign languages, music, and dancing. As time passed the idea that an educated woman was a better mate for an educated man and a better mother for her children took hold. Until the reign of Catherine, most education attained by girls was domestic.[31]

Perhaps most important for the cultural development of Russia was the importation of new scientific, technical, administrative, and military knowledge that brought to the empire a whole new vocabulary. Gradually it was translated and published in a new civil type and in time disseminated. It formed a new Russian language spoken by a small but growing learned elite. The new language and culture coexisted with the old. The absorption of new terms into the language enabled a rapport with the West that by mid-century was beginning to draw more Russians to study in the West, a trend with important consequences during the reign of Catherine the Great.[32]

2

Roots of the System: Catherine the Great

Empress Elizabeth died on Christmas Day, 1741. She was succeeded by Peter III, an ardent admirer of Frederick the Great of Prussia. His love of things German and disdain for Russia and Russians, as well as his withdrawal from the alliance against Prussia in the Seven Years' War, soon sparked conspiracies against him. His most important reform was the freeing of the Russian nobility from compulsory state service. The "emancipation" of the nobility fostered the rise of an educated elite, some of whom began to question the political and social status quo. The conspiracy against Peter coalesced around his wife Catherine, a German princess. It culminated on June 28, 1762, when Peter was overthrown and Catherine was proclaimed by the Church and supporters as "Empress and Autocrat Catherine the Second." Peter was soon murdered by Catherine's supporters. The only other possible claimant to the throne, Ivan VI, who had grown up in prison, was killed by his jailers with Catherine's approval in June 1764. Although born a German, Catherine had learned Russian in the long years before her ascendency and observed the Orthodox faith. Figure 2.1 shows her at her lesson. During her long reign, she confirmed the emancipation of the nobility from state service and in 1785 provided nobles with a charter that outlined their rights along with a similar charter for merchants and townsmen, crushed a massive Cossack-peasant uprising in 1773–4, carried out a major reform of provincial administration in 1775, opened up New Russia in the south, and participated with Austria and Prussia in the partition of Poland.

"Minerva has ascended the Throne," proclaimed Mikhail Lomonosov on the coronation of Catherine the Great. The learned men of the Academy of Sciences and the University of Moscow identified the new empress with the values of educated West Europeans in a series of public lectures and publications. Catherine was soon to proclaim Russia as a European nation. She shared with Peter the Great the cameralist values of utility, service, and the centrality of the state as fundamental to governance. As a student of the Enlightenment, Catherine was a practitioner of Enlightened Absolutism. Autocratic rule in Russia, she argued, guaranteed effective governance over a vast empire. She continued: "The object of autocracy ... is not to deprive men of their natural liberty, but to direct their actions in such a manner as to achieve the greatest good for all."[1] Whereas Peter used education to produce capable state servants, Catherine saw in education a tool to create a "new man" or, later in her reign,

Figure 2.1 Russian language lesson of Catherine the Great.
Source: Heritage Images/Getty Images.

enlightened citizens who freely served the common good. In particular, Catherine was eager to establish in Russia a middle class both to strengthen the economy and to foster civic virtue. The new empress introduced into Russian education a heavy emphasis on character building or moral upbringing (vospitanie). From Catherine's reign onward, moral upbringing became a major concern of the state in education policy-making.

The Enlightenment marked a sharp break with past approaches to education. Thinkers of the Enlightenment introduced new conceptions of childhood and of child-rearing. Not the tradition ridden family but the state should take the leading role in forming individual character and educating citizens. A student of Enlightenment philosophy and pedagogy, Catherine was familiar with the educational works of Johann Comenius, François Fénelon, and John Locke. All understood the inculcation of virtue to be the main goal of education. Fénelon and Locke agreed that at birth the mind is a blank slate on which the educator could write and that reason governed learning. Comenius advocated the use of moral incentives to promote love of learning in children and rejected punishments of all kinds. Both Comenius and Fénelon supported the education of women since they would be the earliest moral guides of their children. Locke linked the type of education appropriate to a child to the child's future station in life. All preferred that children be educated outside of the corrupting influence of the traditional family.

Catherine chose I. I. Betskoi as her principal adviser on educational matters. Betskoi was steeped in Enlightenment pedagogy. He aspired to create individuals and citizens who transcended their social origins. In his view, the key to human well-being was the moral upbringing of the individual. Betskoi divided education into four elements: physical, physical-moral, moral, and academic. He emphasized the first two elements and subordinated the fourth to them. The sensationalism of the French thinker Étienne Bonnot de Condillac powerfully influenced Betskoi's approach to schooling. Condillac argued that mind is the product of the reactions of the sense organs to the stimuli of the physical environment. It followed that by manipulating the environment, educators could make of a person whatever they wished. Early removal from the family into the controlled environment of the school would result in the formation of new persons, free from the failings of the past. Influenced by Jean-Jacques Rousseau, Betskoi advocated a "natural" education that rested on feeling, observation, and experimentation. The goal was to nurture a child's curiosity and only later to turn to books. It was with these ideas that Betskoi embarked on a number of educational experiments under Catherine's watchful eye.

State and Imperial Patronage Schooling

During Catherine's reign, a number of education projects were jointly financed by the state and by funds from the empress's own coffers and from other benefactors. Betskoi shared Catherine's wish to create a middle class in Russia. In 1763 Catherine approved his plan for an Imperial Educational Institution and Hospital for orphans with him as its director. Its purpose was to educate a body of "useful members of society" beyond the cultural constraints of the nobility and peasantry. Unwed mothers were encouraged to come to the homes to give birth or to drop off illegitimate children under a guarantee of anonymity. Many did. Some poor families abandoned their children on the home's doorstep in hope of giving them a better life. The home staffed male and female nurses, a doctor, midwife, teachers, and clergy. At age 7 the children began to learn to read and write. Between the ages of 12 and 14 they received religious instruction and continued their earlier studies along with arithmetic, geography, and accounting. Girls learned housekeeping. In the final four years of their schooling, girls furthered their knowledge of domestic sciences. Boys at that stage were separated into three groups for specific training: those continuing to further education, those entering a vocation, and those destined for manual work. On their marriage young women received a dowry of twenty-five roubles; all graduates were given a rouble to get a start in life. Similar foundling homes opened in various towns. The state provided only token funding. Most support came from private donors, including Catherine. The homes could also open loan banks, build and operate factories, and purchase and sell real estate. Although planning for the homes promised a healthy environment for the children with fresh air, exercise, and a planned diet, overcrowding and poor sanitary conditions resulted in high mortality rates. In Moscow the rate reached 90 percent at its highest. Less crowding in St. Petersburg held the rate to between 10 and 20 percent.[2]

The empress signaled early in her reign her interest in education for women. In 1764 she set out a plan to establish a school in each province to teach girls reading, writing, and domestic arts. Little came of it. In the same year Betskoi submitted to Catherine his Statute on the Education of Noble Girls. She quickly approved it and named him the school's director. The Smolny Institute for Noble Girls opened in June 1764 in St. Petersburg. Its aim was to create "new women," suitable mates for the "new men." Betskoi had visited the famous school of Mme. de Maintenon at St. Cyr in France. His school, however, differed in many ways from St. Cyr. His was a secular rather than a religious institution and offered a more ambitious academic program than St. Cyr. Girls entered the school at age 5, earlier than at St. Cyr, and were isolated from their families except for rare and strictly supervised visits. Students remained at the institute for twelve years. A Local Council, made up of prominent women, saw to the maintenance of the courses and oversaw the internal life of the school. The institute had some state funding but depended heavily on private benefactors, among them members of the imperial family. Pupils aged 5–9 studied Law of God, etiquette, foreign languages, arithmetic, painting, dancing, music, sewing, and knitting. In addition to those subjects, girls from 10 to 12 years old studied geography, history, and household management. The principles of architecture, literature, and economics rounded out the curriculum in the next two years. The final two or three years of study deepened students' knowledge of previous subjects with a particular focus on ethics, manners, and comportment. Physical punishments were banned. Teachers were to be models to their students as well as their companions. Pupils were divided into pedagogical families headed by a class mistress (*dama*) who oversaw every aspect of the girls' lives.

The Smolny Institute had a philanthropic social component. Poor and orphaned girls from noble families had priority. The plan called for two hundred admissions in four cohorts of fifty girls. Recruitment at first was difficult. The first fifty students were in place only in July 1765. Most of them came from St. Petersburg and were the daughters of courtiers or members of the Guards. The second and third cohorts, however, did include many orphaned noble girls. The first girls from the provinces arrived only in 1773. In January 1765 the Novodevichy Institute for Girls of the Third Estate opened with a similar, though less academically demanding, curriculum. Its plan called for 240 students in four cohorts of 60. Many of the girls were orphans or daughters of retired soldiers. Early problems with recruitment in both institutes were gradually overcome. Securing capable teachers was difficult. Both schools were for some time understaffed. In the early years, nobles and commoners mingled freely in classes. By 1794, 440 noble girls and 410 commoners had graduated from the sister institutes. On graduation each girl received a stipend of fifty to one hundred roubles.[3]

State Schooling

Catherine believed that economic development depended on the fostering of scientific and technical expertise. The reputation of Peter the Great's crowning achievement, the Academy of Sciences, had steadily declined since the 1740s. Chronically underfunded, reduced by the reform of 1747 to a dependent department of state, and staffed largely by artisans instead of scientifically trained personnel, pure research in the academy had been sharply curtailed. Catherine restored some measure of autonomy to the academicians in 1766. It was only in 1783, however, that she appointed Princess Ekaterina Dashkova as the academy's director. Dashkova was one of a number of highly accomplished women in the late eighteenth century in Russia who brought female perspectives to literature, the arts, and politics. They included the botanist E. P. Fadeeva, the translator A. I. Vel'iasheva-Volyntseva, the artist sisters A. M. and E. M. Volkonskie, and writers M. V. Khrapovitskaia and E. V. Kheraskova. Under Dashkova's energetic and intelligent leadership the academy again flourished. Enrollments in the gymnasium attached to it increased. The quality of appointments and of the research of academicians rose. Only the academy's university languished. It finally closed altogether in 1796.[4]

The Academy of Arts, established by Empress Elizabeth, gained independence from the University of Moscow in 1764. The academy's new director, Betskoi, attached a boarding school to prepare students for admission. Its students were drawn primarily from the middle and lower social estates of society, including serfs who had attained a certificate of emancipation from their landlords. As in other educational institutions of the day, orphans and the poor had priority. Students, supported by state stipends, entered the school at age 5 or 6 and were cut off from most family contact. Students studied a broad range of subjects that included modern languages, arithmetic, geography, history, and religion. At the end of the program of nine years, students took examinations to determine who should continue on to the academy itself for another six years of training in painting, architecture, sculpture, engineering, music, and other subjects in the arts. All graduates of the academy attained freedom for themselves and their descendants and a rank on the Table of Ranks. Teachers at the academy also held rank.[5]

In Russia, as in Western Europe at the time, military knowledge was deemed to be part of general learning and not a specialist subject. The Nobles' Land Cadet Corps had functioned since its inception with a broad curriculum much favored by a nobility anxious to be exposed to all the knowledge of the West, however superficially. With Catherine's approval, Betskoi reorganized the Corps in 1766. Children now entered at age 5 and graduated at 18. Russian became the main language of instruction after years of the predominance of German and French. The old problem of a vast curriculum persisted. An attempt to reduce the nineteen general subjects taught along with three specialist subjects and an additional nine out-of-class activities failed. A review of the Corps in 1784 found that few students finished the roster of subjects offered fully, and those who completed a subject had at best a superficial knowledge of its content. The same problem plagued students at the Artillery and Engineering Cadet Corps, formed in 1763 from Peter's artillery and engineering schools. It suffered from an overwhelming curriculum of thirty-five subjects. Attempts to reduce the number in the 1780s foundered on noble resistance.[6]

Early in her reign Catherine had formed an education commission. Although many individuals had previously offered plans for general education, the commission was the first state body to consider the matter. The commission reviewed existing proposals and made a number of recommendations. In March 1764 Catherine issued a "General Statute for the Education of Youth of Both Sexes." It called for the establishment of state boarding schools. The plan envisaged students entering school at age 5 or 6 and graduating at 18. It entrusted the clergy with a major role in elementary education. Catherine, who had a low opinion of the poorly educated clergy, hesitated to implement a project that depended on them. She had by this time decided to convene a Legislative Commission to gather representatives of all social estates, except the serfs, to discuss the needs and wishes of her subjects on a range of economic, political, and social matters, including general education. Catherine prepared a lengthy "Instruction" to guide discussion in the commission. In it she proposed a universal education that incorporated moral and spiritual learning and the schooling of citizens for their divinely ordained social roles. Following the French philosopher Voltaire she divided the populace into those who lead and those who obey. Education should support that fundamental division.

The commission met in 1767 and continued into 1768. Education was not a priority for most delegates, but a few voices were heard. There were calls for schools for nobles to be established in district towns to enable the sons of poor nobles or those who lived far from the capital to gain a suitable education. A few noble representatives showed an interest in peasant education as beneficial to landowners and to effective local administration. The nobles of Dimitrovsk district urged the nobility to pool resources to provide one teacher per one hundred peasant households to teach grammar and arithmetic. "Landlords must learn that they will benefit more from literate peasants," they argued. A few others preferred parish schools to provide religious instruction for peasant children aged 5 to 12. Most progressive were delegates from the nobility of Ukraine who called for universities, local cadet corps, and schools for girls. P. I. Panin, a Moscow noble known for his progressive thinking, urged nobles to subscribe to elementary and secondary schools for girls; delegates from Chernigov, Pereslavl', and Eniseisk argued that schooling of girls enhanced their social presence and better prepared them for their moral duties as mothers. Some merchant delegates supported urban schools for townsmen as well as professional schools that taught Russian and foreign commercial law, geography, and modern languages as well as basic skills like forms of business letters and knowledge of weights and measures in Russia and abroad.[7]

The government answered the pleas of the poor nobility for greater access to education by opening the garrison schools to them in 1774 and providing around a thousand stipends to support their sons. In 1779 a boarding school for nobles opened at the University of Moscow, and more money was made available to the university gymnasium to accommodate more commoners. A state Commercial School opened in Moscow in 1777 to meet merchant demands, and in 1779 a Land Survey School was established. As well, the commission struck a School and Welfare Committee before it was prorogued in 1768. In late 1771 the new committee issued projects for elementary village and urban schools, secondary schools, and schools for the empire's many non-Russian subjects (*inorodtsy*). The proposal envisaged one village school per 100–250 families to provide compulsory education, without estate distinction, to boys from 8 to 12 years of age; parents could choose to permit daughters to attend. The curriculum was limited to reading in Russian and religion. Supervision of the schools was entrusted to the local clergy and nobility. One urban school per 100 families would provide reading, religion, and arithmetic to both boys and girls aged 7–12. The plan also compelled illiterate boys of 17 and under to attend an urban school. The local bishop and provincial governor would supervise urban schools and find teachers for them. The proposed schools for non-Russians were similar to the urban schools but with native teachers and instruction in the local language. At the secondary level the proposal called for a gymnasium in each provincial capital for 240 students, half of whom would receive state subsidies. The curriculum included classical and modern languages, mathematics, geography, architecture, music, drawing, dancing, and law. The gymnasiums would be open to children of all free estates provided they had previously learned arithmetic. That excluded children from village schools in which arithmetic was not taught. Local populations had to bear the costs of elementary education. Secondary, military, and university educational institutions were all to be state funded.

Again Catherine demurred. She was engaged in a prolonged war with Turkey and with the suppression of the Pugachev rebellion and preoccupied with the many problems of provincial administration that in part had fueled the Cossack-peasant uprising. In 1775 she initiated a reform that involved local actors more directly in provincial administration. At the heart of the reform were new boards of welfare charged with the provision and administration of local social services, including education. The existing foundling homes in the provinces passed under the purview of the boards. The reform mandated the establishment of elementary schools with low tuition fees in every city and large town. The curriculum required reading, writing, arithmetic, drawing, catechism, and the study of scripture. Attendance was voluntary. Corporal punishment was banned. The boards of welfare were charged with soliciting funding for the schools. The public showed little interest in schooling, the boards struggled to raise funds, and the nobility again objected to the all-estate nature of the proposed schools. Only a few schools were built under the legislation.[8]

The serial failures of her domestic education initiatives convinced Catherine to look to foreign models. She consulted Melchior Grimm, who recommended a version of the Prussian school reform of 1769. She failed to lure him to Russia to oversee the reform and turned instead to a "Plan for Russian Schools" prepared by F. I. Aepinus, a German member of the Russian Academy of Sciences. The plan was modeled on the Austrian school system that was in part based on the earlier Prussian school reform. A meeting in 1780 with Joseph II, the Hapsburg emperor, convinced Catherine that the Austrian model, which, she believed, had fewer associations with atheism and, unlike the Prussian system, functioned in a multinational empire like her own, was best suited to Russian conditions. She contracted F. I. Jankovich de Mirjevo, who had been instrumental in adapting the Austrian school reform to the Slavic and Orthodox regions of the Hapsburg Empire, as consultant to a Commission for the Establishment of Public Schools that she formed in 1782 to implement the reform.

The Statute on Public Schools was promulgated in 1786. The reform fell short of the vision of Aepinus and the Austrian model. It provided for minor (elementary) schools in district capitals with a two-year program and major (upper elementary) schools in provincial capitals with a five-year program. Schooling was free but not compulsory, open to all social estates, and coeducational. The state provided some initial funding for establishing the schools, but the boards of welfare were to maintain them from interest on capital and public donations. The minor schools were to have two teachers, one for each grade or only one if enrollments were low. The statute mandated six teachers in major schools, but in practice few schools had more than four. Students in the first year of study in the minor schools took reading and writing in Russian, basic grammar, elementary arithmetic, catechism, and religious history. In the second grade they added handwriting and drawing to the previous subjects. Major school students in the first two grades followed the same curriculum as in the minor schools. In the third grade pupils advanced their knowledge of the earlier grades with the addition of history and geography. The fourth grade was two years in duration. Along with the earlier subjects students took preparation of business documents, receipts, and accounts, physics, mechanics, and civic architecture. Students planning to continue into secondary education could study Latin and a modern language, preferably one useful within the empire, such as Tatar, Greek, or Chinese.

Moral education was at the heart of the schools' mission. All students in both minor and major schools received a copy of *On the Duties of Man and Citizens*, a translation of the Austrian Abbot Felbiger's *Instructions of Virtuousness*. It contained material on hygiene and health, management of home and family, and social responsibilities. It proclaimed that social divisions were divinely sanctioned and urged citizens to obey their leaders on whom God had conferred care for their welfare. Love of the Fatherland was the highest virtue: the lower social estates expressed their devotion through hard work and respect, the clergy through the religious upbringing of their charges, and the nobility through model behavior and public service. All should be content with their lot in life. The clergy had no role in the new schools. Lay persons taught religion from books supplied by the state. No religion was taught in the fourth grade at all. Manuals urged teachers to form useful citizens from their charges, to encourage young people to perform their social obligations conscientiously, and to act wisely, honorably, and decently.

The statute incorporated many of the precepts of the pedagogy of the day. It banned the use of corporal punishment: good teaching rested on patience and kindness and the use of small rewards as incentives. It frowned on rote learning: good teachers engaged students in a dialogue through questions, first to one student, then to another, as the lesson proceeded, followed by additional review questions as it concluded. Explanations should be clear and simple; extensive use of blackboards was recommended. The level of the curriculum should be geared to the level of maturity of the students. Whenever possible, lessons should be linked to local conditions and affairs. The statute introduced regular examinations to determine grade advancement.

Imposed from above without public consultation, the new school structure was highly centralized. The curriculum and textbooks were uniform and determined centrally. Teachers' manuals and many of the textbooks were translations of works used in Austrian schools. Jankovich himself translated twenty-seven books in at least eight subjects. The hierarchy of command in the structure passed from the empress through the new Main School Administration, formed from the original Commission on Schools, and down to the provincial governors who had sole responsibility to establish schools. Governors were charged with appointing as their agents directors of public schools, who vetted the moral and academic standards of teachers. District inspectors were appointed to oversee the minor schools. They were also to press boards of welfare to fund schools and encourage private donors to support them. Each school had an elected trustee who reported to the boards of welfare. Teachers found themselves at the bottom of the structure with limited autonomy and subject to the whims of all those above them as well as of the parents of their pupils.[9]

The Prussian and Austrian school reforms had included normal schools for the training of teachers. The Russian reform did not. Some teacher training did take place, however: Jankovich trained twenty teachers who taught in trial schools in the capital in preparation for the reform, and the Alexander-Nevskii Monastery in St. Petersburg opened classes for teachers in 1782. In 1783 its students moved to a major school intended to train teachers. It had 385 enrolments in 1784. In 1786 the school became a teachers' seminary that trained teachers for major schools in the capitals. The numbers trained fell far short of demand.[10] The shortages compelled Catherine to assign seminary students to study in major schools in order to become teachers in the minor schools. The conditions of work and living, especially in district capitals, were uninviting. Teachers enjoyed little respect in provincial society. Housing that was supposed to be supplied for them by the local population was often a cramped corner in a crowded home. The few schools that opened were often housed in existing decrepit, unheated, and crowded buildings. With their limited funds, boards of welfare were slow to pay teachers' salaries. Teachers of the upper two grades of the major schools on paper received four hundred roubles a year and lodgings, heat, and lighting. They entered the Table of Ranks at the twelfth level. Those in the lower grades and in minor schools received far less and joined the Table of Ranks at the lowest rank of fourteenth. Teachers lacked training in the methods recommended by the statute. Rote learning remained the norm, and the ban on corporal punishment was widely ignored. Teacher shortages, lack of public support for the schools, and governors who shunned their responsibilities under the statute resulted in the establishment of a mere 161 minor schools in the empire by 1801. Forty-eight of those were in St. Petersburg, Moscow, and provincial capitals. Half of the district capitals had no school at all. Nobles generally avoided schools where commoners were welcome, as did some of the more prominent merchant families.

The statute made no mention of higher education. Although the major schools were intended to be gateways to university study, the universities filled their places with better-prepared students from the gymnasiums of the Academy of Sciences and the University of Moscow. Catherine commissioned a group to plan for the expansion of universities in 1787. It proposed to raise the level of the major schools to make them preparatory to university entrance and to establish new universities with faculties of philosophy, law, and medicine. The plan called for free tuition for the poor and fees for the better off. Catherine did not act on the recommendations. The school reform, therefore, had neither a solid base of elementary schools, since no schools existed in rural areas, nor an adequate higher education summit. At the end of Catherine's reign in 1796 Russia still lacked a unified educational system.

Church Schooling

Catherine's reign initiated new approaches to education in the empire. While not neglecting professional training, the empress wished to implement a broad humanistic curriculum in schools and to substitute moral suasion and willing participation of students in place of the harsh discipline and compulsion of Petrine schooling. The new attitude soon entered the Church. Church leaders in their quest to improve the social standing of the clergy began to encourage civility and gentility between teachers and students and among students. Teachers were urged to be loving fathers to their charges; corporal punishment was entrusted solely to the director of the seminary. The Church appointed inspectors whose role it was to promote pride among students in their estate and to teach them civil behavior. Changes to the curriculum now made it slightly more relevant to priestly duties. Aristotle's logic gave way to a textbook by F. C. Baumeister that challenged Enlightenment skepticism; Catholic authorities like Thomas Aquinas made room for the works of Feofan Prokopovich and other Orthodox hierarchs. Although Latin remained the anchor of the curriculum, the use of Russian textbooks, often at the insistence of the state, became more common.[11]

Emblematic of the new attitudes was Father Platon. He served as instructor of catechism to Catherine's son and heir Paul, from 1775 directed the Slavic-Greek-Latin Academy in Moscow, and later became Metropolitan of Moscow. Father Platon broadened the curriculum of the academy in more humanistic directions by introducing social and political issues into religious teaching. Through a series of public sermons in the 1760s, he sought to reconcile Enlightenment thought with Orthodoxy. Reason, he argued, as did many Western thinkers, was a tool to the better understanding of God's creation. Science, however, without the virtue instilled by religion was useless and even dangerous. Civil law commanded the human heart only if it rested on God's law. The new dispensation was accepted in seminaries in or near the capitals far more readily than in those in the provinces whose graduates remained far from the Church's ideal of the new cleric.[12]

The confiscation of Church lands in 1764 severely curtailed the financial capacity of the Church to support the seminaries. The state assumed their financing but at a level well below their needs. To make matters worse, enrollments grew rapidly, from 4,673 students in 1766 to 20,393 in 1799. From the 1770s, ordination as a priest, deacon, or sacristan normally depended on at least some attendance at a seminary rather than an exclusive homeschooling. Limited state support meant that parents often financed their sons' training. Poorer clergy could rarely afford to maintain their sons for the full program. As standards rose, bishops chose the best students for preferred positions; students with only partial seminary educations were increasingly relegated to the humbler roles of parish churchmen. By the 1790s every diocese had hundreds of seminarians who were surplus to their needs. The hierarchy persisted, however, in educating the sons of the whole clerical estate in their quest to elevate the social status of its members.[13]

Private Schooling

Demand for domestic teachers (tutors, governors, and governesses) steadily rose from the 1770s to the end of the century. Although more care was given to the quality of tutors as the century wore on, the lack of a reliable supply enabled charlatans to secure places in merchant and noble households without penalty. The number of private *pensions* and boarding schools rose steadily during Catherine's reign. Many foreign-owned pensions remained, especially in the capitals. In 1780 there were twenty-three in St. Petersburg with about 500 students, of whom around 200 were Russians, and 72 teachers, of whom 20 were Russians. In the same year, Moscow had ten foreign-run pensions with 374 students. The language of instruction in most of them was French. Half of the teachers employed in them taught drawing and dancing. The best of the pensions featured a broad range of subjects, but many taught only French, dancing, and etiquette. These were the skills in demand. Girls paid more than boys to study in a pension but were taught less. Russian university professors, teachers, and even students also began to offer teaching services through newspaper advertisements. In addition to tutoring, some educated Russians founded and taught in private schools.[14]

The Enlightenment in Russia fostered the growth of reading groups and learned societies among the public. Such groups often had a strong interest in education and established schools based on various pedagogical theories and methods using new textbooks. The Freemason N. I. Novikov opened two charity schools in Moscow for poor children in 1777–8. Pupils studied reading and writing in Russian, catechism, and the first four functions of arithmetic. True to its roots in Enlightenment thought, the primary purpose of his schools was the building of moral character. Another example of private initiative related to professional vocational education. In the early 1770s, Prokofii Demidov of the Ural mining dynasty funded a school of commerce for the sons of poor merchants. The boys entered at age 5 and graduated at 21. Tuition was free. The curriculum began with basic general education, proceeded to an array of subjects relevant to commercial activities as well as to foreign languages, and concluded with experimental sciences and advanced commercial practices. On graduation the best students were awarded a three hundred rouble scholarship for further study abroad. Graduation from the schools also conferred rank on the Table of Ranks. Many merchants, reluctant to forgo their children's labor for study, preferred to train their sons on the job. Consequently, sons of merchants made up a bare majority of the students, many of whom came from poor noble families or even some serfs who had permission from their landlords.[15]

As planning for the school reform proceeded and state experimental schools opened in St. Petersburg and Moscow, the Commission of Public Education in 1782 introduced strict measures to regulate private schooling. The new rules applied first in the two capitals. Private schools underwent inspections of their curricula and vetting of their teachers' qualifications. Several of the foreign-operated schools failed the inspections and were closed. The commission standardized the length of the school year for all schools and required twice-yearly examinations of students in the presence of the director of schools. Private schools run by Russians were transferred into the state system along with their teachers and students. The Statute on Public Education of 1786 included a supplemental decree on private schools. Schools were ranked as either minor or major and were required to teach the corresponding state-mandated curriculum. All private school founders and teachers had to attain certification of moral standing and of knowledge of their subject at the same level required of a teacher in a state school. Russian language was compulsory in all schools. In addition to the state curriculum, private schools could add courses with state approval and proof that a teacher qualified for the subject was available to teach it. The decree confirmed biannual examinations and reasserted the long-standing requirement that all domestic teachers receive certification.[16]

Enforcement of the decree was lax. The state system was as yet too small to dispense with private schooling. A few inspectors were appointed to track down uncertified tutors and governesses but with scant result. School founders frequently fell well short of the qualifications required of them. Many private schools ignored the approved curriculum. The nobility continued to resist an education shared with commoners. For those who could afford it, homeschooling remained popular. Others found a refuge in nobles' boarding schools. The model was the Nobles' Boarding School that opened in Moscow in 1779. It accepted only sons of nobles from ages 9 to 14 for a six-year program. The curriculum included reading and writing, arithmetic, artillery, fortifications, and foreign languages as well as social graces. Tuition at first was 120 roubles a year but soon rose to 150 roubles. It opened with fifty students. New boarding schools for nobles subsequently opened in eight provincial cities.[17]

Outcomes

The subjection of education to the pragmatic goals of the state begun by Peter the Great and his successors continued under Catherine. During her reign the state, at least on paper, imposed stricter regulation on the operation of schools. The creation of the Commission on Public Schools initiated a process of the centralization of general education in the empire under a single authority. The Statute on Public Education marked a partial return to the all-estate principle of Peter's schools, an effort to overcome the cultural divisions of the society that had opened since the Petrine era and to provide, at least in early education, a common worldview. With a few adjustments to accommodate regional differences in a vast empire, the statute imposed a common curriculum and textbooks in public and private schools. By the end of Catherine's reign, however, the emphasis on social estate was again apparent. At the heart of Catherine's education reform was moral upbringing, anchored by the book required in all schools and in home education, *On the Duties of Man and Citizens*. It sanctioned a hierarchical social order in which good and useful citizens embraced their allotted role in life. The statute also established a practice that the costs of elementary public education be borne by local populations.

The total population of the empire in 1796 was a little more than 34 million. A few more than 20 million were Russians and an additional 11.5 million were Ukrainians and Belorussians. A host of so-called non-Russians (*inorodtsy*) made up the remainder. Beside those figures, the number of students attending school was tiny but growing. In 1788 there was a total of 218 major and minor schools with 525 teachers and roughly 13,500 students. In 1801 there were 49 major schools and 239 minor schools with 766 teachers and 22,200 pupils.[18]

Although the upper and middle reaches of the nobility refused to attend all-estate schools, it is notable that 33 percent of the student body of thirty-eight major schools in 1801 were nobles' children. Of the rest, 14 percent were townspeople, 12 percent merchants, 11 percent soldiers, 11 percent serfs, 8 percent bureaucrats, 5 percent state, crown, and economic (former Church) peasants, 4 percent Cossacks and foreigners, and 2 percent clergy.[19] By the end of Catherine's reign, an additional 2,000 students attended military professional schools and 12,000 more were in garrison schools. In all, about 62,000 pupils attended 544 state educational institutions in 1796. Between 1782 and 1800, roughly 180,000 students, of whom 12,100 were girls, passed through the various schools of Russia.[20] Russia's only university, the University of Moscow, boasted an enrollment of eighty-five in 1785, down from one hundred in 1755. No estimate of the number receiving home education is available, but it did not likely exceed a few hundred. The peasantry was largely but not totally excluded from opportunities for education.

The preference of many of the nobility for French manners and shallow learning was not shared by all. The freeing of nobles from compulsory service motivated some to seek a better education. The state sent others abroad to study. The contrast between the growing prosperity and freedoms of the West contrasted sharply with autocracy and serfdom in Russia. The historian Marc Raeff noted a tendency among some conscience-stricken nobles to substitute service to the people in place of the old tradition of service to the state. Students in the Nobles' Land Cadet Corps formed strong personal attachments. Their broader education caused some to feel greater loyalty to the Russian nation than devotion to the tsar.[21] Both tendencies had consequences for Russia's future.

Although there was little broad public support for the education of girls, a small window had opened by the end of the century. Pedagogues saw the educated woman both as a mother better able to furnish her children with early moral upbringing and as a wife better equipped for household management. Parents recognized the social value of education for daughters. Those who could afford it hired foreign governesses to enhance their marriageability. A number of prominent women provided models for female roles in public life. The major and minor schools were coeducational. Girls, however, entered them thirteen times fewer than boys. Most parents in the larger public saw no need for the education of daughters and were reluctant to lose their help in the home or shop. Girls raised in the foundling homes acquired practical skills relevant both to maintaining a household and to work outside it. The Smolny and Novodevichy institutes for girls began as bold experiments in producing new women equal to the new men that Catherine hoped to create and attracted interest from pedagogues abroad.

By the end of her reign, Catherine's enthusiasm for Enlightenment experimentalism had turned to disillusioned conservatism. The French Revolution brought home to Russian authorities that the benefits of education and the changes in culture and society that it nourished were attended by dangers to order and stability. As a consequence of the upheaval in France, the Russian government required all French residents in Russia to swear to severe all relations with France and those with relatives in France to declare allegiance to King Louis XVI as well. Some 1,500 people, among them many governesses, swore the oath. A brave 48 declined.[22] Even before the end of the old regime in France, Catherine's governance was subject to the criticism of homemade socially conscious educated actors, many the product of state education initiatives. Her last years were marked by arrests of critics and studied neglect of the schools she had recently brought into being.

3

Refining the System: Alexander I and Nicholas I

The reign of Alexander I began early in 1801 with the assassination of his father Paul I; it ended late in 1825 with Alexander's early and unexpected death while on a tour of southern Russia. Alexander was succeeded by his much younger brother Nicholas I. His reign opened amid the Decembrist rebellion, an uprising of disaffected officers that he crushed "at the price of my subjects' blood."[1] Although different in many ways, the brothers were deeply influenced by their father Paul I. Paul came to the throne following Catherine's death in 1796. He was a well-educated and cultivated man with a powerful sense of the injustice of the Russian social order. As a young man he became estranged from his mother Catherine who saw him as a potential rival to the throne. Isolated from the court and increasingly alienated as well from his wife, Mariia Feodorovna, Paul spent much of his time at his estate at Gatchina. There he fell under the influence of Baron Steinwehr, a Prussian officer. Steinwehr enamored Paul with the already antiquated system of Prussian military command. He developed a taste for absolute authority and a passion for the details of parade square drill. When he acceded to the throne Paul brought to his office a strong sense of duty and the temperament of a military martinet. His taste for German ways and his arbitrary treatment of his subjects, especially the nobility whom he aimed to return to state service, led to conspiracies against him and ultimately to his assassination in 1801.

Catherine had separated Alexander from his parents on his birth. She furnished him with an education in the spirit of the Enlightenment. As a result Alexander was a Europeanized Russian who spoke French better than his native tongue. But Alexander also spent time with his father at Gatchina. There he too acquired a love of the military life and the order of the parade ground. Caught between the two worlds of his upbringing, Alexander was deeply conflicted throughout his reign and suffered from feelings of personal inadequacy. The experience of absolute command over men at Gatchina informed the enlightened despotism that marked his reign. At the heart of Alexander's politics lay the principle of legitimacy. He did not oppose constitutional forms of governance peacefully conferred by constituted authority but rejected regimes founded in revolution. In his youth he became deeply aware of the disarray in the administration of the empire, an awareness deepened during his many tours of the country throughout his reign. His ideal for Russia was not a constitution but a well-disposed monarchy unlimited in its legislative activity but restrained in its actions by laws and traditions as safeguards against despotism.

Nicholas differed little in that vision from his brother but suffered none of the doubts that haunted Alexander. He was raised by Paul in the military atmosphere of Gatchina but learned from his mother respect for the sanctity of the family and the centrality of the dynasty in Russian life. Nicholas's ideal of state administration was the order of the parade square. He had a powerful sense of duty and an obsession with order and unity. Politics and military matters were his constant concerns; the arts interested him scarcely at all except as instruments of politics. He shared none of Alexander's cosmopolitanism. The fact that he was Russian "means everything," he said. He adopted a defensive stance toward Europe and emphasized the differences between Russia and the West. But with the exception of the closing years of his reign, Nicholas was no tyrant. He lived modestly and happily in his family, setting an example of piety and devotion for his subjects. Like Alexander, he understood the function of law in the orderly administration of the state and oversaw the completion of the codification of the law that his brother had initiated. Throughout his reign, in government offices and within his own household chancellery, the so-called enlightened bureaucrats quietly prepared Russia for the "great reforms" of the next reign. In spite of their many differences there was a large measure of continuity between the reigns of the brothers. Education policy was no exception. Nicholas did not abandon Alexander's reforms in education but repurposed them to fit his vision of social order.

Early in his reign Alexander and his "Unofficial Committee" of personal advisors reformed central state administration. The major change was the replacement of Peter's colleges, headed by a board, with ministries, led by a single person. A new Ministry of National Enlightenment replaced Catherine's Commission of Public Education. Although there was a Council of Ministers, there was no cabinet. Instead, Alexander met separately with each of his ministers, and they were responsible solely to him. The Imperial Senate remained as the highest court of the land. In 1810 the Imperial State Council was made the sole body for the promulgation of laws in the empire. The emperor remained the single initiator of legislation and could veto enactments of the council or accept a minority opinion over the wishes of the council's majority. This structure remained essentially unchanged until 1905. Although Nicholas retained the new administrative order, he signaled his lack of trust in those institutions with the expansion of His Majesty's Own Imperial Chancellery. It was the various sections of the chancellery that addressed the most challenging problems of the state. The Second Section took on the enormous task of codifying the empire's laws, the Third Section policed the political security of the empire, the Fifth Section concerned itself with peasant affairs, including planning for the eventual emancipation of the serfs, and the Fourth Section oversaw imperial charities and played the leading role in the education of women.

State Schooling

The administrative reform initiated under Alexander I was inspired by the spirit of systematization that characterized the administration of Napoleonic France. The goal of the reform was to organize all the affairs of state under central authority in order to facilitate economic and social development. Education was central to the project. A major motivation for the education reform was the raising of the level of competence of the civil servants at all levels. A significant influence on the reform were the Education Statutes of Poland of 1783. The three partitions of Poland in the late eighteenth century had brought much of Poland and the so-called western provinces formerly controlled by Poland under Russian rule. The Polish statutes had established a ladder system of schools linked from bottom to top. Parish schools in villages provided a basic education for the poorer rural classes. District schools in towns had a four-year program of study and provincial schools in cities provided a seven-year program. At the top of the ladder were the universities of Cracow and Vilna. The secondary schools supervised the operation of the parish schools and universities oversaw the running of secondary schools. The secondary schools and universities catered to the large Polish nobility and wealthier non-nobles. Passage from the parish schools into the district schools in the Polish system was arduous. In 1803 Russia promulgated the Statute of the Imperial University of Vilna along with the Statute of the Schools of the Vilna School District that instituted the Polish system without its Polish nationalist content into the Western provinces. The school statute enabled any student who graduated from a parish school to enrol in a district school.

The next stages of educational reform were the Preliminary Regulations on Public Education of January 1803 followed by the Statute on Schools of November 1804. The statutes divided the empire into six school districts: St. Petersburg (established only in 1819), Moscow, Kazan', Kharkov, Vilna, and Dorpat, each with a university at the top of the educational ladder. Every school district had a curator who exercised broad supervisory powers and represented central authority. A Main School Administration in St. Petersburg consisted of the six curators and a number of the emperor's appointees. The universities were accorded a great deal of autonomy. A rector, elected by the professors from among their own ranks, headed the institution. From 1809, however, rectors were centrally appointed. New professors were elected by the faculty. All educational personnel, except village schoolteachers, were state servants who held rank on the Table of Ranks. Rectors held rank five and professors rank seven. Admission to the university conferred rank eight, and university students were entitled to wear a sword, the mark of nobility. They were supported by state scholarships throughout their years of university study.

The reform built on the existing school structure. Catherine's major schools became gymnasiums, four-year schools located in provincial capitals; the minor schools evolved into two-year elementary schools in district towns. On the bottom rung of the ladder were the parish schools in villages and towns with a one-year program. Each level of the system, as in the Polish model, administered the level below it. Inspectors of parish schools held rank nine on the Table of Ranks and those who inspected district schools held the seventh rank. Professors were also expected to visit schools within their school district regularly. The statute provided for state scholarships to enable promising students in district schools to go on to study in a gymnasium. Under the provisions of the statute, parish schools operated for four or five of the winter months, to accommodate the agricultural cycle, and for eighteen hours a week. District schools functioned for ten or eleven months with a twenty-eight-hour week. Gymnasiums had an eleven-month school year and thirty-hour week.

Parish schools normally had one teacher; they were funded entirely from local sources. District schools had two teachers and were financed by urban estate societies with some support from the treasury. Gymnasiums had eight teachers and were state-funded. Teachers in village and district schools were to be drawn from the graduates of gymnasiums. Each university was required to establish a pedagogical institute to train teachers for the gymnasiums and to mount supplementary pedagogical courses for the best gymnasium students to prepare them to teach in district or parish schools. A *Guide for Teachers of Public Schools* set out the recommended methods of teaching and organization of classes. Rote learning was discouraged. The guide urged teachers to familiarize themselves with the abilities of individual students, to explain ideas patiently, and to develop pupils' powers of reasoning. Corporal punishment was forbidden at all levels. The statute recommended salary levels for teachers, but in practice local authorities determined teachers' pay. Salaries varied from district to district. District schoolteachers were state servants with a rank of twelve. They were eligible for pensions. Gymnasium teachers of science held the eleventh rank, while coveted teachers of foreign languages were awarded the tenth rank.

The curriculum in the schools broadly reflected the ideas of the French utilitarian philosopher, the Marquis de Condorcet. He advocated a ladder system of schools with a coordinated curriculum from level to level. He opposed the traditional classical education with its stress on the teaching of Latin. Instead, he supported a modern curriculum emphasizing the theoretical sciences, modern languages, and applied science. Education, he argued, should serve the needs of the state through the preparation of useful citizens. Accordingly, the Statute on Schools of 1804 placed utility and equality at the heart of the education system. Each grade level was designed both to prepare the pupil for the next level and to be an end in itself by providing a complete and useful education for each of the social estates. The parish schools not only taught reading, writing, and the first four functions of arithmetic but also gave lessons in agricultural economy, natural phenomena, physiology, and health. District schools required the study of *On the Duties of Man and Citizen* that Catherine had sponsored, sacred history, Russian grammar and expository writing, arithmetic, basic geometry, physics, natural sciences, world and Russian geography, and drawing. Local school authorities were urged to add topics to the curriculum that were relevant to local conditions and economy. Students in district schools who wished to continue to the gymnasium could study Greek and Latin. The gymnasiums aimed to train students either for university study or for a useful and productive life after graduation. Their curriculum was based on that of the French *lycée*. Subjects included pure and applied mathematics, experimental physics, history, geography, statistics, natural science, political economy, Latin, French, and German. A cycle of philosophy, psychology, and ethics was also available. Some of the wealthier gymnasiums offered dancing, music, and drawing in addition. The statute also encouraged schools to link theoretical and practical knowledge through excursions in nature or to local industries.

The education reform was ambitious and highly idealistic. The reality fell far short of the framers' vision. A major weakness was funding for the schools. Alexander's reign was one of preparation for war and war. The French invasion in 1812, the burning of Moscow, and the vast sums spent on restoration left little money for education. In

1804 only 2.3 percent of the state budget was allocated to the entire school system. That meager sum fell to 1.3 percent in 1809, 0.8 percent in 1812, and rose to a mere 0.9 percent in 1818.[2] Gymnasiums received full funding that rarely met their needs, but district schools normally received less than half of their costs from the center and relied heavily on local resources. Underfunding meant that teachers' salaries were not guaranteed. The building, maintenance, lighting, and heating of district schools rested on local authorities. Few schools were purpose built; most were housed in converted structures. They were usually cramped and lacked supplies and equipment. School rooms were poorly heated and generally unhealthy for children. Few parish schools were ever created. Peasants and the poor urban estates saw no value in education beyond the ability to read a religious text. Those few students who went to school left as soon as they reached a minimal level of literacy.

Practice belied the stress on equality in the statute. Movement from one level of the system to the next was difficult. Restrictions were soon imposed. In 1811 all pupils from the poll-tax-paying estates (all except the nobility and clergy) were required to secure releases from their masters, guilds, or estate institutions to attend a university. When those who had received releases graduated, their upward estate standing had still to be affirmed by senate decree. In 1819 fees were introduced at parish, district, and gymnasium levels, further limiting access. In 1812 the program of study at the gymnasiums increased from four to seven years. By then the district school had largely ceased to be preparatory to the gymnasium. These measures markedly slowed but did not entirely halt the social mobility that the original reform had envisaged.

The system suffered from severe shortages of competent teachers. The pedagogical institutes mandated at universities by the statute were slow to open: in 1804 in Moscow, but only in 1811 in Kharkov, 1812 in Kazan', and 1820 in St. Petersburg. They provided a three-year course of study after university graduation. Students supported by government stipends were required to teach in a state school, usually a gymnasium, for six years after graduation. Many evaded the requirement. The St. Petersburg Institute for the Preparation of Gymnasium Teachers formed in 1804, later named the Main Pedagogical Institute, produced well-trained teachers but not enough to meet the demand. Most of its students were sons of priests. In 1819 it merged with the newly founded St. Petersburg University. Gymnasiums in more remote parts of the empire found it especially hard to recruit and retain teachers. The ambitious curriculum was impossible to deliver. The lower schools were even more poorly served. The statute called for elementary schoolteachers to be trained in the gymnasiums. Since, however, the upper grades of the gymnasiums had few students and those who did graduate had little inclination to teach in a parish or district school, the results were disappointing. The new universities, apart from Dorpat and Vilna, had difficulty recruiting able professors.

The reformers had hoped that the new state-school system would attract the nobility. It did not. Nobles continued to resist sending their children to school with commoners, preferring home education, private pensions, or military schools. In an attempt to force the nobility into the gymnasiums and universities, the government decreed in 1809 that promotion to the eighth rank on the Table of Ranks and again to the fifth rank required a fixed number of years of service in the lower ranks, the permission of the candidate's superior, and proof of studies appropriate to the rank sought in the bureaucracy. In the absence of such proof the candidate had to pass examinations administered by the universities. Failure was common. In 1810 the gymnasium was made the sole prerequisite for university study in a further attempt to force nobles into the system. Although by 1825 a small majority of gymnasium students came from the privileged estates, nobles generally continued to resist state schooling. Those who attended university to meet the requirements of the 1809 decree rarely graduated. Instead, they passed a number of courses that qualified them for their position in the civil service and received from the university an "*attestat*" that they had passed "all the courses for the necessary knowledge."[3] Non-nobles were rarely granted an attestat. Dormitories for nobles sprang up around gymnasiums and universities as they sought further to isolate themselves from commoners.

Continued pressure from the nobility persuaded the government to establish several educational institutions exclusively for nobles with a status close to that of universities. They provided good living conditions, attracted the best teachers, and conferred rank on their graduates. The model was the Nobles' Pension at Moscow University established in 1779. In 1811 the Russian Lyceum at Tsarskoe selo opened for noble youths with the goal of creating a bureaucratic elite. Four other schools for nobles opened in the provinces between 1817 and 1820, among them the Richelieu Lyceum in Odessa. In 1818 the noble pensions of Moscow and St. Petersburg Universities received the status of universities and conferred ranks on the Table of Ranks from fourteen to ten on their graduates. The highest rank that the universities of the two capitals could confer was fourteen for undergraduates and twelve for candidates (graduate students). In 1822 they were raised to ranks twelve and ten, respectively, Graduates of the four provincial universities received ranks from fourteen to twelve.[4]

From 1812 the cosmopolitan and rationalistic intellectual climate of the early years of Alexander's reign gave way to a conservative religious and nationalistic outlook. The emperor himself was drawn to the mysticism prominent in some European circles in the post-Napoleonic period. Symptomatic was his approval of the Russian Bible Society. It was an offshoot of the nonsectarian but pietistic British and Foreign Bible Society established in 1804 to spread the Christian gospels through publication of the scriptures in the languages of the world. From 1806 the society undertook to translate the scriptures for the non-Russian peoples of the empire. It also collaborated with the Holy Synod in the issue of a cheaper and less cumbersome edition of the Slavonic Bible. In addition it published a Russian version of the New Testament in 1821.[5] Prince Alexander Golitsyn, president of the Russian Bible Society, was also Procurator of the Holy Synod and head of the Main Administration of Religious Affairs of Foreign Creeds that oversaw the several non-Orthodox religions of the empire. He played a role in nurturing Alexander's new religiosity.

In 1816 Golitsyn added the Ministry of National Enlightenment to his several portfolios. In 1817 the offices that he held were merged into a single Ministry of Ecclesiastical Affairs and Public Instruction. Under his direction the focus of education was on a narrow religious upbringing and glorification of absolute monarchy at the expense of the academic and utilitarian curriculum of the 1804 education statute. The long-standing instrument of moral upbringing in schools, the book on *On the Duties of Man and Citizens*, was declared to be morally harmful. Readings from religious writings, especially the New Testament, took its place in lower schools. Natural history and philosophy were dropped from the curriculum, and time spent on history and geography shortened. A reform of the gymnasiums in 1819 saw a sharp reduction in the range of subjects taught. Philosophical subjects were purged and rationalist accounts of natural phenomena forbidden. The Law of God was now mandatory. A heavy dose of classical studies aimed at preparing gymnasium students for university entrance.

Golitsyn appointed members of the Russian Bible Society as curators of the six school districts. The most despised was the reactionary M. L. Magniskii, the curator of the Kazan' school district. He reviewed the university in Kazan', found it wanting, and proposed to close it outright. Dissuaded from such a drastic measure, he settled on purging the university's German professors for alleged teachings contrary to Christian belief. Although many of the Russian faculty were congenitally at odds with their German fellows, some resigned in solidarity at the dismissals. Golitsyn brought in Orthodox clergymen to teach a number of courses in religion. He required students to own a Bible, purged the library of much of its holdings, and made communal readings of scripture compulsory. The result was to halve the professoriate and student body, already few in numbers.

Another Bible Society zealot, D. P. Runich, took over as curator of the St. Petersburg School District in 1821. He accused several faculty members of "teaching in a spirit contrary to Christianity" and attempted to remove four professors. The faculty strongly resisted and the attempt failed. The future emperor Nicholas I, no friend of the Bible Society, commented ironically on the case: "We [the state] need such people, so please throw them out of the university. We have places for them."[6] At other universities Bible Society appointees had little impact. At Dorpat University, Count Karl Lieven did no more than to create a faculty of theology as did A. P. Obolenskii at the University of Moscow. The latter distinguished himself by defining for the first time in Russia the academic criteria for the award of undergraduate, candidate, masters, and doctoral degrees.

The growing influence of mystics within the Bible Society and their willing embrace of all faiths alienated the hierarchy of the Orthodox Church. They mounted a campaign against the society's influence. Alexander, alarmed by revolutionary movements in Western Europe and by the rise of secret societies in Russia, many of them associated with Freemasonry, began to see the Bible Society as a danger to traditional order. He banned the Masonic lodges but continued for a while to tolerate the Bible Society. In April 1824 he separated the Ministry of National Enlightenment from all the religious offices that had engulfed it and replaced Golitsyn as minister with the nationalist Admiral A. S. Shishkov. Shishkov eased the Bible Society-appointed curators out of office.

Alexander's death in November 1825 was punctuated by a rebellion against autocratic rule led by Russian officers, many from the most prominent noble families of the empire. The Decembrists aspired to replace the autocratic order with some form of representative government, either monarchical or republican. The rebels were quickly defeated in the capital by troops loyal to the new emperor, Nicholas I, but the revolt lingered on in the south into January 1826. Nicholas took a firm stand: five of the conspirators were executed. He then set out to placate the nobility by assuring them of their privileged position in society while bolstering a loyal bureaucracy as a counterweight to a nobility he no longer trusted. He blamed the insurrection of the nobles on the "semi-knowledge and idleness of mind" fostered by their education. He disliked the ladder system promoted by the education statute of 1804 because it encouraged social mobility. His education policies rested on his belief that the general aim of all schools was to give a moral education and furnish students with the means to acquire the knowledge each most needed according to their status. Beyond its central moral purpose education should have a narrow utilitarian focus, serve the interests of the state, and separate the social estates.[7]

Nicholas established a Committee on Schools that began work in 1826 on a new Statute on Schools. In December 1827 a decree banned serfs from attending gymnasiums or universities. The school statute, which was promulgated in 1828 and implemented in 1832, drew extensively on the Prussian program for schools of 1763. One-year parish schools provided peasants, craftsmen, and low-status factory workers with reading, writing, arithmetic, and religious instruction. The schools were open to boys aged 8 or over and girls no older than 11. Local authorities could add the teaching of crafts useful for the local economy along with some of the subjects of the first year of the district school. As in the 1804 reform, parish schools were geared to the agricultural cycle, operating during the months between fall harvest and spring planting. Parish schools were funded locally. While movement from parish to district school sometimes occurred, the statute positioned the parish schools as terminal and not preparatory to district schools. The district schools were open to all social estates but were geared to the educational needs of the sons of merchants, artisans, petty officials, shopkeepers, and other townsmen. A few peasants were able to enter the secondary level but not to shed their estate origins. Konstantin Klepnikov attended secondary school in the 1830s, the only peasant in the school. He later recalled that "in school they cut our hair, they dressed and shod us all identically. Thus social distance disappeared." But, he continued: "I took off my peasant clothes and put on the school uniform. I was in no way different from all the other students and all the same I still was a stranger among them." He did not complete the program for lack of means.[8] Separate schools for girls were mandated, but few if any appeared. The statute made parish teachers state employees with the rank of fourteen and raised their salaries. Teachers were expected to have completed the program of a district school.

The district schools offered a three-year program with a six-hour day for six days a week. They operated year round with a lengthy summer break. The curriculum was narrower than that of the 1804 statute. The teaching of classical and foreign languages disappeared as did natural history and physics. Russian history and geography were emphasized. Local authorities could add courses such as agriculture, commerce, or accounting that were relevant to the needs of the local economy. The number of teachers per district school went from two to five. They required no formal pedagogical training but were expected to have a gymnasium education. District schools received a small subsidy, but urban societies and private donors contributed significantly to their funding. Tuition was again free at both parish and district levels.

The gymnasium or secondary school emerged in the reform as a standalone seven-year institution. Its first three years of study were equivalent to the first three years of the district school. The final four years provided advanced study. The gymnasium had the dual purpose of preparing some of its students for university entrance while giving others sufficient knowledge to succeed in state service without further study. Natural sciences remained in the gymnasium curriculum but physics was removed. Applied mathematics took precedence over pure mathematics. Eleven hours a week were spent on the study of Law of God. Latin was the basis of the curriculum for those who were university-bound; Greek was now offered only in gymnasiums located in the six university cities. Gymnasiums had a minimum of ten teachers, who were expected to have a university education. Teachers in core subjects held the rank of twelve and teachers of drawing and penmanship the rank of fourteen. The gymnasiums were funded by the state although donations were welcome.

A new university statute was promulgated in 1835. The declared purpose of the universities remained, as in the 1804 statute, to train capable men for all branches of the state service. Universities remained open to all free estates. Each university had faculties of law, medicine, and philology. The latter was made up primarily of history, language studies, and literature. In medicine the program was five years in length and four years in the other faculties. The statute established a classically based liberal arts and science curriculum as the appropriate preparation for civil servants and gymnasium teachers. Degrees remained linked to the Table of Ranks. The many distractions that had diverted professors from their teaching and research were now removed. Their former duties of supervision and inspection of lower schools passed to the curator of the school district, as did censorship and student discipline. At Nicholas's insistence the government appointed university rectors; the faculty chose deans and faculty appointees, although the minister could also appoint new faculty. The powers of faculty councils were reduced to academic matters only, a relief to most professors. A directorate of the rector, deans, and a *"sindik"* chosen by the curator administered the non-academic functions of the university, oversaw the legality of faculty council decisions, and allocated stipends to students. The statute increased faculty salaries. It remained silent on the content of programs and courses and on the estate composition of the student body.

Since 1804, the universities had suffered from shortages of qualified faculty, low student enrollments, underfunding, and chronic student indiscipline. The meddling of the Bible Society reduced the faculty in some universities further and pushed student enrollments to new lows. In 1825 St. Petersburg University had 50 students and still only 130 in 1830. A cholera epidemic in 1830–1 further reduced the numbers. The enrollment at Moscow University fell from 714 in 1830 to 435 in 1834.[9] To address faculty shortages, a Professors' Institute, established at Dorpat University in 1828, aimed to attract twenty graduate candidates from each of the universities to train for two years as future faculty members. The numbers willing to join the program fell short of the target and did little to relieve the dearth of faculty. The Second Section of Nicholas's chancery, concerned with the codification of the law, trained twelve students to teach law in universities. Vilna University in the former Polish provinces was implicated in the Polish rebellion of 1830 and was closed in 1832. In its place

St. Vladimir University opened in Kiev in 1834 with eighteen professors. Its mission was "to spread Russian education and Russian national consciousness in the Polonized regions of western Russia."[10] From the middle of the decade, enrollments in the universities grew slowly and undergraduate degree completion rates rose, especially in St. Petersburg and Moscow, to 50 percent and 75 percent, respectively.[11]

Administration of the gymnasiums and elementary schools passed under the new statute to the curators of the six school districts who now appointed school directors and teachers in collaboration with local authorities. Curators also oversaw the work of school inspectors who enforced discipline in schools and conformity to school policy. Competent teachers remained in short supply. In 1828 the Main Pedagogical Institute in St. Petersburg was reorganized to recruit and train teachers for the gymnasiums. Candidates were drawn mainly from the clergy estate. Over six years of training, students, who were admitted from age 17 and over, took a general preparatory course followed by study of the subjects they intended to teach, and finally training in pedagogy. On graduation, they were required to teach for eight years in a ministry school. In 1838 the institute opened a section to prepare teachers for district schools. Students from age 16 to 18 years with a parish school education trained for four years. The section closed after nine years as more graduates from the gymnasiums began to enter the teaching ranks. In 1850 faculties of history and philology in universities added courses in pedagogy, which were made compulsory for all aspiring to teach in state schools or in home education.

The prestige of the teaching profession remained low, especially of teachers in parish and district schools. The state had raised teachers' salaries, but local authorities continued to pay them. Pay was erratic and often less than the state required. Local authorities also had to provide housing and board for teachers. The teachers' material dependence opened them to abuse and exploitation from authorities and villagers. Only a fraction of teachers had specific training in pedagogy. All were expected to follow the guidance of the prescribed text, *Guide to the Didactic Science of Teaching*. Few did. Corporal punishment, earlier forbidden, was again permitted. Discipline was strict. Students were subordinate to teachers and teachers to school directors. The set program allowed no deviations. The school year culminated in examinations, the sole criterion of advancement. Endless repetition of facts without any understanding of their significance was the result. A student at a Kazan' gymnasium recalled that most teachers were "rude, denouncing students for impudence. Teaching consisted of cramming; several teachers were distinguished by their violence."[12] In the 1840s, however, a few schools were better run and teaching in the new child-centered methods prevailed in them. They remained the exceptions to the rule.

The minister of education from 1833 to 1849 was Sergei S. Uvarov. It was Uvarov who provided a justification for the autocratic rule of Nicholas I with the slogan "Autocracy, Orthodoxy, and Nationality." He had served as the highly successful curator of the St. Petersburg school district from 1810 to 1819 and was a principal founder and first rector of St. Petersburg University. He was president of the Academy of Sciences and served as a prominent member of the committee that drafted the school statute of 1828. A highly educated individual, Uvarov saw human history as a progression, guided by Divine Providence, toward the civil and political freedom of all citizens. Each nation followed its own path toward this universal moral destination. Uvarov viewed Russia as a European nation but one of its youngest members. He believed that it was essential that Russia absorb accumulated European knowledge while remaining faithful to its own social and political traditions. "One of the most difficult problems of our time," he wrote, "is providing true education, a fundamental necessity of our century, with deep reverence and warm faith in the truly Russian conservative principles of Orthodoxy, autocracy, and nationality."[13] Russia was in his view still too immature for constitutional government. The path to maturity lay through moral, social, political, and intellectual education under the rule of an enlightened autocrat. Education was a principal task of the state. He, therefore, set out to improve the education system at all levels.[14]

Like Nicholas I, Uvarov believed in the separate roles of the social estates. He also supported the goal of Peter the Great of linking nobility to state service and state education. Nobility, in his as in Peter's view, was not necessarily hereditary but could be achieved through merit in state service. Rather than preventing commoners from entering state schools, Uvarov sought to attract more nobles into them. With that goal he subsidized the building of pensions and hostels near gymnasiums, enabling more nobles' sons to live among their own kind while attending the gymnasiums as day students. He also assiduously solicited donations from noble parents to support them. Uvarov believed that the appropriate education of an aristocracy and the best foundation for state service were in the Greek and Latin classics. Under his direction the classics constituted the basis of the curriculum in the gymnasiums and historico-philological faculties of the universities. Continued pressure from the nobility for their vision of an education appropriate to their caste forced the minister to permit nobles to establish at their own expense five-year gymnasiums for nobles only, which eschewed the classics and taught French, dancing, fencing, and horsemanship among a few other modern subjects. There were forty-seven of them by 1849.[15]

Among Uvarov's many accomplishments was the partial restoration of the prestige of the Academy of Sciences. Shocked by the excesses of the French Revolution, Paul I took steps to block cultural contact with the West. A victim was the Academy of Sciences where Paul left vacancies unfilled. Alexander restored adequate funding to the academy, and in 1803 it received a new charter. The humanities were once more added to its mandate, and the academicians were charged with expanding human knowledge, spreading enlightenment, advancing science through new discoveries, and applying knowledge to improve human welfare. Academicians gained greater control over administration and the appointment of fellow members. Uvarov had become president of the academy in 1818. He was skeptical about theoretical science as incompatible with religion but valued applied science. As minister of education, Uvarov issued a new charter for the Academy of Sciences in 1836. Under it the academy was essentially reduced to a government agency as it had been in the reign of Elizabeth. The focus of research should be practical and all discoveries with practical application had to be reported to the government. Uvarov was by no means an enemy of scientific learning. During his long tenure as president of the academy, he attracted many distinguished scholars from abroad and a few from Russia as its members. The academy had a number of successes during his tenure, especially in mathematics through the work of Mikhail Ostrogradskii, Pafnutii Chebyshev, and Nikolai Lobachevskii.

Uvarov also understood the need for commerce and manufacturing, a task that he assigned to the middle social estates of the realm. In 1839 urban schools for the sons and daughters of artisans and other townsmen, but open to all estates and funded by the city *duma* (council), opened to teach the equivalent of the parish school program. Under Uvarov's guidance, parish schools also increased vocational training in agricultural and craft production. District schools began to institute a wide range of commercial and technical courses. Universities added courses in agronomy, agricultural management, forestry, and mechanics, and created model farms along with programs to train teachers for these subjects.

In spite of Nicholas's preference, neither the gymnasiums nor the universities prohibited members of the middle estates from admission. Uvarov encouraged talented commoners to seek middle and higher education, and many in the urban estates sought secondary and higher education as paths to social mobility. State authorities were torn between the need for more educated citizens to further its goals and security on the one hand and growing concerns about the effects of social mobility on traditional social and political structures on the other. The latter gradually prevailed. To deter the aspiring poor, a fee of ten silver roubles was imposed on entering gymnasium students in 1836; the fee was raised to eleven roubles in 1838 and applied both to entering and returning students. Additional increases followed in 1845 and 1848, culminating in a fee of thirty silver roubles in the gymnasiums of St. Petersburg and Moscow. As well, those institutions were enjoined to enforce the regulation imposed in the reign of Alexander I that all members of tax-paying social groups had to secure a letter of release from their guild or other group in order to enter a secondary or higher school. On their graduation they had to apply to the Senate to have their new social status affirmed. The letters of release were not automatic since the departure of a tax-paying member of the group, as earlier seen, placed a greater financial burden on those who remained. The rules were not rigorously enforced, however. In the late 1840s some 57 percent of students at Moscow University were commoners. The average in the empire's universities was a much lower 29 percent.[16]

Nicholas did not share Uvarov's enthusiasm for the classics as the foundation of education. The economic ministries of the government, merchants, and the growing number of industrialists campaigned for a more practical curriculum rooted in commerce, science, and technology. By the middle of the 1840s classics was seen by conservatives as subversive, awakening in students, it was believed, republican ideas. In commercial centers some gymnasiums began to offer courses in commercial law, technology, and natural history. Such courses were modeled on those taught in the German *Realschule* of the day. In non-Russian regions of the empire, teaching in local languages was permitted if it facilitated the commercial-industrial interests of the region. As new courses entered the curriculum of the gymnasiums, others regarded as dangerous were removed. Logic ceased to exist as an independent subject, statistics related to geography was also eliminated because it raised political questions. An important addition to the curriculum was jurisprudence. Knowledge of the law was deemed imperative for those entering state service.

A major step in 1849 was the division of the curriculum in one of the gymnasiums of St. Petersburg into two streams. The first three years of the program provided a common curriculum. In the fourth grade students intending to enter state service took more classes in Russian language and applied mathematics; in the fifth grade they added jurisprudence. Students intending to enter university took Latin and Greek, where it was available, beginning in the fourth grade, and Russian language and geography. Students headed to the physio-mathematical and medical faculties of universities took natural sciences. Other gymnasiums began to adopt this model. By 1852, three types of gymnasiums coexisted. Those teaching natural sciences and from the fifth grade jurisprudence for students entering state service or going on to science or medicine faculties in the university (the latter also took Latin); those teaching jurisprudence with the primary mission of producing state servants; and the classical gymnasium for students entering the historico-philological faculties of the universities.

Other ministries opened schools as well. As early as 1797 the Appanages Department that administered the extensive lands owned by the imperial family opened village schools to train boys as clerks in appanage offices. A plan to send three boys from each local appanage office to the new district schools foundered when few district schools actually opened. In 1828 the Ministry of Appanages ordered that rural schools taught by local priests be established in each local area. Their purpose was to provide basic literacy and training for petty peasant officials. In 1830 the Ministry of Finance established *volost'* (township) schools to train peasants as scribes and clerks for state peasant local offices. The students were meant to learn reading, penmanship, accounting, and Law of God over four years of study. Since the peasants showed scant interest in the schools, the ministry decided in 1837 to conscript one child, preferably an orphan, from each village. Within five years some two thousand pupils attended sixty schools. The completion rates were negligible. Of three hundred students in such schools in Kursk province, for example, only eight students became scribes. The rates were marginally better in villages that engaged in trade or cottage manufacture where literacy and numeracy were of greater value. The volost' schools passed into the jurisdiction of a new Ministry of State Properties in 1837. The ministry now required each village to have a school with a three-year course of basic grammar, arithmetic, and religious-moral training. At first the peasants broadly supported the schools with donations to supplement the ministry subsidy of two hundred to four hundred roubles a year to each school. Teaching in the schools was left to priests who provided a low level of instruction. As a result by 1860 the peasants had largely withdrawn support from the volost' schools.

Military Schooling

By the end of the eighteenth century the traditional amalgamation of military education with general education was abandoned in Europe for more specialized schooling. Russia soon followed suit. The reform of military schooling was high on the state's agenda in the first half of the nineteenth century. Concerns about the quality of military education late in the reign of Catherine II had already prompted a review of the Nobles' Land Cadet Corps by the future hero of 1812, M. I. Kutuzov. Following Kutuzov's recommendations, Emperor Paul I ordered the sharp reduction of the humanities in the corps' curriculum and greater emphasis on military sciences and history. The closing of the corps' theater underscored the new direction. For the first time summer field camps were instituted for the field training of cadets. The corps also added a special children's preparatory section that took in boys aged 4–6. Most were orphans or children of the poorest nobility.

Early in his reign Alexander I recognized the need "to give military educational institutions a new structure, and to unite them under one general branch of state administration under one and the same idea and with one and the same goal."[17] In 1801 he had established nine junior military preparatory schools and eight senior schools in provincial cities across European Russia and the Baltic provinces. Students entered the junior schools at 7–9 years of age. Graduates of the senior schools, on a quota basis, could enter either the Nobles' Land Cadet Corps or a university. The provincial schools were intended for the local nobility and were to be funded by them. In 1805 all military schools were placed under a Permanent Council of Military Schools. In the same year Alexander ordered that every province must open a military school and that graduates should attend a cadet corps. To meet the new demand he established new cadet corps in provincial cities. In 1802 the Corps of Pages was remade into an elite military educational institution with an initial class of only twenty-five students. It offered a seven-year program divided into five years of general education and two years of specialist education for either military or civil careers. Students took Law of God, Russian language and literature, German and French, mathematics, mechanics, physics, statistics, strategy and tactics, artillery, and military law. By 1827 the number of students reached 134. The elite nature of the Corps of Pages was confirmed in 1832. Only sons of fathers in the top four ranks of the Table of Ranks in civil and military service were eligible. By 1837 only those whose fathers were in the first three ranks qualified. A new lyceum at Tsarskoe selo that leaned toward the training of civil servants was also highly elitist. Another important military school, the Nobles' Regiment, opened in 1807. By 1812 some 2,000 students were enrolled in it, and in 1815 more than 3,000 studied there. Over its twenty-five-year history it graduated 9,070 officers.[18]

By the beginning of the reign of Nicholas I, the quality of the officer corps had risen significantly. Its loyalty to the crown, however, was thrown into doubt by the Decembrist uprising, led by a contingent of officers from many leading noble families, which had heralded Nicholas's accession to the throne. The thorough investigation of the motives of the rebellious officers initiated by Nicholas revealed that the tendency of a small number among the nobility to transfer loyalty from state to people as early as Catherine's reign was reinforced by the French Revolution that had advanced the nation as the appropriate object of citizens' devotion. The Russian victory over Napoleon had awakened in many educated Russians a patriotism rooted in the idea of the nation that transcended loyalty to the Romanov dynasty. Convinced that the various military schools did not nurture loyalty to the crown, Nicholas ordered a review of their curriculum in 1826. The result was the General Statute on Military Educational Institutions of 1830. The statute proclaimed that the goal of military education was to instill honor and morality in the students and equip them for practical service. In particular the military school had to provide students with "the ability to serve the Emperor usefully and honorably and lead them to understand that their well-being throughout their life depends on steadfast devotion to the throne."[19] Loyalty to the dynasty, Nicholas insisted, took precedence over loyalty to the nation. The statute recognized three types of military schools: (1) provincial cadet corps and noble regiments; (2) the Corp of Pages and Nobles' Land Cadet Corps in the capitals; and (3) the Artillery and Engineering Corps and the Naval Cadet Corps. In 1836 the program of the several cadet corps was revised to include a one-year preparatory class for 7–9-year-olds, five years of general education, and three years of specialist military training. The curriculum remained relatively broad, underlining the role that military schools still played in general education in spite of the reform. Studies included Law of God, Russian language and literature, German and French, mathematics, natural sciences, geography, history, statistics, law, penmanship, drawing, and drafting. Between 1825 and 1856 the several cadet corps of the empire graduated 17,653 students of whom 14,415 served as officers.[20]

An important educational institution that opened in the reign of Paul I was the Imperial Medical-Surgical Academy. In 1808 it came under the jurisdiction of the new Ministry of National Enlightenment. Beginning in 1808 its faculty were accorded the same rights as those of the Academy of Sciences. From that year the Medical-Surgical Academy had three teaching sections: medicine, veterinary science, and pharmacology. The academy was open to members of all social estates, including serfs who had gained the consent of their landlords. Serfs who graduated were obligated to work for their landlords for six years after which they were freed. The academy received financial support from the Ministry of War and in 1838 came under its jurisdiction. Graduates for the most part served as army and naval doctors.

The garrison schools founded by Peter the Great continued to function in the first part of the nineteenth century. By then their students were mostly the children of soldiers. There were roughly sixteen thousand pupils attending them at the beginning of the century. With the aim of making the army more self-sufficient by supporting themselves through farming, the government began to establish "military colonies" in 1810. Soldiers lived with their families in highly organized settlements where they doubled as peasants. The discipline in the colonies was severe. Violent resistance to them among the colonists grew and most were closed by 1831. While they functioned the colonies offered an ambitious educational and cultural program in cantonal schools. There was an elementary school in every colony where children between the ages of 7 and 12 along with adult illiterates studied Russian language, arithmetic, geometry, drawing, Law of God, physical education, and military drill. A lack of qualified teachers forced many of the colonies to rely on the Lancaster system of teaching, developed first in Britain, in which the senior students taught groups of beginners. A teachers' institute to train teachers for the colonies' schools opened in 1818. The colonies also operated schools for girls. The schools were the only relatively successful aspect of the experiment with military colonies. Observers noted that the children were often proficient in mathematics; many spoke German or French. Outsiders saw the schools as an effort to generate a middle class of citizens as Catherine had also hoped to do. By 1822 around 65,000 pupils attended garrison and cantonal schools and the numbers grew rapidly until the experiment ended.[21]

Church Schooling

The uneasy relationship between Church and state over the former's role in public education intensified in the first half of the nineteenth century. The state sought to engage the Church in public education; the Church sought to preserve its independence. The education reform of 1804 made clergy, nobles, and town societies responsible for the support of primary schools and envisioned the employment of seminarians as teachers in them. Most seminarians failed to meet the required standard for the position, and those who did had little inclination to teach. One area of agreement was around the need to combat the proselytizing of the Old Believers, who were Orthodox sectarians, and of other Christian sects. Women among the Old Believers played an important role in promoting the Old Believer faith. In bodies similar to Orthodox monasteries called *sketes* located in the Trans-Volga region and run largely by women, acolytes received spiritual as well as practical instruction in handicrafts and disseminated their spiritual learning as well as literacy and practical skills among the peasant population.[22] With the aim of countering their influence, the Church in 1805 authorized the creation of church-parish schools taught by priests. In 1814 it permitted all church servants to establish private schools on their own initiative to teach reading, writing, and Law of God under the supervision of the local bishop. The schools were made exempt from the tax for the support of orphans that other private schools had to pay. The Holy Synod strongly resisted a proposal in 1818 to place these schools under the Ministry of National Enlightenment on the grounds that clerics should not be compelled to do secular work. In 1836 the Synod ordered all priests to establish schools in their parishes. The numbers grew rapidly. In 1838 there were around 1,500 church-parish schools and nearly 5,000 in 1853. The volost' schools on state lands were converted into church-parish schools in 1843. Estimates of the number of pupils attending them varied widely but were in the range of 150,000 in 1853, among them some girls. By contrast, the number of primary schools under the jurisdiction of the Ministry of National Enlightenment in 1855 was just over 1,100 with around 49,000 pupils, the great majority of which were located in towns.[23]

The education of the sons of the clergy remained in the hands of the Church. In 1807 a Committee for the Improvement of Ecclesiastical Schools convened to address the many challenges that clerical education faced. The committee affirmed the mandate of ecclesiastical schools as the training of candidates for the clergy. It recommended a move away from the European grammar school curriculum that did little to prepare the clergy for their parochial duties. It proposed less stress on Latin and more on Orthodox theology, church history, and Slavonic and Russian language along with a few secular subjects. The committee also recommended a centralized administration of church schools in place of the local administration of bishops. It proposed a four-tier system of schools with four academies at the top, thirty-six seminaries around the empire, and ten district schools and as many as thirty elementary parish schools in every diocese.

The Statute on Church Schools was promulgated in 1814. According to its provisions parish schools taught reading, writing and the first four functions of arithmetic, church singing, and catechism. District schools offered a four-year program with Latin, Slavonic, Russian, geography, catechism, and parish accounting. The seminaries provided six years of education separated into three sections: first came a two-year course in rhetoric and poetry with readings in classical and a few Slavonic-Russian texts; the second section was philosophy in which students studied logic, metaphysics, ethics, psychology, and history of philosophy; the third section was theology. Four academies topped the structure. They offered a four-year program that comprised a more intensive version of the last two sections of the seminaries. The goal of the academies was to produce a body of Church scholars as well as an administrative hierarchy equal in education and sophistication to their secular peers. The statute preserved the estate nature of church education. It required the sons of the clergy to study in church schools. Although outsiders were not formally excluded, they were rarely received into the system. A Commission of Ecclesiastical Schools now oversaw the whole structure. School councils in the seminaries and academies retained considerable autonomy over administration. While exposure to suspect classical texts was reduced, Latin remained the language of instruction except in the teaching of Scripture, Slavonic literature, and the few secular subjects permitted.

Apart from the academies that were well funded, the system lacked qualified teachers and the reform could not be implemented wholesale. Initially, funding came from a state subsidy and the sale of candles. The state subsidy was soon in part diverted to other purposes and ended entirely in 1817. Competition from private vendors of candles reduced the expected revenue from their sale by half. In the early 1820s the state increased the budget for the Church, but inflation and the growth of the system soon erased the gains. The physical conditions in the schools were poor. Libraries possessed few books, classes were large, dormitories were crowded and filthy, meals were inadequate, disease proliferated, and death rates were high. Teachers' salaries in seminaries were 58 percent of those in gymnasiums. The best teachers left. Priests or graduates waiting for a church placement, usually with no pedagogical training, taught many classes. Consequently, the quality of teaching was low. Thinking was discouraged. One seminarian later recalled that "it was enough to resort to opening one's mouth and emitting some words but, oddly, they lacked any of the sense that they originally had."[24] There were too few stipends for poor students; over time their value declined. As in the previous century, seminarians often begged or roamed the alleys in search of scraps. As before as well, the number of graduates exceeded the church appointments available. In the 1840s the Church placed a cap on the number of admissions to the seminaries. In spite of the cap, 2,178 seminary graduates were without appointments in 1850.[25] Those who wished to join the civil service or army faced barriers. As noted, the clergy estate was exempt from taxes. Anyone who chose to leave the clerical estate had only a few months to secure a new status before being arbitrarily enrolled in a tax-paying estate. Some became home tutors. Many of the best graduates of seminaries preferred to attend a university rather than go on to a Church academy.

In 1836 N. A. Protasov became Procurator of the Holy Synod. He hoped to close the gap between priest and parishioners. He proposed to place greater emphasis on Orthodox theology and to introduce subjects like medicine and agriculture into the school curriculum, better to meet the practical needs of parishioners. The Synod, however, rejected a more practical curriculum as serving state rather than church interests. Protasov persisted. He convinced the emperor to replace the Commission of Ecclesiastical Schools with the Bureau of Ecclesiastical Education composed largely of laymen under his influence. He insisted on the introduction of agronomy and medicine into the curriculum of seminaries, eliminated metaphysics and history of philosophy, and required all teaching to be in Russian. Lack of resources and trained teachers thwarted his efforts. By the end of Nicholas's reign the church reform of 1814 was deemed a failure. Teaching remained ineffective, many of the best seminarians left the Church, and the training of priests did little to prepare them for the realities of parish life. In particular, authorities found that the estate basis of clerical education was restrictive and detrimental to economic and social progress.

Private Schooling

The long-standing uneasy relationship between education authorities and private schools continued in the nineteenth century. Of major concern was the influence on the education of the young by the foreigners who operated most private schools and filled the ranks of home tutors. The underfunded state school system was not only inadequate to meet the educational needs of the country but also failed to provide what many parents saw as an appropriate education for their children. Private schools catered to those expectations. Unable to dispense with private schooling the government sought first once more to certify the academic qualifications and moral qualities of founders and teachers and later to align private with state schooling.

Authorities asserted the regulations on private educators first decreed in 1757 repeatedly. The Statute on Schools of 1804 required founders of pensions to present the director of the nearest gymnasium with evidence of their qualifications to teach as well as a detailed academic plan, a list of teachers with evidence of their teaching competence, an outline of the proposed method of teaching, and a list of textbooks and materials to be used. Secondary-level private schools required the approval of their curricula and staff by a university. The standard of private schoolteachers had to equal that of teachers in state schools and the textbooks they used needed state approval. The class time devoted to moral education had also to parallel that of state schools. All private schools were required by the statute to teach Russian language and Law of God. Founders were free to choose the rest of the curriculum subject to the approval of the gymnasium or university. The statute mandated annual examinations in the presence of inspectors of district schools and regular reports on teaching standards to the director of a gymnasium or university rector. In 1804 there were eighty-eight pensions in Russia with 2,074 pupils and 243 teachers. Twenty-four schools were in St. Petersburg, twenty-two in Moscow, and the remainder in Vilna, Dorpat, Kazan', and Kharkov.[26]

The School Statute of 1828 reiterated most of the conditions of the statute of 1804. It placed greater emphasis on the alignment of private schools with the equivalent state school. Lower schools had to conform to the state district school curriculum, including Law of God, Russian language, the history of the Russian state, and sacred and church history, but could also add courses that addressed local conditions or the particular mission of the school. Teachers of Law of God and of sacred and church history had to have been educated in a church school or to have served for at least three years as a teacher of these subjects in a state school. Secondary-level schools had to conform to the programs of the gymnasiums. Textbooks used in state schools were required at the same levels as in private schools. At year's end, private school students were examined in the presence of representatives of the local school administration. Private schools were subject to twice-yearly inspections by district school directors. In 1831 a regulation required that founders of schools must be Russian citizens.

The tough regulations had little effect on the spread of private schools. The government responded in 1833 with "On Measures against the Increase of Pensions." It banned new private schools in the capitals altogether and permitted them elsewhere only where local school authorities believed they were needed. The measures were ineffective. In subsequent years the growth of private schools exceeded that of state schools. In 1849 there were 431 district state schools with 27,198 students and 1,065 parish schools with 43,203 pupils. In the same year there were 599 private schools of all kinds with 15,244 students. Private schools were of many types. Normally they taught foreign languages along with Russian, arithmetic, history, geography, drawing, music, and dancing. Some offered a foreign language, etiquette, and dancing.

The number of pensions for girls grew faster than those for boys, largely because they were unregulated by the state. Girls' education was deemed a private matter. In the St. Petersburg school district in 1820 twenty-five of the forty-five pensions were for girls and in 1828 forty-five of sixty-two.[27] Pensions charged tuition fees, and many received generous donations from nobles or wealthy merchants. The regulations imposed in 1828 gradually brought private schools for boys into closer alignment with the state system. Curriculum and teaching materials were increasingly similar as were the hours devoted to each subject. Private schools had to have at least three grades and teach an eleven-month school year with a June holiday, and year-end final examinations. The alignment was especially enforced in the capitals where private schools corresponded to the three levels of gymnasium, district, and parish of the state school system.

Home schooling by tutors, home teachers, governors, and governesses had numerous critics in government and society. Nicholas I was especially hostile to private education of any sort. The poet Alexander Pushkin, who had been educated at home by governesses and governors, condemned home schooling as immoral. He deplored the slavish relationship of teacher and pupil and the paucity of learning conveyed. Other leading intellectuals like the historian Nicholas Karamzin agreed.[28] Russians who could afford them hired tutors primarily to teach their children a foreign language, usually French among the nobility and German among the merchants. Most tutors consequently were foreigners. Unable to dispense with home schooling the government sought to regulate it. In 1812 a decree reaffirmed the regulation of 1757 that anyone claiming a domestic teaching role, especially foreigners of either sex, was required to have their knowledge and intellectual and moral qualities certified by a Russian university. Parents who hired uncertified tutors were subject to fines and the tutor to deportation. The regulation was without any means of enforcement and was generally ignored. In 1824 there were 186 home teachers in St. Petersburg province alone who lacked certification. Revolutions in Europe in 1830 further raised anxieties in government circles about the influence of foreigners. A regulation of 1831 required Westerners wishing to teach in Russia to provide documentation regarding their material condition, faith, and general conduct on their arrival in Russia. In the same year a regulation required parents to educate children from ages 10 to 18 exclusively in Russian. Failure to do so could result in the exclusion of a son from military or state service.

In 1834 the government issued a comprehensive statute on domestic tutors and teachers. The purpose of the statute was to limit the number of foreign tutors and draw more Russians into domestic schooling. The initiative was not entirely new. The Foundling Homes began to train teachers, governors, and governesses at the beginning of the century. In 1806 the Home of the Society of Lovers of Labor in St. Petersburg opened and took in fifty girls from the poor urban classes and trained them as governesses. Under the 1834 statute nannies and child nurses who were Russian subjects required no special training but only moral certification. Home tutors had to have graduated from a secondary school and home teachers had as well to pass a special examination administered by a university, lycée, or gymnasium in their subject. All must have been born in a free estate, be Christian, and demonstrate moral character. Foreigners could serve in domestic teaching roles if they provided proof of baptism and other documents from a Russian diplomatic mission abroad. Supplementary regulations in August 1834 aligned the status of home teachers with teachers in the state schools and placed them under the supervision of the director of schools in the local district or of university rectors. Tutors and teachers were ordered to use the textbooks used in state schools. All foreign tutors had to be recertified for a fee that was placed in a pension fund for impoverished aging tutors. Between 1834 and 1843, 4,483 certificates were issued, among them around a hundred foreign governesses in service before 1834; several took Russian citizenship.[29]

Over the years there was an evolution in the languages favored by the elite. French predominated in the eighteenth century but fell under a shadow during the French Revolution. Swiss and German teachers briefly gained prominence, but French soon reasserted itself. German had always been popular among merchants and many government officials. English was slow to arrive in spite of Catherine the Great's hiring of English governesses. By the 1830s, however, English became a language of choice in aristocratic circles. Late in the decade Lady Londonderry on visiting Russia was surprised that among the circle she encountered "many people here speak English. It appears to form a part of every woman's education."[30]

The Petrine paradigm of a governing foreign elite animated the enthusiasm of the nobility for homeschooling by foreigners. For the great nobles the acquisition of a foreign language determined the selection of a tutor. Knowledge of a West European language had value in advancement in both military and civil service. Moreover, acceptance into the highest circles of society depended on proficiency, or better, eloquence in French. Dancing was also an essential element of noble education. Precision of movement and proper bearing on and off the ballroom floor were markers of a good upbringing. Home education played an especially important part in the upbringing of wealthy noble girls. The less wealthy sought the same attainments in pensions. Unlike sons, who normally left their early domestic governor for schools, preferably where dancing was part of the curriculum, girls remained under the supervision of a governess until marriage. In the early nineteenth century, especially among the provincial gentry, the education of noble girls was "geared entirely to getting an advantageous marriage." The goal was to attain "the means to shine in the salon, to be captivating and pleasing."[31] The governess taught good manners and social skills as well as language proficiency to her charges. They were constant companions to them, shaping their leisure time and tending to their moral and spiritual well-being. The treatment of governesses varied from household to household. They were often viewed as tools, means to an end, and easily disposable. In general they had little status in the household and kept a low profile outside of the children's quarters. Competition for qualified governesses before the tougher regulations of 1834 could result in good working conditions, however. In a few cases governesses became permanent members of the family and raised two or more generations of children.

Schooling Girls

During the first half of the nineteenth century, attitudes to the education of women slowly evolved. The "frivolous" education of the social butterfly was gradually replaced by the "sufficient" education appropriate to a woman's status as a wife and mother. Increasingly, a good education for women was seen as a prerequisite for social progress. Observers remarked on the influence of educated women on social behavior. P. D. Boborykin recorded: "Youths were 'polished' and that was no bad thing. And on them women, married or maiden, exercised their moral influence."[32] Among pedagogues and education officials the schooling of girls at all levels of society took on new importance. Girls as well as boys had since Catherine's time received an education in a variety of charitable institutions like the foundling homes. The statute of 1804 on schools opened parish schools to girls as well as boys, although girls attended in very small numbers. District schools and gymnasiums also accepted girls. In 1808 twenty girls attended the gymnasium in Vitebsk, thirteen in Mogilev, three in Novgorod, and seven in Pskov. In 1824 in schools administered by the Ministry of National Enlightenment, 5,835 girls were in school, of whom only 338 attended district schools. Private schools accounted for 3,420 of them.[33] District schools continued to accept girls until 1829 when Nicholas I forbade their attendance. Gymnasiums also ceased accepting girls. No women were permitted in universities.

In 1842 Nicholas ordered the creation of privately operated secondary boarding schools for girls in the western provinces with the aim of countering Polish educational influences on them. By 1854 sixty-one schools with 2,033 girls in attendance functioned in the region. Schools on state peasant lands under the Ministry of State Domains also admitted girls to separate classes to learn to read and write and learn handicrafts. The schools were taught by priests. By 1866 there were 2,754 such schools with 132,582 students, of whom 16,579 were girls.[34] In the 1830s and 1840s, the Literacy Committee of the Moscow Agricultural Society promoted moral-religious education or "pedagogical motherhood" to prepare peasant girls for maternal duties. The society engaged noble women to bring girls to church and generally teach serf girls to be good mothers.[35]

The institutes established and operated by Empress Mariia Feodorovna, wife of Paul I and mother of Alexander I and Nicholas I, played a major role in the education of Russian women. Mariia Feodorovna had taken charge of the Smolny and Novodevichy Institutes in 1796. Catherine had established the two institutes with the motive of developing in women the whole personality. Mariia Feodorovna focused more narrowly on preparing women for the role of wife and mother. The chancellery of Mariia Feodorovna opened to support the institutes as well as other charities under her patronage. Funding came from a monopoly on the sale of playing cards in the empire and a 10 percent tax on theater revenues. She personally donated large sums to the schools and solicited donations from wealthy patrons. By her death in 1828 the chancellery had accumulated a large capital. In addition to the two original institutes, Mariia Feodorovna opened schools for girls in several cities. Admission to the various institutes had a social dimension. In noble estate schools, orphan girls from good military service families or daughters of impoverished nobles were preferred. But the empress also founded schools for different social groups that taught them skills appropriate to their station. All girls, she believed, should be imbued with good morals, have the skills of household and servant management, and practice frugal budgeting. Noble girls required French, dancing, and etiquette, whereas girls from merchant and raznochintsy backgrounds required the practical knowledge to become wives and mothers or teachers and governesses.

Although the salaries of teachers in the institutes were lower than in state schools, Mariia Feodorovna was adept at attracting personnel with professional training. In most of the institutes the program was six years in length (nine in the Smolny). To be admitted, applicants of age 8 or 9 had to be able to read, write, and count. In the lower grades, pupils studied Law of God, reading and writing in Russian, French, and often German, the first four functions of arithmetic, nature studies, drawing, dancing, and music. Senior girls took religion, penmanship, Russian language and literature, rhetoric, logic, algebra, geometry, physics, history, geography, biology, music, and needlework. In addition to that crowded curriculum, the girls were trained in the rules of behavior and morality, manners, comportment, and household economy. At the heart of the education of the *institutki* was the fulfilment of duty. Subordination to the rules and order of the institute was paramount. There were few comforts. Most memories of the graduates were of cold in winter, heat in summer, poor food, and even hunger. Strict supervision and discipline shaped their daily lives. Physical exercise was minimal and little play was permitted. Their patron empress believed that dancing was "a preservative against all human illnesses." E. N. Vodovozova recalled that the institutki ranked themselves by their beauty. The most beautiful would marry first. Since she was ninth in the beauty ranking, Vodovozova expected a lengthy wait before being chosen.[36] Isolated as they were, the girls knew little of contemporary Russian life. Their permitted readings fostered in them a noble ideal of childish innocence of mind and heart and a naïve romanticism. Some institute directors had the seventh commandment, which censured adultery, blanked out of texts to shield students from its meaning. As a result of such cosseting, institutki were ill-prepared for life after

Figure 3.1 Pupils of the Smolny Institute of Noble Maidens in the canteen, 1889.
Source: © Fine Art Images/Heritage Images/Getty Images.

school. Vodovozova admitted that on graduation she had no idea that she needed to negotiate a price with a cab driver or indeed that she had to pay at all. In any case she had neither purse nor money. Although the memories of the early students of the institutes were generally fond, later graduates were highly critical of the education and preparation for life they had received in the institutes, an indication of the changes in the expectations of women over time. Figure 3.1 illustrates the number of young women in residence at any one time.

On Mariia Feodorovna's death in 1828, the institutes passed into the jurisdiction of the Fourth Section of the Imperial Chancellery and her chancellery became the Department of the Empress Mariia Feodorovna. Little in the administration changed. There were three sections: (1) foundling homes and all institutions under the guardianship council that oversaw charities, (2) educational institutions, and (3) archives. The Fourth Section was to play an even greater role in the education of women in the coming decades.

Outcomes

State expenditure on education as a percentage of the budget throughout the first half of the nineteenth century was abysmal. By 1852 it had fallen to 1 percent and had rarely exceeded 2 percent. Spending by local authorities also fell dramatically short of the needs of schooling. In spite of some improvement in the 1850s, of 215 district towns as late as 1860, forty-two provided no funding for elementary education, eleven spent a mere 100 roubles a year, and twenty-seven up to 200 roubles annually. The goal set at the beginning of the century to significantly expand the bureaucracy and improve its quality through better and more education was not met. The number of gymnasiums grew from forty-five with 3,840 students in 1825 to sixty-two with 24,746 in 1854.[37] However, only about 20 percent of students completed the full program. The government restricted university enrollments by limiting the number of non-stipendiary students to 300 at each university. In 1850 only 3,018 undergraduates studied in the empire's universities. At the end of the reign of Nicholas I, the universities and gymnasiums together graduated around 400 students a year. The large Russian bureaucracy alone had 3,000 vacancies a year. The practice of filling certain positions in the military with graduates of the university was abandoned. A son of the emperor admitted that in comparison with the powerful states of Western Europe, "we are poorer not only in material means but in intellectual capacity; and we are especially short of trained administrators."[38] The middle and lower levels of the state service remained mired in ignorance and corruption. However, the elite schools did produce a number of civil servants of great ability. These were the so-called enlightened bureaucrats who planned and implemented the great reforms of the 1860s.

Following the rebellion of the Decembrists in 1825, the nature of the Russian autocracy changed. While appeasing and co-opting segments of the nobility by partially reinforcing the estate structure of society, Nicholas rested his authority on the bureaucracy and on a carefully cultivated military elite. Education and the experience of war and contact with the West had alienated large segments of the nobility from the autocracy. The execution or exile to Siberia of the Decembrist conspirators suppressed but did not end the disillusionment of many young nobles. The opposition passed from officers to intellectuals and moved into the universities and salons of the capitals. It thrived on ideas from the west which Nicholas's censors could not keep out. In the late 1830s and 1840s an intelligentsia emerged, divided in those years into Slavophiles and Westernizers, both highly critical of the autocracy in its bureaucratic form. These were the generation of the fathers, the men of the forties. The miserable conditions in the seminaries and the alienation of seminarians from the rest of society often resulted in drunkenness and disorderly contact but also fostered among some seminarians a more thoughtful opposition to the existing order. The harsh conditions in institutions of education of all kinds, especially in the final repressive years of Nicholas's reign, incubated the sons, the generation of the nihilists who led the opposition to autocracy in the 1860s. The advances in education, however limited, had by the end of the reign of Nicholas I in 1854 given birth to a public opinion that increasingly ran counter to the policies of the regime across a spectrum from moderate to radical.

The passion for French language and West European ways among the nobility was an additional source of alienation in Russian society. Many in the elite lived a dual life. They frequently spoke French better than Russian. Families spoke French among themselves and addressed Russian only to servants. In 1812 it was a running joke that Russian patriots cursed the French in French. Another commentator noted that both the Decembrists and state officials could "set out important matters and thought only in French." Later the historian V. O. Kliuchevskii mourned that the manners, habits, feelings and even the language in which provincial gentry thought were imported, alien, and without organic links to his surroundings.[39] Francomania had its critics in both state and society, and over the first half of the century defenders of the Russian language and culture became more vocal. It needs to be noted that much of Russian schooling was remote from the realities of Russian life. Neither seminarians nor institutki were prepared by their education for life in the Russia of their day. Perhaps the most significant consequence of the experience of education in the first fifty years of the century, with its many problems and failures, was a receptivity to change among society and influential officials.

The great majority of the population of the empire still had no formal schooling by mid-century. Most peasants and many townsmen continued to see limited value in literacy for their children. Those pupils who entered a school rarely stayed for more than a year. It is almost impossible to know what level of literacy they attained or for how long they retained it. Much schooling was informal, administered by priests or family members. Little information about this way of learning exists for the pre-Emancipation period. The efforts of the government to restrict schooling by estates and control what was taught in schools likely made the schools less popular than a more relevant curriculum could have inspired. The emphasis on vospitanie over obrazovanie, especially during the reign of Nicholas I, severely limited the scope and nature of learning.

Nevertheless, the numbers available testify that attendance at schools of various kinds grew throughout the period after allowing for population growth. At a rough estimate there was one student per 1,700 inhabitants in 1800, five per 1,000 in 1840, and thirteen per 1,000 in 1863.[40] From 426 district schools and 718 parish schools in 1830, schools under the Ministry of National Enlightenment increased to 463 to 2,214, respectively, by the end of Nicholas's reign. The number of schools on the lands of the imperial family grew from forty with 805 pupils in 1837 to 376 with 11,394 pupils in 1865. In 1839 the Holy Synod had around 2,000 schools with 19,000 pupils and in 1864 22,300 schools with more than 427,000 students. The numbers, especially for the church schools, are suspect since priests had an interest in appearing to be zealous educators. But the upward trend is clear.[41] The attempt to limit secondary education to sons of the nobility and high officials in the reign of Nicholas was often half-hearted. In 1833 sons of the lower estates made up 19 percent of gymnasium students. The percentage crept up slightly by 1843 to 20 percent and reached 29 percent in 1850. In Moscow and several other cities, commoners made up a third of gymnasium students.[42] Social mobility while gradual was steady.

The change in the perceived value of education for women marked an important turning point in the intellectual life of the empire. Although schooling for women remained largely outside the Ministry of National Enlightenment's system of public schooling, social licence for education for girls grew. Even some peasants were requesting the opening of schools for girls by the 1840s. Women increasingly attained recognition in the intellectual life of the country. Countess E. P. Rostopchina and Evgeniia Tur, both hostesses of important salons, were among Russia's early published female authors. Although preparation for wife and mother remained the objective of women's education, the moral status attributed to women marked an early step toward their further empowerment.

4

Engaging the Public: Alexander II

The death of Nicholas I in February 1855 and the defeat of the Russian army in the Crimea by the British and French coalition that autumn were the catalysts for a period of major reform in the Russian Empire. The war exposed the economic and military weaknesses of Russia in comparison with its West European competitors and placed its great power status in jeopardy. The widespread indifference of the public to the outcome of the war alarmed the government. Nicholas's son, Alexander II, had little choice but to undertake a sweeping reform involving nearly every sector of government and society, a task he carried out reluctantly and under duress. The former model of the Westernized autocrat who guarded the nation and gave his passive subjects his paternal protection was no longer viable. A new model required greater engagement between ruler and ruled. Early in his reign Alexander learned that the majority of the nobility was too self-interested to be a useful force for the needed change. Consequently, the former stress on the bonding between monarch and the elite gave way to a new stress on the ties between the monarch and the people. Unwilling to surrender his autocratic prerogatives, Alexander turned to the bureaucracy as the intermediary between autocrat and public. For their part enlightened bureaucrats sought out allies among progressive aristocrats and moderate members of the educated public to advance reform.

Alexander's reign played out against a backdrop of high expectations and gradual disillusionment, especially among young idealists, as the limitations of the reforms became apparent. The dialectic between radicalism on the one hand and the search for stability on the other did much to shape the unfolding of the reform process. The 1860s in Russia was a time of youthful rebellion. University students campaigned for corporate status within the universities. Sons rejected the cautious liberalism or fearful conservatism of fathers, and daughters fled their homes to live in communes. Fictitious marriages freed young women from their fathers' control. The prevailing culture among the young was nihilism. Inspired by journalists and former seminarians like N. G. Chernyshevskii and N. A. Dobroliubov, the nihilists professed a thorough materialism and utilitarianism. They denounced the past and advocated a communalist future for the country. The dislocated and precarious lives of the raznochintsy informed the nihilist style. Indifference to dress, personal appearance, and moral and social convention marked the nihilist. Most hoped to engage the people in communal initiatives. Some, disillusioned with peasant conservatism, turned to threats of terrorism and then to terrorist acts. In 1866 Dmitrii Karakozov, a former university student expelled for inability to pay his fees, attempted to shoot the emperor as he walked in the Winter Garden in St. Petersburg. The attempt failed, and Karakozov was hanged. Other terrorist plots were subsequently exposed.

By 1870 a new ideology, Populism, spread among Russian youths. Populism had several factions. All shared the belief that the privileged classes owed a debt to the people on whose backs they had built their privilege. The result was the "going to the people" movements of the 1870s. Some activists, inspired by the anarchism of Mikhail Bakunin, went to foment spontaneous peasant revolution by means of agitation. Others sought to meld with the people, both to learn from them and to teach them. The peasant response ranged from indifference to bewilderment to hostility toward these naïve strangers in the first wave of populist youth. A second, much smaller and more patient going to the people, based on "small deeds" to foster trust, followed with greater, if still limited, success. The impatient among the populists turned to terrorism. The terrorist wing of the People's Will made repeated attempts on Alexander's life. On March 1, 1881, they succeeded.

The reforms of the 1860s proceeded under the banner of the all-estate principle. All social groups, including the newly emancipated serfs, were to enter the orbit of citizenship. At the heart of the reforms was the emancipation of the serfs in 1861 that turned serfs into citizens. The emancipation act preserved the peasant commune as a grassroots instrument of governance. A reform of local government in the countryside in 1864 created district zemstvos in thirty-four of Russia's fifty provinces elected by all social estates in a curial system of voting that resulted in noble predominance in most zemstvos. Provincial zemstvos consisted of delegates elected from their own numbers by district zemstvo representatives. The zemstvos were given an array of responsibilities in local affairs, including the building and maintenance of schools, and some limited taxing powers. Below the zemstvos were the volost's, instruments of peasant administration with representation from groupings of peasant communes. The zemstvos functioned in only thirty-four of the fifty provinces of the empire. The remaining "non-zemstvo" provinces remained under governors exercising full central government control. A judicial reform created a system of semi-independent courts and trials by jury in 1864. A municipal reform in 1870 conferred some local self-governance on cities. In the early 1870s a reform of the military introduced universal conscription and an army reserve system.

There was near universal agreement that an education that conferred on citizens the skills needed to compete in the modern world of Europe was essential. The government, however, feared the consequences for the existing political order of an education that fostered Western liberal or democratic ideals. It therefore resolved to maintain a monopoly on the reform and administration of education. The old sense of inferiority to the West, reinforced by military defeat at the hands of Britain and France, encouraged the copying of Western educational models, especially from Germany, that took little account of Russian reality.[1] In the second half of the 1850s the government conducted widespread consultations with the public. *Glasnost'* (openness) was intended to build public confidence in the state, but some dismissed it as "artificial publicity."

The debate over education took place in a profusion of journals devoted to education and pedagogy. Existing societies and several new ones pressed for educational reform, printed and disseminated textbooks and other educational materials, raised funds for new schools, and encouraged local organs of self-government to open schools.

Pedagogical theories proliferated. Since at least the reign of Alexander I the Ministry of National Enlightenment had advocated the child-centered, whole-child pedagogy of the Swiss educator J. H. Pestalozzi but with limited effect on teaching methods in schools. In the late 1850s, N. I. Pirogov, a medical doctor and curator of the Kiev school district, called for a humanistic general elementary education for all as the foundation of citizenship, combined with more specialized secondary education that was universally accessible. He supported scientific inquiry in universities free from government interference. Pirogov was an advocate of the education of women, which he linked to their role as mothers. K. D. Ushinskii, inspector of the Smolny Institute in St. Petersburg, rejected the adoption of foreign models in Russia. He urged the study of Russian conditions and needs and the shaping of an education system that conformed to them. In particular, he opposed the classicism that predominated in the gymnasiums and called for a more utilitarian curriculum that included natural sciences, Russian language and literature, modern languages, and mathematics. Language, he argued, was the heart of any national system of education. "The native language," he wrote, "is precisely the spiritual dress into which all knowledge can be snuggly fitted and transform into genuine possession of all-human knowledge."[2] Politics should be excluded from education. Instead, it should be based on child psychology, comparative social sciences, and Russian conditions. Ushinskii authored a reader for elementary schools that was widely used. V. I. Vodovozov popularized Ushinskii's ideas. N. F. Bunakov also broadly supported Ushinskii's pedagogical views. L. N. Tolstoi, on the contrary, was highly critical of Ushinskii's pedagogical thinking. He deplored the decline of the so-called literacy schools that peasants shaped to their own interests and needs. He rejected government intrusion and that of well-meaning but badly informed pedagogues into peasant education. The stories in the readers of Ushinskii or Bunakov, he thundered, were divorced from the experiences of peasant children and could not engage their interest. Peasants should be free to shape their own schools. In his view the sole criterion of sound pedagogy was freedom.[3] Tolstoi produced his own readers for peasant schools that vied with those of Ushinskii and his followers beyond the end of the century.

State Schooling

A. S. Norov, the liberal-minded minister of education from 1853 to 1858, advocated the reform of education geared to advancing a program of economic modernization. He established a School Committee within the ministry and attracted to it educators like Ushinskii and Vodovozov. He ended restrictions on university attendance; by 1859 women were auditing university lectures. Disturbances within the universities as students sought corporate status, the Polish rebellion in 1861, which gained support among some Russian radicals, and a barrage of criticism from the progressive press, however, frightened the government. The quick succession of ministers of education after 1858 was symptomatic of official anxiety. In January 1862 A. V. Golovnin took over the position. He had the support of the liberal-minded Grand Duke Konstantin, who was influenced by Pirogov. Golovnin published a school reform project in 1862 for public discussion as well as sending it abroad for scrutiny by Western pedagogues. The project proposed the creation of normal schools under the ministry to train teachers and the establishment of primary schools shaped by local needs and financed by local society. The local language should be the language of instruction. Critics of the project found it too bureaucratic and regimented and lacking effective public control. They asked for more participation of teachers in shaping academic matters, a reduction in the powers of curators, and a more active role for the school councils of teachers and parents that the project proposed.

The plan was too liberal for Alexander and the State Council. The latter rejected teaching in native languages. Both the emperor and the council were reluctant to see the demise of the estate basis of education. As a result the Regulation on Elementary Schools of July 1864 strayed far from the wishes of Golovnin and liberal society. The regulation applied in Russia's fifty provinces. Its stated goal was to instil in the populace religious-moral concepts and to disseminate elementary useful knowledge. Again moral upbringing trumped academic learning. The curriculum was mostly prescribed, but the legislation left the funding for the expansion of primary education to private and local initiative. The state established conditions for the opening of new schools but at most provided a one-time-only subsidy to assist a school opening. The regulation applied to a wide range of existing schools: peasant literacy schools, the primary schools of the ministries of State Properties and Internal Affairs, appanage schools, the schools of the mining department, church-parish schools, and the new Sunday schools that had formed to advance adult literacy. The schools were authorized to teach to both boys and girls a ministry-approved curriculum that included Law of God, reading of religious (Church Slavonic) and secular (Russian) publications, writing, the first four functions of arithmetic, and, where possible, church singing. Generally the schools offered a three-year program although the legislation did not specify length, hours to be spent on each subject, or school age. The sexes should be taught separately unless material limitations dictated coeducation. The normal schools for teacher training proposed in earlier drafts were omitted from the legislation. Teachers, both men and women, were to possess vaguely specified professional training and certification of their moral standing. They were to be paid on a centrally set scale but from local resources. Priests were assigned to teach Law of God. Teaching was to be in standard Russian and not in local dialects.

The regulation established district and provincial school boards to administer the elementary school system in the thirty-four zemstvo provinces. The boards consisted of two representatives from the district zemstvo assembly and one member each from the ministries of National Enlightenment and Internal Affairs, the Church, and any other ministry operating its own schools in the district. The chair of the board was elected by the members from among their own numbers. Boards were to seek funding for schools, approve the opening of all private nongovernmental schools and any fees the school founders imposed, certify teachers and oversee their teaching with the aid of school trustees from the local community, and provide ministry-approved textbooks and teaching aids to schools. The bishop, governor, director of schools of the province, and two members of the provincial zemstvo assembly made up the provincial school boards. They allocated the scant funds provided by the Ministry of National Enlightenment, reviewed the workings of the district boards, and removed unsuitable teachers. In non-zemstvo provinces the ministry and other provincial and local officials had the initiative in enrolling local support for the opening and maintenance of schools. The legislation dealt with village and parish schools only and said nothing about the higher level of elementary education, that is, the district schools created by the school legislation of 1804. In all of Russia in 1869 there were still only 458 district schools.[4] Figure 4.1 shows a typical class in a general state school.

The Statute on Gymnasiums and Pro-gymnasiums was promulgated in November 1864. The first offered a secondary-level seven-year program of study and the second four years. The curriculum of the pro-gymnasium was the same as that of the first four years of the gymnasium. As secondary schools, their goal was either to provide a general education suitable for government service (graduates of the gymnasium entered at the fourteenth rank of the Table of Ranks) or to prepare students for higher education. The schools were open to boys of all social estates of 10 years or older who had a parish school education. The gymnasiums were of three types: classical with Latin and Greek (usually located only in university cities), classical with Latin only, and real with a modern and practical curriculum. Graduates of the first two types could go on to universities and of the third type to higher technical institutes. The pedagogical councils of the schools were given extensive control over teaching methods and

Figure 4.1 An elementary class in 1905.

Source: © Keystone-France/Getty Images.

other academic matters. The classical curriculum included Law of God (two classes a week), Russian and Church Slavonic, Russian literature, one or two classical and two modern European languages, maths, physics and cosmography, history, geography, natural history, penmanship, and drawing. The real gymnasiums focused on modern European languages, mathematics in greater depth than in the classical school, physics, cosmography, natural history, chemistry, and, for a fee, dancing and music. The pro-gymnasiums, which usually opened in areas far from university cities, were meant to link elementary to secondary education. They charged a fee, which could be waived for poor students, and provided a few one-time stipends to their better students.

The Statute on Universities of June 1863 sharply curtailed the relative openness the universities had enjoyed in the late 1850s. Only graduates of the classical gymnasiums were permitted to attend; women were excluded, even as auditors. Denied entry to higher education in Russia, many women went to Switzerland or other European centers for university study. The statute denied to students the self-government and corporate status they had sought. Faculty, however, made gains. The statute restored much of the former autonomy of the universities lost under Nicholas I. Faculty councils elected rectors with the approval of the emperor and deans with ministry approval; supervision by district school curators ended. Faculty councils also regained control over academic matters. The reform confirmed the configuration of four faculties, History and Philology, Physics and Mathematics, Law, and Medicine, but expanded the number of chairs (departments) within them to eleven, ten, eleven, and twenty-three, respectively. Tuition was fifty roubles per year in the capitals and forty roubles elsewhere; the treasury increased the number of stipends so that only a small proportion of students paid the full fee. The universities again were charged with overseeing the administration of examinations for entry into the civil service. Graduates received the rank of twelve on the Table of Ranks, advanced graduates rank ten, and masters and doctors rank eight. In 1865 and 1869, new universities opened in Odessa and Warsaw, respectively.

The cautious retreat from the progressive plans of the early reform period accelerated following the failed attempt by Karakozov in 1866 on Alexander's life. D. A. Tolstoi, who was also the Procurator of the Holy Synod and a member of the Supreme Council of Women's Education, had by then replaced Golovnin at the Ministry of National Enlightenment. Tolstoi faced the daunting task of significantly raising the educational level of Russians while preventing that very education from arming them with the tools needed to oppose the autocratic order. The leader of the so-called Westernizing nationalists, Tolstoi found an able ally in M. N. Katkov, a newspaper publisher and powerful arbiter of conservative public opinion. Both were proponents of autocracy in Russia and of a unified empire. Like Uvarov before them, they saw in Western educational standards, with their roots in classicism, the means to instil in educated Russians the discipline required to preserve the empire. Katkov called the Western classical school the "mother" of science.[5]

The new minister began to exert even more central control over the education of Russians. In 1867 all schools apart from those of the Holy Synod came under the direction of the Ministry of National Enlightenment. In the same year, he issued new rules of conduct for university students that empowered the police to monitor student behavior on and off the campus and required university officials to inform the police on student activities. In 1869 he created the office of inspector of schools to supervise elementary education. Inspectors were appointed by district school curators and reported to the supervisor of district schools who was in turn appointed by the minister. Inspectors had extensive powers over school curricula and textbooks; they sat on district school boards, examined teachers and their students, could hire new teachers or fire others for cause, and close schools. A new Statute on Elementary Education in 1874 empowered marshals of the nobility, who were elected by their fellow nobles in the district, either to chair or to name chairs of school boards; they had previously been elected by the board's members. Trustees were removed from the boards and additional ministry officials added to their membership. Bishops and parish priests now assumed a larger role in religious and moral education in the schools.

The school inspectorate was chronically undermanned. Tolstoi requested an additional 142 inspectors but got only sixty-eight. There were three inspectors per province in 1874, but normally one of them became the provincial director of schools with other responsibilities, effectively leaving only two inspectors in each province. In a school year of around 132 days, inspectors had to visit a large number of schools scattered over vast distances. Fifty schools per inspector was set as a maximum, but the ratio in the Moscow school district in 1874 was one to seventy-four, in Kharkov one to 163, and in Kiev one to 141. More inspectors were added from 1876, but the growth of the school network far outstripped the appointment of new inspectors. Inspections that took place were perfunctory at best and often frightening to teacher and students. In addition to inspections, inspectors had to attend school board meetings, write annual reports, and relieve directors of some of their administrative load. As a result, some schools went without inspection for several years. Some zemstvos began to fund inspectors. In 1877 nineteen of the 112 inspectors at work in zemstvo provinces were zemstvo-supported. Although the public reputation of inspectors was often unfavorable, many were able and conscientious educators with higher educations and pedagogical training. An outstanding example was I. N. Ul'ianov, the father of Vladimir Lenin. Others were tyrants who terrorized teachers or petty enforcers of minute regulations.[6]

True to his admiration for classical education as the key to Russia's orderly cultural advancement, Tolstoi promulgated a new statute on the gymnasiums in 1871. It increased the number of hours devoted to classical subjects but also of those spent on mathematics and more modern subjects. Preparatory classes were added and the program extended by a year. He removed all control of curriculum from the pedagogical councils of the gymnasiums. While a proponent of classical education for an elite at the secondary level, Tolstoi was well aware of the need of the economy for a cohort of school graduates with a practical, modern education as well. He had long opposed the real gymnasiums and now looked to Germany for a different model. In 1872 he issued the Statute on Real Schools. The goal of these "real schools" was to provide a general secondary education that addressed the practical needs of the economy and the acquisition of technical knowledge by its students. The new schools were open to all social estates, but in Tolstoi's mind they were aimed at sons of merchants, townsmen, and the more prosperous peasantry. The real school offered six grades. The first four grades provided a general education similar to that of the pro-gymnasiums and district schools. Law of God, Russian language, arithmetic, algebra, geometry, trigonometry, drawing, drafting, geography, history, biology, and physics, all taught at basic levels, made up the curriculum in those years. In grades five and six, students could specialize in mechanical-technical, chemical-technical, or commercial programs of study. Mining and agriculture were available in some real schools as well. A supplementary seventh year was preparatory to entering a higher specialist institute. Unlike graduates of the former real gymnasiums, graduates of the real schools could not enter a university. Real schools were jointly funded by the state, zemstvos, urban, or estate societies. Fees were set locally. Since addressing local needs was the purpose of the new schools, pedagogical councils determined the curriculum and teaching methods. Each school also had a council made up of representatives of the city and the school as well as an honorary curator chosen by the school founders and administratively supported by several teachers. The task of the council was to raise funds and organize factory excursions or farm visits to give students some practical experience.

Although Tolstoi spoke often of improving elementary education, his ministry expended only 20.8 percent of its budget on primary schools. The main burden of support for elementary education remained as before with local actors. In 1869 he permitted zemstvos to open "model" schools of one-class with three years of study and two-class with five years. Inspectors were ordered to promote the opening of one-class schools. The intent was to provide peasant children with a more organized and detailed education than those provided by existing rural schools and serve as models for the reorganization of other schools in the countryside. The plan encouraged zemstvos or peasant societies to provide space and maintenance for the schools; the ministry provided salaries for their teachers. Tolstoi made it clear that the schools were to instil practical skills only and not develop the intellectual or reasoning capacity of pupils. He forbade "any broad understanding of the subjects" taught.[7] In 1874 model schools began to appear but largely in non-zemstvo provinces. Compared to zemstvo schools the model schools were few in number and proved to be less attractive to the peasantry. Consequently, over time the model schools even in non-zemstvo provinces reformed themselves on the example of the more progressive zemstvo schools.

In May 1872 the Statute on Municipal Schools transformed the old district schools by merging them with urban parish schools. The new schools offered a six-year course of study; they admitted children of all faiths and conditions at age 7–10 who had no prior formal education. Each school was to determine its level of education in accord with local conditions and needs. Pupils in the first four years studied Law of God, the reading of church (Church Slavonic) and secular works, writing, and the first four functions of arithmetic. Senior students studied Russian language, applied geometry, biology, physics, mechanical drafting and sketching, singing, and gymnastics. They could also take classes directly relevant to work in local industries. One teacher taught all of the subjects in each class except Law of God, which was taught by lay teachers with special training. On paper, the schools were to have four classes and four teachers, but poor financing and scarcity of teachers dictated that a majority had only two or three classes. The teaching method in municipal schools reflected Ushinskii's influence.

It was child-centered and focused on the practical experience of the student and the application of knowledge to real life. Graduates of the schools were prepared to go on to further applied technological studies, or to work in an office or apprenticeship, enter state service at rank fourteen, or go on to a teachers' institute. The original plan enabled students to enter the gymnasium as well, but the State Council refused to sanction it. As a result, there was no link between the elementary and secondary level of schooling and by 1880 the municipal schools had become essentially terminal.

Zemstvo Schooling

The zemstvos were slow to implement the statute of 1864 that enabled them to establish schools. They had limited sources of revenue and many responsibilities. The nobility, who dominated the zemstvos, for the most part regarded popular education as a matter for the peasants themselves. If nobles took any interest in education at all, they preferred to support secondary schools. In 1868 a third of 324 district zemstvos allocated no funding to schools. Of 584,000 rubles allotted by the government to stimulate school openings in 1869, 160,000 rubles went unspent.[8] The main instruments of peasant education remained the old literacy (sometimes called free) schools operated by priests, retired soldiers, or other local literates. They were legalized only in 1882.

By the late 1860s, however, the work of a number of activists within the zemstvos began to produce some positive results. Between 1867 and 1869 a number of zemstvos, especially in provinces with industries and a market oriented agriculture, began to increase spending on education. Provinces such as Viatka and Perm, where the nobility had little influence in the zemstvos, were especially active. Zemstvos increasingly subsidized existing schools as well as new ones and helped to raise funds from private donors or societies to open more schools or provide textbooks and teaching aids to existing ones. Especially important was the work of Baron N. A. Korf who provided a working model for the zemstvo primary school. His goal was to create a school that instilled practical knowledge, shaped the character and outlook of students, and fostered the natural abilities of each of them. He set a minimum of three years of schooling over eleven months each year. His school day had two three-hour periods with two hours for lunch and recess. One teacher taught all three grades. Pupils learned to read and write and to perform the first four functions of arithmetic. As well, they studied history, geography, natural sciences, and Russian. The main textbook for reading was Ushinskii's *Nash drug* (Our Friend). Korf also wrote a guide for teachers. The Korf school type became the principal model for zemstvo schools. The peasantry grew increasingly supportive of the schools as well.

From the early 1870s the network of schools gradually expanded. Much of the growth resulted from the incorporation of existing schools, especially those founded by peasant communities, into the zemstvo system rather than the building of new schools. Between 1864 and 1882 just under fourteen thousand elementary schools opened under the local initiative of zemstvos, villages, and towns.[9] Peasants, who paid the bulk of land taxes in most provinces, continued to bear the bulk of the costs of schooling. Apart from their tax contribution, peasants provided heat and lighting to schools, and labor for their maintenance. The preference of provincial zemstvos to spend school funds on secondary schools remained. In 1877 they allocated 75 percent of education funds to secondary school institutions. District zemstvos also had a leaning toward support of secondary education. In 1877–9 ten districts allocated 50 percent of funds to secondary schools, thirteen spent 40–49 percent, twelve 30–39 percent, and eleven 20–29 percent; no district spent less than 20 percent on secondary education.[10]

Teachers

The chronic shortage of qualified teachers for secondary and elementary schools hindered the expansion and lowered the quality of the school system. In 1858 the government abolished the Main Pedagogical Institute in St. Petersburg as well as the pedagogical institutes in universities. In their place it established two-year pedagogical courses for university graduates to train them as secondary schoolteachers. Teaching remained relatively unpopular as a profession. The courses attracted few candidates in spite of generous stipends for study and the requirement that candidates need master only a single teaching subject. A regulation on teacher training for gymnasiums and pro-gymnasiums in 1866 reengaged historical-philological and physical-mathematical faculties at universities in the process. They now provided lectures on pedagogy, followed by practice teaching in a gymnasium for a year. Fifty stipends per year at each of the eight universities supported the training; graduates were obligated to teach in state schools for at least six years. The inducements were ineffective; the available places were seldom filled. The shortage of teachers of classical languages in particular forced the government to import graduates from the philological faculties of universities in the Austro-Hungarian Empire. A teachers' institute in St. Petersburg trained Slavs from outside Russia to teach in Russian schools from 1869 to 1883. Some twelve to twenty stipendiary students from Russia studied each year at a special institute in Germany at Leipzig University in a two- or three-year teacher training course. They were required to teach in Russian schools for two years for each of the years spent in the program. In 1867 the Historical-Philological Institute in St. Petersburg, which offered a university level program, set up pedagogical courses. By 1881, 113 students were studying there. In the climate of classical learning the training of science teachers was neglected. Science graduates from the universities without any pedagogical preparation were deemed to be adequately prepared for teaching roles in the real schools.[11] Their lack of preparation for the rigors of teaching resulted in many leaving their posts after a few months.

The training of enough elementary schoolteachers to meet expanding needs was even more challenging than at the secondary level. In 1864 three teachers' seminaries producing a mere sixty graduates a year were functioning. In 1865–6 pedagogical courses began to open in a few district schools in five of the six school districts. The quality of teachers turned out was low, and their numbers fell well below the need. By 1881 there were fifty-one state-funded teachers' seminaries with some 3,100 students. Ten of the seminaries had four-year programs, the majority offered three years of study, and six only two years. The academic level of the four-year teachers' seminaries approximated that of the secondary schools. Students studied geometry, surveying, Russian history and geography, a bit of world history and geography, and basic natural sciences. Religion occupied a large space in the program. The three-year seminaries covered the same subjects less thoroughly. The narrowness and lack of depth of the curriculum in the teachers' seminaries was intentional. Teachers were meant to know only the bare minimum required to teach the prescribed subjects in elementary schools. Rote learning assured that the students acquired no skills in independent thinking. Tolstoi wanted peasants to teach peasants and recruited them to the state-run teachers' seminaries. To isolate prospective teachers from urban influences that might alienate them from the peasantry, many of the ministry's seminaries were placed in remote areas. Students were closely monitored, living a near monastic life. Most emerged unprepared for the realities of teaching in peasant villages.[12]

Teachers' seminaries trained teachers for peasant schools. The creation of the municipal schools in 1872 was accompanied by the establishment of teachers' institutes with a three-year course of study to train teachers for them. The institutes admitted graduates of the former district schools and of the municipal schools that replaced them. They also operated a one-year program to raise the qualifications of former district schoolteachers. The curriculum of the institutes closely shadowed the subjects taught in the municipal schools but in considerable depth. Unlike the rural teaching seminaries where training was minimal, the institutes provided training in child-centered teaching methods, text analysis, and visual aids. The institutes were, however, slow to open. By 1879 there were only eight, and in 1881 they together graduated a mere 110 teachers.

The zemstvos were critical of the state's teachers' seminaries. They successfully petitioned to open their own seminaries at their expense to supplement the state's efforts. By 1871 five zemstvo teachers' seminaries had opened, one in each of five school districts. Another six opened in 1872 and eleven more between 1873 and 1875. Many of their students held state stipends. Apart from opening their own seminaries, the zemstvos began to operate short pedagogical courses for teacher in-service training. They were aided by the Moscow Committee on Literacy that sent experienced pedagogues to conduct summer courses of six weeks to three months in length. Some regions began to require teachers to take summer courses. In 1881, 720 students studied in nine zemstvo teachers' seminaries and 102 students were taking preparatory classes prior to admission. The zemstvo seminaries drew students from a broad social spectrum. They taught the teaching methods advocated by Ushinskii, Leo Tolstoi, and Korf that were largely excluded from the state's seminaries. Although there were tensions between the state and the zemstvos over the purposes and methods of schooling, there was also a good deal of cooperation between them. Most nobles, who prevailed in the zemstvo assemblies, were broadly sympathetic to conservative state education policies and willingly cooperated. It was the many employees of the zemstvos, the Third Element as they were called, who promoted progressive educational and social agendas. They were doctors, statisticians, veterinarians, gymnasium teachers, and below them fel'dshers, elementary teachers, accountants, and other service providers who linked the peasantry to the new institutions of local self-government. The government was wary of them and watched them closely.

The zemstvos and the Committee on Literacy also organized congresses for teachers to raise awareness of progressive teaching methods. The first was in Moscow where some seven hundred attendees took short pedagogical courses. An all-Russian congress of teachers met in Kostroma in 1873 that discussed teaching methods and disciplinary practices that rejected humiliation and the physical punishment of students. Local congresses organized in more remote areas provided teachers there with information on new teaching techniques. The congresses were suspect to the authorities. M. N. Katkov spoke for conservative government officials when he wrote of the congresses: "How is it possible to allow public schoolteachers to speak when it is their duty to listen and be silent."[13] His view prevailed. As state servants, teachers were to practice obedience and refrain from individual initiative. In 1883 the state banned teachers' congresses.

The lot of most teachers was not a happy one. At the apex of the teaching hierarchy, university professors enjoyed high status and were well paid. They also had far greater autonomy than secondary and primary schoolteachers. Secondary schoolteachers had some protections. The statute on gymnasiums and pro-gymnasiums established a norm of twelve class hours a week for a teacher but also paid sixty roubles a year for each extra hour taught per week. Most teachers took on extra hours and sometimes taught in more than one institution or tutored on the side. The state paid the salaries of all regular secondary schoolteachers at the same rate of 750 roubles from year one with a raise to 1,050 rubles in year eleven of service and 1,500 rubles in year twenty-one. Local authorities paid for any courses additional to the required curriculum.

Salaries for primary schoolteachers were low. As late as 1894, male zemstvo teachers earned an average of 270 roubles and female teachers 252 roubles a year in sharp contrast to the pay of secondary schoolteachers. Some got free housing and other benefits. Often the payment of their salaries was split between the peasant community and the zemstvo. Neither was prompt with payment. Teachers often had to plead for their salaries. Those who taught far from the district capital had to travel to collect their pay. The limited education of primary schoolteachers, which often excluded them from acceptance by the local intelligentsia, their dependence on the community for pay and sustenance, and, with the decision of the government in 1871 to allow women to teach in public schools, the gradual feminization of the profession, sealed their lowly status. Women were frequent targets of bullying and other abuses. All teachers were subject to multiple pressures from inspectors, trustees, the local priest, marshals of nobility, and others.

Teachers' relationships with the parents of their peasant charges were particularly difficult. Teachers were outsiders in peasant communities. Even the few years peasants spent training in a secluded teachers' seminary changed them enough to alienate them from the village. Teachers had no voice in the village assembly on which their support and that of their school depended. They were caught between the educational goals set by the state and those of the peasants, which differed considerably. Peasants had means to influence teaching in schools. Attendance was not compulsory; they could withhold their children, delay a teacher's pay, or make the daily life of the teacher a misery. Peasants generally did not oppose basic schooling. However, they had alternatives in the form of the literacy schools that had for long been part of village life. The pedagogy employed in the literacy schools often better accorded with peasant notions of teaching and learning than that of the official schools.

Military Schooling

The Ministry of National Enlightenment and the zemstvos were not alone in advancing education. In 1855 the army established schools to raise the level of literacy in the lower ranks and especially at the level of non-commissioned officer. The results were unsatisfactory. In 1861 D. A. Miliutin became minster of war. Miliutin held progressive views about education and from 1866 was an open opponent of the reforms of Tolstoi at the Ministry of National Enlightenment. He was especially critical of the division of gymnasiums and real schools imposed by Tolstoi. He called instead for a united general education secondary school with classical and modern branches. In 1860 the cadet corps were dissolved (the Corps of Pages and the Finland Corps excepted). The general classes of the former corps remerged as military gymnasiums with a seven-year program. To them were added four-year pro-gymnasiums that were preparatory to the upper three grades of the gymnasium. By 1881 there were eighteen military gymnasiums and eight military pro-gymnasiums. They provided a general education focused on mathematics, the sciences, and modern languages and served as a practical alternative to the civilian classical gymnasium. Under Miliutin, the military specialist classes of the former corps were restructured as two-year military higher schools. In addition, Miliutin established Junker schools with a two-year program open to anyone with a four-year general educational background. These schools accepted non-noble students. The system was topped by a military academy and special courses in the military sciences. In 1867 the Naval Cadet Corps became the Naval School. It admitted a limited number of students at age 14. The school offered a four-year program, consisting of one general and three specialist years. In 1875 a second general year was added. In summer, students were assigned to a navy ship for practical training.[14]

Miliutin's reform of military education was not enough in itself to raise Russia's military capabilities to the level of other European powers. Modern warfare required better-educated officers and soldiers capable of independent initiative under fluid battlefield conditions. As well, the adoption of the all-class principle in public life dictated a major reform of the military. In 1874 universal conscription replaced the old peasant army. Educational attainment was linked to reductions in length of service. With a primary school diploma a conscript served four of the normal period of seven years. A district or municipal school graduate served for three years, graduates of secondary schools for two years, and university graduates for six months. On ending active service, soldiers entered the reserves. In 1875 a recruit entering a company school or training as a non-commissioned officer had to be literate. The army defined literacy as the ability to read both printed books and manuscripts, to pronounce words clearly, and to communicate the meaning of what was read. In 1892 the first four functions of arithmetic were added to the definition of literacy. Illiterate soldiers were required to take literacy classes.

Church Schooling

In his dual role of minister of education and procurator of the Holy Synod, Tolstoi attempted to resolve the issues around the education of the clergy. He wished to abolish the clergy estate and saw in it a ready source of elementary schoolteachers. The church had established some 21,000 parish schools with about 400,000 pupils by 1864, for which Tolstoi sought financial support from the zemstvos. Some zemstvos acceded to his request while others refused. Conditions in the church seminaries, which had encouraged radical views among some seminary students and fed the nihilism of the 1860s, had not improved. Declining finances made seminary life only worse. The state provided some financial relief and struck a committee to reform the seminaries. At the heart of the committee's task was to decide whether seminaries should serve only the parochial needs of the church or educate the children of the whole clerical estate. The committee opted for the former. Only some nine thousand of the roughly sixteen thousand sons of clergy would be admitted to the seminaries each year. The reform left the church elementary schools underfunded and poorly equipped to prepare pupils going on to study in the seminaries. The curriculum of the seminaries was revised to align it more closely with that of the classical gymnasiums. In May 1869 a reform of the academies of the Holy Synod defined their purpose as the promotion of theological scholarship and the training of faculty for the seminaries. The reform opened the academies to all social estates and raised faculty salaries to the level of the universities. While the quality of both the seminaries and the academies improved, the dropout rates were high. Many of the best students left for secular schools including the universities, leaving the poorer students to serve as shepherds to the Orthodox flock.[15]

Private Schooling

Following the death of Nicholas I, the government looked more favorably on private education as a supplement to state schooling. In 1858 private schools were permitted to open in the capitals without any restrictions and in the provinces with the permission of the district school curator. The number of private schools in St. Petersburg quickly rose from 156 in 1857 to 227 and in Moscow from 35 to 52.[16] The 1864 school statute encouraged the foundation of schools by private benefactors. Aiming to raise the quality of private schools, Tolstoi in 1866 ordered school curators to supervise both them and home teachers and tutors more closely. In 1868 he reestablished regulations requiring founders of new schools and their teachers to attain certification of their moral and political reliability. In 1868 Alexander II approved a new regulation on private schooling. The regulation established three levels of private educational institutions. The first level had to have at least six grades taught concurrently each year. These schools could be called gymnasiums and qualified their graduates to enter universities. The second level required a minimum of three grades and provided an education equivalent to that of a district school. The third level offered one to two years of basic literacy. All private school proprietors had to receive character references from

Russian citizens and provide proof of pedagogical training. To encourage diversity, proprietors could establish their own program, but all schools had to teach Law of God and Russian language. If the curriculum included geography and history, units on Russia were mandatory. All programs had to gain the approval of the school district curator. Private schools operated under the supervision of the district school administration and were inspected by state inspectors.

The rules governing private education were tightened over time. A new regulation required that to call itself a gymnasium, a private school had to copy the program of the ministry's classical gymnasiums and employ teachers in the highest three grades who had higher education. In many ways the regulations were superfluous. By this time most private schools were superior to state institutions. Innovation in teaching methods was the mark of many of them. Leading pedagogues often taught in them or founded their own schools. Their methods aimed at the many-sided development of the individual student. From 1865 to 1895 the number of private two- and three-level schools rose from 1,107 to 1,542 and private gymnasiums from 74 to 77.[17]

Professional-Vocational Schooling

Vocational-technical education also made advances, often through private initiative. Before the emancipation reform, noble landlords, with economic motives in mind, opened schools for serfs. Large estates needed office workers and workers with special skills both on their estates and in their offices in cities where many of their serfs worked in urban employments. Literate serfs as well were more likely to take up some work on the side, enabling them to pay a larger *obrok* (feudal rent). Some serfs established businesses and accumulated great wealth, which landlords shared. In the 1840s there existed some seven hundred landlord schools. A striking example of landlord initiative was the Mining and Metallurgy School founded in St. Petersburg in early 1824 by Countess S. V. Stroganova. Peasant children from the family's Perm province estate were brought to train as estate, mine, and factory stewards as well as artisans and farmers. The school was located in the Stroganov mansion in the capital. It was overseen by university professors and teachers from the Cadet Corps. Apart from administrative, mining, and agricultural skills students studied Law of God, history, geography, mathematics, natural sciences, and Russian and foreign languages.[18] In industrial provinces factory schools providing basic literacy to workers' children frequently opened. T. V. Prokhorov, owner of a textile factory, opened a school in 1816 with provision for twenty to forty pupils. They studied reading and writing, arithmetic, and the graphic arts. Many of the readings were from secular works and not exclusively religious. In 1833 he opened another school for fifty pupils. His example inspired others. By 1846 there were in Moscow province thirty-four factory schools with up to 1,300 pupils.[19]

In the wake of the disastrous Crimean War, the need for greater technical expertise was highlighted. Ushinskii in the 1860s called trade schools "moral and economic imperatives."[20] The government, however, was reluctant to see peasants transformed into skilled craftsmen. Advances in vocational-technical learning therefore leaned heavily on private initiative. In the decades following the emancipation, various societies formed to promote technical education. The Imperial Russian Technical Society opened in 1866 and in 1868 formed a Permanent Commission on Technical Education. It established a number of technical schools. In 1869 the government allowed it to open more schools and technical courses in crafts, graphics, and drafting. It also operated a number of general education schools with basic technical instruction. It prepared teaching aids, ran a mobile museum of teaching methods, held conferences, and advocated technical education for women. The Moscow Society for the Dissemination of Technical Knowledge, founded in 1869, established a school section in 1871. It spawned several hundred member societies throughout the empire. It also operated Sunday school courses on technical drafting, a craft school for women and a metal work school. In addition, a host of privately funded technical educational institutions opened.

Schooling Women

While educational opportunities for peasant girls remained limited, women from other social estates achieved striking gains in the post-emancipation period. The "woman question" raised in the 1840s was hotly debated in the 1860s. The reform atmosphere of the 1860s supported thoughts about new roles for women. Some influential commentators such as Pirogov linked the education of women to their roles as mothers. Ushinskii called for the equal education of men and women, one beyond an education needed for family roles. Another commentator, M. L. Mikhailov, argued that a woman's role in society rested solely on her ability and not on her gender. Many professors in the universities supported the admission of women to university study and welcomed them as auditors in 1859.

The Fourth Section of His Majesty's Imperial Chancellery that incorporated the Department of the Dowager Empress Mariia Feodorovna had since 1828 overseen all institutions of women's education. The department had long operated the institutes for noble girls and others for girls of the middle estates founded by Mariia Feodorovna. In 1855 the department opened three levels of schools for girls: the first was for daughters of hereditary nobles and military staff officers, the second for daughters of the personal nobility, middle-ranking military officers, honorary citizens, and merchants, and the third for daughters of the remaining non-taxed groups. The schools of the first two levels offered a curriculum roughly equivalent to that of the male gymnasium but with an emphasis on modern languages, drawing, singing, and dancing. Their graduates received the designation of home governesses. The third level offered a curriculum similar to the parish schools with a stress on handicrafts. Around 1860 there were forty schools under the Fourth Section, thirty-six of which were of the first two types in the capitals and several provincial cities with a total of about 6,800 pupils.[21] In 1858 the Fourth Section established a secondary day school in Moscow that was open to all estates except the peasantry. The goal of the school was to prepare girls for useful social activity. The day school marked a break with the long-established practice in girls' schools of separating children from the family in boarding schools. A second of these Mariia schools in St. Petersburg opened a pedagogical class that in 1863 became a full program with a section for natural science and mathematics and another for humanities. The program was the first to provide systematic pedagogical training for women. The department opened similar girls' gymnasiums in other cities. By 1911 they were serving more than 25,000 pupils.[22] Most of the existing institutes under the department adopted the more advanced curriculum of the day schools in 1862.

Legislation in 1858 by the Ministry of National Enlightenment created two levels of girls' secondary schools. The six-year school was the first state-sponsored women's gymnasium. The required curriculum included Law of God, Russian language, arithmetic, geometry, natural history, physics, geography, history, penmanship, drawing, and various handicrafts. Subjects such as foreign languages, dancing, music, and singing were optional. The three-year school curriculum was close to that of the district school and of the male pro-gymnasiums. In 1868 the six-year program extended to seven years. An eighth year provided pedagogical training that conferred the status of home teacher on graduates and the right to teach in elementary schools, private homes, and the four lower classes of the girls' gymnasiums. The stated purpose of the schools was "to impart to pupils that religious, moral, and intellectual education which is expected of women, especially the future mother of a family."[23] The ministry provided a small subsidy (9 percent of costs in 1899) but most of the funding came from municipalities, local societies, and private donors. Annual fees of thirty-five roubles in six-year schools and twenty-five in three-year schools could be waived by the school founder for poor students. Teachers' salaries were lower in gymnasiums for women than in those for men. The lower costs encouraged municipalities to establish them, and their numbers grew more rapidly than gymnasiums for boys. From 29 with 3,440 pupils in 1865, they went to 100 with nearly 30,000 pupils in 1883 and 143 with over 40,000 in 1893.[24]

The daughters of the clergy, who normally married within the church estate, were excluded from diocesan schools. In 1843 Princess Ol'ga Nicholaevna, convinced that priests' wives required an education to perform their parochial services well, persuaded Nicholas I to sanction a new type of school to be funded from the sale of church candles, private donations, and a royal subsidy under the auspices of the Fourth Section of the Imperial Chancellery. A school with twenty pupils opened in Tsarskoe selo in August 1843. Attendance quickly rose to sixty and a second school soon opened in Iaroslavl'. Over the next twenty years, twenty-two three-year diocesan schools for girls opened. By the end of the century there were more than sixty schools and some thirteen thousand girls had graduated from them. Girls entered the schools at age 10. Tuition was 150 rubles a year, but poor and orphaned girls were admitted free. The schools evolved into two types. Those under the jurisdiction of the Fourth Section followed the model of the original school at Tsarskoe selo. Personnel in them were state servants with fixed salaries and pensions. They were open only to daughters of the clergy. The second type was operated by the Holy Synod and was open to girls from inside and outside the clerical estate. The Synod schools had three two-year grades with thirty students in each grade. The curriculum had a strong religious component and church attendance was compulsory for students. Apart from Law of God and church singing, the curriculum included Russian language, Russian and world history, geography, arithmetic, penmanship, physics and biology, drawing, sewing and other domestic skills, sick care, and medicinal plants. All schools had an orchard and garden and cows and chickens. From 1871, graduates of the schools qualified as home and elementary schoolteachers. In 1888 they became six-year schools closely modeled on the Institutes for Noble Girls but with less stress on manners and more on practical pursuits. The diocesan girls' schools were highly successful. Their intellectual level far exceeded that of the male church seminaries. Many of the schools' graduates opened home schools in villages or were employed in village schools.[25]

The growing number of girls with secondary education fueled a campaign for higher education for women. The brief period of acceptance of women as auditors in universities ended abruptly in 1863. The Medical-Surgical Academy had also admitted women following the Crimean War. Among them was Nadezhda P. Suslova. She and others were expelled from the academy in 1864. The exception was Varvara A. Kocherova, who was allowed to complete the physicians' diploma in 1868 following a public outcry. Some of the more determined women chose to go abroad to study, especially in Zurich but also in Paris. Suslova, for example, completed her studies in Zurich. Switzerland was a center not only of open universities but also of revolutionary societies. The extreme poverty in which many Russian students abroad lived and the idealism about social service that had sent them abroad to study drew some of them into revolutionary circles. Some came to believe that the practice of medicine or other practical activities only relieved the suffering of the people but could not cure it. As Vera Figner, a dedicated populist revolutionary, recalled, their studies could only "treat the symptoms of the disease, and not remove their causes."[26] Several women who had studied abroad were later among those tried for "political" crimes in the 1870s. Although only a tiny minority of women associated with revolutionary causes, much of public opinion in Russia, especially after the attempt on Alexander's life in 1866, looked on young well-educated women as dangerous nihilists.

The minister of war, D. A. Miliutin, not only strongly opposed Tolstoi's classical system of education but also was a powerful advocate of practical education for women. In 1867 he began to sponsor medical courses for women at the Medical-Surgical Academy under the Ministry of War. He then formed an alliance with a powerful group of women activists in the capital pressing for higher education for women. In 1868 a plea by Evgeniia I. Konradi at the First Congress of Natural Sciences in St. Petersburg for support for a petition for higher education for women won the attention of university professors in the capital. Encouraged by their support, a group of women from prominent families led by Mariia V. Trubnikova, Ana P. Filosova, and Nadezhda V. Stasova took up the cause. The three women had already established a society to lodge and support working women, a clothing workshop to provide work for poor women, and a publishing cooperative of women for the printing and binding of books. They soon gathered 178 signatures on their petition that they submitted to the rector of St. Petersburg University. Another 400 signatures were later added. Professors at the university agreed to teach the intended courses, some for no compensation, and prepared a program of study.

A delegation of the women met Tolstoi, who rejected their petition but suggested that a few lectures could be mounted. Having successfully blocked women from attending universities by making the male classical gymnasium the sole avenue to entry, he condescended to support the lectures primarily in order to provide an alternative to study abroad. The women turned to Miliutin who agreed to house the lectures at the Medical-Surgical Academy. A series of lectures in botany, chemistry, Russian history, anatomy, zoology, and Russian literature began in January 1870 with evening lectures four times each week. A fee of twenty-five roubles for a semester or of twenty-five kopeks per lecture helped to fund the lectures. Of the 900 auditors who attended the opening lecture 767 were women. The lectures did not cohere into organized programs of study; they were determined solely by the interest of those willing to teach them. Police often interrupted or suspended the lectures. The worlds of learning and work permitted for women were far apart. An imperial order in 1871 defined the type of work that educated women could take up: teachers at the elementary school level, midwives, and some clerical, stenographic, and telegraphic roles. The occupational restrictions severely limited the usefulness of women's education in the workforce.

In 1869 Tolstoi sanctioned advanced secondary-level courses for women, the Alarchinskie courses. They offered classes in chemistry, physics, mathematics, Russian language, and pedagogy at a level equal to courses in a men's gymnasium. Tolstoi's limited concessions did not stem the flow of women to Switzerland for study. In response, Tolstoi allowed the opening of the Lubianskie Courses for women in Moscow in October 1870. Their organization became more programmatic. They began as higher secondary level courses with an emphasis on the sciences but had evolved by 1878 into the equivalent of the program of the physical-mathematics faculty of Moscow University. A few professors and many doctoral students as well as gymnasium teachers taught the courses. By 1885, 150 women attended the Lubianskie courses. In November 1872 the Guerrier Courses in humanities opened in Moscow to provide young women with a secondary education that qualified them as teachers. The ministry approved the courses but declined to grant its graduates the degree of domestic tutor, so excluding them from teaching.

Concern about the radicalization of women abroad and pressure from Swiss authorities, who deplored the unruly lives of Russian students, moved the government to order all Russian students in Zurich to return to Russia by January 1, 1874, or forgo all educational or employment opportunities at home. Most complied, but a few stayed on to study in Bern or Geneva. In compensation, a government commission formed in 1873 to develop plans to open further courses for women in university cities. The commission made no mention of higher education but focused on raising the level of secondary education for women and expanding elementary education for girls. In frustration, P. G. Ol'denburgskii, who chaired the Fourth Section of the Imperial Chancellery, took up the cause of higher education for women. In the face of the foot-dragging of the Ministry of National Enlightenment, he threatened to open higher courses for women under the auspices of the section. Reluctant to cede control to the Fourth Section, Tolstoi approved higher courses in April 1876. The courses were to be run privately and had no power to grant degrees. Although he gave a meager stipend to the St. Petersburg courses, neither Moscow nor provincial cities gained ministry support for women's courses. Funding rested on private donations and fees. The Bestuzhevskie Courses in St. Petersburg enjoyed wealthy patronage; those beyond the capital did not. Various academic institutions provided space, and professors and others taught for scant or no remuneration. Many of the students, even those from noble families, struggled to pay the fees and to survive with few stipends and limited opportunity for work.

The Bestuzhevskie Courses attracted seven hundred students per year. Most attendees were from privileged social groups. Work appropriate to their qualifications after completing the courses remained hard to find. From 1882 to 1889 only 36 percent of the graduates from the Bestuzhevskie Courses found work as tutors, elementary schoolteachers, or teachers in the lower grades of girls' gymnasiums. Courses opened in Kazan' in November 1876, but few women attended. Kiev enjoyed greater success with some three hundred women attending each year from 1878 to 1886. There, as in St. Petersburg, the courses attained the level of the university. The courses produced a cohort of well-educated women who were for the most part excluded from careers. One newspaper editorialized that to provide higher education and no rights was like training "hundreds of men in the naval arts and dispatching them to the Sahara desert."[27] The exception was the Medical-Surgical Academy. It offered courses in midwifery that qualified graduates as physicians. The shortage of medical personnel in the empire convinced officials in 1880 to confer on them the title of *zhenskii vrach* (woman doctor) and permitted them to practice independently. Of the 698 female doctors in Russia in 1888, only 148 worked as zemstvo doctors or rural private practitioners. The remaining 540 entered private practice, the great majority in large cities.[28] In spite of the precedent set by the Medical-Surgical Academy, Tolstoi firmly resisted the admission of women to the medical faculties of the universities.

Schooling Non-Russians

The Russian Empire incorporated around a hundred languages and dialects, ranging from large national groups with a literary heritage of their own to an array of so-called little peoples in the north, east, and south whose languages were largely oral. The largest linguistic group was the Poles followed by Ukrainians. The decision to embark on mass education in the empire posed the question of how to accommodate linguistic diversity in schools or whether to accommodate it all. During the eighteenth century the government had practiced a policy of administrative Russification. Its goal was not cultural uniformity but the extension of Russian administration and laws across the empire and the affirmation of Russian as the language of governance. The education policies of both Catherine and Alexander had mandated the use of native languages in schools.

The growth of Russian national consciousness during the Napoleonic wars launched a self-conscious policy of cultural Russification as part of the nation-building process. In the western regions of the empire Russification proceeded in fits and starts during the nineteenth century. After the suppression of the Polish rebellion in 1863, an early, largely unsuccessful, effort to encourage the growth of a network of Russian-language elementary schools gave way under Tolstoi to the imposition in 1869 of Russian as the sole language of instruction in secondary and higher educational institutions in

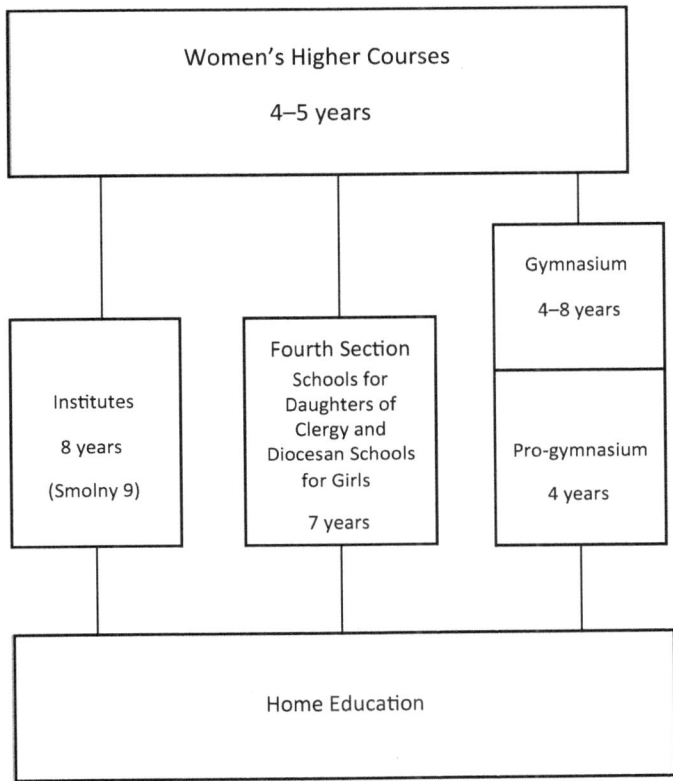

Figure 4.2 Institutions of education for women.

Poland and the western provinces. In Belorussia, Catholic and many Polish schools were forced to close. Bessarabians were required to use Russian in their schools. Similar rules applied in the Dorpat school district in the Baltic provinces. In 1869 the University of Warsaw opened as a Russian-language institution. In 1875, Polish schools and non-Russian schools in the Baltic provinces that had formerly been under the control of local school boards passed into the jurisdiction of the Ministry of National Enlightenment. The influence of the Catholic and Lutheran Churches over schools in those regions was curtailed. In 1876, teaching in Ukrainian was banned in Ukrainian boarding schools. In the Caucasus, Armenians and Georgians had their own schools. In 1867 the Ministry of National Enlightenment placed Armenian parish schools under its supervision. An attempt by the ministry to restrict the autonomy of the schools in 1886 ended in strong local protests and the brief closure of the schools. They reopened after six months.

In the eastern parts of the empire educational policy was driven largely by the competition between Orthodoxy and Islam. Following the conquest of Kazan' in the middle of the sixteenth century, many Muslims, for a variety of reasons, converted to Orthodoxy. In the seventeenth and eighteenth centuries, Muslim villages were often converted by force to Orthodoxy by being arbitrarily baptized, registered as Christian, and incorporated into Orthodox Church parishes. Animist villages often suffered the same fate. Catherine ended the practice and inaugurated a period of toleration that facilitated the spread of Islam throughout the region. Islam had a network of religious schools, the elementary *mekteb* and the advanced *medrese*. Other linguistic groups in the region had oral cultures and no schools. The idea of education as a tool of assimilation into the empire arose early in the eighteenth century. Peter the Great identified the need to translate books into native languages where written languages existed. V. N. Tatishchev, the historian, urged the use of native languages in schools and books. In the reign of Alexander I, the Russian Bible Society had a Church history for children translated into Tatar. The school reform of 1804 that permitted instruction in local languages applied to all non-Russian parishes but had little effect. As elsewhere in the empire, lack of funds and able teachers as well as public apathy conspired to negate the reform effort.

A new initiative arose in the 1860s. The statute on elementary schools of 1864 required Russian as the language of instruction in all schools. Soon an exception was permitted. By the 1860s the many non-Russians in the Volga region who had been forcibly converted to Orthodoxy from Islam or animism were reverting or converting to Islam. By that time apostasy among these baptized non-Russians was widespread. Tatar was increasingly the language of commerce in the region, and the influence of Islam was growing along the Volga and into the steppe beyond it. In the 1870s, Muslim activists initiated a reform movement to modernize and make more secular the traditional curriculum in Muslim schools. A professor of Eastern studies at Kazan' University, N. I. Il'minskii, began in the 1860s to transcribe local languages, which were oral only, in the Cyrillic alphabet. He opened a school for baptized Tatars in which students learned to read and write in their own language written in Cyrillic letters. Students were also introduced orally to Russian in the first two years of instruction. The Cyrillic alphabet served as a bridge between the native and the Russian languages. After the first two years of study teaching began in Russian. The method was extended to other linguistic groups in the region such as the Chuvash, Votiaks, and Cheremis. The Il'minskii system was designed to break up Tatar hegemony through the creation of independent linguistic groups and to slow apostasy to Islam. The Ministry of National Enlightenment supported the initiative.[29] Though controversial, the Il'minskii system was widely practiced in the Volga region, the Caucasus, and Lithuania into the early twentieth century and later served as an inspiration for non-Russian education in the Soviet Union.

Outcomes

The great reforms of the 1860s set in motion forces that the government depended on for its survival as a great power but at the same time threatened to erode public support for autocratic rule. The government sought to find a middle ground between limiting the potential erosion of the social status quo and the risk of slowing economic change. As under previous rulers, the regime of Alexander II placed religious-moral education above academic attainment. The nature and direction of change was contentious in both government and public circles. Within the government, ministerial rivalries developed over the relative merits of classicism in secondary education and a modern, more practical curriculum. The defense of the estate structure of society vied with the need of the government to cultivate talent through limited social mobility. The share of the sons of the nobility and high officials attending the gymnasiums fell dramatically from 70 percent in 1864 to 49 percent in 1884, while that of sons of the urban social estates grew from 20 percent to 36 percent. Boys from the rural estates made small gains from 4 percent to 7 percent, while the clergy's share declined from 2 percent to a mere 1.4 percent.[30] Noble children, however, had schooling options unavailable to other social groups and continued to play dominant roles in state service.

The relaxation of censorship that accompanied the reform facilitated for the first time in Russia widespread discussion of current affairs. Public opinion formed around the many newspapers and journals that proliferated in the reform era. Education was a particular matter for debate. Numerous publications discussed the relative merits of pedagogical methods and teaching materials. The appropriate training for teachers was also contested. The government aimed to preserve peasant culture by providing a bare minimum of religious-moral education that included basic literacy and numeracy but did not encourage independent thought. Its rural teachers' seminaries provided trainees with the barest tools for their task. The ministry was willing to provide urban dwellers with more advanced learning. Although the zemstvos were slow to take up the challenges of elementary education, some of them by the mid-1870s took a more active role both in expanding the primary school network and raising its quality through improved teacher training. Pedagogical courses and teachers' congresses sponsored by the zemstvos gave teachers glimpses of corporate interests that they were to build on in the years ahead. On their part, peasants were beginning to see value in education and becoming more supportive of schools.

In spite of restrictions on their roles in the professional economy, women won significant advances in education at all levels. The initiatives of the Department of the Empress Mariia Feodorovna within the Fourth Section of the Imperial Chancellery touched girls and women of all social estates. Women advocates found allies in professors and some government officials in support of higher education for women. The determination of young women to pursue professional education abroad despite the many hardships they had to endure forced the government's hand. Although the Women's Higher Courses conferred little official professional standing for most of the students, women graduates of the Medical-Surgical Academy who had the right, if limited, to practice set a precedent for further female advancement in the professions. A profession deemed suitable for women was the teaching of young children. The future feminization of the teaching profession had its roots in the reform period.

The stubborn adherence of the Ministry of National Enlightenment to classical education in the gymnasium, the only avenue to university study, and the demotion of professional-vocational education from the gymnasium to the real school provoked the economic ministries of government to pursue their own initiatives in education.

They were abetted by the growing number of professional societies that supported more practical approaches to public education than classicism offered. By the end of Alexander II's reign a growing and more confident public opinion was critical of both the government and the emperor himself. Alexander accepted the need for further reform to appease public opinion. His concession took the form of a consultative assembly of delegates elected by the citizens. Immediately following his approval of the assembly in 1881, he was assassinated by members of the populist People's Will.

5

Reasserting Authority: Alexander III and Nicholas II

Alexander III was more conservative and far more resolute than his father. Like his grandfather, Nicholas I, he came to the throne in a time of crisis. The new emperor's principal tutor had been Konstantin P. Pobedonostsev, who was named Procurator of the Holy Synod in 1880 and remained his mentor throughout his reign. In spite of an early career as a progressive legal reformer, Pobedonostsev had become an advocate of autocracy as the form of government most appropriate for Russia and an ardent opponent of constitutional forms of government. Pobedonostsev and his pupil Alexander believed that the reforms of the previous reign were responsible for student unrest, widespread social agitation, and the revolutionary terrorists who had murdered his father. Under the old banner of Autocracy, Orthodoxy, and Nationality, Alexander reasserted autocratic authority and the influence of the Orthodox Church. He rescinded few of the reforms of the 1860s but tried to limit their effectiveness through administrative and police measures. He sought as well to enhance noble privilege in governance and in access to secondary and higher education. Alexander did not seek greatness but only to perform his duties as he understood them conscientiously. He was most comfortable in the privacy of his family and fiercely defended its prerogatives. He was an imposing figure, a huge man with great physical strength and commanding presence.

His son and successor, Nicholas II, saw his father as the ideal embodiment of a Romanov monarch. Nicholas was a slight figure and felt himself to be inferior to his father in every way. A year before his early death, Alexander dismissed his adult son as an "absolute child." On learning of his father's death and his accession to the throne in October 1894, Nicholas exclaimed: "I am unprepared to be Tsar" and lamented that "I know nothing of the business of ruling." Much of the preparation that he had was at the hands of his father's tutor Pobedonostsev who instilled in his pupil the same principles that had guided the reign of Alexander. Nicholas pledged on ascending the throne "to preserve the principles of autocracy as firmly and steadfastly as did my late and unforgettable father."[1]

During the early years of his reign Nicholas followed his father's example but, in spite of his pledge, without his firmness and resolve. By the time of his coronation in 1896, however, a new image of the monarchy began to emerge. It marked the culmination of the rise of Russian nationalism since the war of 1812 and the apotheosis of the idea of a mystical bond between tsar and people. Nicholas was the only Russian autocrat to abandon the long-established role first played by Peter the Great of a Western-style conquering monarch. Instead he fostered the ideal of Russia's Muscovite past. At the heart of the new dynastic discourse lay the coronation in 1613 of Tsar Mikhail, the first of the Romanov rulers. His coronation signaled divine sanction for the Romanov dynasty and legitimized the personal rule of the family. Descendants of Ivan Susanin, the legendary Russian peasant who died concealing the hiding place of young Mikhail from his Polish pursuers during the Time of Troubles, were featured guests at Nicholas's coronation banquet. A gala performance of Mikhail Glinka's opera about Susanin, *A Life for the Tsar*, followed the banquet. All things Muscovite were promoted. Nicholas dismissed notions of popular sovereignty. In a speech in 1896 he characterized the hopes of Russian liberals for constitutional government as "senseless dreams." The tsar alone spoke for the nation. The role of education was to reinforce the bond between throne and people and to emphasize the differences between Russia and the West.[2] In a memorandum on education of 1902, Nicholas subordinated academic learning to moral upbringing in the spirit of Orthodoxy and respect for monarchy, fatherland, and family. He envisioned a terminal elementary school for the lower social estates, a variety of terminal secondary schools to train needed personnel, and the existing classical gymnasium as the sole avenue to university study.[3]

Elementary Schools

Under the influence of Pobedonostsev, Alexander moved Dmitrii Tolstoi from the Ministry of National Enlightenment to the Ministry of the Interior and appointed I. D. Delianov as minister of national enlightenment in 1882. The real authority in matters of education was, however, Pobedonostsev. He believed that even the limited social mobility that the Tolstoi system permitted destabilized society. Education should not impose international academic standards on the school system but should be more practical and favor Russians and the Orthodox over non-Russians and other religions. In particular he wished to give the Church a larger role in elementary education. In 1881 he removed church schools from the supervision of secular school boards and entrusted them to the Holy Synod. In the next year the peasant literacy schools were legalized and came also under the authority of the Synod in 1891. A regulation on church-parish schools of 1884 created one-class two-year schools and two-class four-year schools. Their mandate was to "strengthen the Orthodox faith and Christian morality among the people and impart useful elementary knowledge."[4] The one-class school taught Law of God, church singing, reading and writing in Church Slavonic and Russian, and the first four functions of arithmetic. The two-class school added some Church and Russian history. Priests and deacons were mandated to teach the classes as part of their parochial duties, but a morally certified layperson could be appointed as well. In practice, neither priests nor deacons were prepared to teach for free; soon the majority of teachers came from among the non-ordained. Graduates of the church-parish schools were accorded the same exemptions from military service as those of secular schools. In 1893 the Church appointed an inspector in each of thirteen dioceses and in 1895 added another thirteen. The state provided a steadily increasing subsidy for the support of church-led primary education. By the end of the 1880s the government spent more on church-parish schools than on ministry schools. Their numbers grew from about 17,000 in 1888 to 27,000 in 1893.[5] Some zemstvos also subsidized church-parish schools that were cheaper than their own or transferred secular schools to church jurisdiction. An important stimulus to the drive for schooling was a famine and cholera epidemic that swept through the Volga region and beyond in 1891. In spite of government resistance to social initiatives, a vast public relief effort emerged. The response to the famine stimulated civic organizations to address pressing social needs. Many activists blamed the ignorance of the peasantry for the famine and saw in education a remedy.

Although the expansion of the church-parish school network outpaced the growth of zemstvo schools, zemstvo financial support for schools grew steadily. Formerly, the bulk of support for schools came from the peasantry. In 1887, however, zemstvo support for education for the first time surpassed peasant communal financing. In 1890 the zemstvos spent 7,500,000 rubles on schools; village societies invested only 1,700,000 rubles.[6] A significant portion of the funds consisted of subsidies to church-parish schools. Nevertheless, from 1878 to 1898 the number of zemstvo schools rose from around 10,000 to 17,000 with the largest growth in the 1890s.[7] By the turn of the century, peasants were beginning to favor zemstvo over church-parish schools. By then most zemstvos had stopped funding the latter. The priority of religious-moral instruction over academic attainment was common to both church and secular schools. Ironically, the teaching of religion in the zemstvo schools, where priests were paid, was often superior to that in church-parish schools where they were expected to volunteer their time.

A highly restrictive statute of 1890 on the zemstvos limited their autonomy further. Under it the proportion of noble members rose from 89 percent to 94 percent on district zemstvo boards and from 61 percent to 75 percent on provincial zemstvo boards. Provincial governors now had the authority to veto decisions of the zemstvos. The goal was to weaken the influence of the so-called Third Element in the zemstvos who were driving reform and seeking to expand their authority. The change had little result. From 1880 to 1890, the zemstvos spent on average 5,900,000 rubles on education; that average more than doubled between 1891 and 1895 and reached 32,200,000 roubles in 1896.[8] In 1893 a Senate ruling recognized an enhanced role for the zemstvos in setting the school curriculum.

In the early years of Nicholas II's reign, the old education policies of his father remained in force but were less rigidly applied. Since the need for universal elementary education was widely recognized within both the government and the public, the pace of expansion of primary schooling accelerated under Nicholas. The Treasury increased funding, at first mostly to church-parish schools but later to ministry and zemstvo secular schools. A Statute on Church Schools in 1902 began the closure of the literacy schools or their conversion into church-parish schools. The Church gradually lost the influence it had gained in the previous reign over the curriculum in secular schools, although priests still taught Law of God in them. Where a secular school already existed, the Church was now required to get the permission of local education authorities to establish a church school. Church-parish schools remained important, however, in cities. In 1903 the Church extended the course in one-class schools from two to three years although the teaching program remained unchanged at fifteen hours per week on religious subjects and sixteen on secular topics. The Church also established a few two-class four-year schools with a curriculum that added geography, natural history, drafting, and drawing to the curriculum. Fears about too much knowledge, especially for peasants, remained. Teachers in the church schools were instructed to teach only the prescribed curriculum and not to presume "to communicate their wider knowledge of any subject" to their students.[9] Urbanites increasingly recognized the value of education. In cities, demand for school places outstripped supply. In 1895 St. Petersburg schools rejected 5,846 applicants, Moscow another 2,983, and Odessa, Kiev, and Kazan' also had shortages. By 1902, however, the rapid expansion of the primary school system had markedly reduced refusals.[10]

The expansion of the elementary school network was also sustained by growing peasant demand. Peasants sought literacy for many reasons. Traditionally, they associated literacy above all with the reading of religious texts. Reading sacred works was seen as a key to a better life and an aid to salvation. The scarcity of Russian translations of the Bible until late in the century made a grasp of Church Slavonic mandatory. A son who could read was able to take part in the church service, a matter of pride for parents. Religious sectarians valued reading. As seen earlier, Old Believer women were known as able and willing teachers of reading skills, a matter of concern for the Church and a spur to their own schooling efforts. Peasants also began to grasp that reading had important secular uses. From the time of the emancipation, reform that brought autonomy to former serfs a mass of information and legal documents essential to the work of peasant administration and the survival of communes accumulated. Peasants had to deal with government officials and other outsiders on a daily basis. They needed to know what they were agreeing to or what they were signing. Numeracy enabled accurate accounting and was a shield against corruption and cheating. Literacy, therefore, served the collective interests of peasants. But individuals also began to discover the value of literacy. The army reform of the 1870s that introduced conscription initially linked length of service to educational attainment. These inducements were only abolished in 1906. As well, a literate conscript enjoyed a head start in gaining NCO rank.

At first, literacy provided little advantage to a family in traditional agricultural regions. Wherever market forces began to shape the economy, however, the advantages of literacy became apparent. Increasingly, peasants in economically dynamic regions turned to state and zemstvo schools to provide the levels of reading comprehension that the rote learning of the literacy schools did not provide. In that calculation, girls fared poorly. Peasants broadly opposed coeducation, but the provision of separate classes for girls was expensive. Girls in peasant agricultural economies traditionally took on household chores and the care of younger siblings early. "Why literacy?" a peasant asked. "You don't need it to make cabbage soup." Girls were also an asset to the peasant household economy. Said another peasant: "If you send her to school, she costs money; if you keep her home, she makes money."[11] Some peasant girls did go to school, especially in areas with economic opportunities outside the home. In the Moscow school district in 1880, the proportion of girls to boys in all primary schools was two in ten. For most girls their value at home outweighed the advantages of their schooling.[12]

Peasants valued literacy but sought to manage its effects on traditional peasant life. Literacy served as a defense against the encroachment of values and practices from beyond the village. Its purpose was to enable effective functioning in peasant society. Literacy should not alter but assure the survival of the essence of peasant life. Peasants preferred poorly educated teachers and maintained a bias in favor of religion as the basis of learning. They judged embellishments such as storytelling or poetry in school to be frivolous distractions from the essential task of learning to read and to count. Many parents believed a year in primary school was sufficient to meet their goals for their children. On the one hand, they limited the length of schooling of their children in order to gain the advantages of basic literacy while, on the other, controlling the impact on village culture that school learning might have. Too much schooling, they feared, spoiled children for agricultural work but did not prepare them for other employment, As a result, the upper grades of schools were poorly attended or often empty. From 1901 to 1915 the percentage of boys in third grade hovered around 19–20 percent and of girls between 11 and 15 percent of the total number of students in school. Boys in the second grade made up from 30 to 38 percent of the total and girls from 34 to 36 percent. Zemstvo and church-parish schools had similar rates. In the 1880s about 10 percent of all pupils graduated. A study of 1896 of the 34 zemstvo provinces found a graduation rate of around 9.9 percent in both zemstvo and church-parish schools.[13] Figure 5.1 captures somewhat romantically both the anticipation and trepidation of a peasant boy on the threshold of learning.

Secondary Schools

There was little disagreement between the state and society about the need to expand elementary education. The battleground was over secondary education. Pobedonostsev supported the boys' classical gymnasium as the sole gateway to higher education. He vehemently disapproved, however, of Tolstoi's policy of advancing the most able students from the lower social estates into the gymnasium. In 1885 the minister of education, Delianov, proposed to restrict admission to children whose social origins were no lower than that of merchants of the second guild. The emperor rejected the proposal but approved a significant increase in fees and the reduction in the number of stipends for gymnasium preparatory classes. He also proposed to reduce the number of gymnasiums by turning some of them into real schools. In June 1887 Delianov issued his notorious "cooks' circular" to exclude children of "coachmen, menials, cooks, washerwomen, small shopkeepers, and the like" from the gymnasiums.[14] The circular caused a public uproar. The policies were intended to reduce the percentage of commoners and also in part designed to reduce the high dropout rates from gymnasiums and increase the rates of graduation. From 1886 to 1890 the graduation rate did increase by 22 percent while the secondary school population shrank by 17 percent.

Figure 5.1 Nikolaj Petrovic Bogdanov-Bel'skij, "Study from Life," *c.* 1903.
Source: The Print Collector/Getty Images.

Public criticism of the classical gymnasium became more strident toward the end of the century. Under public pressure, the ministry eased the restrictive policies imposed by Delianov, resulting in an increase in overall enrolments in gymnasiums in 1895 by 3,500 students over the previous year.[15] Parents demanded more say in the curriculum but were refused any representation on the schools' pedagogical councils. Whereas parents preferred a more utilitarian approach to learning, most teachers saw education as an end in itself. They along with school directors resented public interference in academic programs. Teachers in turn wished to reduce the extensive powers of directors over them and further increase the competence of the pedagogical councils, consisting of teachers. Teachers, directors, and parents alike deplored the so-called number system of grading in the gymnasiums and real schools. Under it, for the first twenty minutes of every class an individual student was singled out to recite the previous night's homework. The students received a number from 5 to 1 for their performances; their scores were tallied quarterly and again at year's end to determine advancement to the next grade and ultimately eligibility to write a graduation examination. While the student was grilled the rest of the class sat idle.

The nature of the final examination that led to the certificate of maturity was also disputed. The examination depended heavily on the ability of the student to translate from Russian into Greek and Latin. A new minister in 1898 struck a commission of district education delegates to address the problems of the secondary education system. Delegates consulted locally and took their findings to plenary sessions of the commission. The discussions were extensive, but the changes were modest. The goal of secondary education was defined as teaching youth to work deliberately and with clarity and precision. The number system of grading was retained but subordinated to the "conscientious" review of individual cases by the pedagogical council whose powers were increased. Teaching was now to be informed but not dictated by government fiat. Teachers were tasked with primary responsibility for the success of their students. The certificate of maturity remained, but Greek and Latin were dropped from the examination.

In 1901 P. S. Vannovskii was named minister of education. He resumed the expansion of the network of gymnasiums after years of stagnant growth. Twelve new ones were added; by 1904 there were 251 with about 102,000 students. The number of real schools also grew by 51. In 1895 the real schools had a total of 17,500 students and in 1905 51,500.[16] Vannovskii worked toward a better balance in secondary education between academic and practical learning. He planned to create a unified secondary school. The first phase of the planned reform saw restructuring of the first four grades of the gymnasium with subsequent changes in the upper years to reduce the program from eight to seven years. Greater emphasis was given to Russian and modern European languages. Vannovskii also intended to drop the certificate of maturity. The plan posed a major threat to the Tolstoi system. It would have permitted graduates of the real schools and of the growing network of commercial schools to enter the university. The result would be a decline in the percentage of nobles and an increase in that of professional, commercial, and industrial groups in higher education.

In 1902 a new reactionary minister of the interior was named, who forced Vannovskii's resignation within a week of his appointment. The latter's plans were largely scrapped. The maturity certificate remained, and graduates of commercial schools were blocked from university enrolment. The promising alliance forged by Vannovskii early in the new century between the Ministry of Finance and the Ministry of National Enlightenment was broken as the latter realigned with the conservative Ministry of the Interior. A few changes were made. The teaching of Greek was now restricted to one gymnasium only in each of the university cities, and Latin was dropped in the first two grades of the gymnasium and not introduced into the real school. The gymnasium retained eight grades and the real schools six. The first two years of the gymnasium and real school were made coterminous and students were more easily able to transfer from one into the other.

Universities

A new statute on universities of 1884 greatly increased the powers of the school district curators at the expense of faculty councils. The faculty lost the say they had enjoyed in appointments under the previous legislation. The Ministry of National Enlightenment now appointed rectors while curators appointed deans. The ministry also named professors to vacant chairs and assigned inspectors of students. The latter were supervised by the curator and worked with the police to oversee student behavior. A decree of May 1885 denied students the right to engage in activities in common or to incorporate in any form. As under Nicholas I, uniforms for university students were made compulsory. Tuition fees rose by a multiple of five. An attempt to assassinate Alexander III in 1887 resulted in the closure of five universities and two higher technical schools and in hundreds of arrests of students. Quotas on Jews in gymnasiums and universities were imposed in July 1887: no more than 10 percent of the student body within the Pale, 5 percent outside the Pale, and 3 percent in the two capitals.

The university statute subjected university students to intolerable living conditions. About half of the student population existed in dire poverty with no reliable means of support. A lack of student dormitories forced them into cramped and unhealthy quarters. New rules of student behavior in 1885 placed students under close police supervision both within and beyond the university. Persecutions and expulsions were common. The university statute allowed students no corporate organizations. That prohibition ran counter to student culture that had since the 1860s evolved a consciousness of shared belonging and common interests or *studenchestvo*. Students doggedly maintained a number of corporate bodies deemed illegal by the authorities. The *kruzhok* was a study circle where students met to discuss topics often forbidden by the authorities; *zemliachestva* were groups of students from the same geographical region of the empire that helped to integrate newcomers from that region into the university community; the *skhodka*, modeled on peasant communal organizations, was a representative body signifying student collective responsibility and decision making.

In 1899 student unrest morphed into a student strike. Repression came swiftly. More than 1,300 students were expelled. A law of July 1899 provided for expelled students to be forcibly enlisted in the army. The War Ministry objected that the army was not a reform school. Rules in the summer of 1899 increased the number of inspectors in the universities but softened their mandate. They were not to oppress students but to address their needs. Students were required to attend only the university in the school district of their residency. Some hostels for poor students were built but with little effect on student unrest. On their part, professors chafed under the restrictions of the new university statute. They wanted a return to faculty elections of rectors, the right to appoint faculty and discipline students, and autonomy in research and teaching, free from state regulation. In their view the formation of a national culture depended on the production within the universities of pure knowledge on which character was built. While opposed to government educational policy, professors feared revolution from below even more. They blamed government policy and police repression of students for student unrest but sought to avoid confrontation with the state and to reform the system from within rather than to overturn it.

A second student strike in 1901 sparked the Ministry of National Enlightenment to ask the universities to inquire into the causes of the disturbances. The universities recommended allowing students to form societies, restricting the powers of inspectors, creating university courts for student discipline, and assuring university autonomy. The then minister, Vannovskii, agreed to permit students to establish dining clubs, reading rooms, and mutual aid societies for the distribution of state and private funds to the most needful students. The traditional student corporate bodies remained banned, however. More strikes followed in 1902 and 1904. Expulsions continued. In 1904 the concessions to students made in 1901 were withdrawn. By then student disturbances were spreading into the gymnasiums. Although many expelled students joined the growing revolutionary movement, the focus of studenchestvo or student corporate action within the universities remained on the perceived needs of students. Student organizations worked with revolutionary parties only to the extent that the parties were prepared to advance student corporate causes.[17]

Women's Higher Courses

With the accession of Alexander III, the women's higher courses came under scrutiny. Conservatives not only blamed the universities for revolutionary unrest but also saw the women's higher courses as seedbeds of subversion. At first, new admissions to the courses were suspended pending a review. Against the advice of the review committee, Delianov closed the courses in Moscow in 1888 and those in Kiev the following year. Only the Bestuzhevskie courses in St. Petersburg survived thanks to the influence of the many grandees of the capital who patronized the courses and argued that they preserved "traditional moral and social values." The courses now fell under the same rules as the universities. The Ministry of National Enlightenment appointed all their managerial and administrative personnel, including the director and the trustees. It also approved teachers and supervisory staff. It was made explicit that the goal of the courses was not to prepare women for professional careers but "for life, mainly family life." The total number of auditors was restricted to four hundred and non-Christians to 3 percent of the total. Thanks to the restrictions the new class of 1889 was 90 percent Orthodox. Students from noble or high official families represented 77 percent of the total and 13 percent had merchant backgrounds. The closures of the higher courses and medical courses for women drove them abroad once more. In 1888–9 more than one hundred women enrolled in Swiss universities.[18]

Nicholas II exhibited a more favorable attitude to the education of women than had his father. Educational opportunities for women expanded rapidly during the early years of his reign. In 1897 the Medical Institute for Women opened in St. Petersburg. In 1904 it was given equal status with university medical faculties. Its graduates soon were granted equal rights with male physicians in state service, barring rank on the Table of Ranks. Women doctors could practice privately and serve as doctors in female religious, educational, and children's institutions such as orphanages. They could also practice medicine in villages for female and male patients. In general they were paid less well than male counterparts. In 1905 some five hundred women were studying at the Medical Institute.[19] The restrictions on the Bestuzhevskie Higher Courses for Women were lifted and in 1901 their graduates were permitted to teach the senior classes in girls' gymnasiums. Higher Courses were again permitted in Moscow and later in other cities, reaching twenty in 1910 with roughly twenty thousand students.

Women in the higher courses were passionate in their studies. E. I. Time recalled the buffet in the school in St. Petersburg where ardent discussions often took place. "Life," she said, "put before us many complex questions, but our ties of friendship helped us to navigate them. Every one of us formed our own opinions and tastes: later our paths diverged, but we always agreed on one thing: the search for the truth and meaning of life."[20] The *kuristy* of the 1880s distinguished themselves sharply from the nihilist women of the 1860s. E. A. Andreeva-Belmont recalled meeting some of the women of the older generation: "They were already old, ugly and shorn, they smoked and dressed in some sort of grey overalls. I did not want to be like them."[21] Her attitude to the pioneers of women's emancipation in Russia was testimony to the change in Russian society that increasingly recognized the public roles of women. Memoirists invariably expressed their gratitude to the professors who taught them, often for little or no remuneration. Young men of the intelligentsia were often intrigued by the *kuristy*. V. V. Veresaev remembered standing on the street opposite the building of the Higher Women's Courses in St. Petersburg observing with eager curiosity the women with their "inspired and serious faces." He longed to meet them and engage with them in good conversation.[22]

To address the chronic shortage of teachers in secondary girls' schools, the Department of the Empress Maria Feodorovna collaborated with the Ministry of National Enlightenment to found the Women's Pedagogical Institute in St. Petersburg in 1903. It had historical-philological and physical-mathematical sections of four and a half years of study to train teachers for female secondary schools and home tutors. Gymnasiums for girls continued to grow faster than those for boys. In 1902 there were three girls' schools for every two boys' schools. Figure 5.2 sets the types of schools providing elementary education early in the twentieth century.

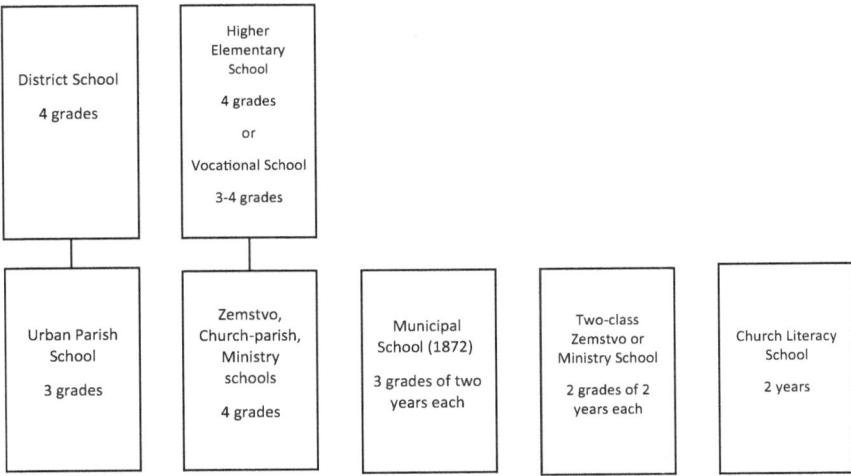

Figure 5.2 Types of elementary schools in the early twentieth century.

Professional-Vocational Schooling

In spite of various obstacles placed in its way, professional, technical, and vocational education also expanded in the last decades of the nineteenth and early years of the twentieth centuries to meet the growing needs of an expanding market and industrial economy. Conservatives in the government feared that the mass education of workers would ultimately subvert the monopoly of ruling groups on education. As well, some industrialists, who drew on foreign technicians for specialist expertise, gave little support to technical education in Russia. In 1895 only 8 percent of some 27,000 factory and plant operations in the empire provided technical education to their employees.[23] The economic ministries, however, recognized the need for professional and technical training. The Ministry of Finance ran several technical schools as did State Properties, Railways, Army, Navy, and Agriculture. The zemstvos also began to establish trade and agricultural schools as well as medical educational institutions. From 1884 to 1903, the zemstvos created forty-nine elementary and secondary agricultural schools.[24] A number of general zemstvo schools also had agricultural sections. A plan in the late 1880s to provide technical education for women came to nothing, but in 1901 the Ministry of National Enlightenment opened a department to oversee existing schools for women's technical education. It counted 129 such schools with just over 9,900 students.[25]

Professional-vocational education at the secondary level also fell under the suspicion of conservatives. Critics maintained that the curriculum of the real schools gave students more education than was needed for people best suited by their social origins for vocational careers. In 1888 Delianov issued a new statute on real schools that eliminated the professional elements of the curriculum and reduced them to lower trade schools. The six years of study remained. He also introduced three types of specialist vocational schools. The first type trained assistant engineers; it had a four-year program with mechanical, chemical, construction, agricultural, and mining sections and admitted students who had completed the fifth grade of the reformed real school. The second type trained skilled foremen; it had a three-year program and took students from the sixth year of the urban schools. The third type produced skilled workmen; it admitted students after two or three years of primary schooling and offered three-year courses for locksmiths and carpenters among others. The new schools were unpopular. The aspirations of young people were high in an expanding economy. The vocational schools were at best a last resort for students not accepted elsewhere. Only a few such schools opened, two between 1888 and 1893 and another eight from 1894 to 1898.

Organizations of civil society also continued their efforts to advance technical expertise in the empire. From 1872 the Russian Technological Society had within it a Commission on Technical Education with branches in several cities. It promoted professional and technical education but saw general education as the prerequisite to professional studies. The commission operated Sunday and evening courses for workers in various enterprises, sponsored public readings on technical subjects, and opened libraries. It also organized a series of congresses on technical and professional education from 1889 to 1904. At the most basic level, both rural and urban primary schools were free to offer training in crafts and skills relevant to the local economy, and many did so. In addition, many private groups opened professional and technical schools with programs between six and nine years. Private donors between 1897 and 1901 invested 2.5 million roubles in commercial and trade schools and courses.[26] The government issued statutes to govern elementary and higher craft schools in the early 1890s and a law in 1902 on craft and technical schools and courses. In 1903 municipal schools were authorized to open craft courses, often against the wishes of parents who wanted a general education for their children as a pathway to social advancement.

In 1894 the Ministry of Finance took jurisdiction over all so-called commercial schools. In 1896 it organized them into four groupings. The first were commercial schools at a secondary school level. They offered either three- or seven- and eight-year programs that combined general with commercial education. The second were trade schools with three grades that taught vocational courses. Trade classes and commercial classes that served as refresher courses for those already employed comprised the third and fourth groups. The schools and courses were funded by the ministry, zemstvos, merchant and craft guilds, and private donors. Graduates of commercial secondary schools could attend the higher technical institutes. There were ten higher institutes under various ministries that delivered higher technical education. The Technological Institute, the Institute of Civil Engineers, the Institute of Mining, the Institute of Forestry, and the Institute of Ways and Communications were located in St. Petersburg. Moscow boasted two technical institutes: the Petrovskii Academy of Agriculture and the Moscow Technical School. Kharkov and Kiev had one each. The Academy of Arts and the two Military Academies in St. Petersburg rounded out the list. A proposal to open professional schools for women within the Ministry of National Enlightenment in 1888 came to nothing. In spite of government and social initiatives, the level of technical education available within the empire and the ranks of professional and technical specialists was by the beginning of the twentieth century far below what was needed to energize and modernize a still heavily agricultural country.

Church Schools

In his role as Procurator of the Holy Synod, Pobedonostsev was a critic of the existing statutes on Church seminaries and academies. In his mind they were too secular in their orientation and encouraged mobility out of the clerical estate. A new statute for the academy in 1883 gave greater authority to the bishop and rector at the expense of the faculty, revised the curriculum to strengthen religious content, and modestly increased the budget. In 1884 he formed a committee to consider reform of the seminaries. A new statute on the seminaries was promulgated later in the year. It, too, gave bishops greater authority and expanded religious studies in the curriculum. Classicism remained as an important element of the curriculum, however. The new dispensation did little to solve the problems in church education. By the 1890s, morale among students reached new lows. Plans for further reform produced little result. Graduations from the academy declined and the number of deacons in parishes who had completed the seminary fell from 88.1 percent in 1890 to 63.8 percent in 1904. The better students often left to study in secular institutions. By 1900 11.4 percent of university students were from the clergy estate.[27] The mood among the majority of bishops by 1905 was relatively liberal. They recognized that the clergy were outcasts from the rest of society and supported their full integration into the nation. They also favored the expansion of the church-parish school system, which the Church undertook in 1904, as a means better to integrate church and society.[28]

Outcomes

The reign of Alexander III and the years to 1905 overseen by Nicholas II were years of missed opportunities for Russia. The healthy forces present that held promise for the future were systematically suppressed through administrative and policing measures. While there were important gains in education, they fell well short of what was needed and possible. From the mid-1860s to the mid-1890s the number of elementary schools grew from 27, 000 with 700,000 pupils to more than 80,000 with 4,000,000 pupils. By 1904 there were 81,000 elementary schools of all types with 4,700,000 pupils.[29] Of the total, 94 percent were one-class schools with one- to three-year-programs, 4 percent were two-class schools with four to five years of instruction, and 2 percent were multigrade schools with six years of study.[30] The rapid growth of the population in this period far outstripped the capacity of elementary schools to accommodate it. In the Moscow and St. Petersburg school districts in 1882, there was one school per 2,900 inhabitants; in 1894 it fell to one in 3,100. In major cities only one in five children of school age and in the provinces one in six could be accommodated in the schools (boys at two in seven and girls at one in twenty). About a third of school-age children were literate in that year.[31] If literacy was proving useful to peasants it was also of great value to urban working people. As one observer noted: "They do not take illiterates in the trades." A survey in 1896 found that 90 percent of workers in restaurant service were literate, as were 86 percent of bakers, 85 percent of sausage makers, and 84 percent of coachmen. Even stevedores had a literacy rate of 54 percent. The census of 1897 counted 2.6 million workers in industry, transport, and trade, of whom 53 percent were literate.[32]

Much of the initiative for the expansion of education came from the institutions of society. Zemstvo expenditure on education grew from only 5 percent in 1868 to 14 percent in 1895 and was to reach 31.1 percent in 1914. Fearing to lose control of the direction of education, the state responded. The allocation of the state budget for education at all levels grew from 2.69 percent in 1881 to 3.22 percent in 1900. Government expenditure on primary education lagged until 1895 when it reached two million roubles then leapt to five million the following year, doubled that number in 1900, and continued to increase. Qualified teachers remained in short supply. Those who taught, especially at the primary level, were inadequately prepared for the demands of modern schooling.

The initial growth of secondary education under Alexander II was sharply curtailed in the reign of Alexander III by ever higher fees with fewer stipends, reduction of preparatory classes, and quotas on Jews. In spring 1887 there were just under 71,000 students in 241 male gymnasiums and pro-gymnasiums in the empire. The numbers fell to about 62,000 in the fall of that year and to 59,000 in 1889. A slight increase followed in 1890.[33] The number of pro-gymnasiums declined from 70 in 1887 to 58 in 1894 and those of gymnasiums from 176 to 166. By 1895, 13.3 enrollees per 10,000 of the total school population were in secondary school and only 7.6 percent of them were from the peasantry. The census of 1897 revealed that only 1 percent of the population was enrolled in general education secondary schools or military academic secondary schools in that year.[34]

Alexander's policies altered the social composition of students in gymnasiums once more in favor of the elites. The number of the children of noble and high officials attending gymnasiums increased from 49.2 percent to 56.3 percent, and those from the urban estates decreased from 35 percent to 31.3 percent. The period also witnessed rising demand for a more practical education. Between 1885 and 1897 the numbers attending real schools increased by 18 percent. The percentage of nobles in them declined from 40.7 percent to 38 percent and that of the urban classes rose from 41.8 percent to 43.4 percent, and peasants from 10.9 percent to 12.7 percent. The elites also held their own in the universities. In 1900 the total number of students in the universities of the empire was 13,548. Half were the sons of nobles and high officials. A little less than a third came from the urban estates and just over 11 percent from the clergy. Peasants, Cossacks, and foreigners made up the remainder.[35]

At all levels of the education system the rate of graduation was low. In municipal schools in 1884 only 4.8 percent of students completed the four-year program. In 1894 the number rose to 7.3 percent. A survey in 1896 found that in both zemstvo and church-parish schools in the thirty-four zemstvo provinces, the rate of completion was 9.9 percent.[36] Secondary school graduation rates were equally low. In 1898 only 3.8 percent of students in real schools graduated. Two-thirds of students in the gymnasiums left before graduation. The women's gymnasiums suffered from graduation rates even lower than the men's. In 1893 completion rates in female gymnasiums in six school districts ranged from a high of 14.7 percent in Kharkov to a low of 8.6 percent in Kazan'. Rates in pro-gymnasiums for girls fell, for example, to 12.5 percent in Orienburg and 7.5 percent in Odessa.[37] The flight of students from the church seminaries enabled those who remained to secure a church position without having to graduate; accordingly graduation rates in them fell. The goal of many students in the universities was to secure an attestat by completing the minimum requirements for entry into state service rather than to complete all of the requirements for a degree. The higher technical institutes did little better. In 1904, for example, only 1,000 of about 13,000 students graduated from institutes of engineering.[38]

Private education remained popular as parents sought alternatives to the conservative curriculum of the gymnasiums. Private gymnasiums were required to teach the program of ministry gymnasiums and in the three senior grades employ teachers with a university education. They were free, however, to add courses beyond the required state curriculum and often practiced more modern teaching methods. There were 77 private gymnasiums in 1895. There were also 1,542 lower private schools operating in that year. For the most part they prepared students for admission to the gymnasiums. A number of prestigious gymnasiums for girls opened in the 1870s. Many stressed pedagogy and trained numerous teachers and governesses. The Department of the Empress Mariia Feodorovna opened the Women's Pedagogical Institute in 1903 to train teachers and domestic tutors, who remained in demand.[39] Foreign governesses, especially English ladies, were popular with the aristocratic elite. Adult education was also gaining support. The Sunday schools that had been closed in the 1860s were again permitted in 1874. Peasant parents were drawn to them when they saw the ease with which their children learned to read. Between 1892 and 1897, 136 new Sunday schools opened. Most were taught by local teachers or students. Regulation slowed their opening, however. Concern that radicals would use the schools to spread subversion led the government to transfer them to the control of the Holy Synod.[40]

By 1905 various segments of public opinion were at odds with state policy. Conservatives, especially those among the nobility, felt threatened by the rapid economic development that was changing the balance of social and economic forces in the empire. They were influential at the highest levels of government and in the zemstvos. The rising commercial, industrial, and professional classes were highly critical of an education system that failed to meet their own and the state's practical needs and resented the constraints on their activities imposed by government. They longed for greater corporate and individual autonomy as well as a voice in governance. Women chafed at the inequalities of education and their exclusion from most professions. Industrialization gave birth to a working class, a proletariat, which by the late 1890s was beginning to organize to protect and enhance worker rights. In many parts of Russia there was growing peasant land hunger, which added to traditional grievances against authority.

The student disturbances at the turn of the century were only a symptom of wider public dissatisfaction with the regime of Nicholas II. Groups of politically like-minded citizens began to organize and to articulate their concerns through a vibrant press.

They also started to forge tactical alliances among ideological factions to present a common front to the state. Progressives among the new economic and professional groups who sought constitutional reform as an antidote to revolution joined forces in the Liberation Movement in the first years of the twentieth century. They evolved into the Constitutional Democratic Party founded in 1905. The more conservative advocates of reform among them soon formed the Octobrist Party toward the end of 1905. New illegal political organizations offered ideological formulations around which to organize worker and peasant movements. The Russian Social Democratic Party was by the end of the century adapting Marxism to Russian conditions. Early in the new century it split into two factions, the Bolsheviks and Mensheviks, who differed about the nature and pace of social revolution. In 1902 the old populist factions coalesced into the Socialist Revolutionary Party that advocated agrarian socialism and peasant revolution.

As long as the coercive powers of the state remained intact, however, society could do little to oppose authority effectively. The disastrous war with Japan begun in 1904 altered the balance. As defeats in the East amassed, the prestige of the regime fell. With a large segment of the army at war in the Far East and the general decline of morale among soldiers in home barracks at the news from the front, the coercive powers of the regime were severely hampered. The workers of St. Petersburg lit the fuse that set off the revolutionary explosion. The growth of the work force in the capital was not matched by the supply of affordable housing. Low wages condemned workers to live in deteriorating conditions, crowded into corners of rooms occupied by other impoverished families. A strike at the Putilov works in January 1905 sparked a walkout in sympathy in other enterprises of some ten thousand of the capital's workers. A priest, Father Gapon, who was involved in organizing worker unions while also in the pay of the secret police, led a march of workers with their families to present a petition to the tsar from his loyal subjects that asked for his intervention on their behalf. The march took place on January 9, a Sunday. The authorities had erected barriers to block the major streets leading from the worker districts to the Winter Palace. As workers approached the barriers some of the officers commanding the soldiers ordered them to fire. Around 150–200 men, women, and children died, and many more were wounded. The old regime tottered but did not fall.

6

From Revolution to Revolution: The Duma Period

Bloody Sunday set off a spring and summer of strikes and peasant disorders that culminated in a nationwide general strike supported by nearly the whole of society in October 1905. Reluctantly, Nicholas II was forced to concede to demands for an elected representative parliament. The October Manifesto offered a lower house, the Duma, elected on a broad franchise, and an upper chamber, the State Council, partly elected by conservative groups and partly appointed by the emperor. The concession split the opposition forces. Workers, supported by various revolutionary factions, continued their resistance, especially in Moscow, but were brutally crushed in December 1905. Peasant unrest intensified as well after the manifesto and continued into 1906. Petr Arkadevich Stolypin was named minister of the interior in April 1906 and prime minister in July. He was a highly capable politician, statesman, and staunch patriot. He adopted a two-pronged policy of repression of unrest in the countryside and partnership with center and right forces in the new Duma to advance a cautiously progressive agenda. The repression, especially in the western provinces and the Baltic provinces, was brutal. Stolypin followed rural pacification with a major land reform that allowed peasants to consolidate their communal holdings into single blocks of land to form individual farms. Some peasants embraced the offer, but the commune remained the dominant form of peasant land tenure. He also opened crown lands for sale to peasants and encouraged peasant resettlement in Siberia and Central Asia to relieve land hunger in the European Russian provinces.

Elementary Schools

Between the granting of constitutional government in the October Manifesto and the convening of the First Duma in the spring of 1906, the government promulgated the Fundamental Laws of the Russian Empire. The Fundamental Laws blurred the distinction between a fully constitutional order and the supremacy of the law on the one hand and the absolute authority of the autocrat on the other. The left-leaning liberal Constitutional Democratic Party (Kadets) formed the largest faction in the First Duma, which convened in May. There were several groupings to its left. The delegates were in an uncompromising mood. A leading member of the Kadets declared that the

Fundamental Laws made the law in Russia a "joke."[1] On education, nearly all sides agreed on the need for universal elementary schooling. Progressives of various stripes wanted the removal of religion from schools, teaching at the elementary level in the language of the student, and a unified school system. Opposition to the Fundamental Laws soon led to prorogation of the Duma and new elections. The Second Duma was nearly as radical as the first. It produced a bill for free universal primary education. Under its provisions local authorities were to take responsibility for opening the needed schools and managing them under Ministry of National Enlightenment supervision. Schools were to be located within a radius of three *versts* of one another in order to overcome distance as an obstacle to attendance. The schools were to provide a four-year course of study, and classes should have a maximum size of fifty students. The treasury would provide an annual grant of 390 roubles per fifty students. The Duma, which continued its opposition to the constitutional arrangements imposed on it, was prorogued before the bill was passed. The Ministry of National Enlightenment, however, pursued its basic provisions.

Stolypin was committed to modernizing reform in the empire but was determined to reassert government control over the modernization agenda. He perceived the Duma as an obstacle but neither could nor wished to abolish it. Instead, he staged a coup by greatly narrowing the franchise for Duma elections to assure a more politically moderate body of delegates. The Third Duma, elected on the new franchise, convened in November 1907 and lasted until June 1912. It proved, for the most part, to be a willing and able partner of Stolypin's government. The major party in the Third Duma was the Octobrists. They were right-leaning liberals dedicated to making the concessions contained in the October Manifesto function in the public interest. The reactionary United Nobility occupied the political right in the Third Duma. The reform of education was a priority for Stolypin and his parliamentary allies. Although the Third Duma succeeded in passing only two education bills, one authorizing state credit for schools in 1908 and a second supporting a school construction fund in 1909, it built in the course of its debates the foundations of a system of universal elementary education. In March 1911 the Duma passed legislation to make elementary education compulsory. The deeply conservative State Council, however, rejected mandatory schooling along with most of the other provisions of the bill, including the inclusion of women on school boards, teaching in the native tongue in primary schools, the transfer of church-parish schools to Ministry of National Enlightenment control, the right of graduates of primary schools to go on to secondary schools, and the right of non-Orthodox citizens to teach in non-Russian schools.

The opposition of the State Council slowed but did not prevent important education reforms. The school funding bill of 1908 marked a major change in state policy toward elementary education. Since the reign of Peter the Great the government had placed the burden of funding primary schooling on local populations. Under the new legislation the government gave local district zemstvo and urban duma authorities a period of ten years to submit a plan for the provision of free universal primary education in their district or municipality When the plan was centrally approved, the legislation provided for transfers from the treasury of 760 roubles per fifty students in non-zemstvo provinces and 390 roubles per fifty students in zemstvo provinces in one-class schools. From 1907 to 1913 the budget of the Ministry of National Enlightenment increased from 45,900,000 roubles to 97,000,000 roubles, about 40 percent of which went to primary education.[2] The ministry plan envisaged, as had the bill in the Second Duma, the presence of a school within three versts of all settlements; if that proved impossible the school should include a residence. The plan called for provision for some 14 million students in 280,000 school complexes at a cost of 17 million roubles a year.[3] The money went to district zemstvos. The government saw provincial zemstvos as more liberal than their district counterparts and froze them out of school funding. Although the Duma refused to subsidize church-parish schools, the State Council demurred; in 1909 the Duma reluctantly voted two million roubles to church-parish schools and raised teacher salaries in them to the level of those in secular schools. Legislation had previously established a minimal salary of 360 roubles for teachers with a raise of 60 roubles after five years of service.

Although zemstvos and city dumas remained responsible for the building and maintenance of schools, central state funding of academic programs left them with little influence over curriculum and teaching. From 1910 to 1914, members of the zemstvo were entirely excluded from the supervision of schools. Teachers, curriculum, and the content of school libraries were centrally controlled. The role of inspectors was enhanced to enforce the policies. By 1911 the Ministry of National Enlightenment had agreements with 398 (90 percent) of district zemstvos but only 218 (35 percent) of town dumas. Fifteen percent of the 441 district zemstvos had by that year established schools with a certified teacher within a three-verst radius of all villages; that goal was in the reach of another 62 percent of districts within five years and of 30 percent within six to ten years. Town dumas were laggards. Only 195 of 984 of them had submitted plans by 1913.[4] In spite of a push beginning in 1905 to raise the elementary school course from three to four years and to create more two-class five-year schools, progress was slow. In Moscow province in the 1909–1910 school year, only 6 percent of schools offered a four-year course. On average, 23 percent of zemstvo schools provided four years of schooling.

The goal of creating a unified school system with continuity from primary to secondary education remained elusive. In 1906 the urban schools further increased the vocational element of their programs. They had remained unpopular with parents because they were not a gateway to secondary education. In 1912, however, an attempt was made to make them a bridge between primary and secondary schooling. Urban schools were reconstituted as four-year higher elementary schools. All those pupils who had graduated from a parish school could be admitted to a reformed urban school. The schools could be single sex or coeducational and were open to children of all social estates. They provided a general education that in 1913 was supplemented with the introduction of foreign languages. The vocational element did not disappear: in addition to general education, urban schools could offer trade courses to serve local business needs, pedagogical courses, training for postal and telegraph services, accounting, construction, and electronics. Teachers in the urban schools either had a higher education and certification from a pedagogical institute or had secondary education in a specialist theoretical or practical subject. Rather than one teacher for all subjects as in primary schools, teaching was done by subject. Students in these higher elementary schools could transfer after their second year into the third year of the gymnasium or real school after passing a foreign language examination. By 1915 there were 1,547 of these schools. The emperor and the State Council, ever fearful of social mobility, objected to the role of the higher elementary schools as preparatory to secondary education; obstacles to passage from one to the other consequently remained.[5]

Secondary Schools

During the upheaval of 1905, parents' committees had voluntarily formed in many secondary schools to restore order amid the revolutionary chaos. The government recognized their role as equivalent to trustees. Teachers gained greater control over the curriculum through the pedagogical councils. No longer did the councils have to select textbooks from a ministry list. The real schools in particular introduced more science subjects and reduced the religious content of the curriculum. Coalitions of parents, local education authorities, merchants, and industrialists also opened needed secondary schools in rural areas in the year of revolution. A reaction soon followed. The government remained torn between its recognition of the need for schooling and a profound reluctance to acknowledge the consequences of economic modernization for education planning. The parents' committees were soon sidelined or closed. Most of the newly established secondary schools in rural areas ceased to operate. Dress codes were reestablished. Competitive entrance examinations for entry into secondary schools resumed. In order to move from the real school to the gymnasium, examinations in Latin and history had to be passed. Textbooks required ministry approval. Those approved were often poor translations from Western textbooks; most science textbooks approved were badly out of date.

In spite of government concerns, the rapid expansion of elementary education required the growth of secondary education in order to prepare teachers for the lower schools. A huge new supply of primary schoolteachers was needed. The ministry's plan called for the opening of around a hundred new teachers' seminaries and teachers' institutes along with seven hundred teachers' short courses.[6] Gymnasiums were also a source of teachers. They, too, expanded. By 1913 there were 232 gymnasiums and 202 real schools for boys, up from 167 and 112, respectively, in the 1890s, and 599 gymnasiums and pro-gymnasiums for girls, up from 280 in the 1890s.[7] The expansion did little to overcome the shortage in rural areas of secondary school options. Peasants increasingly took the initiative in opening secondary schools. Their number grew from thirty-eight in 1907 to ninety-six in 1915.[8] After 1905, private gymnasiums with the right to issue certificates of maturity also proliferated. Some 120 opened between 1905 and 1911. Most were located in urban, affluent areas. Municipalities and zemstvos also opened secondary schools at their own expense.[9] Demand continued to surpass supply. In 1914 the ministry imposed a new academic plan on all secondary schools that reasserted vospitanie over obrazovanie. The religious component was increased as were the hours devoted to classical languages. Time allocated for the natural sciences was proportionately reduced.

Professional-Vocational Education

Government concerns that mass technical instruction would undermine the monopoly of ruling groups on education persisted into the early twentieth century. So too did the work of several technical societies that countered government reluctance. The Imperial Russian Technical Society from 1882 to the beginning of the First World War opened a range of educational institutions, from general education schools offering technical instruction to specialist schools and classes in technology, crafts, graphics, drafting, and electronics in several branches of industry. The Moscow Society for the Dissemination of Technical Knowledge had 878 member societies throughout the empire by 1912 and ran numerous schools and courses on technical subjects. In 1911 the governor of Moscow closed six of its most important sections. The Moscow Society of Engineers and Pedagogues from 1907 operated a secondary-level technical construction school and the Moscow Art Society ran a large school of painting, sculpture, and architecture. Many important professional-vocational institutions were established by private benefactors. They included the Stroganov Central Artistic-Industrial School in Moscow, the Shtiglits Central School of Technical Drawing in St. Petersburg, the I.I. Khoin Secondary Polytechnical School in Odessa, and many others.

In January 1910 a survey found 3,036 different professional-vocational education institutions with nearly 214,000 students in the empire. Only 355 of the schools were at the secondary level. Students in craft schools made up 42.2 percent of the total, 31.6 percent were in commercial schools, 6.8 percent studied in agricultural and cottage industry schools, 6.1 percent in technical institutions, 2.7 percent in art, and 2.3 percent in music. Railroad technology, graphics, health, forestry, and mining pupils each registered below 2 percent. Factory owners were often reluctant to run training schools for workers in their enterprises. Instead, they preferred on the job training. In 1914 the Fourth Duma discussed a bill on women's professional education. It limited the role of women to the teaching of knowledge needed for domestic roles and the training of capable specialists through schools and courses in six branches of women's work. The bill was never passed.[10]

Higher Education

In the wake of Bloody Sunday the government closed the universities and all other institutions of higher education. During the spring and summer, students engaged in demonstrations, signed petitions, and consorted with radical parties, especially the Social Democrats, while safeguarding their own corporate interests. A commission in June 1905 recommended the granting of autonomy to the universities. In late August the government acquiesced to the recommendation but did not abrogate the 1884 statute governing institutions of higher education. During 1906 and 1907 the universities operated in relative freedom. Faculty councils gained considerable powers. Women were permitted as auditors. By 1908, 2,130 women were studying in the universities. The student movement (studenchestvo), which had demonstrated cohesion and resiliency in the years before the October Manifesto, began to fragment in 1906. Pleas by the revolutionary parties for their support were generally ignored. The student body was politically divided; opportunities for socially useful employment after graduation were increasingly available. Concern, however, that on graduation they would become part of an oppressive order weighed heavily on students and preserved some traces of the former radicalism among them.

A reaction against the new order in the universities began in June 1907 when the government issued new rules on student organizations. Again, all corporate student organizations and most meetings were banned. Only meetings directly related to academic studies were permitted. Such meetings had to be approved by the rector and attended by the police. Women were banned from the universities in 1908. A public outcry, however, shamed the government into permitting those already enrolled to complete their studies. Funding to universities was sharply reduced. In 1880 the government had spent 311 roubles per student; in 1912 the expenditure fell to 166 roubles per student.[11] In 1909–10 the Council of Ministers debated a new university statute. While recognizing the failings of the 1884 statute, the members equally opposed autonomy for the universities. They also proposed to restore the male gymnasiums as the sole gateway to university admission. The Duma opposed the council's proposals. The emperor ended the standoff with the appointment in 1910 of an arch-conservative, L. A. Kasso, as minister of national enlightenment. He reactivated the statute of 1884 but did not abrogate the much more liberal temporary rules of August 1905. In 1911 students at Moscow University rebelled against the dictates of Kasso. The police entered the university and arrested and expelled dozens of students. Some professors who defended the students were fired as well. In protest, twenty-five professors and seventy-four junior faculty members resigned in response to the dismissals. Many were later reinstated.[12]

In spite of the tensions in the universities and conservative opposition, the system of higher education expanded rapidly in the prewar years, driven by economic necessity. By 1909 there were ten universities in the empire. In addition, ministries other than the Ministry of National Enlightenment as well as private activists promoted higher education. The Ministry of Trade and Industry was particularly engaged. In 1913 its Moscow Commercial Institute alone had more than four thousand students. Polytechnical education was growing in popularity as jobs in industry grew. The eight institutions of higher education for women open in 1905 grew to thirty in 1915, and the number of students from 5,500 to about 44,000. Higher Education Courses for Women opened in Kiev, Kazan', Odessa, Kharkov, Tiflis, Dorpat, Novocherkassk, Warsaw, and Tomsk between 1906 and 1910. In Moscow in 1909 and Kharkov in 1910, medical sections were added to the women's higher courses. The Bestushevskie courses added a department of law in 1906. Law faculties for women also opened in Kiev, Odessa, and Warsaw. In the 1911–12 academic year some 22,000 women were taking higher courses and 1,400 attended the Medical Institute for Women. Opportunities for women to study architecture, agronomy, engineering, and business courses opened as well. A variety of higher coeducational institutions enrolled up to five thousand women a year. From 1906 the higher commercial institutes under the Ministry of Trade and Industry were coeducational; the Psycho-Neurological Institute in St. Petersburg founded in 1908 accepted women. By 1915 the roughly 44,000 women enrolled made

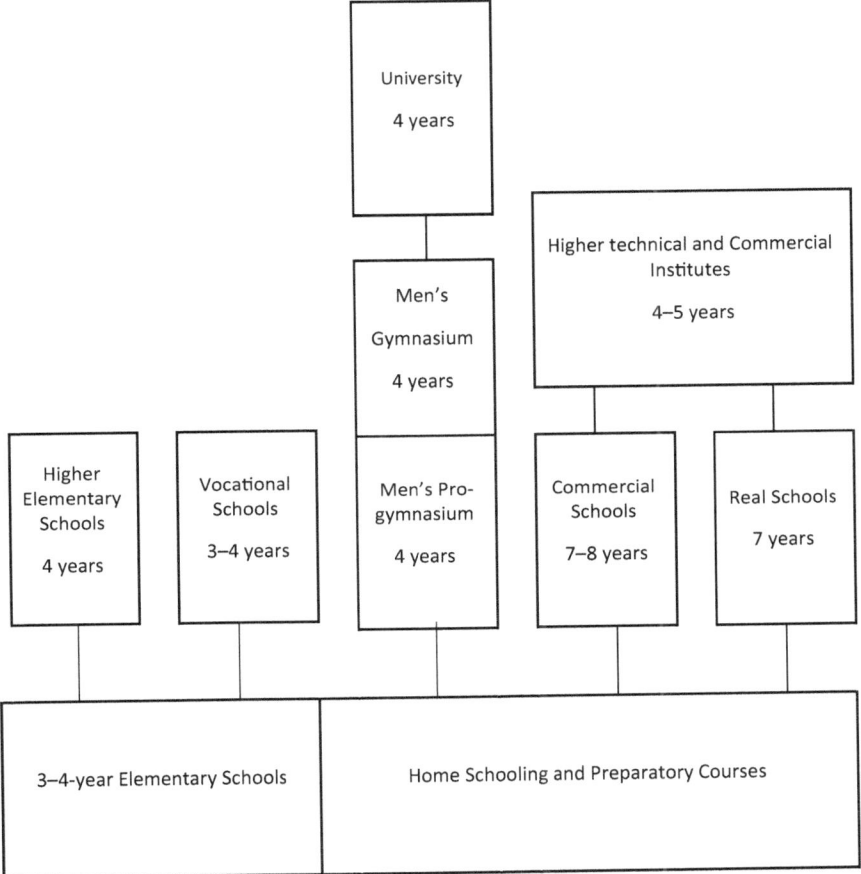

Figure 6.1 The general education system *c.* 1914.

up about a third of the total population of all higher education students. In 1911 the state decreed that the women's higher courses had attained the academic level of the universities. Their graduates were entitled to teach at all grade levels in both male and female gymnasiums and real schools with salaries and pensions commensurate with those of male colleagues. Women also were permitted to sit university examinations and attain the same degrees as men. All rights attached to a university degree except rank on the Table of Ranks were open to women.[13]

Private and municipal universities also began to appear. In 1905 the All-Russian Society for Public Universities opened with thirty branches. It offered mostly secondary-level courses but ran a few higher education courses as well. In Iur'ev in 1907 a Professor Rostovtsev established coeducational university courses. The first of the municipal universities was the Shaniavskii People's University in Moscow. It accepted anyone of either sex at the age of 16 and over but alerted them that classes were taught at a university level. Classes took place in the evening. It also offered preparatory classes for aspirants who lacked a secondary school diploma. Students in the academic section took classes for two hours a night, five days each week. The university offered degrees in history, law, languages, literature, and sciences. It also provided practical training in library science, pedagogy, cooperative administration, and local governance. Students paid from six to twenty-five roubles, depending on their means. In the 1913–14 academic year 5,372 students were enrolled. Other people's universities opened in the empire. By 1914 the number of students in all forms of state, public, and private higher education in Russian exceeded 100,000.[14] Figure 6.1 details the structure of the general education system on the eve of the First World War.

Adult Education

Local education authorities and private sponsors recognized the need for adult education. Sunday schools had operated on and off since the 1850s. They were particularly popular in rural areas and among women. In Moscow province in 1910, 336 men and 2,240 women attended them. They suffered, however, from a lack of teachers and state-imposed restrictions. Public readings also drew large peasant audiences. Here, the government imposed a limited list of approved readings. Literacy committees were active in opening adult schools, providing them with appropriate textbooks, and establishing libraries and reading rooms. A government regulation of 1907 banned these activities; instead, it permitted zemstvos, urban and rural societies, and private individuals to run schools, classes, lessons, and courses for adults under the supervision of school boards. Courses for adults organized by the St. Petersburg Technical Society in 1897 provided lectures by professors in physics, chemistry, mathematics, history, geography, and languages. They became a model for others. By 1911 there were 104 similar institutions in thirteen European Russian provinces.[15] Reading materials were increasingly available through some thirteen thousand people's libraries in 1911 as well as city public libraries, factory libraries and reading rooms, and houses of culture.[16]

Teachers

From the early 1880s, teaching became and remained the fastest-growing profession in Russia. In 1880 there were 24,400 teachers in the European provinces of Russia of whom only 4,900 were women. The government's preference was to hire peasants to teach in rural primary schools. By 1885 peasants made up 35 percent of male elementary schoolteachers.[17] Although many peasants doubted the ability of female teachers to discipline children, the decision of the government in 1871 to hire women as elementary teachers sparked a steady feminization of the teaching profession. In 1880, 27.5 percent of rural teachers were women; by 1894 they made up 41.4 percent. In 1890 around 37 percent of teachers in urban elementary schools were women. By 1911, 52.2 percent of teachers in church-parish schools were women as were 71 percent of teachers in zemstvo schools. Women received lower pay than men and were perceived by society, if not by peasants, as "natural" educators of young children. Government authorities increasingly favored women teachers whom they deemed to be more pliable and politically reliable than men.[18] Although the practice varied from region to region, women teachers who married were commonly dismissed. Conditions for all teachers remained harsh. Salaries were low as was the status of the profession. So poorly paid were they that few teachers could afford to educate their own children beyond the elementary level. The growing presence of women in classrooms was resented by male teachers who complained that women had no families to support and thus were better off than male teachers who did. They also questioned the ability of women to teach technical skills. Teachers of both sexes often felt themselves inadequately trained in teaching skills and methods and unprepared for life in the villages.

In the 1880s, women made up a quarter of all teachers in secondary schools. They were excluded from teaching in boys' gymnasiums but from the early 1880s were allowed to teach all subjects, excluding religion, in the lower classes of girls' gymnasiums. Male secondary schoolteachers were drawn from the universities. Half of university students were the sons of gentry, officials, and high-ranking military officers; they also made up about half of secondary schoolteachers. Seminarians comprised a significant number of teachers at the secondary level as well. To escape the clerical estate many of them entered the historical-philosophical faculties of universities in order to qualify as teachers. Since teaching was one of the few professions open to females, women from the upper and middle estates of society were drawn to teaching. Most had secondary education and some pedagogical training. Of 1,346 graduates of the Bestuzhevskie courses between 1882 and 1896, 514 became teachers, 200 in urban elementary schools and others in secondary schools or as home tutors.[19]

Although conditions for teachers improved marginally before the First World War, they struggled to achieve the professional status they believe their contributions to state and society merited. The state saw them as state servants, not as a corporation of professionals. Their battle for recognition had a long history. Teachers had enjoyed the advocacy of professional pedagogues and educators since at least the 1850s. Pedagogical journals, advancing the latest education philosophies and teaching methodologies, had proliferated in the post-emancipation years. Several societies devoted to advancing schooling in Russia arose from the 1860s. The St. Petersburg Pedagogical Society commissioned reports and held discussions on the needs of education. The government closed it in 1879 on the grounds that its discussions went beyond pedagogical subjects. The St. Petersburg Froebel Society opened in 1871. It was interested in preschool education. The society founded kindergartens on the German model and organized pedagogical courses for kindergarten and primary schoolteachers. Both the Imperial Russian Technological Society and the Society for the Dissemination of Technical Knowledge advocated vocational schooling and created schools for workers with the active participation of teachers. Literacy Committees, formed under the auspices of the Free Economic Society in St. Petersburg and the Agricultural Society in Moscow, provided teaching aids, prepared popular readers, and researched education in Russia. Teachers joined and participated in their work. The Society of Women Educators and Teachers opened in 1870 in Moscow. It built residences, libraries, and reading rooms. When the women's higher courses in Moscow were closed, the society reopened them under the title of "collective lessons." Assets of the closed courses passed to the society as well.

While wanting to improve the quality of teaching in Russia, the government opposed the aspirations of teachers to attain professional autonomy. Consequently, the only organizations permitted to teachers were mutual aid societies that provided various financial services to their members. In 1890 the St. Petersburg Mutual Aid Society opened. It grew slowly but by 1905 had 660 members from among primary, secondary, and higher education teachers as well as some school directors. In 1896 the society established the Ushinskii Commission to study the living conditions of teachers. A Moscow Society for the Improvement of Teachers' Living Conditions in the Primary Schools of the City of Moscow from 1895 also worked to better the lives of teachers. The isolation of rural teachers made it difficult for them to communicate among themselves. Teachers' congresses provided vehicles for them to meet. The Ministry of National Enlightenment had encouraged them in the 1870s but banned them in 1885 on the grounds that they discussed politics at their meetings. The more liberal Ministry of Finance organized the First Congress of Russian Participants in Technical and Vocational Education in December 1889. A second congress followed at the end of 1895. Its discussions went beyond technical education to include the failings of general education. An education section at the All-Russian Industrial Exhibition in Nizhnii Novgorod drew some 4,500 teachers from eighty provinces.

The Ministry of National Enlightenment cautiously allowed a congress of Moscow School District teachers in 1899. Then in 1901 it permitted a national meeting of representatives of teachers' mutual aid societies. It was closely monitored: reports to the congress had to be submitted in advance for approval and ministry officials attended in large numbers. A major topic in the proceedings was the removal of the ban on marriage for women teachers. Despite its precautions the ministry judged the congress to be too radical. The general mood of opposition in society at the beginning of the twentieth century further emboldened teachers. A majority of the 3,198 participants at the Third Technical Congress in St. Petersburg at the end of 1903 were teachers. The congress set out a clear set of demands that would dominate future discussions about education. They included a leading role for teachers in educational policy-making, universal elementary education, public control of schools and school boards, instruction in the language of the pupils, defined legal status for teachers, and an end to compulsory state examinations and revision of disciplinary practices in schools.[20]

The outbreak of the Russo-Japanese war in 1904 opened the floodgates of civic action in the empire. Bloody Sunday in January 1905 and the killing of forty gymnasium students at a demonstration in Kursk in February sparked a rash of parents' meetings demanding more open schooling, an end to religious teaching in schools, parent participation in pedagogical councils, and an end to police surveillance of students. Teachers joined the outcry against the bureaucratic-police school regime. The Moscow Teachers' Association had formed illegally in 1904. It worked during 1905 with Moscow city officials to reform schools and improve the lives of teachers. The association saw self-policing through a court of honor as a step toward professionalization. A similar but more conservative association opened in St. Petersburg in April 1905. An All-Russian Union of Teachers and Education Activists formed in March. It supported the professional demands formulated at the Third Technical Congress but also entered the political arena with calls for civil rights, an end to arbitrary arrest, and freedom of conscience, speech, the press, and assembly.

From the start, teachers were divided over the purpose of the union. Many saw its proper focus as the reform of education and not broader political objectives. At a congress in April 1905, delegates split over whether to form a purely professional organization or a professional-political union. The majority opted for the second option but refused to affiliate with any one political party. In response, the secondary schoolteachers of St. Petersburg withdrew from the All-Russian Union of Teachers and established the St. Petersburg Union of Secondary School Teachers. They rejected the growing radicalism of elementary schoolteachers who were increasingly drawn to socialist ideas. Secondary schoolteachers were predominantly male and better paid than elementary schoolteachers. They aspired to professional status and upward mobility within a reformed but not socialist political order. Women teachers among them were given little say, and their specific needs were subordinated to other demands. The relative conservatism of urban teachers was not confined to St. Petersburg. At the first Congress of the All-Russian Union of Teachers in June 1905, a majority of delegates agreed on a professional-political union. Most urban delegates walked out following the decision. The union now represented primarily rural elementary teachers. The fragmentation of the teachers' movement could not be repaired. Powerful gender and class divisions among them prevented the building of a common front. Membership in the union began to drop. Teachers in Moscow and St. Petersburg supported the general strike in October, but the October Manifesto that promised reform satisfied many among them. Professional goals remained, but political differences undermined corporate identity and hindered progress toward their realization. The promising teachers' organizations of 1905 had largely ceased to function by 1907.

The political turmoil of 1905 had placed rural teachers in a difficult position. By that year peasant attitudes toward teachers had somewhat mellowed. Many teachers provided services apart from teaching that made them useful and more acceptable to the peasantry. Propagandists from the populist Socialist Revolutionary Party were active in the countryside, seeking to enlist peasants into the political struggle. An independent Peasant Union formed to pursue peasant interests. Since it was more moderate in its demands than the socialist parties, many teachers saw it as a safeguard against peasant violence and cooperated with it. The union engaged teachers in reading the latest news to peasant audiences, interpreting manifestos from the various contending parties, explaining events in the capital and elsewhere, and writing petitions to the government on behalf of peasants. It was a role that many teachers preferred to avoid, but curious and persistent peasants made evasion difficult. The fall and winter of 1905–6 witnessed the greatest turmoil in the countryside. A harsh reaction followed. Arrests and executions subdued the peasantry into silent resentment. The authorities blamed teachers for the role that some had embraced and others had forced on them. The numbers of teachers fired, arrested, or killed were officially underreported. In the Baltic provinces alone some two thousand teachers were purged. The result was severe teacher shortages and school closings. Male teachers were more often purged than females, further advancing the feminization of the profession. From 1908, teachers were more firmly brought under central control. More inspectors were appointed who policed relations between teachers and peasants.[21]

The failure to attain professional standing was reflected in teachers' salaries, which they believed did not recognize their value to society. In 1894 teachers in zemstvo schools averaged 285 roubles a year. In 1911 the average had risen to 380 roubles. Male teachers in urban schools received on average 528 roubles in 1911 and women 447 roubles. By 1911 most teachers in rural schools had free accommodation. Legislation in 1909 raised salaries, provided for increments for years of service that reached 125 roubles after twenty-five years, and mandated subsidies for housing. Some zemstvos introduced raises of 60 roubles after each five years of service.[22] Although from 1908 the state heavily subsidized elementary education, the money went to local dumas and zemstvos that then paid teachers. Often payments were late or did not meet the sum set by the legislation of 1909. Even when paid regularly, teachers' salaries fell far below those of other government, zemstvo, or municipal employees. In 1905 salaried government officials earned around 2,000 roubles a year. Zemstvo statisticians were paid around 3,600 roubles, lawyers earned from 2,000 to 10,000 roubles annually, a qualified agronomist got 3,000 roubles, and even doctors, whose status was also relatively low, earned around 1,200 roubles a year.[23]

Regulations on hours of teaching were more notional than real. The standard was twelve hours per week, but directors could ask for more. For each additional class a teacher was paid sixty roubles a year. The pay of most teachers whether married or single was less than their living costs. The difference was made up by outside work. Many teachers tutored to supplement their incomes. In 1907 the Duma established a class size of fifty students per teacher. Elementary school classes in 1911 ranged from forty to forty-four students per teacher. The comparable number of students to teacher in Germany was sixty-five. The consequence of the cap, however, was a massive shortage of school places. In 1910 nearly a million children of a school age population of around twelve million were refused registration, about half as the result of overcrowding.[24] The municipal schools that in 1912 became higher elementary schools averaged sixty to seventy students per teacher. The ministry set the limit at one hundred.[25]

Schools in villages were often housed in rented buildings roughly converted into classrooms. Government subsidies for new schools were too low to build a healthy environment for learning. Where schools were built the work was often done on the cheap with poor materials and shoddy workmanship. Few provided recreational spaces, cloak rooms were tiny, and toilets primitive; classrooms were poorly ventilated. Secondary schools also suffered from poor sanitary conditions. Bad conditions facilitated the rapid spread of infectious diseases. In Moscow school district in 1914, 72 percent of schools used kerosene lanterns for lighting, 70 percent relied on traditional Russian stoves for heating, and 91 percent had unheated toilets. Both teachers and students, especially in rural schools, suffered these conditions with little or no medical care. The free housing that teachers were afforded was most often a small, inadequately furnished, and freezing room in a peasant cottage. Diets were poor. A study in one province discovered that after five or six years of teaching the percentage of teachers in good health declined from 64 to 27 percent.[26]

In order to meet the stated goal of universal elementary education, some 15,000 teachers a year over ten years were required to fill new posts and another 8,000 to fill vacated positions. In 1914 pedagogical institutions were graduating about 5,000 teachers a year for rural schools. To meet the vast gap, all graduates of general secondary schools, graduates of higher elementary schools, and of the secondary schools of the Holy Synod were declared eligible to teach. The Ministry of National Enlightenment established pedagogical classes in gymnasiums to provide some specialized teacher training. The ministry also increased the number of teaching institutes to twenty by 1913 with more than 1,400 students. A proposal in the Duma in 1907 to elevate the teachers' seminaries that prepared rural elementary teachers to the level of secondary schools was not adopted. Several zemstvos, however, took the initiative and raised the seminaries' standards. By 1913 there were seventy-one teachers' seminaries with about 7,000 students, 67 percent of whom had rural origins. The Holy Synod opened church-parish teachers' schools with a three-year program accommodating 500 students in 1913. Evening and summer courses designed to raise the qualifications of practicing teachers proliferated with both private and public sponsors. There were 116 pedagogical courses of varying lengths in 1907 and 129 in 1913.[27]

Most secondary schoolteachers were either university graduates or graduates of state pedagogical institutes. The latter offered a four-year program to train teachers for the classical gymnasiums. Most of the students in them were former seminarians seeking a way out of their social estate. The P. G. Shelaputin Pedagogical Institute opened at Moscow University in 1911. It trained male teachers for gymnasiums over a two- or three-year course. The St. Petersburg Pedagogical Academy was a private institution that opened in 1907. It also trained secondary schoolteachers. The Society for Experimental Pedagogy, privately sponsored as well, opened in 1910 and evolved into a four-year teacher training program by 1913.

Only a small number of teachers received adequate pedagogical training. As a result, the quality of teaching remained low or even declined with the rapid expansion of the school network. Although the Ministry of National Enlightenment officially supported a child-centered education at the elementary level, the reality in the classroom was more often rote learning and harsh discipline. Even the best-prepared teachers were constrained by inspectors, trustees, or demanding parents. After 1907 the ministry began to increase the number of inspectors. It was aware that many inspectors were unqualified for their duties. To raise the standard of inspection, in 1912 it required inspectors to have a higher education degree and the pedagogical qualifications of a higher elementary schoolteacher. Not all inspectors were obstructive but their general reputation was bad. To teachers they represented the central control that educators resisted.

The government placed moral probity in their teachers above academic learning. Inspectors were mandated not only to monitor the classroom but also more urgently to inquire into the private lives of teachers. Women teachers in Moscow were subject to an 11:00 p.m. curfew. In 1912 in Chistopol'sk, the school board, of which inspectors were members, required women teachers to provide proof of not only their political reliability, a common requirement in many school districts, but also medical certification of their virginity.[28] Teachers whose students showed signs of initiative or undue curiosity were often sanctioned. It is little wonder that teachers complained of being treated like slaves. At the secondary level, teachers were closely monitored to assure that they did not stray beyond the rigidly set curriculum. The state feared the awakening of intellectual curiosity in students. Teachers were forbidden to answer students' questions or to encourage initiative among them. Private schools or schools under the jurisdiction of ministries other than the Ministry of National Enlightenment were more open to the new teaching methods and innovations in curriculum.

Non-Russian Schools

The question of the language of instruction in primary schools in non-Russian areas remained contentious. In the last quarter of the nineteenth century, the old markers of identity, tsar and Church, were being supplemented, or in some quarters supplanted, by allegiance to the nation. The theme of nation was prominent in popular culture and in elite responses to it. Progressives from Ushinskii on had stressed the importance in early schooling of the native language in child development. Russians of all political leanings believed that Russian should be taught to non-Russian children from the first year of schooling as a subject of study, if only orally at the beginning, and that Russian should be the sole language of secondary and higher education. Most also complacently assumed that the Russian language was a welcome bearer of culture and civilization to the "less developed" peoples of the east and south.

Pressures for stricter policies of Russification intensified as Russian nationalist sentiment grew in the years before the war. The rise of nationalism among Russians was met with the growth of national consciousness among many non-Russians. The imperial bureaucracy took a pragmatic approach to language policy. While Ukrainian remained banned in schools, competition with the Catholic faith and Polish language in Belorussia persuaded the government to encourage the development of the language and culture of Belorussians. In the Volga region and the Caucasus, the Il'minskii method, developed in the 1860s in the Kazan' and Orienburg school districts, was still in use in some schools as a tool of Orthodoxy against Islamization. Il'minskii's followers advocated the use of the native tongue of the pupils, transcribed into the Cyrillic alphabet, as the language of instruction during the first two years of schooling along with Russian as a language of study. They believed fervently that Orthodoxy could fully penetrate the heart of non-Russians only if they imbibed it in their native tongue. They understood Russification to mean the acquisition of Orthodox religion and Russian religious culture. Nationalist criticism of the Il'minskii method intensified in the late nineteenth and early twentieth centuries. Conservatives viewed the elementary school as an instrument of Russification, which they understood as the acquisition of the Russian language. The alternative method to the approach of Il'minskii to teaching language by the 1890s was the "natural method," first developed in the United States. The natural method eliminated the use of the native language entirely. In Russia, natural method teachers indicated objects or performed actions naming them in Russian and requiring the child to repeat the names. The method purported to duplicate the way children naturally learned their native tongue.

Wherever the Il'minskii method was used, pressures to replace it with the natural method grew.

The parties of the left and center in the first three Dumas supported early instruction in the native language. The elementary education bill that the Third Duma forwarded to the State Council included provision for the use of the native tongue of children in the first two years of schooling. The State Council removed it. In the Fourth Duma, however, the Octobrists took a more conservative approach and supported instruction in non-Russian languages only in a handful of cases and only in the first year of school. Proponents of the Il'minskii method mounted a determined campaign in its defense. In this they gained the support of many members of the Orthodox Church hierarchy. At the Kazan' Missionary Congress in 1910, delegates recommended that in all dioceses with missionary activities, the study of native languages be mandatory in church seminaries. The congress endorsed the use of the Il'minskii method in all non-Russian schools and ordered that a church circular of 1899 mandating the Il'minskii method in non-Russian church-parish schools be enforced.[29] The urgings of the congress, however, had slight effect in non-Russian schools where the natural method was often used. The Ministry of National Enlightenment remained ambivalent. The matter was not resolved before the revolution but reemerged in the Soviet era.

Last Chance

The death of Kasso in 1914 and the appointment of P. N. Ignat'ev as minister of education early in 1915 initiated the final attempt of the old regime to reform the education system. Ignat'ev's planned reform was sweeping. He supported public initiative in education, freedom of teachers in choosing teaching methods, the removal of the Church from education, and equality of all in access to education at all levels. He supported compulsory primary education, advocated a more practical curriculum than the present system provided, and sought to link schooling to living experience. He promoted a ladder system of schools by uniting the gymnasium and the real schools into a seven-year school open to graduates of elementary schools. Students in the new secondary school could enter one of three divisions: classical, modern languages, or natural science. The programs prepared graduates either to enter the workforce or to progress to higher education. He planned to expand professional and technical education to train specialists to meet the country's many practical needs. A new statute for the universities sharply reduced the power of school district curators and increased those of rectors who would again be elected by faculty councils. He identified the primary function of universities as research and not the training of state servants. He provided for the admission of women to universities with the permission of the Council of Ministers. In June 1915 the Council approved the admission of women to the faculty of physics and mathematics at Kazan' University, the faculty of medicine at Tomsk and Saratov universities, and the faculty of law at Tomsk University.[30] The statute was submitted but not ratified. Intrigues within the imperial court undermined the confidence of Nicholas in his minister; Ignat'ev resigned in 1916, his plans for reform largely unfulfilled.

Outcomes

The advances in education during the reign of Nicholas II were impressive. Between 1908, when the push for universal education began, and 1914, the number of schools rose from around 50,000 to almost 81,000. Literacy among the Russian population significantly increased. Among rural males it grew from 39.3 percent in 1897 to 45.2 percent in 1907 and 53.2 percent in 1917. Among rural women the figures were 13.4 percent, 17 percent, and 22.6 percent, respectively. Urban men boasted literacy rates of 69 percent in 1897, 74.1 percent in 1907, and 79.8 percent in 1917. Members of the noble and clerical estates of both sexes had attained literacy rates of 90 percent and 95 percent, respectively, in 1917. In the same year the average literacy rate among urban dwellers of both sexes was 64 percent and among the rural estates 36 percent.[31]

Much remained to be done. School participation rates remained low. The school census of January 1911 found that only 30 percent of 8–11-year-olds were in school and 45 percent of those were in urban schools. In 1917 a third of all school-age children were still not in school. Parental choice and not the conditions of schooling most often determined the length of children's stay in school, although distance from schools and the costs of suitable clothing were an impediment for some families. The efforts made to remove obstacles to school attendance, especially in rural areas, did little to improve rates of participation. The plans made in 1908 to place schools within a radius of three versts began to alleviate the problem but were only partly realized by 1917. Distance affected girls' attendance more than boys' as parents feared for their safety. Girls also were more likely to be kept at home to care for younger siblings or to attend to household chores. The increase in the number of female teachers, however, helped to reduce fears for the safety of girls over time.

There were fewer obstacles to school attendance for rural boys than for their sisters. Peasant boys did not normally engage in heavy agricultural work until the age of 15. The school age of 8–11 years and the length of the school year, which was adjusted to seasonal agricultural work rhythms, therefore, especially facilitated school attendance for boys. School began in September. The youngest students arrived first. Basic reading was the focus of teaching in the early weeks of the term. Older boys began to arrive in October when the emphasis shifted to more advanced exercises. Child labor laws in the 1880s had also set age limits on adolescent employment in factories and other enterprises. As a result, the years for many boys between age 12 when they left school and 15 when they could enter the workforce were often idle, and complaints of delinquency, especially among town boys, were common.

At all levels of the education system the rate of completion while improving remained low. Following 1905, interest in advanced elementary education grew as a changing economic environment offered opportunities that required greater knowledge. Of those enrolled in municipal schools, 59.6 percent graduated. Graduation rates in secondary and higher education institutions also rose after 1905 but fell well below the rate in municipal schools. In 1911, 10.8 percent of boys and 7 percent of girls in zemstvo schools and 10.7 percent of boys and 8.2 percent of girls in church-parish completed the full course of study.[32]

Rural literacy rested on one, two, or at most three years of schooling. Rote learning remained common in Russian classrooms. Questions about the meaning of literacy and its retention among students arose. Teachers regarded reading aloud as mechanical reading or recitation and distinguished it from reading with comprehension. Mechanical reading served ritual religious purposes but did little to enhance knowledge. Various studies of retention of reading skills and acquired knowledge after leaving schools were carried out after 1880. A survey among teachers in the thirty-four zemstvo provinces in 1911 looked at retention of knowledge in a variety of areas. Most reading among former pupils after leaving school was for religious or entertainment purposes and not for advancing one's knowledge or for self-improvement. Writing skills appear to have declined more rapidly than reading skills. However, there is evidence that few forgot how to write. They wrote ungrammatically and reproduced local dialects in their spelling but could still write meaningfully. The ability to solve simple problems in arithmetic orally remained high, but the capacity to perform written operations low. Stories from the Bible were retained but little understood. Most remembered prayers.[33]

A mere 1–1.5 percent of peasant children went beyond elementary school. A very few continued to higher elementary education or to a trade school. In 1897 only 20 in 10,000 rural males and 10 in 10,000 rural females had a secondary or university education. In 1911 one village boy or girl in 100 went beyond elementary school and 29 in 10,000 proceeded to secondary school. Male peasants in pro-gymnasiums and gymnasiums in 1905 represented 10.6 percent and reached 20 percent in 1914 of the student body; in real schools from 1876 to 1914, peasant males rose from 7.6 percent to 32.1 percent of attendees. Impressive as the increase was in terms of percentage, the actual number of male peasants in secondary schools in 1914 was roughly thirty thousand.[34] Ben Eklof observed that "mobility through the system was both extremely limited and *adequate*," in that it met the expressed needs of peasants and the capability to attend to those needs.[35]

One consequence of the spread of literacy among the peasantry was the growth of reading for pleasure. Fairy tales and the lives of saints were popular. The *lubok*, a simple illustrated booklet or print, was the main instrument of such reading. Peddlers marketed them on behalf of publishers at fairs. Increasingly, peasant tastes included secular works along with traditional religious readings. A commercial literature written for peasants, increasingly by peasant authors who understood the tastes and reading levels of their audience, was well established by the end of the nineteenth century. With the easing of censorship in the first years of the twentieth century, commercial literature began to flourish. Exposure to schooling weakened the hold of superstition on the peasantry. Interest in science grew. A powerful driver of changing tastes among peasant readers was the growing market economy in Russia that valorized success and mobility. Ambitious peasants internalized those capitalist values, despised by Russian intellectuals. Equally alarming to the educated were the themes of crime and rebellion that captured the interest of peasant readers.

The intelligentsia and those who aspired to it, including most teachers, deplored the rise of popular literature. Nor did they share the peasants' enthusiasm for the market. Peasants, they argued, were incapable of choosing for themselves what to read; the duty of the cultured was to lead the peasants toward high culture. At first the

St. Petersburg and Moscow Literacy Committees published books for the people, with the participation of Leo Tolstoi and Ivan Turgenev, among others. Later, Tolstoi joined with the publisher I. D. Sytin in an enterprise named *Posrednik* to write and publish books for popular reading. Other publishers followed suit. Lenin in 1905 prophetically advocated control over publishers, bookstores, libraries, and reading rooms in order to remove inappropriate literature. Teachers were positioned to influence peasant reading and to distribute useful and edifying works. Their efforts did little, however, to halt the flow of popular literature. Popular, commercial literature was what peasants preferred to read for pleasure.

The Great Reforms of the 1860s put Russia on a path, however reluctantly followed by the autocracy, which by 1917 had restructured the economy, reshaped the relationship of state and society, and altered the balance of political power. The changes included a growing market economy; expanded credit for large and small investors and savings societies; new property rights and inheritance reform; a major step toward representative government; rapid advances in literacy and education, especially among urban social groups, including workers; tactical collaborations between some state officials and society to advance the public good; a proliferation of institutions of civil society; and growing civic consciousness. The changes were gradual and steady but unwelcome to the tsar and many of his appointed officials who distrusted public initiative and frustrated it at every opportunity. The advances in public education were particularly notable as the goal of universal primary education came into sight. A major weakness, however, was the lack of any systematic plan for scientific and technological education and its application in the economy. Some progress was made. In 1899 the number of students in higher technical education was 7,334; in 1913 the number reached nearly 25,000. For a vast empire with a population of about 170 million in 1913, this was a pitifully low number.[36] In spite of the efforts of some of the tsar's ministers, the fears among conservatives that science undermined religious belief condemned Russia to enter the First World War with a large technological deficit compared to its German opponent.

The pattern remained unchanged during the war. The fruits of the growth of civil society and civic consciousness were particularly evident in the work of voluntary societies in the war effort. The Union of Zemstvos and the Union of Towns formed in 1914 and amalgamated in June 1915 to form the Union of Zemstvos and Towns. It administered hospitals for wounded soldiers, organized refugee relief, and as the war went on, secured procurement orders for the military. The War Industries Committee, organized by leading industrialists, worked tirelessly to coordinate domestic industry in order to meet the needs of the military, sometimes in collaboration with the government but often in the face of government interference. The Progressive Bloc in the Duma together with various municipal zemstvos, and supported by some government ministers and members of the State Council, made a number of demands on the emperor, including a call for the formation of a government enjoying public confidence. Nicholas responded by proroguing the Duma. Workers in St. Petersburg demonstrated in protest against the closure. Moderates, fearing popular violence, acquiesced, however. Ill-equipped at the beginning of the war, the army suffered further deprivations in spite of the effort on the home front to supply it. The economy proved unable to sustain the war effort and support the population. By the end of 1916, food shortages threatened stability in the cities. Radicalism born of anger at the authorities and fear in the face of defeat first dulled then obliterated the promise of the prewar period and set the stage for the collapse of the regime.

7

Schooling for Socialism: Revolution to Cultural Revolution

Russia's war began with the humiliating defeat in late August 1914 of its First and Second Armies by German forces in East Prussia. Early successes during the fall of 1914 and winter of 1915 on the Austrian front were reversed in the spring when German troops reenforced Austrian positions and opened a second front in Poland. A war of attrition began. Russian casualties in killed, wounded, and captured were high, approaching 50 percent. The rates among officers were especially severe; university students were drafted to replace them. Morale among frontline troops was low and discipline already strained. As Minister of Education, P. N. Ignat'ev, observed at a Council of Ministers meeting in August 1915: "There is no more army, only an armed people."[1]

The breakdown of the authority of the old regime culminated in February 1917. On International Women's Day a demonstration in St. Petersburg to protest bread shortages, instigated mostly by women, soon brought out factory workers in sympathy. The protests escalated. From the front, where he had unwisely taken direct command of the army, Nicholas II ordered the violent suppression of the disturbances. A struggle for the loyalty of troops garrisoned in the capital ensued. They, fearing deployment to the front, sided with the demonstrators and refused to leave barracks. Nicholas ordered frontline troops to the capital to end the rebellion. His officers refused to obey the order. Accepting his now almost universal lack of support, Nicholas abdicated in favor of his brother Michael. When he declined the crown the imperial regime was no more.

A Provisional Government composed of liberals and moderate conservatives assumed the task of restoring central government authority. It did not neglect education. The new government assured universities of autonomy, ended the role of the Church in public education, placed all vocational and elementary education under the Ministry of National Enlightenment, guaranteed teaching in the native languages of students, declared its intention to devolve control over primary education to local authorities and to create boards of community leaders, parents, and senior students to administer secondary schools. The plans were not realized. The difficulties the government faced were enormous. It was unelected and rested its authority on a promise of the election of a constituent assembly charged with writing a constitution for the new political order. Organizing a fair election in the chaos of a losing war proved difficult; it was postponed, raising public suspicion about the intentions of the government. To legislate on critical matters, however, without the sanction of voters was unacceptable to moderates. Peasants agitated for a badly needed land reform. The Provisional Government failed to act and lost the trust of the peasantry. Pressed by its Western allies and fearing the consequences for order at home of the "armed people" returning from the front, the Provisional Government pursued the war effort.

The Petrograd Soviet, which represented workers and soldiers, had formed at the same time as the Provisional Government. Various socialist factions competed for influence over it. The result was a period of "dual power" between the Soviet and the Provisional Government. The Soviet's "Order Number One," which urged soldiers to obey only those orders approved by the Soviet and abolished the old forms of address of officers, legitimized the long-standing enmity of the soldiers toward their officers. The order destroyed any chance of regaining command of the army and rejuvenating it as a fighting force. Unrest grew over the summer months. The membership of the Provisional Government drifted leftward with the incorporation of a few socialists into responsible posts. A renewed Russian campaign against the Germans collapsed. A failed attempt at a military coup in late July by General Lavr Kornilov was thwarted by workers and soldiers.

The revolutionary parties had not made the revolution in February. Not ideology but anger and desperation had given birth to the poplar radicalism that precipitated the collapse of the old order. As the doubtful authority of the Provisional Government dissipated, however, the opportunity to shape popular anger and disillusionment presented itself to the socialist parties in the capital. The Socialist Revolutionary Party enjoyed a strong following among the peasantry. It advocated an agrarian socialism that had only limited appeal among workers. The Menshevik wing of the Social Democratic Party were orthodox Marxists who believed that Russia was passing from a feudal into a capitalist phase of development which in time would prepare the ground for socialism. They rejected what they thought of as premature revolution. Lenin, who had returned to Russia in April, benefited from this default of practical alternatives to Bolshevism. Lenin skillfully tailored the Bolshevik program to address the needs of the population: land for the peasants, bread for the urban population, and a separate peace treaty with Germany that sacrificed large parts of the old empire. He pressed for an immediate seizure of power. Together with Leon Trotskii, Lenin orchestrated a strangely peaceful seizure of the Russian capital in October 1917.

The Bolsheviks had secured Petrograd with relative ease but faced opposition throughout the empire. The anti-Bolshevik Moscow Soviet was subdued by force. The new Soviet government permitted the election of the constituent assembly, promised by the Provisional Government, to proceed. The vote overwhelmingly favored the Socialist Revolutionaries. A feverish night of debate in January 1918 ended around dawn with soldiers dispersing the delegates and closing the meeting place for repairs. The closing of the constituent assembly made civil war inevitable. There were several reasons for the ultimate success of the Bolsheviks in the war. They greatly benefited from the incompetence and lack of coordination of their rivals. The Bolsheviks occupied the center of the country and commanded much of its remaining industrial capacity. The opposition operated from the periphery and suffered from long lines of communication and lack of war matériel. The brief intervention of foreign troops in support of the anti-Bolshevik forces prompted a patriotic response that induced some former tsarist officers to support the Bolshevik forces. Under Trotskii's leadership the Red Army became a formidable force. The Bolsheviks understood the value of organization and mass mobilization. They also were prepared to sacrifice territory to focus their efforts to win the civil war: in March 1918 the Soviet government had negotiated a separate peace with Germany that included a significant loss of territory; the European peace settlement at the end of the war imposed further territorial reductions with the independence from Russia of Finland, Poland, Estonia, Latvia, and Lithuania. Finally, the Bolsheviks were prepared to employ whatever brutal means needed to gain their objectives.

The civil war left the country in a state of exhaustion and near breakdown. It was fought under the banner of War Communism during which all of the resources of the country were organized around the war effort. After a brief period of workers' control in factories, Lenin reimposed one-man management to organize production more efficiently. The harsh program of grain and animal requisitioning had by 1921 alienated much of the peasantry. The regime was particularly alarmed when in early 1921 the sailors of Kronstadt rebelled on behalf of Soviet rule but without Bolshevik control. The rebels were defeated, but their message was heard. With peace established by the end of 1920, Lenin turned to the task of relieving the hardships of peasants and workers, who were beginning to chafe at Soviet rule, and restoring the economy.

In spring 1921, he declared his New Economic Policy (NEP) that ended requisitioning and partially restored capitalism at the retail service level of the economy while preserving state control over large industry, banking, mining, and foreign trade. Recovery required professional expertise. Lenin acquired it by courting the so-called bourgeois specialists. Socialism, he believed, had to be built on the wide cultural foundations that capitalism had bequeathed. Under NEP, class struggle gave way to an uneasy policy of class conciliation. Managers, engineers, professors, and other experts from the old regime again gained prominence in the new order. Both economic recovery and the enlarging of the industrial proletariat, the class bearers of socialism, through the expansion of industry rested on the cooperation of the specialists. Lenin died in early 1924. NEP, while unpopular with many devoted communists, endured until Stalin consolidated his position as leader of the Party.

The Unified Labor School

The new Soviet government was structured around people's commissariats that took over the functions of the tsarist ministries. In 1918–19 the People's Commissariat for National Enlightenment (*Narkompros*) assumed control over all educational institutions except technical schools for adults. Narkompros was a vast enterprise with seventeen departments for the several levels of schools, different types of schooling like home or technical education, experimental pedology, school medicine and hygiene, and construction of new schools, among others. Although it had jurisdiction only in the Russian Republic of what was soon to become the USSR, most of the other republics took their lead from Narkompros in matters of education. The exceptions were Ukraine and Belorussia, which developed competing educational models. Narkompros inherited a network of schools from the old regime along with a severely diminished cadre of teachers. The war and civil war had also left thousands of children orphaned or displaced, many of whom had received no education at all.

The school that the leaders of Narkompros, A. V. Lunacharskii, M. N. Pokrovskii, and N. A. Krupskaia, envisioned was far from the school of the tsars. In general they shared the criticisms of the tsarist education system that progressives like Pirogov and Ushinskii had long before raised. As Marxists they attached the utmost importance to education. Marx regarded education as an instrument by which the ruling class asserted social control and perpetuated the existing class order. With the end of the class struggle and the overcoming of the alienation of producers from the product of their labor under socialism, he saw education as the key to the final transformation of society and the development of a new man. But he left little guidance in his writings about the form that education should take under socialism. In general he argued that its purpose should be to reduce the gap between mental and physical labor. Labor should constitute an integral part of learning. Lenin underscored the central role of Party and state in education. "We openly declare," he said, "that a school outside life, outside politics is a lie and hypocrisy." He called teachers "the main army of socialist education."[2]

With the broad objective of transitioning from an agricultural to an industrial society, Marx's Soviet disciples saw in polytechnical education the best way to achieve the master's objective. Soon, however, differing views emerged about what the content and methods of a polytechnical education should be. In October 1918 Narkompros issued the Declaration on the Unified Labor School. It provided for the merger of all existing schools into a single system of free, coeducational schools that formed an unbroken chain from elementary to secondary and tertiary levels. It declared that education and labor were inseparable. The elementary school provided five years of education for 8–13-year-olds and the secondary school a further four years. The two levels of schools were to provide general polytechnical education that incorporated socially useful labor as a means through which students gained familiarity with the various forms of production. In 1923 a new school statute created four-year, seven-year, and nine-year schools. Graduates of the seven-year schools (incomplete secondary) could enter technicums and those of the nine-year schools (complete secondary) universities. Polytechnical schooling, in the vision of Narkompros, aimed to develop the whole child physically, psychologically, intellectually, aesthetically, and socially with the goal of transforming human nature within a collectivist order. Narrow technical-vocational training was banned until at least age 14. Labor in the polytechnical context meant hands-on work in a school workshop or garden or, if possible, in association with a farm or factory. Activities such as nature walks to teach biology or excursions to local institutions to enhance social studies were recommended. Music, singing, dancing, drawing, and other arts were encouraged in order to shape aesthetic tastes and values. Class reconciliation and not class struggle informed the education system. Lunacharskii saw the unified labor school as a microcosm of a classless society. While disseminating Marxist ideology the goal was to exclude the class struggle from the classroom and make all children regardless of their social origins into self-conscious socialists. Moreover, Soviet pedagogues saw education as a continuous process that went on beyond the classroom and moulded literacy, upbringing, and cultural development into an organic whole within the being of each citizen.

Narkompros attached great importance to coeducation. Not only did it confront family influences centered around the gender division of labor and the traditional ideal of the homemaker, but it also equally challenged the unfairness of the double burden borne by women at work and at home. Schools were expected to treat boys and girls equally without any differentiation in labor roles. Equally important was preschool education that freed women to enter the workforce. Even in the difficult conditions of the civil war, some 25,000 children were reported to be in preschool institutions by the end of 1920.[3]

Krupskaia, with the active participation of S. T. Shatskii, a noted pedagogue who saw productive labor as the nucleus of social organization, took the lead in shaping the curriculum of the unified labor school. The work of the American pedagogue John Dewey and his student William Hearst Kirkpatrick strongly influenced their choice of a method of instruction. Dewey's pedagogical thinking is complex and cannot be reduced to a few sentences. Soviet pedagogues took from him the concepts that best suited their purposes. Dewey was a pragmatist who rejected the notion of an unchanging human nature. Individual character formation was influenced by the environment. Children were not passive receivers of knowledge. Instead, they learned best when they interacted with their environment and participated in the process of their own learning; experimental and problem-based learning formed the most effective methods of childhood education. He supported the empirical scientific method as the best means to uncover the correlations between events in the environment and change in individuals. Ideas were in his view plans of action, tools to make sense of the world that had to be tested to determine their validity in practise Teachers were not just instructors but also facilitators and guides who created opportunities for children to discover on their own. E. N. Medynskii, a Soviet pedagogue, captured the understanding of Soviet school reformers when he celebrated Dewey, who "places productive labor at the center of the educational system and motivates the need for it, like Marx, using historical-economic arguments."[4] Dewey's follower Kirkpatrick developed the project method of learning in which the curriculum was organized around a subject's central theme. By working through the project, children directed their own learning with the teacher as guide. His influential essay "Project Learning" appeared in 1918.

From these sources Krupskaia forged the "complex method" of teaching for Russian schools. At the elementary level the complex method avoided the separate teaching of subjects. Instead, subjects were merged in themes related to the child's own milieu. The broad themes were Nature, Society, and Labor. All subjects were to be examined through the lens of these themes. Each grade in the school saw the incorporation of a secondary theme within the framework of the first theme. In grade one, for example, the secondary theme was the Child and in grade two the Village or Urban District of the child. In the second grade the child learned Nature through the exploration of local plants and animals, Society through familiarity with local social institutions, and Labor through exposure to the local economic infrastructure. In subsequent grades the foci turned to Province, Country, and the World. In the complex method the skills of reading, writing, and arithmetic were acquired by the child through doing rather than through instruction. It was left to teachers to devise activities useful for the development of the themes and relate them to subjects.

Narkompros initially provided neither a compulsory curriculum nor guidance for teachers to follow. Marks were prohibited. At the secondary level of schooling some separation of subjects was required. The themes of nature, society, and labor remained, but some subjects were explicitly taught within the themes. The primary influence at the secondary level was the "Dalton Plan," a method devised by an American, Helen Pankhurst, in 1919. Under the plan, subjects were divided into monthly assignments. In the version adopted in the Soviet Union, students were expected to work on the assignments in groups in order to discourage individualism. A group contracted to complete an assignment on a timetable its members selected and had to finish it to move on to a new task. The curriculum at the secondary level was biased heavily toward the social sciences with a secondary role for natural and physical sciences. Since social studies dealt with current real world issues, they leant themselves better to activity teaching. Thus, themes included ideologically based topics such as "Class Contradictions in the City" or "Peasants and Landowners." The themes severely narrowed for students the scope of any given subject, reducing it to one aspect of the larger subject or even to a single topic within it.[5] As in the elementary school, mathematics at the secondary level was not taught separately; students acquired it as an adjunct to other subjects. The study of literature focused on the class nature of the work under discussion. The secondary school curriculum included no history other than a handful of ideological-sociological precepts.

In the real world, schools bore scant resemblance to the ideals of Narkompros. The obstacles to their realization were vast. Many provincial education departments dismissed central directives as utopian; local Soviet officials often judged the activities recommended by the complex method to be a waste of time and money. Most parents agreed. They valued reading, writing, and arithmetic over the experience of excursions or the refinements of aesthetics. Many teachers got on with teaching what parents wanted them to teach. Although the schools did not conduct anti-religious propaganda, the absence of religion was of concern to many. Resistance to coeducation among parents, especially in rural areas, remained high. Many questioned the need for compulsory education for daughters. As a result, girls dropped out of school by the third or fourth grade at a higher rate than boys. Parental pressures on teachers led to separate seating for boys and girls in classes. Rather than an equal curriculum, many schools continued to teach girls traditional household skills and boys workshop crafts.[6]

The ravages of the civil war had left behind thousands of orphans who had received no formal education; they often subsisted in gangs and were generally viewed by the authorities as juvenile delinquents. A. S. Makarenko, a pedagogue, led an initiative to school some of these children. Makarenko believed that labor was central to the intellectual and moral development of the child. He held that only in society through collective education could children attain their full potential. Personality was formed by transference of knowledge and values from the collective to the individual. With these principles to the forefront, he established a colony or cooperative for orphaned children, the Gorkii Colony and later the Dzerzhinskii Labor Commune. The children were given considerable autonomy in their own organization and activities. Students were divided into departments with their own heads. The heads took part in decision making within the colonies. The goal was to produce an individual capable both of leading or following. Some three thousand children passed through the colonies before they were closed. For all their success in the chaos of the postrevolutionary period, Makarenko's views had little influence on general education policy under Stalin before his death in 1939.

Damages inflicted in the civil war had left many education facilities in ruins. Funding was inadequate for the support of what remained and nonexistent for rebuilding. Space, supplies, furnishings, libraries, textbooks, teaching aids, lighting, and heat were chronically in need. The prescribed labor activities required school gardens and workshops, tools and machinery. Factories had limited resources and could not easily supply the needs of the schools. Rather than expanding, the underfunded elementary school system contracted sharply from between 76,000 and 81,000 schools with 6 million students in early 1921 to a mere 49,000 schools with 3.7 million pupils in October 1923.[7] Only a few schools offered the mandated four years of compulsory schooling. From 1919 to 1922 in the Russian Republic, the average number of years in school was 2.3 in rural and 3.1 in urban areas. Only about a third of rural children went on to the second grade. In cities, 17 percent of students did not attend beyond grade one. Only 23 percent of rural boys and 15 percent of rural girls completed four years of schooling, whereas around half of city children finished the prescribed number of years.[8] Rather than transforming into unified labor schools, most of the old gymnasiums and real schools continued as they were, taught the old subjects by the traditional methods, and persisted with religious instruction. Under NEP the practices in schools changed little. The old school subjects, except classical languages and religion, continued to be taught by the traditional methods of drill and testing. The prescribed social studies were rarely taught; the same fate befell physical education, art, and music. Science, too, was often neglected. Whatever socially useful labor there was consisted largely in janitorial tasks around the school.

Teachers were in a particularly difficult position. They had greeted the Bolshevik seizure of power in November 1917 with a strike. During the civil war they were often vilified as members of the class enemy. Many received no pay following the strike and abandoned their posts. Shortages of teachers were the principal reason for the many school closings of the period. Those teachers who remained received salaries from local Soviets well below prewar levels. Although Party and state leaders during NEP defended teachers as the friends of the people, they remained suspect in the eyes of local Party zealots. Teachers had not been consulted about the Narkompros curriculum and prescribed methodology, and many were completely unaware of them. Narkompros attempted to mount short teacher training programs to inform teachers, but to little effect; those charged with teacher training were as incapable of teaching the complex method as teachers were of implementing it. The teachers' seminaries and institutes of imperial days, renamed pedagogical schools and pedagogical institutes with two-year and four-year programs, respectively, remained but were ill-suited to teach new classroom methods or to meet the rising demand for teachers. In the absence of training, many teachers faked something on paper to satisfy the authorities and went on teaching in the old way. In any case, few had time to learn if they cared to do so.

A decree of December 1918 declared a war on illiteracy; it required all citizens of the Russian Republic between the ages of 8 and 50 to learn to read and write in their native language. The working day was shortened by two hours without loss of pay for those adults attending literacy classes. Teachers were expected to devote themselves to the campaign, a heavy drain on their time. Secondary schoolteachers who had graduated from higher institutions of education had been taught nothing about how to prepare teachers to link labor to learning. About a third of elementary and secondary schoolteachers in the mid-1920s had no specialist education; a mere 20 percent had pedagogical training and only 10 percent had higher education.[9] There were few inspectors; those that there were little understood the complex method and could give scant guidance to teachers. Like teachers, inspectors were poorly paid and often could not even recoup their travel expenses.

The governance of schools was also in flux. Initially, students were granted minority representation in school Soviets (councils) and were encouraged to elect class committees. They discussed school matters, ran their own disciplinary courts, and frequently complained against their teachers. The Statute for the Unified Labor School of 1923 abolished governance of schools by a consensus of students, teachers, and community and placed it instead in the hands of the school director and local education departments. It did not, however, end student pressure on teachers. Communist youth organizations had standing in schools. In 1922 the Young Pioneers was formed. During the 1920s roughly 20 percent of children aged 10–14 joined the Pioneers. Educators saw the Pioneers as a substitute for the family with its traditional values and expectations. The children took great pride in their distinctive white shirts and red scarves. One young woman who was seen attending church was stripped of her scarf at a formal gathering of students in the schoolyard. "I fell down on my knees," she remembered, "and begged them not to take the scarf from me," but to no avail.[10]

The Komsomol, or Communist Youth League, for older students was already well established at the national level and had representation on committees of school welfare in secondary schools. Its members were indoctrinated in Marxism and heavily engaged in ideological activities, often to the detriment of their school work. Since children of NEPmen (those engaged in the market economy), priests, kulaks (rich peasants), and nobles were unlikely to be admitted to secondary and higher education or to join the Komsomol or Pioneers, the members of these youth groups were from working and peasant backgrounds and strongly committed to the socialist future. Although during NEP they made up a minority of elementary and secondary school students, they were aggressive in their oversight of teachers and set the tone for other students. Central Party organs continued to speak on behalf of teachers as sympathetic to Soviet power and as part of the toiling masses; local party organizations continued to count them among their class enemies, making teachers easy targets for youthful zealots.[11] Creeping elitism associated both with membership in youth organizations and with parents who were Party members emerged among schoolchildren as early as the 1920s. Such students were often deferred to by others.[12]

Central funding for the unified labor schools plunged during NEP. Local authorities lacked the resources to make up the deficit. On average about 12 percent of local budgets went to education, well below prewar zemstvo outlays. The result was a steady decline in the number of schools and teachers between 1920 and 1928. In 1921 the authorities began to urge parents to supply school materials voluntarily and also permitted schools to impose school fees. By 1925, 35 percent of children attended school for free; about a third of all revenue of secondary schools came from fees. In addition, roughly a third of primary schools in Russia signed contracts with unions, cooperatives, or state agencies for financial support. Narkompros responded in the 1926–7 school year by banning fees in elementary schools and restricting them at the secondary level.[13]

The failings of the unified labor school were grounds enough for harsh criticism, but the ideal school of Narkompros activists faced larger challenges. Powerful factions within the Party rejected its very premises. Should the schools focus on the creation of "new persons" or of knowledgeable people? A major concern of critics was the relationship between the unified labor school and institutions of higher education. Some officials outside of Narkompros wanted a curriculum that was preparatory to university study. The subordination of subjects to themes mandated by the complex method left students poorly prepared for higher specialist training in specific subject fields. In 1926 the universities imposed oral and written admission examinations in Russian language and mathematics. Around 60 percent of applicants failed mathematics and only a few, to the consternation of Party officials, did well in a supplementary examination on principles of Marxism. Various attempts by Narkompros to support the complex method by issuing detailed instructions about how to implement it gained little sympathy on the ground. Provincial education departments and local school boards were sympathetic to teachers' demands for more traditional approaches to instruction. Increasingly, departments and boards, while notionally retaining themes, arranged teaching around subjects. Prescribed textbooks and the once forbidden homework made their appearance.

Krupskaia continued to defend the complex method but was compelled to accept a new curriculum that retained themes while allowing more emphasis on subjects; she conceded that subjects no longer had to be connected at all times to the themes. Pressure continued, and Narkompros further compromised. In mid-1926 a new curriculum allowed the teaching of reading, writing, and arithmetic in the first two elementary grades as separate subjects outside of themes. In grades seven and eight, more room was provided for mathematics, physics, and chemistry, and history began to reappear as a subject in all grades. In 1927 yet another curriculum, which was made obligatory, placed ever greater emphasis on subjects over themes. Homework was now required in secondary schools but limited to five hours a week in grades five and six and six hours in grade seven. New textbooks to support the curriculum were published. Teachers and local education departments welcomed the new direction.

Professional-Vocational Schooling

A major point of contention within Party circles was the striking of a balance between general education and vocational training to prepare desperately needed skilled workers in multiple fields. Lenin recognized the technological deficit inherited from the old regime. In 1918 he argued that in modern society "it is necessary to master the highest technology or be crushed,"[14] a sentiment that Stalin was later to echo. Narkompros advocated general education without specialized professional training before the age of 17. Professional-vocational education should begin only following graduation from the unified labor school. Lenin agreed that the upper years of the unified labor school should not be reduced to trade classes but in 1919 called urgently for the spread of professional-technical skills training among the masses. Industrialists, engineers, and parents of worker and peasant backgrounds liked the old imperial vocational schools and supported the continuation of vocational training. In February 1920 the Party introduced labor conscription and endorsed the creation of courses and schools to prepare conscripts as qualified workers. A number of day (four-year) and evening (six-year) technicums were formed. Limited financing, lack of equipment, and poorly qualified teachers reduced their effectiveness before 1925. Ukraine and Belorussia went their own way. They established a single system of vocational schools that provided seven years of general education followed by two to three years of professional-vocational training. Their schools conferred on graduates a qualification for work in a specific field or for admission to higher education in a technicum, university, or polytechnical institute.

A successful initiative in the Russian Republic was the factory-plant apprenticeship school (FZU), formally under the supervision of Narkompros but normally financed locally. The FZUs originated in 1918 following a decree that all workers between the ages of 15 and 17 have an education. At first education clubs set up in factories by the Komsomol gave basic literacy instruction to adolescent workers and provided political, cultural, and technical education as well. By 1922 the Ninth Party Congress required factories to employ a set percentage of youths and to provide opportunities for them to raise their production qualifications. Factory managers disliked the requirement that roughly 5 percent of their workforce should be adolescents with reduced work days and adult wages. Unions resented the competition of FZU students with their members. Such concerns were pushed aside, however, and the FZU, financed by the factory but administered by the Main Committee for Professional Education of Narkompros, became a fixture of education in the USSR. In theory the FZU set the same educational standard as the seven-year unified labor school; in practice most offered four years of general education and technical training. In addition, about a hundred Factory Seven-year Schools that provided a general education and production training also functioned by 1927–8. They were linked primarily to steel and textile works. In 1929–30, 1,115 technicums with 237,000 students and 2,711 FZUs with 323,100 students were operating.[15] Proponents of vocational education celebrated the FZUs along with the many technicums as effective instruments for the training of a new generation of qualified and class-conscious workers. In addition to the schools, professional-technical courses expanded from the mid-1920s. In 1928–9 there were just more than 2,000 such courses attended by 180,000 students.[16] The Komsomol also supported Schools for Peasant Youth as a counterpart to the apprenticeship schools for workers. They were general education schools at the level of grades five and six of urban schools that also provided specialist agricultural training. By the end of 1924 about 200 Schools for Peasant Youth were running. Their numbers in the Russian Republic reached 767, with 73,000 students in 1927.[17]

In the early 1920s the number of women in professional-technical education was very low: in industrial technicums women made up only 5.1 percent of enrollments, in agricultural technicums 14.6 percent, and in FZUs 16.5 percent. In 1927 the Central Committee urged the Komsomol to attract more women into production and vocational schools by providing a set number of places for adolescent girls. The directive had little effect. In 1928 the Central Committee complained about the lack of response and issued detailed directives to attract more girls into production, to raise the qualifications of girls already employed through special courses, and place women in jobs commensurate with their qualifications. Again the results were disappointing in technicums but better in the FZUs where by 1929–30, 31.6 percent of FZU students were girls.[18]

The scarcity of qualified teachers limited the effectiveness of vocational schools and courses. Most often teachers in technicums and FZUs were worker specialists with jobs in industry teaching part-time and lacking pedagogical training. Part-time teachers made up more than 75 percent of instructors in technicums and 54 percent in FZUs.[19] Efforts to overcome the shortage of teachers of technology met with limited success. The Petrograd Herzen Institute mounted the Petrograd Higher Technico-Pedagogical Courses in 1923 to prepare teachers in electro-technical, mechanical, chemical, agricultural, and construction professions. Similar courses soon were offered in Moscow. A statute in 1924 created pedagogical courses in higher agricultural, industrial-technical, and artistic educational institutions in Moscow and Petrograd that enabled students to remain for a year to learn teaching techniques. Few students applied, and the courses soon closed. Another initiative saw the opening of faculties of pedagogy in higher technical institutes to prepare teachers for technicums and factory-plant apprenticeship schools. These, too, soon folded for lack of applicants. More successful was the merger in 1923 of the former Prechistenskii Practical Institute with the Moscow Institute of Public Education into the Karl Liebknecht Industrial Pedagogical Institute to prepare teachers for technicums and FZUs. Over twenty years it trained several thousand teachers in technical and socioeconomic fields of study.

Higher Education

A major challenge for the communist regime during the period of the NEP was access to higher education. On the one hand, the realization of the Party's economic goals required the expansion of higher education. In general, educators sought to provide all classes of society with a good education. On the other hand, students from intelligentsia and white-collar families, many of whom had little sympathy with Bolshevik objectives, predominated in universities. To fill the higher posts of government with them was politically dangerous. The Party was anxious to create a proletarian intelligentsia that in time would replace the old tsarist-trained intelligentsia and their children but without lowering educational standards and alienating those groups on which economic recovery still depended. The answer to the dilemma was the policy of *vydvizhenie* (acceleration) by which workers and peasants were promoted into higher education and managerial positions. One manifestation of the policy was the Red Directors, communists placed in managerial positions for which they usually lacked qualifications but were supported by a bourgeois specialist deputy.

In order to prepare workers and peasants for admission to higher education institutions the Party in 1918 created worker faculties (*rabfaks*). Students in rabfaks were workers and peasants no younger than 16 (most were over 20) who had been employed in manual labor for three years. Most of them had four years or fewer of schooling before admission. Party and trade union organs, factory committees, and Soviets nominated candidates. Most nominees were Party or Komsomol members. The rabfaks aimed to prepare their students for university study. Their graduates competed with secondary school graduates for places in institutions of higher education (VUZs) but enjoyed a large preference over them. In 1924 only 650 of 30,000 secondary school graduates attained places in higher education while 12,850 places went to rabfak graduates or nominees of the Party and unions. In 1926/27 some 50,000 students were in the rabfaks and 90 percent of them were from worker or peasant backgrounds. Rabfak graduates made up almost a third of higher education students in 1928; 26 percent of enrollees in that year were workers.[20]

Not all workers and peasants in higher education came via the rabfaks. Secondary schools had significant numbers of children from the working classes, some of whom found their way into higher education. There were, however, no formal quotas by social class, and many committed communist students came from white-collar and professional families. Bolsheviks, however, distrusted the many "social aliens" among university students and ideological opponents on faculties. The period following Lenin's death saw a major purge of the universities in 1924, reducing the percentage of "social aliens" from nearly 37 percent to 19 percent. Women students, many of whom had middle-class origins, were reduced from 38 percent of students in 1924 to 28 percent in 1928.[21] Faculty were not affected by the purge.

The universities and higher technical institutes relied heavily on professors from the old regime. Demand for their services gave them a good deal of leverage in their dealings with the authorities. Their resistance to incorporation into the Teachers' Union led to a compromise by which they formed a Section for Scientific Workers within the union that provided them with considerable autonomy. Their wish to have a free hand in university administration was not, however, met. By 1921 all institutions of higher education fell under the control of Narkompros. It appointed rectors who administered universities with the assistance of a small governing body; it in turn appointed deans and junior faculty. Student members of the Komsomol were represented on departmental committees, deans' advisory councils, and curriculum committees. They exercised considerable influence over university affairs. Faculty members in the social sciences resisted calls for programs informed exclusively by Marxist ideology with considerable success. Concern about controlling the ideological content of higher education led as early as 1918 to the establishment of several communist universities. The Zinoviev Communist University and the Sverdlovsk Communist University among others were designed to train cadres for Party and government work. Institutes of Red Professors established in Moscow and Petrograd in 1921 graduated their first classes in 1924. In 1925 the Central Committee required all large institutes of higher education to establish chairs in the history of Bolshevism and Leninism. Efforts to increase the number of communists on university faculties had little result, but women made significant gains. One product of the revolution was the merger of the Shaniavskii People's University with the Women's Higher Courses in Moscow to form the Second Moscow University. By 1926 women occupied 32 percent of junior faculty positions in universities.[22]

Concern within the economic commissariats about the quality of the graduates of VUZs pushed the social-political criteria in play in the purges of 1924 into the background from 1925. In response to criticism from the Supreme Soviet of the National Economy (*Vesenkha*) in that year, secondary schools introduced measures to improve the academic performance of their graduates. The universities and higher technical institutes ended the nomination system of admissions and required entrance examinations for all applicants. Rabfak graduates still had priority but had to pass the examinations to enter. The stiffening of entrance requirements saw a decline in enrolments in the VUZs of the Russian Republic from 117,000 in 1925 to 107,000 in 1928. White-collar applicants outnumbered other social groups. Their numbers in VUZs grew from 35.8 percent to 39.4 percent between 1924–5 and 1927–8. Workers increased from 20.7 percent to 26.5 percent of students in that period, communists from 10 percent to 17.1 percent, and Komsomol members from 9.5 percent to 20 percent, while peasants remained at 24 percent. Different types of VUZs had different clienteles. Pedagogical, agricultural, and medical schools had large numbers of peasant and white-collar students and few communists. In pedagogical and medical schools over half the students were women. Few women attended socio-economic or engineering schools which were favored by rabfak graduates and communists. Adult workers made up 40.7 percent of engineering students in 1927. White-collar students made up 18 to 20 percent of students in economic and engineering schools. As in the tsarist past, graduation rates were low. Only 6.3 percent of students in engineering VUZs and 7.6 percent in socioeconomic schools graduated in 1925. Between 1918 and 1928 only about ten thousand communists graduated from institutions of higher education.[23]

Cultural Revolution

The many compromises made by Narkompros to include more vocational content in the unified labor school curriculum failed to satisfy the growing number of communists who were critical of NEP. The criticism of the schools turned on the nature and meaning of science. Lunacharskii and Krupskaia maintained that science entailed the pursuit of knowledge for its own sake; it encouraged independent thought and critical examination of received truths. Science was the basis for the development of the whole person and cultured citizen and not a narrowly utilitarian pursuit. Critics of that view saw science as a pool of knowledge useful for the manipulation of the material world; children should be taught it as the instrument to achieve the technical goals that were key to the realization of a communist society. The Komsomol disliked the general secondary school as a nest for bourgeois sentiments, especially its upper two grades. They wanted the bulk of students who completed the first seven grades at age 15 to enter vocational or industrial schools. Only the best of them should go on to higher education via a rabfak or technicum. Even Vesenkha, in pursuit of more skilled workers, had a preference for the Ukrainian vocational approach to education. Its leaders saw general education and the promotion of a humanistic culture as a barrier to the expansion of vocational education. Others went further. V. N. Shulgin was head of the Institute of Educational Research in Moscow. An advocate of pedology or the study of children, Shulgin focused on the study of a child's social environment and its relationship to their learning, behavior, and ideology. His goal was the revolutionary transformation of human nature that Marx foresaw with the realization of a classless society. He believed the present school environment only perpetuated the status quo. He hoped to merge labor and education completely, making the school unnecessary. Only the social environment of Pioneers, Komsomol, and factories along with early engagement in socialist construction was the appropriate milieu for the transformation of children. He famously predicted the "withering away" of the school. Young communists, anxious to create a new proletarian culture, saw the alliance with the bourgeois specialists as an impediment to their hopes and longed for a renewal of the class warfare that had characterized War Communism. These undercurrents during NEP surfaced during the "cultural revolution."

NEP and the system of education that supported it had been a temporary compromise, "one step backward to go two steps forward," as Lenin had put it. Its fate was tied to the larger political arena that by 1927 had dramatically changed. Hostile statements made abroad in that year sparked a fear among Party leaders of impending foreign intervention in the Soviet Union. The Fifteenth Party Congress in December called for an accelerated pace of industrialization to counter the threat and more funding for education to support it. At the same time, however, the congress rejected the critics of Narkompros. Stalin, for tactical reasons, disagreed. He adopted a critical stance toward Narkompros. He began to advocate the proletarianization of higher education and called for class war instead of the class conciliation that lay at the heart of the policies of Narkompros. He fostered doubts about the loyalty of the bourgeois specialists. Rumors and fears that they were collaborating with foreigners to undermine the regime spread.

In 1928 more than fifty engineers and managers in the town of Shakhty were arrested and tried for colluding with former owners of coal mines, now living abroad, to sabotage the Soviet economy. The incident quickly became a tool of Stalin in his battle with the so-called Right opposition that favored continued collaboration with the bourgeois specialists. The trial sparked a campaign against them. It extended to the VUZs with the dismissal of professors and to a new purge of "social aliens" among university and secondary school students. The policy of accelerating workers (vydvizhenie) was enhanced. In the autumn of 1928, 65 percent of admissions to higher technical institutes (VTUZs) went to workers; more special preparatory courses for them were mounted. As well, one thousand communists were enrolled in VTUZs and another three thousand sent to rabfaks over and above their normal intake. These were the first of the many "thousanders" to be accelerated into higher technical schools. The First Five-Year Plan of 1927 set the goal of higher education for 110,000 Communists.[24] In July 1928 the best of the VTUZs were transferred from Narkompros to Vesenkha. In March 1929 the factory apprenticeship schools also passed to the control of Vesenkha.

The instigation of class war against the bourgeois specialists and in the schools was part of a larger drive to force the collectivization of agriculture through the promotion of class war among the peasantry. The Party believed that traditional peasant agriculture through the cultivation of individual plots periodically reallocated by the village commune was inefficient and an impediment to the realization of socialism. Their ideal was a form of collective agriculture employing machinery on a large scale. The First Five-Year Plan envisaged the rapid expansion of industry. Vast amounts of money and manpower were needed for the task. Collectivization was seen as the most effective means to control a peasantry that the regime believed to be hostile to its interests and to squeeze the needed resources for industrialization out of peasants through a return to the requisitioning policies of the civil war period. Most Communists saw the need; few believed it possible. Stalin ordered the impossible task of collectivization to begin in 1929 and pursued it at an accelerated pace. An attempt to turn poor and middle peasants against rich peasants (*kulaks*) stumbled over village solidarity. Instead squads of committed communists were dispatched to arrest and deport the kulaks en masse. Collectivization was largely accomplished by 1931.

Throughout 1928 and 1929 the assault of the Komsomol and other Communist bodies on Narkompros continued. Lunacharskii and Krupskaia defended general education over narrow vocational schooling, but in vain. They were forced into yet more compromises. In July 1929 Narkompros abandoned the ideal of socially neutral education and embraced class war. Its leaders conceded that teachers should be active agents of social change and engage in public campaigns as directed by the Party. A new curriculum in that year tied the complex themes to class struggle, industrialization, collectivization, and anti-religious propaganda. In effect, Narkompros denounced the unified labor school and accepted the factory apprenticeship school, the factory seven-year school, and the school of peasant youth to be the appropriate tools for advancing socialism. Defeated, Lunacharskii resigned as Commissar late in the year.

His replacement, A. S. Bubnov, named Shulgin head of teacher training. His philosophy and methods dominated schooling for the next couple of years. Socially useful work beyond the school lay at the heart of the new pedagogy. Shulgin's methodology required that children take part fully in adult life and mandated the project method of teaching adapted to Soviet needs. It meant the commitment of children from various grades, working in group assignments or brigades, to fulfilling the Five-Year Plan through socially useful work such as anti-illiteracy or anti-drunkenness campaigns and employment in factories or collective farms. Child labor returned to the fields. The schools did not wither away, but classroom study was minimalized. The teaching of subjects was incorporated into projects or preparation for projects. Students received project assignments at the school and reported the results on the project's completion. The projects were varied, ranging from political and anti-religious propaganda to fundraising for industrial or agricultural purchases. Set textbooks disappeared, but loose-leaf pages on various current issues were issued nearly monthly to suggest projects. Evidence about how many schools actually pursued the project method is scant.

While the general school faded, vocational education flourished. Having gained control of the FZUs, Vesenkha moved to increase enrolments in them massively. The intake for 1930 exceeded the set target of 57,000, a doubling of the numbers in 1928–9. A third of the new students had graduated from the seven-year unified labor school.[25] The push for specialized training increased. Only the elementary school any longer provided general education. The recruitment of students from the old secondary grades to apprenticeship schools left grades eight and nine bereft of students. In 1930 Narkompros agreed to convert the two upper grades into schools of vocational training or technicums. Later that year all schools were required to form an attachment to an industrial or agricultural enterprise. The Schools for Peasant Youth were renamed Schools for Collective Farm Youth. They trained tractor and combine operators for the new Machine Tractor Stations, which provided collectives with needed machinery, mechanics, dairy farmers, and others. A new School for Commercial Services arose to train accountants and clerks for farms and enterprises.

Under Vesenkha higher education institutions also became highly specialized. At first technical institutions of higher education had to attach themselves to an industrial enterprise and provide practical work to students. The curriculum required an equal division of time between theoretical study and practical work. Other institutions of higher education also had to provide work experience for students. In summer 1930 an additional refinement divided all higher education institutions into specialized schools under the administration of government agencies or economic departments to train for the competencies required by each agency or department. The number of VUZs skyrocketed from 152 in 1929–30 to 537 in 1930–1, although many of them were simply independent departments within old institutions.[26] The intake of workers and Communists, who were poorly prepared, into higher education resulted in the lowering of academic standards. In order to speed specialists into the workforce, the length of programs in technical institutes was shortened to four years, and the many new VTUZs offered only three years. Theory was largely ignored. Lectures were seen as antiquated. In 1931 a group-laboratory method brought the project method into higher education. Student brigades undertook projects under a professor's supervision. Graduates educated in the brigade system, it soon became apparent, were ill prepared for the complex tasks of building a modern economy. The practise of the method virtually assured the incompetence of most graduates. Elena Gorokhina, who studied at the Medical Institute through the brigade method recalled that "one student, the brigadier, took exams for the entire group of twenty....The test would either give credit to everyone in the group or doom the whole lot to failure." Her group was blessed with a swot who took all the tests and invariably passed.[27] Stalin by far preferred the *praktiki*, specialists who had learned their trade on the job rather than in schools, to graduates. They still made up about a third of engineers and half of technicians in 1930.

Between 1928 and 1930 the number of elementary and secondary schools grew from 85,000 to 102,000 and enrolments from 7.9 million to 11 million. The schools for collective farm youth burgeoned from 768 with 73,000 enrollments in 1927 to 3,500 with 529,000 students in 1930. Factory-plant apprenticeship schools increased from 903 with 100,000 students in 1927 to 3,265 with 600,000 students in 1930; including their merger with trade schools, enrollments exceeded a million in 1931–32. An even greater number of skilled and semi-skilled workers were receiving training in short factory courses and on the job. The factory seven-year schools also rapidly expanded so that by 1931 they accounted for half of working youth enrollments at the secondary level. Although skills training played a large role in them, the apprenticeship schools at the secondary level also devoted time to general education. The percentage of female students went from 40 percent in 1927 to 46 percent in 1930, and more workers and peasants attended secondary school than previously. The rapid expansion resulted in overcrowding. Schools often resorted to two or more teaching shifts each day.[28]

As in the past the system was severely underfunded. Between 1928 and 1932, from 75 to 80 percent of all funding for education came from local authorities; half of it went to elementary and secondary schools. Inflation ran at more than 40 percent in these years so any increase in central funding was offset. Rapid expansion spread scarce resources even thinner. Underfunding left schools without adequate means for vocational training. Only a small minority of schools in 1931 had a workshop. Few schools for collective farm youth had garden plots. Factories were meant to supply materials and equipment as well as work placements but often did not. Factory managers resented the disruption of maintaining links with schools. They found the students they took to be of little use in production and used them in marginal tasks if they used them at all. The effort to transform the senior classes of secondary schools into technicums foundered for lack of equipment, appropriate space, and teachers.

Teachers during the cultural revolution were in a particularly difficult position. As with the complex method, they had little understanding or training in the project method. Even those who attempted it lacked sufficient resources to effect it. The qualifications of teachers remained low. In 1931 only 9 percent of elementary teachers had attended an institution of higher education; three-quarters had attained a secondary education of dubious quality. Among secondary schoolteachers 42 percent had some kind of higher education but 48 percent had completed only secondary school. Many of those with higher education had attended accelerated, academically thin programs in the race to meet the demand for teachers. The vast majority of teachers lacked any pedagogical training. Reliance on teachers from the old regime remained high. Teachers who had begun their careers before the revolution made up 33 percent of primary and 45 percent of secondary school instructors. Only 31 percent and 18 percent of teachers at those levels, respectively, had begun to teach after 1928. Among elementary schoolteachers only 14 percent were members of the Party or of the Komsomol.[29]

Teachers occupied an uncomfortable intermediary position between the regime and the citizenry. During the cultural revolution, the regime made many demands of them. The adult literacy campaign imposed a heavy workload beyond the school. The campaign often included anti-religious propaganda. Teacher participation in it alienated them from the many believers among the peasantry. Failure to participate brought down on them the wrath of local communist authorities. The latter demanded all sorts of supplementary work from teachers, forcing them to do accounting or double as telephone operators. The white-collar background of teachers could lead to their purging as kulak sympathizers. Pay depended on local authorities and was often late. A central pay raise for teachers passed through the hands of their local masters who pocketed a portion. The rest was erased by inflation. Sexual abuse of teachers was often recorded but rarely remedied.

With forced collectivization many teachers fled rather than be assigned to a *kolkhoz* (collective farm). Others left from exhaustion or frustration. Graduates of pedagogical technicums often failed to take up their assigned teaching posts. New employment opportunities arising from rapid industrialization made teaching comparatively less attractive. Enrollments in the teaching technicums in Moscow province fell by 50 percent in 1930 and the Herzen Pedagogical Institute in Leningrad got only 75 percent of the expected applications.[30] Teaching in factory schools fell often on anyone willing to take on the task. Skills training was provided by experienced workers who had no pedagogical training. University faculty were suspect and subject to periodic reappointments. The expansion of higher education, however, left academics in demand. In 1927-8 there were 18,000 higher education teaching positions; the number rose to 47,000 in 1930-1 and 51,000 in 1933. Demand was so great that many professors worked at more than one institution. The opening of multiple research institutes offered additional places for specialists. Ideological concerns about the loyalty of faculty continued. Communists made up only around 13 percent of VUZ teachers in 1931-2. However, a new generation of university trained communists was in the making. Of ten thousand VUZ graduate students in January 1933, 50 percent were communists and another 20 percent Komsomol members.[31]

Outcomes

The NEP represented a tactical retreat from the idealism of the early days of the revolution and civil war. The goal of economic recovery and a period of social stability was at least partly met. Education was the outlier. Radical experimentation was the order of the day. It rested philosophically on Marxist thinking about the merger of intellectual and manual labor and the transformation of human personality in the collective. It drew extensively for its methodologies on the latest pedagogical theories from the West, especially the United States. Divisions among communists over the purposes of scientific knowledge were present from the beginning. Ideological concerns over the compromises of NEP merged with the practical need of the state to industrialize rapidly. Those who were dissatisfied with the compromises of NEP seized the education agenda during the cultural revolution of 1928 to 1931. The emphasis on general education of Lunacharskii and Krupskaia yielded to a preference for specialist vocational training that was supported by the need for skilled workers as the industrialization drive consumed the country's energies. Neither the complex method of the unified labor school nor the project method of the supporters of vocational training were widely practiced in schools. Whatever the merits of the methodologies, the educational level of the population inherited from Tsarist days, inadequate teacher training, and above all the meager funding provided for education at all levels doomed the experiments from the beginning.

The period of NEP was not without achievements. Rates of literacy rose. By 1929 literacy in Russia was 62.8 percent (81.9 percent in cities and 57.8 percent in villages). As early as 1926 literacy among workers reached 83.7 percent compared to only 64 percent in 1918.[32] A wide-flung network of schools at all levels and of different types had come into existence. The number of primary and secondary schools grew from 85,000 to 102,000 from 1928 to 1930 and their enrollments from 7.9 million to 11.3 million.[33] The school year had been extended to ten months in most Narkompros schools. The number of students repeating grades fell from around 20 percent in 1925 to 5 percent in 1930. Dropout rates remained high, especially in rural regions where only 5 percent of children aged 12–14 attended secondary school.[34] Advances in secondary and higher education were also impressive. Developments in professional-vocational education had begun to reduce the technology deficit. In 1928-9, 41 percent of the 645,000 secondary students in grades above seven were in training for industrial work. By 1932-3, from 60 to 70 percent of the 1,724,000 secondary school students were in technical training. In the same years the number of students in higher education rose from 167,000, of whom 31 percent were in engineering programs, to 394,000, of whom 50 percent were pursuing careers in engineering.[35]

The Party strongly supported the education of girls and women. In spite of attitudinal obstacles among the population to coeducation, advances were made. The percentage of girls in general schools rose from 40 percent in 1927 to 46 percent in 1930. Repeated efforts by the Central Committee to increase the number of girls in vocational training, however, had little effect. In 1930 a mere 13.9 percent of students in industrial technicums were girls, up from 11.4 percent in 1925; the greatest increase in female enrollments was in the FZUs where 31.6 percent of students were girls, an increase from 20.8 percent in 1925. In higher professional technical schools the percentage of women declined from 31.9 percent in 1925 to 29.8 percent in 1930, although the large increase in enrollments overall meant many more women students in absolute numbers were in attendance compared to 1925.[36] With the revolution women gained equality with men in the universities. Their numbers grew both among students and in the professoriate.

By the beginning of the 1930s the acceleration of workers and peasants into higher education had transformed the face of the political and managerial elite. The proletarianization that the cultural revolution featured had also permanently shifted the balance of power in the cultural professions from the old intelligentsia to a red intelligentsia composed largely of former workers and peasants. By 1933, of the roughly ten thousand students in graduate studies, 50 percent were Party members and another 20 percent were in the Komsomol.[37] Once in place the Party and state *apparat* (bureaucracy) settled into a new status quo. Although they were to experience wild upheavals in the coming years, their leading position in state and society was secure. The "new class" denounced by Milovan Djilas in 1957 was already in formation.

8

Retrenchment: Stalin to Chernenko

Party leaders realized by the beginning of 1931 that the education policies of the cultural revolution were a hindrance to the fulfilment of the next Five-Year Plan. The earlier phase of plant and infrastructure construction was transitioning to a focus on production; the new phase required more skilled workers than had the building phase. The cultural revolution had drawn many skilled workers out of the factory and into administrative political work to the detriment of production. In March 1931 the Party ordered all workers who had left the factory in order to take part in political campaigns to return to factory work. By May 1931 some 31,000 skilled workers had returned to their enterprises. The many shortcomings of Shulgin's experiments in education were increasingly evident. A sharp fall in standards in education accompanied the cultural revolution. Secondary schools were in despair about the quality of applicants from the lower grades. The low skills' level of the first engineers educated in higher technical institutes during the cultural revolution alarmed the economic ministries. The newly minted engineers had no production skills despite the emphasis placed on the practical in the Shulgin scheme. At every level the gap between the ideals of Shulgin and his supporters and the reality in the schools was exposed. The Sixteenth Communist Party Congress of 1930 declared the need to raise not only the number but also the quality of economic and technical cadres through better preparation of students at the secondary level. With that in mind, as early as 1929 the Party had announced the creation of the ten-year school at the very time that the cultural revolution had begun to funnel students in the upper grades of secondary schools into vocational training. In order to increase the pool of students for ten-year secondary and higher education, the Party in August 1930 adopted the goal of moving toward universal compulsory education to age 15. All children aged 8–10 and all young people aged 11–15 who had not completed the four-year school were compelled to do so. Children in urban areas were required to complete seven years of education.

The disorder in the schools during the cultural revolution and its consequences for the economy and social order had alienated parents, teachers, students, and industrial managers. Parents wanted basic literacy and numeracy for their children and some measure of discipline in school life. Teachers were bewildered by the ever-changing directives from the center. They, too, longed for greater control over curriculum and discipline in learning. In any case, most schools lacked the facilities to carry out prescribed initiatives. Factories had neither the means nor the will to fulfill the many obligations that the experimenters expected of them. Students assigned to factories were of little use in the production process. Passionate student campaigns around social issues disrupted work schedules and annoyed employees. At the beginning of the 1931 school year, the Central Committee of the Communist Party condemned the policies of Narkompros that rejected the teaching of subjects and academic content. "It is necessary to wage a decisive struggle against thoughtless scheming with methods … especially against the so called project method."[1] The Party repudiated the doctrine of the "withering away of the school" in 1931. The heart of the project method, the Shulgin Institute, closed in 1932. A new course for Soviet education was in the making. Stalin was likely directly aware of the problems schools faced in carrying out the project method. His own daughter attended a model school in Moscow. That school enjoyed a privileged position but was still unable to provide the facilities needed to support the labor components required by the project method. Most local education departments had by 1932 dropped any pretense of providing a labor component. In 1933 the pedagogical institutes began to close the sections devoted to training instructors for labor classes.

Change to the theory and practice of both politics and education followed quickly. The bourgeois specialists were again restored to favor in both industry and academia. Social value (ability) replaced class origins as the principal basis for advancement. The structure and discipline of Stalin's education reforms suited teachers and parents and served the interests of the emerging new class of administrators and professionals. In spite of efforts by Khrushchev to revive in part the unified labor school of the 1920s in order once again to promote social mobility among workers, the general principles of Stalin's education reform persisted until the advent of Mikhail Gorbachev in 1985.

General Elementary and Secondary Education

The school that Stalin built marked a major departure from the unified labor polytechnical school of the early Soviet reformers. Although they clashed over the best means to achieve the goal, reformers like Krupskaia and Shulgin shared a belief in the transformation of human beings into conscious and willing socialist citizens through Marxist upbringing and the experience of socially useful labor within the collective. Stalin replaced that ideal with the lesser goal of the creation of a New Soviet Person through strict discipline in school and society, indoctrination, enforced obedience, conformity, and unquestioning loyalty to the Party and its leader. The school was in his conception a microcosm of a disciplined and hierarchical society. Under Stalin, the polytechnical ideal of the unified school gave way to two educational streams. The first enabled a relatively small number of students to acquire an academic education. The second placed the great majority of pupils on a vocational path. Social mobility slowed but did not end. The vast expansion of the economy and state sector assured the social advancement of meritorious workers and peasants. But the distinction between manual and mental labor was reaffirmed, and social capital, that is, native ability, parentage, place of birth, and political access, increasingly determined position and success.

In August 1932 the Central Committee ordered that grades eight to ten be reestablished in the general school. Although the linkage of school to factory and collective farm remained, the committee delineated teaching from work. In 1933 it created its own Department of Schools to which the Commissariat of National Enlightenment was effectively subordinated. Under the department's direction, teaching and individual grading by subject returned to primary and secondary schools as did required textbooks, lesson plans, homework, and year-end examinations. History returned as a separate subject and literature, geography, social studies, and other subjects were taught through the lens of history. Chronology was stressed. Teaching of the basics, the enforcement of discipline, and persistence in learning now informed school life. The school year and school day were standardized. Every detail, including the type of chalk, pen or pencil, and the quality of paper, was specified. Class journals recorded attendance, behavior, class performance, and completion of homework. Students kept personal day books in which they outlined assignments and their activities outside of school hours. Teachers recorded a daily grade in the day books, which the home room teacher and child's parents reviewed weekly and signed. The conduct mark, familiar in tsarist schools, returned. In 1935 the Komsomol issued its Disciplinary Code that in many ways echoed the old tsarist code for students. The tsarist ritual of "Day of Knowledge" or "First Bell," a celebration of the first day of school, was revived and practiced in many schools. In 1935 a decree ordered a festival on May 25, the final day of school, of "Last Bell" to be followed by a "leavers" ball.[2]

In 1936 the Central Committee closed the chapter on experimentalism in education with a ringing denunciation of pedology. The attack on pedology was in part motivated by a wider campaign to impose Party control over the larger world of scholarship. The pedologists' belief that a child's physical and social environment along with biologically inherited traits determined their learning capabilities resulted in the classification of students according to their learning potential and the creation of special schools or parallel classes for their education. The science of "defectology" partially informed pedolgy. Pedologists' broad definition of mental retardation contradicted the Party's belief in the equality of all persons. Socialist consciousness and not biology determined educational outcomes. The Central Committee ordered the closing of most of the special schools and an end to instruction in pedology in teacher training. Most of the children in special schools were quickly returned to regular school classrooms. Many teachers objected to the return of difficult students to their charge and ignored their needs or tried to get rid of them. The authorities met such reluctance with the charge that "there are no poor pupils, only poor teachers."[3] Teachers who had successes with difficult students were publicly praised. The burden of socializing children bore heavily on teachers and, to a lesser degree, parents. Teacher and parental protests did result, however, in the restoration of some special classes for the more vulnerable students.

Although they supported a very different political and social structure, schools under Stalin increasingly resembled their tsarist predecessors. Codes of student conduct departed little from the tsarist originals. Although education authorities condemned rote learning, the examination system based on set textbooks that they imposed in 1935 encouraged memorization as the best path to success. Teachers resorted to the old patterns of repetition of material and testing of the student's recall of it. Command of given facts determined grades. Upbringing played as large a role in Stalin's schools as in the schools of the tsars. Law of God gave way to a powerful ideological socialist element in the curriculum. Children's organizations reinforced broad ideological commitment. In the last years of the empire, boys' military societies called "Play Regiments" that stressed drill and calisthenics sprang up in schools and churches.

In the Soviet Union the Octobrist organization for the youngest children was oriented to fun and leisure. The Young Pioneers, founded in 1922 for children aged 10–14 and from 1936 aged 11–16, originally were affiliated with culture clubs, factories, orphanages, and other social organizations. From the early 1930s, however, they were formally attached to schools and given the task of increasing "conscious discipline among children and especially in schools."[4] On initiation, Pioneers from 1936 onwards swore fealty to country and Party. Most pupils enrolled in the Pioneers. Pioneer Palaces, providing spaces for leisure and cultural activities of members, began to be built in the mid-1930s and were mandated for all medium and large towns. Ideological work within them continued. The Komsomol for teenagers and young adults embraced far fewer members but played a large role in political indoctrination in secondary and higher education. Figure 8.1 shows the growing ubiquity of Stalin's image in education.

Figure 8.1 Students listening to their teacher tell a story at a kindergarten for miner's children in the Soviet Union, 1948.

Source: © Sovfoto/Universal Images Group/Getty Images.

Inevitably, Stalin's ideal of the school was seldom fully replicated in real life. Authorities issued multiple and often contradictory directives. Schools lacked the resources to meet many of the requirements, especially for out-of-class student activities. In the mid-1930s the Party invited criticism of the school system. A flood of complaints poured in from parents, students, and teachers, ranging from late pay to poor facilities, shortages of school supplies, absenteeism, and uncooperative local officials. The tide of criticism reflected on Narkompros. Despite a campaign of self-criticism within Narkompros, most department heads were arrested in 1937. Regional Narkompros officials also were heavily purged.

Teachers

Teachers at all levels of the system were in demand. The number of students in elementary and secondary schools burgeoned from about four million in 1928 to thirty-one million in the late 1930s. By far the greatest increase was in secondary schools. Some twenty thousand teachers were needed annually merely to fill vacancies.[5] The two-year pedagogical schools and four-year pedagogical institutes turned out about one hundred thousand graduates from 1930 to 1935, far short of the need. To make matters worse, despite the requirement that they work for two years after graduation, half of institute graduates did not enter the profession. Opportunities for work elsewhere in the economy, especially for women, drained the ranks of potential teachers. While the number of women in other professions grew during the 1930s, the number of women in teaching declined from 62 percent in 1932 to 56 percent at the end of the decade.[6] To meet demand, students in pedagogical courses were awarded an early graduation and sent to schools at best only half-prepared for the task they faced. Experienced urban teachers who agreed to work in rural areas for two years were guaranteed a return to places in city schools at the end of the agreed term.

The average age of teachers was low. Among elementary teachers in 1933, 5 percent were 17 or younger and 15 percent were aged between 18 and 19 years. Relations between older and younger teachers were often tense. Younger teachers were more likely to leave the profession for other work or further education. The regime much preferred the more reliable older teachers. In the early 1930s, however, the authorities were concerned that around 36 percent of all teachers were from backgrounds other than peasant or worker. Such "social aliens" were once again suspect and vulnerable to dismissal. Later in the decade, however, the leadership, out of need, defended teachers of politically suspect origins. In any event, by the late 1930s the political reliability of teachers had markedly increased. Although few teachers were Party members, the numbers of them who had joined the Komsomol grew steadily during the decade among the youngest cohort of teachers.

In 1936 new standards for teachers were established. An elementary schoolteacher was expected to have completed the junior seven-year section of the general school and to have had an additional four years of pedagogical training. Secondary schoolteachers were required to have completed the senior ten-year division of secondary school and to have graduated from a pedagogical institute or a university. All practicing teachers were to be recertified to meet those standards. Between 1936 and 1941, 1,725,000 teachers had met a certification commission. Only 3 percent failed to meet the criteria.[7] Although their salaries were raised in 1930 and again in 1936, teachers, especially in rural areas, experienced material shortages. Local authorities continued to regard them as low in status and often withheld part or all of their salaries. Teachers were not allowed to form professional organizations and had no collective means to defend their interests. Compared to other professional groups they felt underpaid and underappreciated. As a result, many teachers left their posts to pursue better rewarded careers.

Most teachers welcomed the end of educational experimentation that had often placed them at odds with parents and with local authorities. They also were grateful for the restoration of their authority in the classroom. There was, however, a cost. In return for some measure of control in the classroom, teachers under Stalin lost any say over curriculum. They accepted that the transmission of prescribed knowledge and not the provision of students with the tools for independent thought was their lot. Narkompros dictated course content and lesson plans. Every lesson had to instill Party-mindedness. Teachers resented their lack of autonomy and the need to place communist upbringing above academic learning. Vospitanie, they believed, should take place outside of the classroom. While what was taught was prescribed how to teach it was not. And since few had formal pedagogical training, many resorted to rote teaching. As noted earlier, examinations, which largely determined student advancement, encouraged memorization of the prescribed texts.

Stalin's schools placed a heavy burden on teachers that extended well beyond the classroom. Political activism took precedence over the duties of teaching. Teachers were expected to play a major role in collectivization and other state campaigns. Excellence in teaching was less valued than political conformity, acceptance of official values, and active participation in state objectives. Teachers were mandated to oversee the lives of each of their students both in and beyond the classroom. Visits to parents were mandatory and detailed reports on each student required. The restoration of their authority over pupils subjected them to blame for lack of student discipline, common in schools of the 1930s, and for poor results by their charges in compulsory examinations.

The lack of corporate protections left teachers on their own to mediate among the demands of the state, the wishes of parents, and their own sense of worth and dignity. In doing so, they gained some agency in shaping the playing out of Stalinism in their schools. The fact that they were desperately needed to fulfill the objectives of the regime afforded them some leverage. Coercive measures to keep them in place, for example, were mostly ineffective. The purges that devastated Party ranks and professionals in 1937–8 touched teachers relatively lightly. It is estimated that around 3 percent of teachers were removed, but many fought back and were reinstated. Although men made up some 40–45 percent of teachers, the regime saw the profession as passive and "feminine" and of little danger to Party interests.

Children whose parents were arrested were often expelled from school or persecuted by other students if they remained. Perhaps because they were not regarded by the regime as threating, women teachers often protected such students and fostered their further education. Many children whose parents were purged were sent to orphanages.

When Al'dona Volynskaia's father was expelled from the Party, teachers at her school questioned her about her mother who soon also disappeared. Al'dona was first sent to a children's reception center and then transferred to an institution in Odessa where some five hundred children whose parents had been arrested were gathered. From there they were despatched to various orphanages or children's homes. When Al'dona arrived at her new home she and her companions were conducted straight to the dining hall. There "the tables had been set with food, and every bowl had more than a dozen flies floating in it. At that time none of us could eat the soup. Later on we would eat it, even if another child had spit in it."[8]

Professional-Vocational Education

Vocational education also underwent major changes under Stalin. The factory-plant apprenticeship schools (FZUs) until the end of 1932 had, by providing general education along with technical training, enabled graduates to go on to further education instead of entering the factory workforce. In spite of a stipulation that on graduation students must remain at work in the factory for at least three years, some 35 percent of students in higher technical education institutes had come directly from the FZUs without the three-year interval. Party officials deplored the steady drain of FZU graduates out of the factory and into rabfaks, technicums, and higher technical institutes at the expense of production. In 1933 they redefined the role of the FZU as the preparation of workers for production work in narrow specializations. The FZU was now required to accept only students who had completed the seven-year school and to enforce the rule on work in the factory for three years after completion. The training period was sharply reduced. General education subjects and general technology subjects were proscribed. Eighty percent of study or work time was devoted to the specialization and 20 percent to theory directly related to the specialization. A shortage of willing graduates of seven-year schools left many FZU places empty. Students who might have attended FZUs to prepare for further education now avoided the new narrower version of them. As a result, only just over 35 percent of students in 1934 in FZU programs had a seven-year school qualification. The low educational level of entrants convinced the Party to increase the length of training programs.

In addition to the FZU schools, various branches of the economy opened their own vocational training schools. An example was the schools of the railways established in 1934 to train machinists, station masters, and other employees. The schools provided three-year courses equivalent to grades five to seven of the general schools. Students received full boarding and stipends. Graduates were required to work in the field of their training for at least five years. A whole system of short courses for workers on the job had evolved as well. They had a general education focus that encouraged adult workers to seek to continue on to further education, a goal no longer supported by the regime. As a result, they were replaced by technical minimum circles that all workers who had not graduated from a FZU or other technical school were required to take. The training provided in the technical minimum circles raised the technical knowledge of workers but did not qualify them for further education and so kept them in production.

The circles were supplemented by Stakhanovite schools for shock workers, schools of masters of Soviet labor, and other forms of adult worker instruction within the factory or collective farm.

Shortages of teachers of technical specializations were acute. The removal of general education from the FZUs in 1933 saw many teachers leave. Of those who remained in 1935, less than 50 percent had professional-pedagogical training. On-the-job engineers, technicians, and master workers made up the other half of the teaching contingent. In August 1931 the Supreme Soviet ordered the training in special courses of teachers for special technical and general technical disciplines in urban centers. Some of the economic branches also opened short courses to raise the teaching qualifications of instructors. The Moscow industrial-instruction technicum graduated 908 technical instructors from 1922 to 1937. They comprised a mere 7 percent of the total number of technical instructors. The railways ran their own pedagogical-technicums from 1932. Learning on the job remained common in Soviet industry, however.

Higher Education

During the cultural revolution, universities and higher technical institutes suffered severe disruption; many ceased to function. Stalin resolved by the beginning of 1930 to turn all institutions of higher education into centers of science and technology. In 1930 provincial universities were formally closed and then reorganized. The Central Committee in April 1931 mandated the universities to teach primarily pure science and mathematics and to prepare university professors to teach them. In the 1931–2 academic year the newly reopened universities taught almost nothing except science. Only a handful of institutes in Moscow and Leningrad taught any humanities or social science subjects. The department of oriental studies in the University of Vladivostok was the sole nonscientific department in the Russian Republic. In 1934, however, the Party established departments of history at the universities of Moscow and Leningrad with the primary role of preparing history textbooks. Although the stress on class struggle was reduced, courses on Marxism-Leninism were mandatory in all higher education institutions. In 1938 the *History of the Communist Party of the Soviet Union (Bolshevik): Short Course*, commissioned by Stalin to answer important ideological questions, was made required reading in all higher educational schools. Police monitored and recorded the activities of students through special departments established in each institution.

The Committee on Higher Education, founded in 1932, undertook an extensive review of higher technical education. Institutes that failed to meet the review's standards were either reduced to lower schools, merged with better institutes, or closed. The students in each were also examined; weaker students were weeded out, placed in evening courses, or sent to lower-level technicums. The quality of applicants began to improve. In 1932 only 16 percent of applicants had finished secondary school; in 1937/38 a majority had done so. Consequently, dropout rates declined, from seventy students per hundred in the period from 1928 to 1932 to forty/forty-five per hundred in the period from 1933 to 1937.[9] The committee also reviewed all faculty members. Many young faculty who had been advanced thanks to their class origins rather than their abilities were removed. The firings left some higher technical educational institutes (VTUZs) without any staff. Even the most prestigious schools under the Commissariat of Heavy Industry faced a shortage of 282 professors in 1934 due to the review. Some 500 heavy industry graduate students also lost their places.[10] The laboratory-brigade method of the cultural revolution was first made optional and then abolished and grading of individuals restored. The number of specializations was vastly reduced and greater attention given to theory. Faculty were expected to devote half their time to research. In September 1932 a decree required that all VTUZs and technicums devote 80–85 percent of teaching time to theoretical and technical subjects. Attention to theory marked a partial break with the preference of nearly all regimes in Russia since the eighteenth century for applied over theoretical science. The principal objective, however, remained assimilation of Western knowledge and not innovation. Stalin preferred the practical and remained suspicious of higher education. The inadequate funding to technical education provided under his leadership slowed the expansion in expertise required to meet the needs of a rapidly expanding economy and complex society.

Outcomes

The 1930s witnessed an explosion in the number of schools and of students. The budget for schools quadrupled over the decade from ten roubles per student to thirty-eight roubles. By 1939–40 the total number of students in schools of all kinds reached thirty-one million. In 1938–39 more than twelve million of them were in secondary or higher education. The percentage of girls in school increased from 40 percent in 1927 to 48 percent in 1938. The proportion of women in vocational education also rose significantly. In 1931 the Party adopted specifications for the building of schools developed at the All-Russian Congress on School Construction in 1929. The number of new schools, however, did not keep up with the rapid expansion of the school population, and facilities in rural areas lagged far behind those in urban centers. They, too, suffered from lack of appropriate space, too few teachers, and two or more teaching shifts. With the abandonment of class criteria in advancement, social capital in terms of urban residency, education level of families, and social connections played a larger role in social mobility. The percentage of workers in higher education fell sharply from the heady days of the cultural revolution to 33.9 percent in January 1938. Peasants accounted for another 21.6 percent, a number far below their percentage of the total population. Students of white-collar and professional parentage made up 42.2 percent of higher education students but only 17 percent of the population in 1938.[11]

For all its struggles and the turmoil within the system, schooling under Stalin attained impressive results. School attendance blossomed and literacy rose. While in 1926 only 47 percent of children aged 8–11 had basic literacy skills, some 95 percent of people over the age of 9 were literate in 1939. Teachers chafed under the material condition of the schools but broadly shared the goals of the state and performed their jobs adequately in trying circumstances. Thanks to rapid economic expansion, both general and vocational education offered opportunities to all for social advancement. Students had little say in what or how they learned but saw education as a path to jobs and status. They also were motivated by participating in a process of national development and social progress. The growing technical intelligentsia were assured of a privileged position within state and society. Optimism about the future was high. Shared objectives with the state provided the best teachers with space to make prescribed materials more palatable to students. Soviet citizens educated in the 1930s had highly positive memories of their school experience. Soviet schoolchildren during the 1930s had great faith in Stalin and were loyal to him. In assessing the Stalin school it is well to remember that many of its features were replicated in other countries. Strict discipline, rote learning, patriotism, low teacher qualifications, and underfunding were features of education throughout Europe and beyond in the prewar years.

There were negative consequences of schooling under Stalin. The humanities and social sciences were almost entirely subsumed in courses on Marxism-Leninism that enforced acceptance of prescribed values. Human needs were neglected. The focus of education was material production in which individuals were reduced to objects or cogs in an ideologically driven machine. Creativity and initiative withered under a regimen of duty, routine, and increasing competition in school and in society. Suppressed during the war, the negative sides of Stalinist education were to preoccupy reformers in the postwar world.

Schooling in the Second World War

Between the beginning of the war in Europe in late summer 1939 and the German invasion of the USSR in June 1941, a number of changes took place in the Soviet education system. Although various attempts to introduce some military training into the schools had gone on since the early 1920s, schools were lax in enforcing them. A law on universal conscription in September 1939 recommended basic military training for middle school students and pre-call-up training for seniors. Training was made compulsory in September 1940, but the content of the training and who was to provide it was not resolved before the German invasion. The concern of the regime to promote foreign language skills in the population, both to increase access to Western knowledge and to improve outreach into a hostile world, moved the regime from the mid-1930s to adopt foreign language teaching as a priority. Lack of foreign language teachers, however, had resulted in little progress. In September 1940 the Central Committee decreed that at least one of English, French, or German must be taught from the fifth grade of secondary school by 1943. The decree also set targets for an intake in pedagogical foreign language institutes of 5,500 students in 1940 and 10,000 by 1942. All higher education students were now required to take four-year courses of two to three hours per week in a foreign language.[12]

Change also occurred in vocational education. The Third Five-Year Plan called for the training of 1,700,000 qualified workers. The FZUs had in the first two years of the plan graduated a meager 320,000 trained workers. The Presidium of the Supreme Soviet in October 1940 addressed the problem with the establishment of labor reserve schools. A Main Administration for Labor Reserves oversaw the new initiative.

Republican and local organs of the Main Administration administered the schools. The plan called for the recruitment of urban and rural youth to train for a wide range of specialist occupations in two-year craft schools. A few less demanding specializations were assigned to six-month schools. In all, around four hundred specializations were taught. Students received full government support and on graduation were required to serve for an unbroken period of four years in state enterprises on regular salaries. Whereas the FZUs were voluntary, the labor reserve schools had planned recruitment that included the drafting of young people into them. Graduates of the schools could be deployed wherever the government chose in order to assure a territorial distribution of needed personnel. Around 900 FZUs were converted into labor reserve schools; a total of 1,549 were soon operating. In addition to the labor reserve schools in 1940–1, about 4,000 secondary specialist vocational schools with a million students and 250,000 graduates annually were in operation.[13]

Prior to the German invasion and under the terms of the Nazi-Soviet Pact of 1939, the USSR annexed Western Belorussia, Western Ukraine, the Karelian province of Finland, the Baltic States, and Moldavia. Polish general schools in annexed territories were quickly converted into Soviet four-year elementary schools and seven-year incomplete secondary schools. Polish gymnasiums and lycées were redesignated as ten-year complete secondary schools. Teaching was in Polish. Schools in Western Ukraine in which Polish had been required now adopted Ukrainian as the language of instruction in schools. Much the same occurred in Belorussia. Shortage of Belorussian language teachers, however, slowed the process there. By the end of 1940 Russian was taking over from local languages as the language of instruction in secondary schools in occupied areas.

The German invasion in 1941 inflicted extensive damage on Soviet schools. More than 80,000 school buildings were lost. In the USSR there were 191,545 general schools in the 1940–1 school year of which 113,180 were in the Russian Republic. At the beginning of the next school year the numbers fell to 116,548 and 90,610, respectively.[14] Classroom time was sharply reduced as teachers and their students were assigned to harvest crops and carry out other manual tasks. Many districts shortened the school year. Male teachers were frequently drafted. Female teachers were assigned to production or to local government or Party administration. Teacher shortages required an increase in school day shifts, but teachers evacuated from German occupied areas helped to fill some of the vacancies. In 1941–2 Narkompros issued a shortened curriculum as a temporary expedient. The numbers of pupils, especially among senior students, were nearly halved. Many students had left to take work or to join the armed forces. In response, the government opened part-time Schools for Working Youth that operated primarily in Leningrad and Moscow. Students attended three-hour class sessions three times a week to study two or three subjects at a time from the general school curriculum. In 1944 evening classes were introduced in rural areas in which students worked through the curriculum of the seven-year school for four hours each night for five nights a week.

Indiscipline among students had plagued schools in the 1930s. The war made matters worse, prompting the government in 1943 to issue a decree on "Rules for Pupils." The rules may have been in part influenced by the work of A. S. Makarenko who, as we saw, had operated camps in the 1920s for the many orphans in post-revolutionary Russia. After years of neglect of his ideas, the Party press began in 1940 to praise his approach as "a dynamic weapon in the communist upbringing of the younger generation."[15] The new rules were similar to previous student codes but stressed individual immersion in the collective enterprise as the highest civic virtue.

In the same year the Party ended coeducation in elementary and secondary urban schools. The decision referred vaguely to differences in the nature and timing of male and female development in justification of the policy. In 1934 Stalin had remarked on the success of the education system in producing good pilots, engineers, and agronomists, but its failure to teach a woman "much about bringing up children and preparing her for family life."[16] A goal of the reform was better to prepare males for their roles as fathers and soldiers and females as ideologically conscious mothers and educators of the coming generation. The curriculum reflected the goal. Boys were to receive training in topography, map reading, and orienteering; girls were destined to study pedagogy, needlework, domestic sciences, hygiene, and child care. In part, the change was inspired by continuing concerns about classroom discipline.

Those concerns continued. In March 1944 Narkompros issued a decree "On Strengthening Discipline in Schools" that increased measures available to deal with problem students, including transfer to special regimen schools. At the same time, socialist competition, which had been introduced into schools in 1929, was abolished. It pitted teams of students against each other in achieving grades or completing projects or socially useful work. Now socialist competition was condemned as encouraging teachers and students to conspire in order to win the competitions and to inflate grades. The old five-point grading system of tsarist times was restored. Behavior was again subject to grading. Only a mark of five for behavior qualified a student to take the newly imposed certificate of maturity examinations that seven-year and ten-year school leavers were required to pass. Gold and silver medals that conferred privileges on their student recipients were also introduced. The attempt to introduce single-sex education in city schools produced limited results and considerable criticism. Facilities, already overstrained, were not easily found for the additional classes; many schools resorted to separate male and female shifts. Teachers were equally in short supply. Discipline in both boys and girls schools was hard to enforce. Critics of the reform regretted what they regarded as a retreat from gender equality in education.

During the war, students performed a wide variety of services outside of the school. They were urged on by a wartime propaganda that muted the socialist message and replaced it with an appeal to Soviet patriotism. Defense clubs prepared citizens for anti-air raid and anti-chemical defense work and engaged in fire control; rural students opened garden plots and worked on collectives; some sixty thousand students in Leningrad worked on the city's defenses during the siege of 1941, sometimes under fire. Where schools functioned conditions in them were grim. One student recalled moving from one school to another during the siege to escape the cold: "It turned out to be worse there. On top of the cold, there was no light." For eight months from June 1941, the catacombs of Odessa served as schools. Students brought their own slates and sleeping bags, made their way through the dark tunnels to their classroom by following a thread, and lit the classrooms with paraffin lamps that they fashioned from bottles and wicks.[17] School production mastery workshops (UPMs) organized in schools and factories taught basic technical skills through the making of clothes for soldiers, mending of shoes, fixing of furniture, manufacture of tank, gun, and grenade parts, camouflage covers, stretchers, and other needed commodities. Girls comprised from 65 to 75 percent of UPM participants. The labor reserve schools played a major role in maintaining wartime production. Young men and women filled places in production vacated by workers drafted into the military. As occupied areas were gradually recovered, the labor reserve schools moved in to provide four years of minimal general schooling and a narrow production qualification to the many orphans left by the war.[18]

The strains of the war had undermined parental authority and threatened the stability of families. Beginning with the 1944–5 school year, the regime lowered the entry age of pupils from 8 to 7. The regime hoped that schooling at an earlier age would substitute for failing family upbringing. In addition, more mothers would be freed for work. Instead of graduating at age 15, students would complete the seven-year school at 14 and go on to technical training or join the workforce. The change also sought to lower dropout rates. Fourteen-year-olds were thought to be less likely to leave school before completion than 15-year-olds. The authorities mounted special summer programs in advance of the reform to prepare teachers for the double cohort of young pupils as well as to take on the many older children in occupied areas who had received no schooling during the war.

Postwar Schooling

The USSR during Stalin's last years was a dark and repressed place. A cult of the leader largely replaced the earlier idealism of creating a communist society. Marxism at best received lip service. Concentration camps overflowed with returning soldiers taken as prisoners of war and others whom Stalin deemed suspect. Peoples such as the Crimean Tatars, who had been displaced as "traitors" during the war, were not allowed to return to their homes. Perhaps the only bright spot in the gloom of the postwar Soviet Union was the rapid reconstruction of the school system. By September 1947, 99.6 percent of the prewar total of schools were functioning in the Russian Republic. Ukraine and Belorussia had each restored 92 percent of their prewar school total. The number of teachers had fallen from nearly a million and a quarter in 1940–1 to just over a half million in 1943 but grew to over a million by September 1945. A shortfall of teachers remained. Their hours of teaching were extended and class sizes increased. To cope with the very large primary school cohort of pupils, persons without formal teaching qualifications filled the gaps. Short pedagogical courses did little to raise the general level of teaching. While the elementary school recovered quickly secondary education lagged behind. Teachers were slow to return. Primary schoolteachers were often pushed into secondary teaching without the required training. In all on September 1945, 26,100,000 children attended Soviet general day schools or 75 percent of the prewar figure.[19] The rapid recovery of primary education was rebuilding a base for secondary schooling in the years to follow. Population losses and forgone births during the war, however, portended a demographic crisis in the postwar period.

The death of Stalin in March 1953 initiated a period known as the "Thaw." After a brief power struggle, Georgy Malenkov became first among equals within a collective leadership. In a little more than a year, however, Nikita Khrushchev emerged as the undisputed leader of the Party organization and his friend Nikolai Bulganin became premier, that is, leader of the government. The principal feature of the Thaw was de-Stalinization. It included the rehabilitation of many but not all of Stalin's victims, a greater openness in discussions about past failings, and the liberalization of economic policy. In February 1956 at the Twentieth Party Congress, Khrushchev delivered his "secret" speech, in which he denounced the cult of the leader, repudiated the terror of the purges, and blamed Stalin for the drastic losses in the first months of the Second World War.

By 1950 the large dip in the birth rate during the war years was already apparent in falling enrollments in elementary schools. The demographic deficit lasted into the 1960s; at the lowest point the school-age population declined by nearly half. In 1953 about thirty million students were enrolled in general education schools. The great majority of 7–11-year-olds were in attendance in the first four years (elementary) of school, about two-thirds of eligible children aged 12–14 remained to complete the seventh class (incomplete secondary), and around 20 percent of 15–17-year-olds were enrolled in the ten-year program (complete secondary). Coeducation was restored in 1954. Part-time and correspondence education also had grown rapidly, and the labor reserve schools had both stabilized and improved the offerings of their craft and agricultural schools. The postwar strain on facilities and teaching resources was alleviated as pupil numbers dropped. Military training for boys that had begun before the war continued in the postwar years.

General Schooling

In the eyes of Party and many educational authorities, the abstract and heavily academic nature of Stalin's general school curriculum was a cause for concern. Even before the dictator's death, the Nineteenth Party Congress in 1952 had called for a more polytechnical approach to general education. In 1954 Narkompros mandated one hour of labor per week in a school workshop or garden plot for pupils in grades one to four and two hours in grade five. In 1955 practical classes of two hours per week in agriculture, mechanics, and electricity were required in grades eight to ten. Time spent on Russian language and literature and on mathematics was abbreviated to accommodate the labor component. The sciences and mathematics again turned away from theory to practical applications, and lessons on the technical and production aspects of enterprises in the region of the school were mounted. The new curriculum encouraged excursions to factories and collective farms. The commitment to the ideal of education for all was exemplified in the creation in 1956 of a network of boarding schools that within a decade accommodated 2.5 million students. The curriculum was roughly the same as that in day schools but more flexible in implementation. Preference in entry went to orphans, children of widows or of unmarried mothers, invalids, and children from large families. They also took on problem children. Parents' Committees helped to maintain ties between children boarding in the schools and their families.

The desired reincorporation of labor into school curricula was slow. A majority of schools stuck to the old curriculum. Training in agriculture proved to be feasible, but there were obstacles to acquiring an industrial job placement. General school students showed little interest in manual labor. Motivated in part by the educational ideals of the revolution, Khrushchev in 1958 proposed a further reform of schooling intended again to narrow the gap between mental and manual labor and link school more closely to life. Although the discussion focused on the ideological and social goals of the reform, the changes also sought to address the growing shortages in the production workforce due to the wartime demographic dip.

The reform, to be implemented gradually from 1959, made eight years of schooling required for those aged 7–15, an extension of a year. The new school was renamed the incomplete secondary labor polytechnical school. The ten-year complete secondary school remained but was extended to an eleventh year. The additional eighth or eleventh years, respectively, were devoted to polytechnical studies that included domestic sciences for girls, school workshops for boys, lectures on labor and production, projects providing work experience, factory and farm visits, and an array of extracurricular activities largely through the Pioneers organization. Employers were also expected to provide opportunities for students to gain production experience. The curriculum called for manual labor training in grades five to eight of two to three hours a week and in the senior grades no fewer than twelve hours each week. Further reductions in the class time for Russian language and literature, mathematics, and foreign languages made room for the additional labor components. The school day and school year were also lengthened. On graduation at age 15 or 16 students were to engage in socially useful labor. Part-time study was expanded. Graduates of the eight-year school were encouraged while they worked to continue part time toward a complete or specialist secondary education either in evening shift secondary schools or general labor polytechnical schools, which provided three years of training for a specific branch of the economy or of the cultural sector, or in a technicum or other vocational educational institution. Employers were asked to release workers to enable part-time study. Before being admitted to higher education, all but the most able students were required to have at least two years of work experience.

Increased ideological study accompanied the return to polytechnical education. The purpose of education was defined as assisting in the building of a communist society through the preparation of students for socially useful work, provision of a good grounding in various fields of learning, and the inculcation in them of a materialist worldview. Although labor skills were important, so too was general culture through exposure to literature and the arts. In order to enhance the cultural level of the population, special schools for the gifted, mostly in music, ballet, and art, were established. The diminution of time spent on foreign languages in general education found compensation in the establishment of around six hundred foreign language schools by 1970. Scientists pressed for schools for the gifted in scientific fields but were rebuffed.

Khrushchev's attempt to reshape the workforce and revitalize ideological commitment met with widespread criticism. Some of the old problems recurred. Factory managers were reluctant to take students on. One complained that "most of the students were more trouble than they were worth to him as workers."[20] Of particular concern to the Party were changing attitudes of youth toward manual labor. As the eleven-year (complete) secondary school expanded, more and more graduates aspired to go on to higher education. The economy, however, needed more middle-level technicians and not high-level specialists. The requirement that graduates perform two years of labor before applying for higher education did not slow demand. Institutes of higher education saw a large increase in applicants. To accommodate them, evening and correspondence programs blossomed, accounting for 79 percent of the 1,400,000 increase in higher education enrollments between 1958 and 1964.[21] The result was falling academic standards in higher education and growing resentment among faculty about the heavier workloads.

The problem of access was exacerbated by growing stratification within Soviet society. Stalin's education policies, however disruptive, were elitist. They fostered the growth of an intelligentsia, a considerable proportion of whom now made up the ruling stratum and the economic and cultural elite on whom the regime depended. It was their predominance that linked the educational reforms of the 1930s to the conservative consensus of the Brezhnev years. The rapid expansion of the elite assured a considerable level of social mobility. Expansion was, however, slowing by the 1960s. The social status of parents was increasingly linked to the educational fate of their children. At 20 percent of the population, children of the intelligentsia made up 50 percent of higher education students in the mid-1950s.[22] The rural-urban split was also growing. While seeing the danger stratification posed to building communism, the Party also had no desire to alienate those on which the country depended.

Khrushchev's erratic performance resulted in his removal in 1964 as general secretary of the Party and his replacement by Leonid Brezhnev; Alexei Kosygin, a specialist in light industry production, became premier of the USSR. The new regime quickly curtailed the amount of required work training at all levels of schools without fully abandoning it. Schools were still designated as polytechnics. Four hours per week were now devoted to labor theory and practice, largely in school workshops. Placement of students in factory or farm work was for the most part abandoned. Grade one pupils learned about tools and materials. By grade four, students did some carpentry and machine training in workshops within the school. Girls took domestic science and handicrafts. To mitigate the apparent gender gap and appease critics, girls received some mechanical training while boys did some domestic science.

In order to address the challenge of social stratification in education, the Party opened two fronts. The first sought to increase the pool of college eligible students by setting the goal of universal complete secondary education by 1970. In spite of too few places in grades nine to eleven in urban areas and too few students to fill grades nine to eleven in rural schools, by 1970 more than 60 percent of 20–29-year-olds had a complete secondary education. To facilitate entry into higher education for the less advantaged the Party in 1969 created preparatory departments to prepare young workers and peasants for study in higher education. The program had some success. By 1976, 97,000 students had completed the preparatory courses. The dropout rate, however, exceeded 55 percent.[23] The expansion of complete secondary education was not matched by the complementary expansion of institutions of higher education. Competition for places increased, and the social capital of parentage played an even larger role in admissions. The bottleneck created at the university level only highlighted the problem of social stratification.

Professional-Vocational Schooling

The second front in the battle for educational reform was an effort to make vocational schooling and work more attractive. The newly formed State Committee for Professional and Technical Education oversaw the conversion in 1959 of the labor reserve schools along with some FZU schools into professional and technical schools (PTUs). The committee established programs of study, teaching methodologies, equipment standards, and the trades to be taught in the schools. The administration of the new schools fell to the republics. The schools were linked to enterprises and were partly self-financing from their own production. They accepted graduates of the incomplete secondary schools into four- to five-year courses with full-time and part-time sections in urban areas and one- or two-year courses with an agricultural focus in rural areas. Urban PTUs also ran short courses in certain specializations. Brezhnev recentralized the administration of the PTU system in 1966 and in 1969 ordered the schools to move toward providing secondary level education. From that year the PTU was to provide a general education equivalent to the eight-year school as well as a trade certificate. The best graduates were eligible for admission to an institution of higher education. The goal of the latter provision was to attract a better class of student into the vocational stream.

The reformed PTUs at first proved to be popular. From 1977 graduates of the complete secondary school could also go on to attain vocational training in a PTU. The schools evolved along three lines. Some provided one or two years of training in a simple trade to anyone who applied. A second provided longer courses in more complex trades for graduates of the eight-year school. A third type trained eleven-year school graduates in one- or one-and-a-half-year courses in technical specializations. PTUs also operated part-time and ran boarding schools as well as day and evening schools. Males predominated in the schools. In 1970 they made up 72 percent of students. The greater emphasis of the Brezhnev regime on light industry, however, began to draw more women into the PTUs over time. By 1979 there were 3,676 secondary PTUs with around two million students. They comprised half of all the students in vocational education. By 1984 the number had doubled.[24]

As production in the USSR in the 1970s edged toward greater mechanization, the technological future became more uncertain. Rapid change required both flexibility and rapid on the job training. The regime counted on the PTUs to furnish graduates with both deep and broad knowledge that facilitated easy adaptation to changing production needs. Their hopes were not met. The reformed PTUs did not attract better applicants. The better students in general schools chose other paths; the weaker students filled the PTUs. Many of them were not capable of meeting the demands of the curriculum. Throughout the 1970s the average school leaving grade of PTU students barely exceeded a pass, although grading standards were deliberately slack. Absenteeism in the schools was common, discipline was poor, and student participation in organized cultural and social activities low. Many of the students had no intention of working in the trade for which they were training. Some 20–30 percent of graduates failed to report to their assigned places of work after graduation. Those trained on the job performed significantly better in their work than did PTU graduates. By the mid-1980s, public opinion had turned against the PTUs.

While the PTUs were intended to train lower level workers, it was the role of secondary specialist schools (SSUZs) to train students for middle level technical work. Although a few of them, particularly those providing arts education, were highly prestigious, academic standards in the SSUZs were generally low. In 1975, 40 percent of students in SSUZs were training for jobs in industry and construction; 17 percent in agriculture; 12 percent for law and economics; 11 percent for health, physical culture, and sports; 9 percent for education; and the remainder for transport. Enrollments were strong, with some 4,700,000 students in SSUZs in 1978. But many applicants were poorly prepared and required preparatory courses before being admitted. Like the PTUs, the SSUZs were scorned by educated society. Their low repute influenced the social composition of the student body. The great majority of SSUZ students came from worker and peasant backgrounds, further exacerbating social stratification in a society professing social equality.

Teachers

The expanding school system required an ever-growing corps of teachers. The Academy of Pedagogical Sciences of the Russian Republic was established in 1943. It included various branches of educational research including History and Theory of Pedagogy, Teaching Methods, Defectology, Natural Sciences, and others. It became an all-union institution in 1966. As in the past, much was demanded of teachers. Official pedagogy in the USSR placed full responsibility for the success of students on their teachers. Teachers were expected to be steeped in Marxist-Leninist theory, be masters of their subject specialization, and skilled pedagogues. In addition, they were to be influential activists in their community.

In teacher education, ideological upbringing trumped subject content. Prospective teachers spent more hours on political courses than on education theory, psychology, and teaching methods combined. A directive of 1967 noted: "The graduate of the pedagogic school is the warrior of the ideological front, the bearer of party ideas."[25] The role of teachers was to convey effectively a body of knowledge dictated from above; the role of students was to memorize it. The successors to the tsarist teachers' seminaries and teachers' institutes were the pedagogic colleges and pedagogic institutes. Pedagogic colleges prepared elementary schoolteachers at a level of education comparable to that of the complete secondary school. They offered two types of programs. The first admitted students with eight years of general education. Prospective primary

Figure 8.2 Russian teacher holding a book as she presides over a lesson that children carefully read along. Note that here the teacher follows while pupils read aloud from the textbook.
Source: © Margaret Bourke-White/The LIFE Picture Collection/Getty Images.

schoolteachers took a four-year program; kindergarten teachers studied for three-and-a-half years. The second program type took students with a complete secondary education into a two-year course centered on pedagogical training.

The goal of providing universal complete secondary schooling required the training of a host of subject specialists for the higher grades, that is, teachers of mathematics, the sciences, languages, and others. The pedagogic institutes admitted students who had attained a complete secondary education as well as graduates of specialized secondary schools. They trained subject specialists in a four-year program for one specialization and a five-year program for two. Universities also trained subject specialists for secondary schools. Their students underwent five years of study for one subject specialization. Secondary schoolteachers who came through the universities graduated with little or no pedagogical training and were poorly prepared for the rigors of the high school classroom.

Although there were excellent teachers who found ways within the rigid structure to inspire their students, the general quality of teaching was poor. Elementary teachers began their training at age 15 and graduated at 19. It was difficult to instill in them the skills required for teaching in elementary schools where problem students were routinely placed in regular classes. Secondary schoolteachers who had received their training in pedagogic institutes often had a weak grasp of their subject specialization.

University-trained specialists knew their subject well but lacked training in teaching methods. Practice teaching was more fictional than real as students were used to fill the many vacancies and so received no supervision from experienced mentors. Although about 60 percent of university graduates became teachers, the profession was often their second choice. The better students attained the best job opportunities elsewhere in the economy. Teaching for many was a default. On graduation teachers were assigned to postings. Those sent to remote areas often did not report.

The authorities did their best to raise the image of the profession in the eyes of the public. Institutes for the Improvement of Qualifications had existed since 1938. By the mid-1960s there were one hundred of them offering refresher courses. They provided information on new developments in subject matter and methods. Teachers required recertification every five years and took course upgrades if found wanting. Salaries were linked to educational qualifications, length of service, and the location of schools. Rural teachers were paid less but received free housing, heating, and lighting. Teachers could also get additional pay for conducting extracurricular activities or taking positions of responsibility. After twenty-five years of service, teachers could retire with 40 percent of their full salary. Teachers also were awarded honors and decorations. The best in the eyes of the authorities could receive the highest orders of the state, such as the Order of Lenin and the Order of the Red Banner of Labor.[26] Occasional pay raises did little to improve teachers' standing relative to other professionals. After a brief hiatus the feminization of the profession resumed. Seventy percent of teachers in 1970 were women and their predominance grew in the next decades.

Military Education

The Soviet Union developed an elaborate complex of higher military schools and institutes for officer training.[27] An important source of students for officer training institutes were the Suvorov and Nakhimov schools. The Suvorov schools were founded in 1943 to educate the sons of officers killed during the war. The students were admitted at age 10 and given a complete secondary education along with military training that qualified them for officer training schools. Most graduates of Suvorov schools entered the armed forces. There were eleven schools by the end of the war and some 4,500 graduates. The decline in the number of orphaned boys in the postwar period saw the opening of admissions to the schools to sons of serving, retired, and reserve officers and even of civilians. The age of admission went up to 11. Following a further reorganization in 1963, students were admitted at age 15 or 16 into a three-year program, reduced to two years in 1969. By 1970 only eight Suvorov schools remained. Three Nakhimov schools also first opened in 1943 to educate sons of naval officers killed in action. By 1944 there were five schools. Age at admission ranged from 10 to 14 years. Only one school remained by 1955. It now admitted boys at age 15 or 16 who received a general education and naval training. Over time fewer and fewer graduates of the Suvorov and Nakhimov students went on to officer training. Increasingly they became the preserve of the sons of the elites. A third institution founded before the Second World War was the Moscow Military Music School. Students entered it at age

15 for a general education and music study. They went on to musical careers in the military.[28]

Special Education

Schools for children with physical disabilities existed in the Soviet Union from 1918. Their availability then and in the 1980s varied greatly from region to region. Guidelines called for the screening of 1-year-olds, again at 3 years of age, and once more on enrollment in school at age 6 or 7. Those identified with a disability were placed in special day schools or often boarding schools designed for a particular condition. They provided a general education of 8–12 years and training in a suitable vocational skill. Graduates of the schools had to be employed in a factory, workshop, or on a collective farm. In the 1920s and into the 1930s, children with learning disabilities also attended special schools. Stalin's attack on pedology in 1937 resulted in most of them being returned to regular classrooms. The notion of learning disability was dismissed. Good teaching would remedy slow learning. That proved to be difficult. The presence of slow learners in classes that proceeded at one pace left many behind. Up to 10 percent of pupils in the 1950s repeated one or more grades. The Khrushchev reform of 1958 again provided more schools or classes for pupils with learning disabilities and mandated screening to assign pupils to appropriate learning environments. A lack of standards of assessment as well as limited availability of special schools, however, meant that to the end of the Soviet Union, students without visible disabilities but who struggled in school often remained in regular schools. As in the 1930s, teachers often passed them through the system to enable them to attend vocational schools.

Higher Education

Brezhnev took a special interest in higher education. Between 1964 and 1975 he oversaw the establishment of twenty-four new universities for a total of sixty-six. Universities, however, made up only a small proportion of all higher education institutions (VUZs). There were 866 of them in 1978. Universities taught and conducted research in the humanistic and pure sciences. All students taking those subjects were listed under the humanities. They along with students in colleges of arts, music, law, economics, and teacher training made up just over 40 percent of all students in the early 1970s. Practical and applied subjects, such as law, medicine, engineering, agriculture, and others, were taught in specialist VTUZs. Technical institutes and colleges accounted for just under 40 percent of all higher education students. Around 11 percent of them were studying agriculture and 8.5 percent medicine. The applied sciences offered just under a hundred technical specializations. All higher education institutions were considered to be equal in status although some enjoyed higher prestige than others in public opinion.

Most institutions of higher education fell under the jurisdiction of the newly formed Ministry of Higher Education. A few, such as health studies, were administered elsewhere. Institutions of higher education enjoyed little autonomy. Rectors of VUZs were appointed by the ministry. An Academic Council, consisting of a deputy rector, heads of departments, some professors, representatives of the Communist Party, the Komsomol, trade unions, and ministry officials, assisted rectors. The Academic Council appointed deans from among the faculty. Brezhnev increased Party control over the administration of VUZs. In 1977 all rectors, 65 percent of Doctors of Science, and 51 percent of Candidates of Science were Party members.

Students competed for higher education places. Those with references from the Party, Komsomol, or trade unions were given preference, but only if they met the examination standards. The days of accelerated advancement for workers and peasants had long passed. Two years of work experience between secondary school and admission to higher education was, however, expected of applicants. Tuition was free. Students had to choose a specialist subject at the beginning of a five-year course of study; it was very difficult to switch specializations mid-course. Courses in programs were prescribed. Electives were few, optional, and additional to required courses. Workloads were heavy and reading lists long. Lectures were the main tools of instruction; there was little discussion. Success in examinations rested on regurgitation of the materials studied. Individual thought and initiative were frowned upon. On graduation, students were assigned to any job in any place in the Soviet Union. Although there were penalties for noncompliance, no shows were common. Surveys in the 1970s revealed that only 15–20 percent of students intended to work in production upon graduation and 50 percent intended to go on to do graduate research. The basic degree was a diploma. After an additional three years of study, final examinations, and the presentation and defense of an original piece of research, the degree of Candidate of Sciences was awarded. Doctors of Science were few. Many more years of successful independent research were required to qualify for the doctorate.

Communist Upbringing

Upbringing (vospitanie) in communist ideology, morality, and Soviet patriotism was an essential component of schooling at all levels. Upbringing referred to character training and the development of personality. The Twenty-Second Party Congress in 1961 had set out a blueprint for the creation of the "new persons." They would hold a scientific worldview, have experienced a labor upbringing, be steeped in communist morality, proletarian internationalism, and socialist patriotism, and act as soldiers in eliminating the remnants of capitalism and unmasking bourgeois ideology.[29] At the lower levels of education, ideology was not made explicit. Instead, subject content was manipulated to instill desired patterns of belief and behavior. The moral and ideological values of all subjects were stressed. Biology taught materialism and ultimately atheism. Chemistry was a tool of communist construction. Each class had a tutor who encouraged collectivism in the carrying out of school duties and organized events of cooperation. Tutors worked with youth organizations to organize extracurricular activities that promoted collectivism, duty, and Soviet patriotism. The Octobrists for younger children, the Young Pioneers, and the Komsomol served to engage pupils both in and outside of the school in activities that reinforced the values of labor, community, and socialism.[30] Secondary school students were required to take courses on Soviet law and a Social Studies course that included Marxism-Leninism among other subjects in their final two years of study. The also took a course in Ethics and the Psychology of Family Life. Conspicuous for its absence in the curriculum was sex education. Students might learn the basics of human reproduction in biology classes, but the emotional and psychological aspects of sexuality were ignored.

Doubts about the effectiveness of the teachers of ideological and political courses led Brezhnev in 1966 to establish institutes for the training of social scientists who were charged with the task of socializing students. In the Soviet context, "social sciences" referred to ideological training. In 1967 a Laboratory of Sociological Research on Problems of Student Upbringing was established within the Leningrad Institute of Complex Research. In the same year the Central Committee underlined the perceived crisis in ideological training. It called for the preparation of teachers capable of leading students in the deep and creative study of the classics of Marxism-Leninism and of fostering the independent work of students. The Central Committee positioned the Komsomol as central to linking ideological work in the classroom and its realization in society. It should organize Lenin readings, bring students and Party leaders together, organize courses and seminars, and promote student participation in patriotic activities. In the early 1970s the Komsomol established centers in institutions of higher education to link theoretical and practical social sciences to the practical activities of students. At the same time the ministry established in VUZs a program called sociopolitical practice. It combined lectures with practical work. Every student was required to undertake a project that arose from issues discussed in the social science curriculum. Students were assessed on the level of their activism.

Concern that students studying technical subjects might focus solely on their specialization to the neglect of ideology led in 1974 to increased hours of study of Marxism-Leninism and examinations in scientific communism in all higher and specialist secondary schools. All freshman students attending VUZs also took a course of 120 hours or more in the History of the Communist Party of the Soviet Union. In their second and third years they took Marxist-Leninist Philosophy (90–200 hours) and Political Economy (140–250 hours), and Foundations of Scientific Communism (80 hours) in year five of their studies.

These and subsequent measures to enhance ideological studies had little practical effect. The efforts of social science teachers and Komsomol activists to engage students in ideological discussions or projects were met with indifference by most students. The relevance of ideological training to their future personal and professional lives was not apparent to them. Only those who hoped to join the Party took much interest in the required courses. Others did enough to pass and quickly forgot what they had studied.

Non-Russian Education

As a multiethnic entity, the USSR was compelled to address the question of language in schools. From the beginning, Lenin declared the equality of languages. He shared

Il'minskii's conviction that true conversion to a religion or ideology was possible only if received in the native tongue. He rejected Russian as a state language or even its imposition as a compulsory language of study in schools. Consequently, Soviet policy guaranteed non-Russians an education in their native tongues. The policy of *korenizatsiia* (indigenization) set as its goal the merger of all nations into a single socialist community, but only after national cultures had had a chance to flourish during the stage of the building of socialism. Culture, however, was narrowly understood as restricted to language. The content of education to be delivered in non-Russian languages was to be uniformly socialist. National in form, socialist in content was the heart of Soviet language and cultural policy.

The regime undertook a major effort to enable the flowering of the languages and literatures of non-Russians. Linguists created fifty-two new and sixteen reformed alphabets for oral languages, for the most part based on the Latin alphabet. Traditional written languages were equipped with modern vocabularies. The translation and publication of textbooks in the languages of minorities began immediately. By 1931, textbooks existed in seventy-six languages of the USSR. Stalin embraced fully Lenin's formula. "If we want to raise the broad masses to a higher level of culture," he wrote, "we must develop the native language of every nationality maximally."[31]

The task was challenging. There were far too few native teachers. Many schools for non-Russians had Russian teachers who did not know the language of their pupils. Some schools in mixed ethnic regions had pupils speaking two or more languages, without a teacher for any of them. Russians living in non-Russian areas were encouraged to learn the native language. Few did. Instead, they attended Russian-language schools, usually located in urban centres. Russian and non-Russian children rarely mingled. Many non-Russian schools did not teach Russian as a subject of study as educators expected. In some areas Russian was mocked by locals, raising ethnic tensions. In 1938 the Central Committee made Russian a compulsory subject of study in non-Russian schools. Although Stalin sharply rebuked instances of Great Russian chauvinism, Russian was increasingly positioned as the language of culture bringing superior civilization to backward peoples. In 1945 Stalin glorified the role of the Russian people in the victory over Nazism. At Stalin's death, however, most peoples who had a written language received primary education in their own language. As well, twelve ethnic groups had seven-year schools and six had ten-year schools that were taught in their native languages. Higher education was conducted in Russian.

The reform of schools in 1958 removed the provision for the compulsory teaching of Russian in non-Russian schools but also rejected the principle that children should be educated in their own language. Instead, non-Russians could choose freely their preferred language of learning. Parents recognized that social and professional advancement required Russian language facility and often opted for Russian as the preferred language of instruction with the native language as a subject of study. The Twenty-Second Party Congress confirmed the provisions and named Russian as the "inter-nationality language of communication." Brezhnev supported Khrushchev's claim that the nationality question had been resolved: socialist content had rendered national in form superfluous. The Community of Peoples was now united, with Russian as the shared language. Russian was believed to be not only the language of science and technology but also the most effective vehicle for the understanding of Marxism-Leninism. Recall that Lenin, on the contrary, had believed that only the native language could imprint the ideology of Marxism on the human heart.

Instruction in native languages did not disappear. Around fifty languages remained as languages of instruction in the 1980s. Parental choice varied widely. Kazakhs opted heavily for Russian for their children. Ukrainians, except in Kiev, preferred Ukrainian. Russian, however, was increasingly promoted through special elective courses in schools and extended hours of Russian instruction. The methods of teaching Russian were standardized. In 1966 the republican ministries of national enlightenment were amalgamated into a single Ministry of Education at the union level and a single Russian language and literature curriculum was implemented.

Outcomes

The Brezhnev years witnessed the economic decline of the USSR. Central planning was proving to be an ineffective instrument to meet the needs of a society of growing complexity and sophistication. The outreach of the military was overstretched and unaffordable. Bureaucratic routine and police repression of dissidence stifled innovation and independent thought. Revelations about the Stalinist past undermined the credibility of a Marxist rhetoric that even Party leaders no longer believed. Greater knowledge of conditions in the West subverted carefully crafted tales about the horrors of capitalism. Careerism was both rife and despised by citizens.

The achievements of the regime in advancing education in the USSR from the mid-1930s to the middle of the 1980s were largely quantitative. Between 1927 and 1985, enrollments in all institutions of education grew by 453 percent while the population increased by 188 percent. Much of the gain was in the postwar era. From 1960 to 1970, for example, school enrollments grew by 45.5 percent while the school-age population expanded by 19.1 percent. The goal of providing universal secondary education for school-age children was nearly complete by the end of the 1970s.[32] Educational opportunities for girls expanded rapidly, especially in the postwar period. Although 72 percent of PTU students in 1970 were males, the emphasis on light consumer industries under Brezhnev fostered a steady increase of women in vocational roles. Women also made impressive advances in secondary education. They outnumbered men in specialized secondary education in both urban and rural areas by the early 1970s. General secondary schools in cities had more female than male students, although males remained the majority in rural general secondary schools.[33]

By practically every measure, quality in education was low. The industrialization drive was accompanied by a massive demographic shift from rural to urban areas. By 1975, 61 percent of the populace was urban-based and the percentage grew rapidly in subsequent years. The school-age population in the countryside shrank, leaving a host of "pygmy" schools with small enrollments. Rural schools made up 75 percent of all schools but served only 40 percent of the school-age population. By the 1980s, the physical conditions in schools were worsening. Twenty-one percent lacked central heating, 30 percent did without running water, and 40 percent lacked indoor toilets.[34]

The growth of the urban population overwhelmed the schools. Many operated two or even three shifts each day. Few had the facilities needed to meet the requirements of the curriculum, especially workshops to support vocational learning.

The rapid expansion of elementary and especially secondary education placed heavy strains on teaching resources. The feminization of the profession resumed in the postwar period. By the mid-1980s, 70 percent of teachers were women. The stress in teacher training at pedagogical colleges and institutes was on communist upbringing. Subject specialization and pedagogy were secondary concerns. Political activism outside the classroom was as central to the mission of teachers as their work within the school. Students in training had little or no practice teaching before placement in a school. Rural regions struggled to find and retain teachers. Teachers trained for work in secondary schools often knew their subject specialization well but lacked pedagogical training. Short pedagogical courses mounted by education authorities were often poorly organized or out of reach of the teachers who most needed them. In spite of efforts to raise the prestige of the profession through awards and medals, pay remained low. Teaching was often a second career choice. It should, however, be noted that poor training does not necessarily mean poor teaching. Although supervision was close and the curriculum and methods largely prescribed, teachers had been mandated since the reforms of Stalin to assert authority in the classroom. While some no doubt abused their powers, others turned them to serve the best interests of their charges.

Although the emphasis on vocational training and narrow specialization in higher education following the Second World War served the broad interests of the state adequately, complaints about the quality of graduates from secondary and vocational schools were endemic. Heavy teaching loads and the emphasis on prescribed specializations in institutions of higher education inhibited research and innovation. Only a handful of institutions engaged in research, and only one or two institutes rose to international standards in research. The unfolding age of the computer in the West had largely passed the Soviet Union by in the early 1980s. The economy rested heavily on manual and middle-level vocational outputs; mechanization remained low.

The rapid growth of secondary education was not matched by the expansion of higher education. Of great concern to the Party as early as the 1960s was the changing attitudes of students toward employment. More and more school graduates aspired to continue into higher education at a time when the economy needed middle-level workers and not more specialists. Since the number of places in universities and technical institutes grew only slowly, competition for admission increased. Growing social stratification shaped educational opportunity. Although children of workers and peasants broadly aspired to occupations higher than those of their parents, their expectations were modest. Even those who aspired to higher education were victims of the bottleneck at the university level. By the 1980s, the family background of students was closely related to academic achievement. Children of workers and peasants were far more likely to drop out of school after grade eight than those from intelligentsia backgrounds, and only a few of the children of workers and peasants who managed to graduate with complete secondary schooling went on to higher education.

The efforts of the regime to shore up communist upbringing in education brought diminishing results. Marxist-Leninist ideology appeared remote from the lives and careers of citizens. As belief in communism faded, nationalism among Russians and non-Russians crept in to replace it. The policy of korenizatsiia, with its stress on ethnicity, weakened older religious identities and strengthened national consciousness at the expense of communist ideology. Korenizatsiia did produce a *lingua franca* but also fostered native languages adapted to modernity. By the 1980s, Russians were slipping into a minority in the Union, causing growing unease among them and fueling Russian nationalism. Ethnic tensions rose and played a significant part in the last days of the Soviet Union. Ethnic division combined with the economic crisis and ideological disorientation heralded the last attempt to redeem the Bolshevik experiment.

9

Ends and Beginnings: Gorbachev to Putin

By the early 1980s, the Soviet Union was in a demographic and economic crisis. The labor force was declining in a labor intensive economy. In 1975 roughly 42 percent of Soviet industry was not mechanized. Ten years later the percentage was still 35 percent. Urbanization and the growing predominance of the nuclear and often single-child family resulted in a drop of 10 percent in school enrollments between 1970 and 1980. Students and their parents aspired to higher education as the road to social status, but the large number of higher education graduates could no longer be absorbed into the white-collar workforce. Seventy percent of needed labor was in blue-collar occupations. Few youths, however, were interested in manual labor. Recruitment and retention of young workers were difficult. Between 20 to 30 percent of graduates of professional-technical schools did not report to their assignments and 40 percent changed their occupation after graduation. Productivity was low and the work often shoddy. The Soviet economy had been built on extensive development through the expansion of raw material and manpower inputs. Further growth depended on a transition to intensive development through more efficient use of existing resources and of modern technology to raise productivity. The sclerotic bureaucratic machinery of central planning was ill-adapted to oversee the needed changes.

The Education Reform of 1984

In 1984 the government undertook yet another school reform. The reform did not represent a radical break with the past but sought to adapt an existing system of schooling to meet changing economic and social needs. The old pattern of positioning education as a function of the economy within the context of communist upbringing persisted. The planning process included a wide public inquiry that disclosed a great deal of dissatisfaction with existing schools. In early 1984 Mikhail Sergeevich Gorbachev became chair of the school reform commission. As Second Secretary to the Communist Party, he appointed new leadership to the Ministry of Education to effect the reform. The resulting "Fundamental Guidelines for the General and Vocational Schools" of April 1984 were in part a return to the Khrushchev reform of 1958. The goal was the old one of linking life to learning through labor. The reform aimed to persuade as many students as possible to choose a career that did not require higher education. All students were to acquire a skill in a common manual occupation. The reform envisaged raising all professional-technical schools to the secondary level and doubling the percentage of 15-year-olds entering them out of general education schools from a third to two-thirds by 1990. General schools were encouraged to provide vocational guidance to direct students toward entering the professional-technical schools (PTUs) at age 15.

In offering more general education along with vocational training, the reformers saw the secondary-level PTU as the fulfillment of the ideal of the unified labor polytechnical school of the 1920s. The legislation required a labor component in grades ten and eleven of the complete secondary school as well as in the first eight grades. Graduates of complete secondary education were also encouraged to enter a PTU for a year of vocational training. The reform mandated that all schools be attached by law to a base enterprise. Schools signed contracts with a farm or factory that obligated the enterprise to equip the school workshop and provide the materials needed for the workshop's production. The enterprise also had to make available on-the-job work for senior students, provide them with suitable clothing and meals, and certify the skills that they acquired. Production Training Combines, formed in 1974 to facilitate school-factory collaborations, were now charged with linking all schools to an enterprise. Some 2,700 of these combines were functioning in 1985–6.

The reform reduced the school age from 7 to 6. Combined with an expansion of preschool care and longer elementary and secondary school days, the lowering of the school age enabled more mothers to remain in the shrinking workforce. Teachers received a raise, a lighter teaching load, and improved in-service training. The reform called for the gradual introduction of new courses into the general school curriculum. Some of the courses aimed to address social problems: alcoholism, divorce, and the strains of family life. Courses in computing were especially promoted. All senior secondary school students were now required to take "Principles of Information Science and Computer Technology." New, more practical and engaging textbooks were commissioned.

Gorbachev became First Secretary of the Communist Party of the Soviet Union in March 1985. He believed in the communist ideal and hoped to invigorate it through a two-pronged policy of *glasnost'* (openness) and *perestroika* (restructuring). The aim of glasnost' was to engage the Soviet public in constructive criticism within the framework of Party leadership. He hoped to find allies within the public, and particularly among the intelligentsia, to break the hold of an entrenched conservative bureaucracy that he held responsible for the decline of the USSR. Openness would expose the crimes and failures of the Party in the past and establish a basis for reform. The political objective of perestroika also targeted conservative opposition to reform within the Party through its democratization. Its economic goal was to invigorate the planned, state-owned economy by injecting into it elements of the market. In particular, Gorbachev hoped to break up large and inefficient industrial and farm monopolies by promoting certain capitalist features like self-financing, entrepreneurship, and pay linked to productivity. Although he opposed individual private ownership, he encouraged the growth of for-profit cooperative enterprises.

Gorbachev wanted to make every citizen "a fighter for perestroika."[1] The school, as envisioned in the reform of 1984 in which he had played a prominent part, was central to that goal. Its role was to mould the psychology and thinking of youth to the principles of restructuring. Labor remained at the heart of his vision. The school should combine general with polytechnical education and be fully aligned with industry and agriculture. The youth organizations, Octobrists, Pioneers, and Komsomol, would liaise between the worlds of school and work. Upbringing in communist ethics in school was an essential feature of his vision. The curriculum contained a heavy labor component from grade seven on. Forty percent of teaching hours in grades seven to nine were allocated to labor training. In grades eight and nine, students were required to train for work in construction, metalworking, or agriculture. Openness in schools meant that teachers should be free to tell the truth about the errors of the Party. Gorbachev believed that a major failing of the old system of education was its neglect of the development of the human personality. The old school had required students blindly to accept Party dictates; it had led to indifference in school and work. The reformed school should encourage the growth of independent thinking and personal initiative and meld individual will with the collective good.

In April 1985 the ministry issued the "Standard Rules for Students." The rules were an attempt to reinforce social discipline. Problems with absenteeism, drugs, sex, and other frowned-upon behaviors were common in Soviet schools in the 1980s. Under the new rules, students in the first four years of school were to learn about working people and the jobs that they performed. Those in grades five to nine were urged to take part in socially useful and productive labor and choose a future occupation. Students in grades ten and eleven were expected to perform productive labor and master the skills of the occupation they had chosen. The rules created a four-point grading system for behavior, conscientious study, and socially useful labor. A student who received an unsatisfactory grade in the ninth year could be excluded from writing the state leaving examination. The rules incorporated many of the features familiar from earlier versions: respect for elders, standing to answer a teacher's question, industry, patriotism, comradeship, and courtesy.

In June 1985 the government announced that the Soviet Union's three million teachers would be recertified by 1990. Beginning in 1986 each year, 20 percent of the teaching corps underwent a complex review and were rated on a scale from one to four. Most were renewed, some ordered to take in-service training, and a few dismissed. Future salary increases were tied to the review. Teacher-methodologists were appointed locally to counsel teachers in classroom techniques. As earlier, honors and titles were awarded for excellence in teaching. In the new atmosphere of openness, teachers themselves organized to address the issues the profession faced. A "Pedagogy of Cooperation" movement called for a broad coalition of students, teachers, parents, and education administrators to reform the school. A Creative Union of Teachers formed as a counterpoint to the official teachers' union. The *Teachers' Gazette* (*Uchitel'skaia gazeta*) emerged as a forum for discussion. Teachers organized so-called Eureka clubs to promote innovation in teaching among their members.

The Academy of Pedagogical Sciences came under heavy criticism for its conservative and conformist educational agenda. In an effort to reduce bureaucracy and unify a rambling educational system, a major reorganization of the administration of education in March 1988 saw the merger of the Ministry of Education, the Ministry of Higher and Middle Special Education, and the State Committee for Vocational and Technical Education into the State Committee for National Education of the Soviet Union headed by Gennadi Iagodin. His views were deeply influenced by the pedagogy of cooperation movement. Like Gorbachev, he sought to motivate and not to compel students to learn. Authoritarian teaching methods were antiquated, he urged. Teachers should have a part in choosing and developing instructional methods, the writing of textbooks, and in appointing their leaders. The differing needs of students should be met with greater flexibility. Committees of teachers, students, parents, and representatives of community organizations should have a greater say in the hiring of staff and the financing of schools. The reformers announced in 1989 the opening of several lyceums beginning in 1990 to provide alternatives to general education schools and stimulate the reform of curricula and methodologies. Not all teachers agreed with the changes. At the All-Russian Congress of Teachers in 1988, reformers and conservatives clashed, and the congress failed to produce a consensus on the way forward.

The reform for all its good intentions had little effect on practice in schools during the years of glasnost'. The plan to start pupils in school at age 6 instead of 7 was slow to proceed. The heavy workload required in the first year of school proved to be difficult for 6-year olds. The workload in all grades was arduous. The entrenched communalist mentality limited attention to individual students' needs. Classes continued to be conducted as collectives. Students moved forward together and usually, in the lower grades, kept the same teacher. There were no individual schedules and few options. The class as a collective also prevailed in senior grades. Youth organizations continued to foster conformity. Most students aged 6 or 7–10 belonged to the Octobrist youth organization and moved on from ages 11 to 15 into the Pioneers. A smaller group was recruited at age 16 into the Komsomol where they remained until age 25. Each class had a youth detachment divided into links. The school brigade comprised the class detachments. The detachments competed among themselves in behavior and socially useful activities. Group criticism forced flagging individual members into line. Far from promoting individualism and personal initiative, the school fostered group conformity. The revised textbooks that were promised were slow to materialize. In 1988 history examinations were cancelled for lack of suitable textbooks.

The reform faced larger obstacles. The funding for education in Imperial Russia and the Soviet Union had for most of its history been based on the "leftover" principle. Once the needs of other sectors were met, education received what remained. The shrinking economy saw funding for education in the Soviet Union decline from 11 percent of the state budget in 1970 to 8 percent in 1986. Pledges to increase funding in 1988 were not met. The goal of reducing class sizes from forty to thirty students could not be realized. Some eight million students attended schools with two shifts. Many schools had difficulty finding a base enterprise where students could do their required labor. A few successful partnerships formed; they were the exceptions. As ever, factory managers were reluctant to take students on. Those who did take students provided menial and exploitative work for which they paid no wage. The addition of general education subjects to the curriculum of professional-technical schools, which were meant to be the incarnation of the unified labor school, placed too great a burden on students, most of whom were not academically inclined. Whispers reached school authorities to go easy when grading the students. A mere one in three students desired a career in manual work. Only around 10 percent of graduates of the general secondary schools went on to work in the vocational speciality they had learned in school. A paltry 24 percent of graduates of the PTUs took up the occupation for which they had trained. Far from seeing the reformed PTUs as the ideal that Gorbachev intended, the public looked down on the PTUs, which they associated with weak and badly behaved students.

The return of vocational training to the general school was unpopular as well. In the eyes of the public, the general school produced citizens and the vocational school trained workers. The large labor component in general schools made it difficult for academically strong students to prepare properly for higher education. Once more universities expressed fears about threatened standards. In February 1988, Yegor Ligachev, one of the more conservative members of the Party elite, launched a broad critique of the school reform of 1984. The reform, he said, had failed to provide guidelines for the democratization of the school system, with the result that little change had occurred. He complained of the inadequacy of funding for facilities and equipment for an expanding school network. Low-level vocational training, he regretted, was pursued at the expense of strong scientific and technical knowledge. In the same month, plans for the integrated secondary school were shelved and compulsory labor training in general schools ended. Once again students would receive nine years of general education followed by academic and vocational tracks. Enrolments in the PTUs sharply declined. The general education component in them was pared back. Most remained attached to factories for whom the schools once again trained narrow specialists. The last attempt to revive the ideal of the unified labor school had ended in failure.

Collapse of the Soviet Union

The circumstances of the disintegration of the Soviet Union are complex and can be treated only briefly here. The Brezhnev regime had paid little heed to accountable budgeting. Military overextension, chronically low industrial and agricultural productivity, and rising demographic and social stresses resulted in massive state debt. Gorbachev's plan to return to the economics of the New Economic Policy with a partial restoration of market forces was too timid to address the deep economic malaise the country faced. The USSR lacked the financial infrastructure needed to expand the market significantly. A fall in oil prices only exacerbated the problem. As the various republics increasingly asserted their autonomy, tax revenues that had once flowed to the center were sharply reduced. Citizens had accumulated considerable savings, but industry was unable to produce enough products to buy. Too much money was in pursuit of too few goods. To bolster its own revenues, the state printed more money. The result was the runaway inflation that marked the early post-Soviet years.

The Party faced a crisis of legitimacy. Its ideology had long lost widespread support, and its inability to organize the economy further undermined public belief in the country's leaders. Gorbachev's efforts to democratize the Party through elections to responsible posts badly split the leadership. Their quarrels went public, underlining Party weakness. Glasnost' had already exposed the failings of the past. The democratic centralism that Lenin had imposed on the Party was antithetical to real democracy. In an effort to build a foundation of support for reform outside of his squabbling party, Gorbachev arranged for competitive elections in March 1989 to a new Congress of People's Deputies. Candidates ran singly and not in organized parties. Although communists did gain election, so too did many noncommunists from a variety of organizations and backgrounds. It was a huge assembly of 2,250 members. It choose a smaller group of 542 delegates to conduct congress debates. In 1990 the congress elected Gorbachev president of the republic; he also remained First Secretary of the Party. The idea of the one-party state was fatally compromised. Each of the republics also held elections of people's deputies, further eroding central control.

The decline of communist ideology and of the monopoly on power of the Party left a partial vacuum in the Soviet Union and beyond. Gorbachev openly encouraged reformers in the states within the Warsaw Pact. Where reform was resisted, emboldened publics in Poland, Czechoslovakia, and elsewhere in the pact grew more assertive. Reform turned in 1989 to open resistance. Most of the revolutions in the Eastern European countries were bloodless, Romania excepted. Communist leaders in East Europe realized that the Soviet Union would not intervene in their defense as it had in 1956 and 1968 and relinquished authority. National self-determination in the satellite states fed nationalist appetites in the Soviet Union. Interethnic strife broke out. There were hostilities in parts of Central Asia and the Caucasus. In March 1990 Lithuania declared its independence. Independence was delayed, but in January 1991 a conservative effort to restore order in Lithuania, in which fourteen people died, failed, and the three Baltic States quickly seized de facto independence. Their determination to leave the union was less apparent in other republics of the USSR. The final impetus for separation came from within the Russian Republic itself. By now a slight minority in the Soviet Union, Russians increasingly saw at least parts of the USSR as drags on their own development. The charismatic people's favorite, Boris Yeltsin, had become the president of the Russian Republic. The old communist order had equated Russia with the Soviet Union. Yeltsin did not. He behaved as if Russia was truly an autonomous republic and began to act independently of the Soviet government. A plebiscite in March 1991 asked Soviet citizens to decide whether a reformed USSR as a federation of equal republics that guaranteed human rights and freedom of the nationalities should be instituted. The Baltic States, Moldova, Georgia, and Armenia, already independent, did not participate in the plebiscite. Of the rest, 80 percent of voters opted for a renewed federation. The new Union of Soviet Sovereign Republics was to be declared on August 20, 1991.

Military leaders and conservatives had been shocked by the abandonment of their East European buffer. They now feared that the new political order favored by the public in the plebiscite spelled the end of Soviet power. On August 19 they staged a coup. While they hoped to persuade Gorbachev to abandon the reforms since 1985, they also wanted him to retain the presidency. He rejected their plan. Yeltsin seized the initiative. He succeeded in organizing enough support among a relatively passive public to arrest the leaders of the coup. Soldiers refused to resist those who supported him. Yeltsin banned the Communist Party in the Russian Republic; other republics followed suit, then one by one seceded from the Union. Its president, Gorbachev, now without a state, resigned his office in December 1991. The non-Russian states set out on their own courses. In the new independent Russian Federation, 80 percent of the population was Russian.

The Russian Federation

The leaders of the Federation faced daunting tasks: a transition from an authoritarian state to a European-style democracy and from a centralized planned state economy to a market economy. The Soviet Union had not been swept away on a wave of popular protest but had gradually disintegrated. Consequently, popular support for radical political and economic change was muted at best. The impetus for change came from above and not from below, a well-established precedent from the tsarist past. The immediate effect of the collapse of the USSR was a severe goods shortage. Factory production, already low, fell further amid the uncertainty of the transition. Goods once produced in other republics of the old Soviet Union were cut off. The impending breakup of the collective and state farms and the reluctance of peasants, in the face of low agricultural prices, to buy and to farm the land independently created a food crisis. Prices for scarce goods rocketed; inflation reached 2600 percent in a single year. Personal savings were quickly wiped out; pensions went unpaid; and the purchasing power of salaries tumbled. A black market second economy provided some relief but also deprived the state of revenues. Tax evasion was chronic; national income sharply declined. An attempt to enable all citizens to become shareholders through the issue of vouchers to invest in businesses and industries foundered on corruption and the unwise choices of vulnerable people who sold their vouchers merely to survive. Cheap imports of consumer goods that flooded in from the West undermined the recovery of domestic consumer industry. Domestic output by the mid-1990s declined to 55 percent of output in 1989.

Many members of the old Soviet elite were well placed to take advantage of the economic disorder. Fortunes were made. In 1995–6 the state and the new oligarchs colluded in the transfer of remaining state enterprises into private hands. Vast fortunes were transferred abroad while needed capital investment in Russia flagged. Crime was endemic. Murder rates rose as gangs protected their territories. The Russian mafia functioned with near impunity and spread its operations abroad. The general populace were the victims. Public misery spawned debilitating social problems. Alcoholism, suicides, a health crisis, falling life expectancy, and a plunging birthrate reduced the population by 4 to 144 million from 1992 to 2002. Physical and mental disorders among children drove an expansion of special schools from 59 in 1993 to 105 in 1998 and their students from 10,400 to 17,308. In the same period the number of students with learning problems in special classes grew from 117,300 to 190,000.[2] Child abandonment and the rising numbers of orphans saw nearly 600,000 children living in homes or foster care in 1997. Flight from the countryside forced the closing of just under 2,500 rural general schools. Many of the best scientific and technical minds emigrated. Although the birthrate has improved slightly in recent years, it is estimated that the population that numbered 143.4 million in 2015 will shrink to 128.6 million by 2050.[3]

Political restructuring was equally troubled. Citizens showed little confidence in the country's political and legal institutions. Public involvement in political reform was minimal. Again, change came from the top. A product of Soviet authoritarianism, President Yeltsin was unable to curb an authoritarian impulse. He made no effort to build a political party that could support his reform efforts. The State Duma, which was left over from the reforms of Gorbachev, soon clashed with the president. In September 1993 Yeltsin prorogued the Duma. Its members refused to disband and garnered some popular support. An armed conflict ensued with the loss of many lives. Yeltsin emerged victorious. In December 1993 the country approved a new constitution and elected a new parliament. The constitution created a federal state within a strong presidency. The parliament comprised an upper house of representatives from the autonomous republics and Russia's eighty-nine provinces and a lower house, half of whose representatives were elected in their districts and half appointed from party lists according to a proportional formula. Two antidemocratic parties, a right-wing nationalist party and the Communist Party, held the most seats. They gave little support to reform but were hindered by the limits on the powers of the legislature. The road to power was through the executive. The Communist candidate in the 1996 presidential election threatened a return to Soviet power. He was narrowly defeated when an uneasy coalition of oligarchs, successful entrepreneurs, and liberal intelligentsia persuaded a small majority of voters to reelect Yeltsin. In the wake of the election, Yeltsin's health declined rapidly. Several appointed premiers led the government in his stead. The last of them during Yeltsin's presidency was Vladimir Putin. He won the failing president's endorsement as his successor.

The Law on Education of 1992: General Schooling

Education reform proceeded against this tumultuous economic and political background. The political class and bureaucracy were heavily absorbed in shaping a new political order that came into being with a new constitution and election in 1993. The education reformers worked largely in isolation from that process. They produced the Law on Education in 1992 without a clear political or economic roadmap to shape its provisions. The law provided compulsory education to age 15; guaranteed an annual allocation of 10 percent of national income to the support of education, a guarantee that produced at most half that sum in future; banned political and religious groups from state schools; and legalized religious and private schools and home education with accreditation by the ministry. It established standards for teaching methods and textbooks but also empowered schools to choose among them for themselves. Provisions were made for the assessment of teaching staff. The law assumed a federal political structure within which federal and regional elements would cooperate. The federal level took over supervision of school financing and established a program for educational development. The central ministry and regional education administrations undertook cooperation agreements for the joint administration of education. The new curriculum embraced federal, regional, and school components. The existing pedagogical councils and parent committees in schools were retained. To them was added a school council made up of teachers, students, and parents with the mandate to discuss all issues pertinent to the operation of the school.

The Law on Education rested on a number of principles that were in part a reaction against the old centralized, egalitarian, and politicized school order. The principles of decentralization and regionalization promised the devolution of educational administration onto republics, regions, municipalities, and schools. Democratization sought to foster the accountability of education administrations to the public and to engage parents and students in the running of schools. Diversification pointed in a number of directions. Instead of a single moral or ideological point of view, the curriculum would provide multiple perspectives through a program of civic studies. Private schooling, home education, and alternative state schools would permit choice in education. Instead of a single curriculum for all taught at a uniform pace, diversification would allow both choice among schools of various types and streaming within schools. The principle of humanization focused on attention to the needs of individual children. The development of the rounded personality was fundamental to the reform. More humanities subjects aimed to balance the prior emphasis on science and technology but without displacing them. The reformers understood the importance of the latter to a market economy.

The reform also addressed the issue of language instruction in non-Russian schools. A survey of practices in the autonomous regions showed how far the early pledges of the Soviet government to provide education in the languages of the students had deteriorated. Only Tatars, Bashkirs, and Georgians were able to complete their education in their native tongues at the end of the Soviet period. Nine other groups enjoyed instruction in their own language for more than two but fewer than eleven years. Another ten linguistic groups received instruction in their languages for one or two years. The remaining forty-three groups had none. In 1991 an Institute for National Problems in Education formed to prepare materials for nonliterate minorities. Teacher training and in-service institutes were expected to provide national content for their curricula. The constitution of 1993 guaranteed the equality of languages. All citizens were free to choose their language of communication, upbringing, and instruction. Ethnic republics were free to use their own language. Thirty-four languages received status as state languages. All were required to use the Cyrillic alphabet. Russian was designated as the sole state language across the whole of the Russian Federation.[4]

Alternative schools, both state and non-state, proliferated in the 1990s. Experimental programs, often based on poorly understood and badly implemented methods, came and went. So-called profile schools that featured in-depth studies of particular subjects were popular. There were 7,580 of them by 1997 with 1.5 million students. In the same year the number of state lycées, which normally emphasized humanities, and gymnasiums, which featured the sciences, counted 594 with 406,000 students and 952 with 768,000 attendees, respectively. As well, there were 540 private schools, located primarily in large cities, with 50,500 students. The number was tiny beside the 21 million children of school age (6–17) in the federation. Private schools charged tuition. Both alternative state and private schools could select their students and suffered less from the social problems that engulfed general state schools.[5]

Reform did not come to all parts of the education system. Chronic underfunding by the regions hit preschool education particularly hard. Crèches and kindergartens, which had frequently been associated with a manufacturing sector, went into decline. Local authorities had to assume the costs; private providers proliferated. What had once been cheap became expensive as fees for child care grew. The preschool network of the USSR had facilitated the employment of women. Working families were particularly damaged by the reduction and expense of preschool services. Special education for those with disabilities remained unchanged. The old system of boarding schools, each devoted to a particular physical disability continued but with diminished financing. Disabled children were kept out of sight, separate from family and community. The training of special needs teachers was neglected. Although the ideas of Lev Vygotsky about the source of disabilities in genetic and social factors were revived, few steps were taken to apply them to the care of the disabled or learning challenged.

Vocational Schooling

Vocational education was especially problematic. The Soviet system of professional-technical schools as the first level of vocational education with one- to three-year programs in narrow specializations, and technicums at the second level, with two or three years of combined academic and vocational study, remained. In the 1990s many technicums upgraded to colleges providing a longer and broader general and vocational education. However, their offerings were mostly irrelevant to the needs of the changing economy. In 1999 a law reduced the number of specializations in vocational schools from 1,250 to 257. Although enrolments in the professional-technical schools declined, they remained significant. In 2000 there were 4,180 PTUs with 1.6 million students.[6] To adjust the curriculum to the needs of the market, vocational teachers would have to retrain *en masse*. That was costly. Low pay discouraged the recruitment of new staff. Youth unemployment was particularly high. Employers in the growing service sector of the economy preferred to hire graduates of the general schools rather than vocational school graduates. Ineffective as they were, however, the government saw the PTUs as a social safety valve that kept weaker students off the job market for a few more years. In 1997, however, the federal budget for PTUs was decreased and then devolved onto the regions.

Higher Education

Plans for higher education were as ambitious as those for general education. The reformers aimed to increase access to higher education through maximizing opportunities for attaining general complete secondary education. Under the State

Committee for Science and Higher Education, higher education institutions acquired the right to own their own property, to develop their own governance statutes, to control admissions, and set their own curriculum and specializations. Financing, staffing, and administration were the institutions' responsibility. The reformers aspired to equalling world standards under the UNESCO indicators of performance quality in Russia's higher education institutions.

The obstacles were many. Administrators of higher education institutions had no training in budgeting or financial management. Promised loans for students did not materialize. The imposition of fees in many of the better secondary schools deprived children from poorer families of opportunities for adequate preparation for university entrance. In addition to economic hardship, universities were expected to provide a whole range of new subjects suitable for a democratic and market oriented society. Late in 1993, most funding responsibility for them passed from the center to regional governments. The federal government provided funding only for a few high-demand specializations. Local authorities hurried to upgrade institutes into universities or academies to enhance their status. Most did so with no change in teaching personnel. Some hundred such upgrades took place in a single year, half of which involved teacher training institutes. Regional financing proved to be unreliable. Consequently, VUZs were required to seek alternative funding that resulted in a host of contracts with outsiders and questionable arrangements. Fees for optional courses and for special services proliferated. Opportunities for corruption were plentiful. University applicants were required to take only an admissions examination in the subject they intended to study. Bribes for admission were commonplace. Few faculty engaged in research, burdened as they were with heavy teaching loads and lack of research funding.

Church Schooling

The campaign of atheism following the Revolution had not entailed the total suppression of the Church. The Moscow Patriarchate had been restored in 1918 and the Church had survived in a greatly diminished form in the Soviet Union where it was permitted to operate a few seminaries. The Law on Education of 1992 forbade religion in schools, and a majority of the general public resisted any return to indoctrination of any kind in education. Nevertheless, some regions initially permitted priests into their schools. The constitution granted the right to adherents of Orthodoxy, Islam, Judaism, and Protestantism to promote their faiths. A Law on Freedom of Conscience and Religious Associations in 1997, however, recognized the special role of Orthodoxy in "the history of Russia [and] in the formation and development of its spirituality and culture."[7] The law permitted religious instruction in state schools but only outside of the education program and on a voluntary basis. While it also recognized the importance of other religions, Orthodoxy was the only Christian faith specifically mentioned in the law.

In 1991 the Church established the Synod Department for Religious Education and Catechization. Adult-education Sunday schools had revivified following the fall of the USSR. In 1992 the Church and the Ministry of Education signed a cooperation agreement and vetted a course to be taught in Sunday schools called The Law and Commandments of God. The scheme was poorly funded, and the role of the Church in the Sunday schools remained undefined. The Church persisted, however, and gradually turned the Sunday schools into a principal tool for popular religious education. The schools were open to children from age 4 or 5 and to all adults. By 2000 there were some 2,600 Sunday schools in operation with 30,000 adults and 80,000 children attending.[8] The Church also began to establish its own network of schools coordinated by the Russian Orthodox Church Education Committee. Orthodox schools with grades from kindergarten to eleven combined courses about Orthodox religion and culture with the state general school curriculum. By 2018 the system included two Orthodox Christian Academies, two Orthodox Christian Universities, thirty-five seminaries, and twenty-two Orthodox Christian theological schools and provided schooling from preschool to doctoral degrees.[9]

Obstacles to Reform

The deficiencies of the education reform and its implementation were soon apparent. The reformers had no control over the shrinking economy and had little say in setting federal and regional spending priorities. Gross domestic product (GDP) in the Russian Federation contracted every year between 1991 and 1999. By 1999 spending on education had declined to 3.2 percent of GDP. By 1994 federal funding for education represented only 13 percent of the total, the remainder falling to the regions. Regionalization of the administration of education opened disparities between better and badly off districts, threatening to fragment the system. Conditions in the schools raised mere survival over reform. Thirty-six percent of schools operated two or three shifts a day. Another 40 percent had large building repair arrears. Many rural schools still lacked electricity and running water. Soaring inflation made budgeting of already inadequate funds challenging for school administrators who lacked management training. Economic hardship gave birth to a host of social problems. The stresses of poverty, alcoholism, drugs, family breakup, and rising death rates placed on schools and teachers a debilitating social welfare role. Weakened immune systems were easy marks for contagious illnesses. Drug use among students and widespread sexual diseases were commonplace. Observers noted that from 50 to 70 percent of pupils were incapable of progressing in school due to physical and mental disorders.[10] The Pioneers and Komsomol had organized much of the extracurricular life of students in Soviet times. Their exclusion left students to form their own groups. Many of them were antisocial. Right-wing organizations found ready recruits among disillusioned and struggling students.

The Law on Education had failed to delineate clearly the responsibilities of the federal, regional, and school partners for schooling. By 1995, seventy-three of eighty-nine regions had established their own education programs. Such decentralization threatened extreme regionalization. Although the federal level set overall standards, the ministry found it difficult to evaluate the regional and school components. These went in many directions and potentially raised the danger of further fragmentation and widely differing standards. The rise of alternative schools with a heavy emphasis on institutions for the gifted raised concerns about educational equality. Extending choice for some threatened to limit the extent of provision for all students. Critics pointed to the risk that the general schools would become a dumping ground for the academically less able. Others worried about standards in private schools. The Law on Education provided for accreditation of schools. Inspectors were to review and license them. There were, however, too few inspectors, and many of those on the job were poorly trained. At least in the early years of the reform some schools operated without a license.

If decentralization and diversification posed problems, so too did the principle of humanization. The infant market economy had little regard for the well-rounded personality. Parents and their children wanted training that would result in lucrative jobs. The humanities subjects in the new curriculum were seen by many as luxuries. Only foreign languages were viewed as useful instruments for future success. At higher levels, law, management, and computer technology dominated specializations. Conservatives used standards as a weapon against reform. They argued that programs diluted by an emphasis on the humanities weakened the sciences and lowered standards. A survey found that 45 percent of parents believed humanization was harmful.[11] Teachers should be strict and demanding rather than equal partners with students in learning. A study in 1991 had found that 70 percent of parents wished their child to enter an experimental program. A repeat study in 1996 saw that number drop to 35 percent. As the reform unfolded it became evident that the idea of democratization in education was an imposition from above that was not welcomed or understood by the public. In most schools the boards established by the Law on Education, with some exceptions, did not work. School heads often curtailed their roles in favor of top-down administration.

Teachers

The Achilles' heel of the reform was teacher training. The success of the reform rested heavily on preparing teachers to act as "change agents" in schools, a task for which their previous training and experience ill-suited them. Although many pedagogical institutes reinvented themselves as pedagogical colleges or universities, the training they provided remained largely unchanged from Soviet times. The same was true of in-service training. While many consulting agencies offered seminars and workshops, access to them was limited. Many teachers could not afford to take time off for supplementary training; often the costs of travel to and accommodations while in the course were prohibitive. Some teachers did receive training in new methods but on resuming or taking up their posts soon reverted to the old ways. Most teachers were unaware or badly informed about the objectives of the reform. Established teachers saw no reason to change their approach. Younger staff, who were more open to innovation, clashed with their elders and with school heads. Some regions hired methods teachers who traveled from school to school advising teachers about new ways of instruction. They had minimal effect.

Decentralization included the devolution of the federal portion of teachers' salaries to the regions. Some of the money disappeared. Teachers' salaries fell to 45 percent of what they had been under the soviets. Often these meager salaries were in arrears. In 1997 the Duma allocated three billion roubles to pay what was owed. Within a year arrears had again accumulated.[12] To scratch out a living, teachers often took on heavy overloads. No time remained for preparing new and innovative materials or even to refresh old notes. The low salaries made recruitment onerous. Some 40 percent of students who attended pedagogical colleges or universities did not teach. Their goal was preparation for a higher degree and not a career in teaching. There were many vacancies in schools, especially in rural areas. Teachers routinely left the profession at the first opportunity. Retirees in need of income often returned to the classroom. They were firmly wedded to the old methods.

Even teachers eager to innovate met obstacles. The preparation of textbooks and other teaching materials takes up to eight years. Their distribution over a vast network of underfunded entities took yet more time. Teachers were urged to produce their own materials; few had either the ability or the time to do so. Instead, the old texts prevailed as did the old attitude that the text is the curriculum. The preparation of textbooks was often in the hands of the same people who had prepared Soviet texts. Many of the new textbooks that were produced were overburdened with facts and dull to read. The expectation that teachers, who had no experience of democracy, would democratize the school and classroom was unrealistic. No guidance was given; no textbooks on the ways of democracy were available. The more aware doubted that it was the role of the school to train students for democracy in any case. The rejection of enforced upbringing went deep. Teachers felt and, in fact, were undervalued by society. They made their feelings known. In 1998 a strike involved 1.8 million teachers. The results of labor action were few.

Retrenchment Again

Vladimir Putin assumed the presidency of the Russian Federation in 2000. He oversaw the recentralization of control over education as part of a larger program of the recentralization of political power within the federation. In a series of moves that culminated in 2004 with a change from the local election of regional governors to their appointment from the center, he undermined regional autonomy in the federation without fully abandoning the federal structure set out in the constitution of 1993. He was abetted by the failure of the constitution to delineate clearly the responsibilities of the center and the regions. From the beginning of his presidency Putin systematically eliminated any institution or political position that threatened the authority of the presidency. Under his guidance, Russia has become a quasi-federal state under a political system called variously "illiberal democracy" and "managed democracy." Elections are regularly held, but only token rivals are able to run for office. Cracks in "managed democracy" have recently appeared, but President Putin's authority is not yet seriously threatened at the time of writing. He presides over a hugely corrupt political and social structure in which economic disparity is among the highest in the world. He assumed office just as the economic crisis of the 1990s was ebbing. After several years of strong growth built largely on gas and oil revenues, the country entered a new period of financial stress from which it has been slow to recover.

The failure of the reformed school system was obvious by the mid-1990s. A conservative reaction set in. Not all elements of the 1992 reform were abandoned, but a gradual return to the old educational order in a modified version began. In the late 1990s the central state began to reassert its role as the director of education. A "Doctrine on Education" embodied the new conservatism but had little practical effect in the schools themselves. The same was true of new rules for changes to school organization and other directives. Putin has taken a strong interest in education, especially in the presentation of Russian history to students. His focus from the beginning has been on Russian nation-building. In a speech in 2013 at the Valdai International Discussion Club, he outlined his vision of Russia and the role of education in supporting it. He rejected both the Soviet and Imperial political models as well as what he called the "extreme, western-style liberalism" of attempts to civilize Russia from abroad. Quoting the nineteenth-century conservative thinker Konstantin Leont'ev approvingly, he pointed to Russia's "blossoming complexity" and went on to describe Russia as a "state-civilization, reinforced by the Russian people, Russian language, Russian culture, the Russian Orthodox Church, and the country's other traditional religions." In light of subsequent developments, it is interesting that he praised the Soviet attention to minority language rights and called for a return to that tradition. Ethnic and religious identity, however, had to be merged, he argued, into a common civic identity of shared values that assured unity in diversity. The highest value of citizens he defined as patriotism. He rejected a past in which little value was placed on individual human lives. The future rested on developing educated, creative, physically and spiritually healthy people. The principal role of education, he asserted, was to educate the individual as a patriot. The method was to restore the role of Russian culture and literature in education. He saw in teachers a force for civic patriotism and national unity: "The community [of teachers] speaks the same language—the language of science, knowledge, and education, despite the fact that it is spread out over an enormous territory." He added that support for this community "is one of the most important steps on the path toward a strong, flourishing Russia." He deplored the moral decay of the West and revived the siege mentality of "encirclement" in Soviet days and the threat of the "liberal virus" to Russian values that had troubled Nicholas I.[13] Russia, he had already declared in 2012, was in a fierce competition with the West over the very soul of the Russian nation.

The general demographic crisis continued to take a heavy toll on the education system under Putin. Between the 2000–1 and 2014–15 school years, the number of secondary school graduates fell by half from 1.46 million to 701,400. The total number of enrollments in higher education fell from 7.5 million in 2008–9 to 5.2 million in 2014–15. By 2021 the number is estimated to fall to 4.2 million students.[14] Shrinking enrollments were accompanied by the closing of nearly 7,800 schools between 2000–1 and 2006–7. After a brief rise, spending on education went down as well. After reaching a low of 2.94 percent of GDP in 2000, expenditure on education rose to 4.1 percent in 2008 only to recede to 3.86 percent in 2012 and down again to 3.7 percent in 2016.

A bright spot has been the recovery of preschool enrollments (age 3–7). Between 2005 and 2017 the percentage of preschool children attending a school rose from 53 percent to 83 percent. The sharp reduction in the number of students in the system has mitigated the impact of the decline in financing, but Russian spending on education is well below that of France at 5.4 percent of GDP, the United Kingdom at 5.5 percent, or the United States at 5 percent. A major cause is budgeting priorities. The Russian Federation spends 70 percent of its budget on unproductive expenditures (that lower or make no contribution to GDP) like the military and only 10.5 percent of GDP on productive budget expenditures like health and education.[15]

In 2001 the government adopted the "Conception for the Modernization of Education." It aimed to reform the practise of education by 2010. A plan followed in 2003 to establish universal educational standards, school leaving and college entrance examinations, and new course curricula in all subjects. The general goal of the plan to make education again into a tool for the country's modernization proved to be unpopular with the public. Many saw it as a return to the organizational and workplace planning that had characterized Soviet practise. The plan also proposed to improve teacher training by, among other things, providing computers to teacher training institutions and to improve the living conditions of teachers. Teachers ceased to be municipal employees as in the 1992 reform and again became state servants. Attracting young people into teaching remained difficult. In 2007, 17 percent of teachers were retirees and another 30 percent were in their preretirement years. Primary professional education remained a major concern as well, as shortages of qualified blue-collar workers amassed. Large businesses began to incorporate vocational training institutions into their own structures, a step not available to middle and small business owners. Facing the draft into the army on leaving school rather than entering the job market, 17- or 18-year-olds had little incentive to learn their trade well. Only 25 percent of vocational school graduates entered the profession for which they had trained. In 2005 the state transferred all but 250 of about 3,800 primary professional schools to regional administrations. The numbers going on to secondary professional education remained relatively steady although tuition fees rose rapidly in these years.[16]

Dissatisfaction with the education system remained high in the public. A survey in early 2012 found that 72 percent of respondents were dissatisfied with the education available to them, and 39 percent declared that it was impossible to get a good education in Russia.[17] The government responded by completing the process of recentralizing education that it had tentatively begun. The primary source of legislation on education was now presidential decree. A council under the presidency was established to advise education authorities and coordinate education at various levels. The Ministry of Education and Science and the Department of Science and Education Policy within the Ministry oversaw the functioning of the laws on education and regional ministries of education implemented policies at the local level. Municipalities were required to provide schools and free access to them. The Ministry of Health administered medical and pharmaceutical education, the Ministry of Defense ran Military Higher Education Vocational Schools, and the Ministry of Justice saw to education in correctional institutions.

The new round of reforms set out to modernize general education at all levels through better facilities and upgraded skills in teaching and management practices.

The main instrument of the new order was the Law on Education of 2012. The law required all constituent bodies of the Federation to conform to federal laws on education. Schooling had already been made compulsory through grade eleven in 2007. The new law provided for public and free preschool, primary general, basic secondary general, upper secondary general, and established a uniform curriculum which individual schools could enhance by deepening certain areas of study. The law permitted full- and part-time learning, distance learning, e-learning, gymnasiums, lyceums, homeschooling, and private schools. More than 99 percent of students, however, attended state schools, of whom 7.8 percent went to gymnasiums that, as in the past, specialized in the sciences and 5.6 percent to lyceums that generally offered humanities. There were also schools for the gifted, especially in the arts and a few in the sciences.[18] Among the latter was the Sirius Center for Gifted Education in Sochi, a personal project of President Putin. The law took an individual approach to child learning. As well, education was inclusive. Special needs students were normally to study in general schools but had the right to request to be trained in special needs schools.

Teachers in the New Order

Preschool and elementary teachers usually train at post-secondary pedagogical colleges where they earn a diploma of Middle Level Professional Education. Secondary school teachers train at universities or tertiary-level teacher training institutes. All teachers in upper secondary school grades must hold a specialist or master's degree. Their training included an academic study of a specialist subject and pedagogical and methodological courses as well as a practical teaching internship. The law of 2012 established rights for pedagogical employees. Teachers are eligible for refresher courses every three years, are entitled to a paid leave at the end of ten years of service, and can retire early. Rural teachers receive housing. Teachers' salaries are set at no lower than the average salary of all workers in their region. Many of these promises have been honored in the breach as underfunding has continued to fall disproportionally on teachers who continue to work in poor facilities and under-resourced classrooms. The feminization of the profession that began in the late nineteenth century continues. Some 85 percent of teachers are women. Although some teachers no doubt strive to fulfill the mandate of the law to develop the personality and foster the individual self-determination of the child, the evidence suggests that teacher-centered learning remains the dominant mode of instruction in Russian schools. Compulsory state examinations at the end of grade nine and again at grade eleven induce most teachers to teach to the examinations. Such learning entails a good deal of memorization.

Vocational Education

The reform of general education was accompanied by changes in vocational education better to meet the changing needs of labor. In order to bring greater unity and focus to vocational learning, the former PTUs and professional-technical lyceums were merged into technicums and colleges. In particular, vocational training was to incorporate information and computer technology at all levels. The vocational schools provide basic and higher technical education and in some cases a middle-level blend of the two. Enrollments in the lower level continued to be low as they had been in the PTUs since 1991. Blue-collar workers remain in short supply. Admissions to middle- and upper-level technical training were generally steady. The higher vocational schools supply the economy with much needed technicians, accountants, teachers, nurses, and other middle-level workers.

Higher Education

Higher education in the 1990s fell into disarray as institutions struggled to find new resources and adjust to a market economy. Bribes to secondary school teachers to raise grades were followed by bribes to university admissions officers, and further bribes to professors for grades. In addition, admission fees were exorbitant at many institutions. Some institutions and their faculty maintained their integrity, but corruption in the system was widespread. Investigations have shown that one out of nine of the members of the Duma had plagiarized or ghostwritten their theses. Some 30 percent of theses accepted by universities were bought.[19] In order to curb cheating to gain admission to universities, the government established a compulsory Unified State Examination in 2009. The examination is created centrally and administered in a network of some 5,700 examination centers in the regions. The examination not only helped to address the corrupt practises around admissions but also gave easier access to applicants who previously had to travel to several universities in order to sit their entrance examinations. Although questions are still leaked in advance and answers sometimes corrected by corrupt examiners, the unified examination has greatly improved university practises and standards.

The 1990s had seen a proliferation of higher education institutions. Few conducted research and the standards of instruction were low. The Putin regime has put a good deal of effort into raising the level of higher education in the country. Russians place a high value on education. In 2015, 54 percent of Russians between the ages of 25 and 64 held tertiary degrees.[20] In 2012–13 a performance review resulted in the reduction in the number of higher education institutions through closings or mergers from 1,046 to 896 in 2016. Further closings followed. The rush in the early 1990s toward narrowly utilitarian specializations ebbed at the turn of the century, and the traditional faculties have rebounded. Russia had earlier become a signatory to the Bologna process that sought to align higher education standards and degrees throughout Europe. In 2007 universities began to move away from the old five-year specialization degree and to the four-year bachelor and two-year master's degrees standard in the West. Both degrees require final state examinations and a thesis based on original research. An additional three years of study and the defense of a thesis is required for a Candidate of Science degree. The degree of Doctor of Science requires from five to fifteen years of further work and research and a dissertation. Five independent accreditation agencies work to assure adherence to the Bologna standards in areas such as engineering and law. The Federal Services for Supervision in Education and Science provides accreditation for institutions of higher learning for six-year periods.

The government set the goal of placing five Russian universities into the top 100 of world rankings by 2020. At the timing of writing, only the Lomonosov State University of Moscow has attained that distinction. The government has sought especially to raise the research profile of higher education. It has created fifty specially funded and research focused National Research Universities of National Innovation and nine Federal Universities to coordinate research geared to address regional socio-economic needs. Two National Universities, Lomonosov Moscow State University and St. Petersburg State University, operate under the direct control of the federal government. They administer their own admission examinations independently of the unified state examination required of other universities.

Demographic decline was accompanied by falling higher education enrollments by 32 percent from 2000 to 2013. A small recovery followed. With some success the government has attracted students from abroad to boost student numbers. As well, in 2014 Russia joined the Global Education Program that enabled Russian graduate students to study at 288 universities abroad. By 2014 there were around 300 private universities in operation in Russia with 884,700 students or 16 percent of total enrollments. Most specialized in niche subjects rather than competing with state institutions.[21] Since 2014, a suspicious government has taken a hard line on private higher education institutions, closing some and harassing others with a stream of petty regulations. Foreign funding of such institutions has been blocked.

The cost of higher education in the Russian Federation is rising. Between 1995 and 2006 the percentage of students paying tuition rose from 13 percent to nearly 58 percent.[22] Parents or adult students can apply to a bank for an "education credit," applicable to tuition, food, lodging, and textbooks, at a low rate of interest. Access to higher education, especially in rural areas, remains limited and costly for many. The quality of secondary education in rural schools lags that in urban areas, and rural students are often poorly prepared to face the unified state examination. The focus in schools on general education also ill-prepares rural students for vocational and higher education studies in agriculture and drains the most able away from the countryside into the cities. Only 12 percent of rural youth want to pursue a career in agriculture and a scant 8 percent would choose to work in a village. The low level of agricultural science contributes to low productivity in agriculture and imposes a major drain on the economy.[23] Figure 9.1 illustrates the school network in the Russian Federation in 2018.

Upbringing

The socialization of citizens into a set of shared values and outlook is a feature of most polities. A contentious issue in education since the end of the Soviet Union has been moral upbringing in schools. The stifling upbringing in communist morality that characterized the old order has made the Russian public wary of any attempt to use the school to instill a single ideological or religious point of view. Under Putin the focus

190 A History of Education in Modern Russia

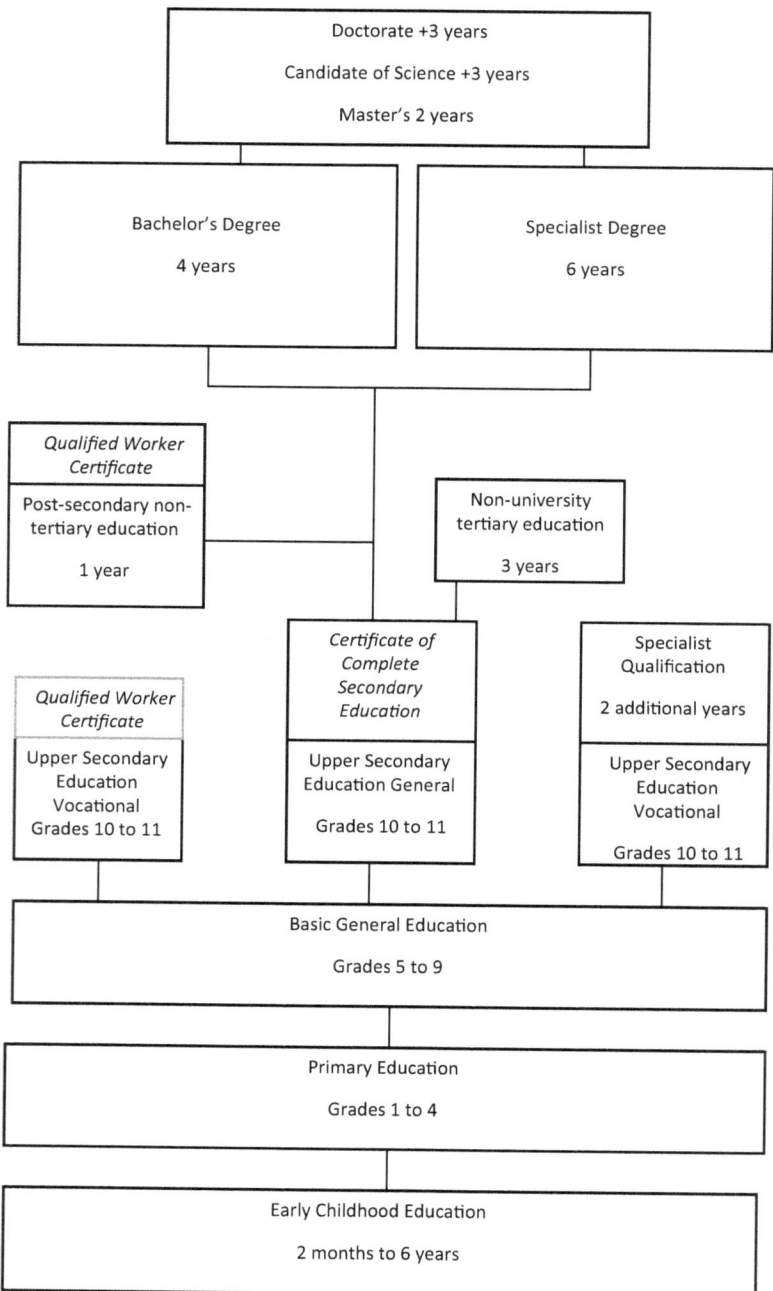

Figure 9.1 The education system of the Russian Federation in 2018.

of upbringing has become patriotism. In 2009 the Federal State Standards of General Education were promulgated. They were revised in 2016. The standards included a section called Conception of the Spiritual and Moral Upbringing of School Students. The conception set out the national values that informed upbringing in and beyond the school in alliance with family, civil society, and religion. Although it recognized the values of particular ethnic, religious, and cultural groups in the Russian Federation in shaping the identity of Russian citizens, it asserted that national unity rested on the sharing of a set of Russian historical values. These included: patriotism defined as love of Russia and of Russians, love of region, and service to the country; social solidarity built around trust in the institutions of the state and civil society and belief in justice and honor; civic mindedness incorporating respect for the rule of law, duty to the fatherland, deference to older generations, interethnic peace, and freedom of conscience and religion; love of family, industriousness, science, and ecological awareness; Orthodox religion, Russian literature and arts; and concern for humanity through promotion of world peace, respect for cultural diversity, and international cooperation. On this footing, the integration of the individual into society and the formation of the spiritual and moral personality were the foundations of social capital. The conception called for the incorporation of moral upbringing into the entire school program.[24]

These were worthy ideals, but the place of religion in the school remained contentious. The Orthodox Church had continued to press for access to schools beyond the voluntary courses they had won in 1997. The Church took every opportunity to present Orthodoxy as an essential element of Russian culture and identity. Many proposals and rejections were made until a compromise was reached. In 2010 a pilot project was launched in nineteen Russian regions. Parents of children in grade four (ages 10 or 11) could choose from six modules: Fundamentals of Islam, Judaism, or Buddhism, Orthodox Christianity, World Religion and Culture, or Secular Ethics. In the pilot, 60 percent of parents choose the secular model. Materials for the modules were hastily prepared, and teachers had almost no advance training in their delivery. In spite of the poor quality of the modules, the project was declared a success in 2012. From September of that year, all students in fourth and fifth grades were required to take one of the six modules. The confessions concerned had the right to approve the syllabi of the modules but had no direct input into their writing. The approach in the modules focused on the history and culture of the religions in question and not on theology. They provide education "about" and not education "in" religion. Secular teachers teach the modules for one hour per week. Christianity is represented solely by Orthodoxy. The school curriculum is built around inculcating in students the values of traditional Russian culture. But religion remains contained in a cultural and not theological box and is taught in one grade only.

More recently, the Strategy on Development of Upbringing in the Russian Federation until 2025 calls for the adoption of "traditional moral values," readiness to defend the Motherland, and the nurturing of patriotism and collectivism. Collectivism again serves as an antidote to Western individualism. A collectivist mentality subordinates the needs of the individual to the interests of society and state. The core of moral upbringing under Putin is a patriotism that transcends religious and ethnic identity. In the fall of 2015 the president ordered the creation of a national student movement to shape the character of young people through instilling the values intrinsic to Russian society. It has been portrayed as a new form of the Young Pioneers of Soviet days. Participants receive what is called a military-patriotic education. A second initiative came from the Russian army in the form of a program called the Young Army. These youth associations give training in military tactics and patriotic history. Priests of the Orthodox Church provide religious instruction to Young Army youth. The Suvorov and Nakhimov schools founded in 1943 have again become more numerous and, along with other cadet schools, are an important focus of military-patriotic education.

Since the foundation of the Russian Federation, the writing and teaching of the nation's history have been tumultuous. At first, historians focused on creating a history outside of a Marxist framework. They expended much energy on correcting the falsehoods of the old historiography and exposing the darker aspects of Soviet history. The result was a cacophony of interpretations of the past in multiple textbooks. The chaos required the suspension of the matriculation examination in history in 1998. Historians largely turned away from political history and toward the study of the relationship of the individual to society. Their goal was to humanize the writing of history. Society was often portrayed in history texts as a counterbalance to state oppression. While Russian historians were reshaping the history of their nation, non-Russian ethnic historians were writing their own histories. These were often critical of Russians.

The move in the 1990s to recentralize education included the compulsory teaching of Russian history in schools. The Ministry of Education established a Compulsory Minimum of the Content of Education for Secondary Schools and selected recommended textbooks that met this minimum. In 2000 the parliament issued a sharp criticism of the writing of history for schools, which had failed to produce a "comprehensive theoretical framework" for its teaching.[25] It demanded greater unity and set requirements for content and level of teaching. The document was abandoned after widespread public protest. The State Council of the Russian Federation took over from the Ministry of Education the role of shaping the history curriculum for schools. A working group set out a strategy for the next ten years that had the goal of socializing students through historical and literary selections. Existing textbooks were discarded. In 2002 the government sponsored a textbook-writing competition. Successful textbooks should reflect "state-oriented opinion." A textbook for grade nine and another for grade ten were selected. They stressed patriotic upbringing. Other textbooks with different perspectives were still available, however. Only textbooks approved by the ministry were centrally paid for, but other textbooks could be used at the users' expense.

As Putin's authoritarian tendencies hardened and his emphasis on patriotism, built on a vision of the values and experience of the Russian past, gelled, he grew impatient with the diversity and sometimes critical evaluations of the nation's history. In 2007 and again in 2014 he gathered a number of historians to express to them his views on the function and writing of history. The humanities, he argued, must play a central role in the education of children and transmit the "best traditions and values of the national culture."[26] Although he insisted that he did not wish to standardize historical thought, he demanded the clear presentation of the facts. He portrayed history as scientific, in that it consists of verifiable facts not subject to interpretation or alteration. He also pointed to what he called the proud history of multiethnic and multiconfessional polity in Russia, which historians should stress. His persistent musings resulted in 2013 in the formation of a group to produce a single history textbook without "any internal contradictions and ambiguities."[27] The ideal textbook would foster patriotism, civic responsibility, and tolerance toward other nationalities. It should teach youth to take pride in Russia and its heroes of the past. In particular it should emphasize Russia's heroic military efforts to safeguard a besieged and threatened nation. The project managed to produce three different approved textbooks for use in October 2015; all adopted a standard view of Russian history and culture. At the same time textbooks in a variety of subjects were assessed and discarded if deemed insufficiently patriotic. The publishing house of *Prosveshchenie*, owned by an old friend of the president, has emerged as a dominant force in the publication of textbooks.[28]

One of the participants in the single textbook project was Olga Vasilieva, a scholar of the Russian Orthodox Church. She serves as the minister of education and science. In her past reflections she has expressed a favorable view of the Stalin era. She refers to his crimes as "shortcomings" and praises him for his attitude to the Orthodox Church and his promotion of patriotism and Russian pride. "I'm for the return to the best traditions of the Soviet school," she says.[29] Criticism of the Stalin period and particularly of his performance immediately before and during the war is condemned. A law of 2014 made it a crime to rehabilitate Nazism and criticize Soviet activities during the Second World War. "Lying about history" could cost the accused three years in prison or forced labor. Textbooks now validate the seizure of the Crimea from Ukraine and support the rebels in Eastern Ukraine.

Surveys and sociological studies have cast doubt on the success of Putin's program of military-patriotic indoctrination. Sociologists distinguish between constructive and negative patriotism. The first rests on the liberty to hold points of view that differ from official versions of the country. Negative patriotism is blind and inflexible identification with a fixed and relentlessly positive picture of the nation that is promulgated by authorities. Society is essentially excluded from participation in nation-building. A recent article concludes that the "uneven nature of Russians' patriotic self-identity shows that external events play a large role in the formation of patriotism, while Russian society consolidates not through the cultivation of positive values, but on the basis of negative factors whose impact leads only to blind—and not to constructive—patriotism."[30] Love of country remains, but identification of citizens with the patriotic values advanced by the state is nebulous.

Non-Russian Schooling

Since speaking positively in his speech to the Valdai convention in 2013 about Soviet policy toward minority languages, Putin has experienced a change of heart. He has spoken critically about nationality policy in Imperial Russia and the Soviet policy of korenizatsiia. The Constitution of 1993 guaranteed the equality of the languages spoken in the Russian Federation. While the teaching of Russian was compulsory, the teaching of non-Russian languages was left to the autonomous regions. They had the right to establish their own state languages along with Russian. In the academic year 2015–16, 90.5 percent of schools in the Russian Federation taught only in Russian, 4.4 percent provided a mixture of Russian and a non-Russian language, and 5.1 percent taught children in a non-Russian language. Some Russian language schools taught non-Russian languages as a subject of study to 1.6 million children, and roughly 57,000 children studied non-Russian languages on a vocational basis or in hobby clubs. In total, 2.3 million of 14 million school children throughout Russia studied non-Russian languages and only a quarter of them studied them as the language of instruction.[31] Ethnic Russians who lived in areas where the study of non-Russian languages was required of their children often complained. A group of activists in 2015 in Bashkorostan, Buriatia, Tatarstan, and Komi opined in a letter to the leadership that the compulsory study of the local language hindered their children's learning of Russian.

As early as 2009 the right of secondary school students to sit state examinations in their own language was removed. The many school closures often fell on schools providing minority languages. In the same year as he spoke favorably about non-Russian language rights, Putin also declared the Russian language to be the "fundamental basis of the unity of the country."[32] Recentralization under the Law on Education of 2012 eliminated the regional cultural component of the 1992 legislation. The right to choose the language of instruction in schools was declared in the new law to be available only "within the opportunities offered by the education system." By 2015 only twenty-four state languages were used as languages of instruction in any grade and seventy-three were taught as subjects of study. In a speech in July 2017 Putin said: "To force someone to study a language which is not his native tongue is impermissible." The constitutional right to study in non-Russian languages was, he argued, a "voluntary right."[33] Following Putin's declaration, the education law was amended to make minority language lessons in ethnic republics optional and limited to two hours a week. Parents were required to request the option for their child. In September 2017 the General Prosecutor's Office conducted an audit in non-Russian republics to assure that ethnic languages were treated as optional only. In Bashkorostan and Tatarstan they found that they remained compulsory but with reduced hours. The course teachers were fired en masse. Demonstrations followed and several arrests were made. In Tatarstan rallies were banned and students who took part in "illegal" demonstrations were threatened with expulsion from the university.

Minority ethnic groups undertook an online campaign against the changes. In June 2018 they formed the Democratic Congress of the Peoples of Russia to advocate multiculturalism and federalism. The hypocrisy of the regime is blatant. While it is impermissible for a Russian to be compelled to study a language not his own, it is compulsory for a non-Russian to do so. The idea of the "Russian World" that establishes the duty to protect the use of Russian in the Federation and beyond its borders opens a window to Russian intervention in Ukraine, the Baltic States, and other bordering states with Russian minorities.[34] It is akin to the Imperial Russian doctrine from the late eighteenth century of the duty to defend the rights of the Orthodox beyond its borders. Ethnic tensions were central to the fall of the Russian Empire as well as to the liquidation of the Soviet Union. In those cases non-Russians made up a near or small majority, residing largely on the Russian periphery. Non-Russians in the Russian Federation make up only 20 percent of the population and, except for the Caucasus, are surrounded by Russians. Secession is unlikely, but their alliance with Russian liberals could be decisive in bringing down the authoritarian regime of Vladimir Putin in the future.

Outcomes

The reforms of perestroika, including the education reform of 1984–5, sought to rescue a failing political order. They looked to the past rather than to a reformed future. The most important consequence of the Gorbachev years for education was glasnost'. The new openness enabled a wide public discussion of education reform as well as the formation of several movements and organizations that brought together pedagogues, teachers, and parents to advance reform. The Pedagogy of Cooperation movement played a major role in shaping the education reform of 1992. The collapse of the Soviet Union in 1991 and the creation of the Russian Federation not only created opportunities for radical change in schooling practises but also posed an array of challenges to the success of reform.

The education reform of 1992 took shape amid a political crisis during which the constitution of the new country was hotly debated. The reform was in large part a reaction to what had gone before. Its foundations were the principles of decentralization, democratization, diversification, and humanization, all intended to counter the authoritarianism of the past and nourish a democracy of the future. Whatever the merits of the reform, and they were many, the obstacles to its realization were overwhelming. The old problems of underfunding limited the possibilities for change. Neither the reform nor the constitution established clear principles of cost sharing among the center, regional, and local school authorities. The transition from a planned to a market economy precipitated a crisis, marked by economic dislocation, unemployment, and hyperinflation. School curricula under the reform required inputs from the center, the regions, and schools. The result was widespread differences from region to region or even within regions.

The success of the reform rested on the capacity of teachers to support its principles in the classroom. They were poorly equipped to succeed. Even the most capable lacked the textbooks and teaching aids needed for the task. The reformers saw the classroom as a catalyst of democracy. Teachers had no experience of democracy and many doubted that its promotion was the proper role of the school. Parents also quickly soured on the reform. They wanted their children, especially in a period of economic crisis, to acquire the basic skills of literacy and numeracy needed in the new economy. Many curricular changes and new teaching methods appeared to them as frivolous or even harmful. By the mid-1990s the education reform was widely regarded as a failure. The pattern, familiar from the past, of partial, not total, retreat from reform reasserted itself.

At the heart of the Russian Federation from its inception lay the task of nation-building, the reconstruction of a Russian identity in place of the Soviet ideal of the citizen. Decentralization in such a large state potentially compromised national unity. Following his ascendency in 2000, Vladimir Putin has recentralized administration in the Russian Federation, including the education system. The curriculum and the textbooks that support it are geared to a nationalist agenda. Vospitanie in Russian schools is constructed on patriotic themes. Even science or mathematics textbooks have been rejected for insufficient patriotism. While upbringing in school hours is secular in nature and in the hands of teachers and not priests, the state increasingly asserts the close association of Russian identity with Orthodoxy. A proposed constitutional amendment in 2020 asserts that Russia's citizens traditionally believe in God. While limited in its access to classrooms, the Orthodox Church uses all means available to it to shape young minds. School after hours and school vacations are devoted to patriotic indoctrination, often including religious instruction.

Thanks to oil and gas revenues, Putin was able to improve funding for schools and universities and to stabilize the system. Teacher preparation and compensation have been enhanced. The fall of the price of oil and economic sanctions following the annexation of Crimea, however, have placed new financial strains on the education network. Spending on education decreased by 8.5 percent between 2014 and 2016 and has not since recovered. The continuing decline of the population also threatens the vitality of the education system.

After the chaos of the reform period, most Russians are more or less satisfied with the status quo in education. Not all the initiatives of the reform of 1992 have been lost. Putin has learned from the mistakes of the past. The narrow scope into which his predecessors squeezed education deprived it of its capacity to keep up with changing administrative and economic needs. While recentralizing control over schools, Putin has encouraged considerable diversity within the state system, from general schools to lycées and gymnasiums as well as specialist arts, science, and technical schools for the talented. Diversity will broaden the capacity for knowledge transfer from abroad and for domestic innovation. The role of private elementary and secondary education is limited. A mere 1 percent of students study in private institutions.

The achievements of the education system in Russia are notable. In 2011, 94 percent of the population aged 25–64 had completed at least upper secondary education. The comparable average in OECD countries was 75 percent. Since 2002, youth literacy has stood at 99.7 percent. The universities are in the process of aligning their degrees and standards with those of the European Union. They are attracting increasing numbers of foreign students, a goal of Putin, and their research profile is gradually improving. Computer literacy has blossomed. Putin is particularly interested in artificial intelligence, which he sees as the key element of economic success and state power. Private universities account for about 16 percent of all students in tertiary education but pose little competition to state universities.[35] Putin views private universities as seedbeds of Western liberal ideas. They exist under constant threat of closure.

Opposition to the Putin regime has increased in recent years. It comes from major urban centers and the non-Russian nationalities. The language rights of even the largest ethnic groups are under pressure. Putin has reasserted the formula first advanced by

Khrushchev that Russian is "the language of the state-forming nationality" while also declaring the equality of all ethnic groups.[36] The rise of opposition has been met with increasing censorship and police repression. Rigged elections and state control of the media confine the opposition to the streets and some social media. Putin does not appear to be grooming a successor. Instead, a successful referendum in the summer of 2020 has approved legislation that is intended to allow him at the most to remain as president until 2032 or at the least to preserve his influence over policy-making until that year. Among many other things, the referendum secured the place of patriotic education in schools and affirmed Russia's ancestral faith in God. Even with a change in the regime, however, changes in education policy are likely to be limited. As in the past, there is little public support for experimentation in schooling, especially on Western models. Distrust of the West is deeply engrained in the Russian psyche, the product of centuries of incursions from Teutonic Knights to Poles, Swedes, French, and Germans. Patriotism fueled by historical memory will remain a mainstay of the state and of the education system that sustains it.

Conclusion

The cameralist model that provided the underpinnings of the Petrine state has left its mark on all subsequent regimes. It lingers on in the Russian Federation today in Putin's depiction of Russia as a "state-civilization." Russia has been far from the "well-ordered police state" of the cameralist ideal, but the interests of the autocratic, communist, and managed democratic states that succeeded one another and their leaders have been paramount since the time of Peter. The role of the public has been to serve the state in return for sustenance and security. Even the most benevolent of the rulers equated the "general good" with the success of the state and perpetuation of their governance. Education in modern Russia has served primarily as an instrument for the advancement of state interests.

Successive regimes in Russia have been caught between the need to educate a larger and larger segment of the population, both to compete internationally as a great power and to support an ever more complex economy and internal administration, and the desire to preserve the political and social status quo. At least some social mobility through education was required to meet the first condition, but too much social mobility undermined the second. The result of the tension between the two imperatives has been a recurrent pattern of educational reform followed by a partial retreat in which some aspects of the reform were kept. Advancement was halting and slow, but advancement there was. The pattern of reform and retrenchment ultimately served both the autocracy and the Bolsheviks badly. It is difficult to assess the role that the constraints imposed on schooling by the autocracy and the communists played in their downfall, but the importance of the educational deficits that accumulated in both tsarist and Soviet Russia should not be overlooked. The failings of obrazovanie were matched by the generally dismal results of vospitanie. Love of country has been a mainstay of the resilience of the Russian population since at least the invasion of Napoleon in 1812. But the pinched morality of the Law of God under the tsars and communist morality under the Bolsheviks, both reinforced by police surveillance, promoted indifference and alienation, stifled creativity and initiative, and fostered deceit and avoidance of civic responsibility. Putin's patriotic-military education seems destined to repeat the established pattern.

Education in Russia was rarely a budgetary priority. Underfunding has been chronic and has undermined the implementation of nearly every reform initiative. The exception was the brief push in the post-1905 drive for universal elementary schooling. The result of underfunding has been a history of substandard facilities, inadequate textbooks and teaching aids, insufficient teacher training, low teacher pay, double or triple shifts in schools, and teacher burnout and turnover. Although the status of teachers has improved over the decades, teachers struggled to secure professional standing and the prestige that professional recognition confers. The percentage of women among teachers has risen steadily since the 1880s. Putin has recently improved conditions in the schools and for their teachers. The standard of teacher training has risen and pay stabilized. But budget constraints grow as the Russian economy shrinks.

The dominance of the state in directing education policy has not meant that authority has had its own way. The implementation of reform from the top has rarely been complete. Size, administrative complexity, and underfunding provide part of the explanation for failures. But public reception of reform initiatives has also played a major role. Passive resistance to unwelcome change has thwarted or modified the implementation of directives from the center. Local authorities and parents have routinely ignored orders from above. The role of teachers has been particularly significant. For the most part they were receptive to the replication of the top-down authority of the state in classroom relations. They were, however, perennially the unfortunate mediators between the state and the public. Pressured from both sides, they shaped practice in the classroom as best they could to accommodate conflicting demands.

It is difficult to predict the future of education in the Russian Federation. For all its many faults, the system of education in Russia and the Soviet Union, especially since the early twentieth century, has had remarkable success in a relatively brief period. The literacy rate in today's Russia is among the very highest in the world. The numbers of citizens with tertiary education also exceeds that of nearly all other nations, an achievement clouded by the widespread corruption of the 1990s. Russian and Soviet scientists and technicians have achieved landmark successes, notably the space program that began with Sputnik in 1957 and continues today. Particularly praiseworthy has been the history of the education of girls and women in Russia. Under the royal patronage of Catherine the Great and later of Mariia Feodorvna, girls of various stations in life received basic and sometimes excellent educations. The painful sacrifices that young women made to attain educations abroad in the 1860s and 1870s and the hard-won battle of determined women for women's higher education in Russia resulted in a cohort of women professionals that far exceeded that of other nations of the day. The role of male professors and some state actors in sustaining the women's higher courses illustrates the advanced social consciousness of the Russian intelligentsia in spite of a repressive school system. The emphasis of the Soviet regime on equality of education for women maintained that tradition but never solved the problem of the double burden of work and family. It remains to be seen whether equality of opportunity in education for women will survive in the Russian Federation.

In the 1920s and again in the 1990s, Russian pedagogues and educational activists undertook the radical transformation of education. In both cases the experiments were poorly executed but also foundered on lack of resources, inadequate teacher preparation, and public resistance. At present, the direction of schooling in the

Federation rests heavily on the will of Vladimir Putin. While supporting it adequately, he is imposing on schools a narrow militarized nationalism that is increasingly reinforced by an expanded role for the Church. Many parents are suspicious of any kind of indoctrination, but citizens are largely excluded from actively participating in constructing Russian nationhood. Putin's language policies have already alienated many non-Russians. The corruption of the regime, its increasingly brutal suppression of dissent at home, and its cynical policy abroad may gradually galvanize an opposition and inaugurate a new beginning. Whatever the future, the eternal questions of the purpose of education and whom it should serve will rise again to the top of the political and social agenda.

Glossary

apparat	The Communist Party and state bureaucracy in the USSR
commune	A peasant community unit with shared obligations to state and landlords until the emancipation and to the state thereafter
defectology	The study of physical and mental disabilities in the USSR
directors of schools	In much Western parlance, school principals
Duma	The lower house of the parliament created in 1905
duma	City councils created in the reforms of the 1860s and 1870s
estates	The legal division of Russian society into nobility, clergy, merchants, townsmen, and peasants, each with its distinct rights and obligations toward the state
fel'dsher	A doctor's assistant or paramedic, usually working in rural areas where doctors were scarce
foreign quarter	A suburb of Moscow where foreigners were usually required to live in the seventeenth and early eighteenth centuries
Fourth Section of His Imperial Majesty's Own Chancellery	One of six sections established by Nicholas I under his personal direction. The fourth section dealt with various charities such as orphanages or care of the disabled and included the Department of the Empress Mariia Fedorovna that oversaw the education of women in various institutes
FZU	Vocational training schools located in factories or other industrial enterprises in the USSR that offered a mix of basic general and vocational schooling for teenagers
glasnost'	Openness that permitted public discussion of policy both in the early reign of Alexander II and under the Communist Party leadership of Mikhail Gorbachev
historical-philological faculty	Used in Russia to designate the faculty of arts
Holy Synod	The governing body of the Russian Orthodox Church, created in 1721, made up of churchmen but headed by a layman appointed by the emperor
inorodtsy	Non-Russian subjects or citizens in Imperial Russia and the USSR
institutki	Students and graduates of the several institutes for the education of girls in Imperial Russia under the Department of the Empress Mariia Feoforovna

korenizatsiia	A policy of integrating non-Russian nationalities into the Soviet Union through regional language and cultural policies
kruzhok	A student circle often engaged in the discussion of forbidden topics
kuristy	Students in the higher women's courses
Law of God	Religious instruction in the schools of Imperial Russia
lubok	A small publication with pictures and simple texts on folk and religious themes, popular with peasant readers
marshals of the nobility	An elective office created in the reign of Catherine the Great that endured until 1917 to engage the nobility in local administration
military colonies	Highly regimented agricultural colonies with soldiers doubling as peasants established by Alexander I to make the army more self-sufficient, which were hated by the colonists and gradually abolished by Nicholas I
Narkompros	People's Commissariat of National Enlightenment with responsibility for education in the Russian Republic of the Soviet Union
NEP	The New Economic Policy implemented in 1921 by Lenin to restore economic stability in the Soviet Union
NEPmen	Businessmen during the period of the New Economic Policy who engaged in private trade and small-scale manufacture, viewed as greedy and unscrupulous by many in the public
nihilism	A movement in Russia in the 1860s that rejected the past and sought to rebuild Russia on the basis of science, utility, and communalism
obrazovanie	Education in the sense of academic learning
obrok	A fee paid by peasant households to a landlord in labor or cash
obuchenie	Instruction or training
Old Believers	An Orthodox religious sect that rejected the church reforms of the seventeenth century and actively propagated their own interpretation of the Orthodox creed
pedology	The study of children's behavior and development in late Imperial Russia and the USSR
perestroika	A restructuring of the Soviet economy and society envisaged by Mikhail Gorbachev in the 1980s
poll tax	A tax imposed by Peter the Great on all adult male peasants and townsmen but not on nobles or clergy
populism	A movement in Russia in the 1870s and 1880s seeking to establish peasant socialism in Russia by means of revolutionary agitation and propaganda or terrorism

Procurator of the Holy Synod	A state official appointed as the secular or lay head of the Holy Synod, the governing body of the Russian Orthodox Church
PTU	Professional technical schools providing training in a variety of technical skills at basic and secondary levels
Pugachev rebellion	A massive Cossack-peasant uprising along the Volga River and in the Ural mountains in the early 1770s led by Emelian Pugachev
rabfak	A worker faculty to prepare workers for entrance into tertiary education instituted in the 1920s to accelerate workers into education in order to generate a proletarian intelligentsia
raznochintsy	Individuals who had separated from their natal social estate, usually through the acquisition of a measure of education, and who lived in occupations requiring a good level of literacy
rectors	University presidents or vice-chancellors
skete	Old Believer monastery, usually run by women who gave both spiritual and practical instruction
skhodka	A meeting of the members of a peasant commune at which joint decisions were taken on matters like allocation of taxes or land redistribution among communal families but also referring to secret meetings of university students in imitation of peasant practice
Slavophiles	An intellectual movement beginning in the 1840s whose members broadly rejected the reforms of Peter the Great and advocated a return to the values of pre-Petrine Russia
SSUZ	Secondary specialist vocational schools under Brezhnev that trained PTU graduates at a higher level
studenchestvo	Corporate solidarity among university students in pursuit of their collective interests
Sunday schools	Schools begun in the late 1850s for part-time adult education that the state at different times tolerated or banned. In the Russian Federation, Sunday schools operate under the auspices of the Orthodox Church for youth and adult religious instruction
Table of Ranks	A system of ranking civilian and military state servants, as well as those in court service, introduced by Peter the Great, with fourteen ranks, the top six (later four) of which conferred hereditary nobility on their holders and the remainder personal nobility
technicum	A vocational school, usually at the secondary level of education

third element	Salaried employees of the zemstvos such as agronomists, statisticians, and others viewed by many conservatives as agents of liberal or radical change
Uniate Church	Formed at the end of the sixteenth century in Western Ukraine in a compromise with Rome that permitted the continued use of the Slavonic liturgy and rites in return for recognition of the authority of the Pope over it
UPM	School production workshops organized in factories and schools during the Second World War in which students learned skills and produced materials in support of the war effort
verst	A Russian measure of distance equal to 1.066 kilometres or 0.66 miles
Vesenkha	The Supreme Soviet of the National Economy was the highest state institution for the management of the economy at first in the Russian Soviet Republic and later in the Soviet Union
volost'	An administrative unit comprising several peasant communes, a township
vospitanie	Moral upbringing or education embracing both personal and civic-moral obligations
VUZ	Institution of higher education within which technical institutions were sometimes referred to as VTUZs or higher technical institutions
vydvizhenie	The acceleration of workers and peasants into higher education with the goal of creating a proletarian intelligentsia
Warsaw Pact	A formal alliance of the Soviet Union with its East European satellite states
Westernizers	An intellectual movement beginning in the 1840s whose proponents accepted the Westernizing reforms of Peter the Great and advocated further Europeanization of the country
zemliachestva	A support group for students coming from the same region of the country
zemstvo	Rural administrative units elected on an estate basis formed in 1864 at district and provincial levels that provided limited self-administration to local populations
zhenskii vrach	A female doctor

Notes

1 Facing West: Peter the Great and His Successors

1. Nicholas A. Chrissidis, *An Academy at the Court of the Tsars: Greek Scholars and Jesuit Education in Early Modern Russia* (DeKalb: Northern Illinois University Press, 2016), 91.
2. Paul Bushkovitch, "Change and Culture in Early Modern Russia," *Kritika*, 16, no. 2 (Spring 2015): 292.
3. For a detailed analysis of this evolution, see Max J. Okenfuss, "From Social Class to Social Caste: The Divisiveness of Early-Modern Russian Education," *Jahrbücher für Geschichte Osteuropas*, 33, H. 3 (1985): 321–8.
4. Quoted in Patrick L. Alston, *Education and the State in Tsarist Russia* (Stanford, CA: Stanford University Press, 1969), 4.
5. Richard S. Wortman, *Scenarios of Power: Myth and Ceremony in Russian Monarchy*, vol. 1 of *From Peter the Great to the Death of Nicholas I* (Princeton, NJ: Princeton University Press 1995), 5–6, 63, 107–9.
6. Igor Fedyukin, *The Enterprisers: The Politics of School in Early Modern Russia* (Oxford: Oxford University Press, 2019), 11–13. The projector phenomenon was common in seventeenth- and early-eighteenth-century European states.
7. Ibid., 60–3, 72–5, 87–94.
8. Ibid., 46–7.
9. E. K. Sysoeva, *Shkola v Rossii xviii-nachala xx vv. Vlast' i obshchestvo* (Moscow: Novyi khronograf, 2015), 34–8.
10. Alexander Vucinich, *Science in Russian Culture: A History to 1860* (Stanford, CA: Stanford University Press, 1963), 65–71.
11. Lindsey Hughes, *Russia in the Age of Peter the Great* (New Haven, CT: Yale University Press, 1998), 309.
12. W. Garth Jones, "Russia's Eighteenth-Century Enlightenment," in William Leatherbarrow and Derek Offord (eds.), *A History of Russian Thought* (Cambridge: Cambridge University Press, 2010), 77–8.
13. Fedyukin, *The Enterprisers*, 134–5, 155–9.
14. Igor Fedyukin, "Nobility and Schooling in Russia, 1700–1760: Choices in a Social Context," *Journal of Social History*, 49, no. 3 (2016): 558–84; and Igor Fedyukin and Salavat Gabdrakhonanov, "Cultural Capital and Education in St. Petersburg: The Noble Cadet Corps, 1732–1762," *Journal of Interdisciplinary History*, 46, no. 4 (Spring 2016): 485–511.
15. Vucinich, *Science in Russian Culture*, 80–2.
16. D. I. Fonvizin, "Chistoserdechnoe priznanie v delakh moikh i pomyshleniakh," in V. Petrov (ed.), *Naslednik vstal rano i za uroki sel.... Kak uchili i uchilis' v xviii v* (Moscow: Lomonosov, 2010), 76.
17. Chrissidis, *An Academy at the Court of the Tsars*, 193–4.
18. Hughes, *Russia in the Age of Peter the Great*, 309.

19. The Regulation is treated in detail in James Cracraft, *The Church Reform of Peter the Great* (London: Macmillan, 1971).
20. Gregory L. Freeze, *The Russian Levites: Parish Clergy in the Eighteenth Century* (Cambridge, MA: Harvard University Press, 1979), 79–80.
21. Ibid., 91–3.
22. Ibid., 98–9.
23. M. V. Danilov, "Zapiski artelerii maiora," in Petrov (ed.), *Naslednik*, 49–50.
24. S. V. Sergeeva, *Teoriia i praktika chastnogo obrazovaniia v Rossii (poslednaia chetvert' xviii-pervaia polovina xix v)* (Moscow-Penza: MPGU, 2003).
25. Hughes, *Russia in the Age of Peter the Great*, 305.
26. J. L. Black, *Citizens for the Fatherland: Education, Educators, and Pedagogical Ideals in Eighteenth-Century Russia* (Boulder, CO: East European Quarterly, 1979), 21 and 30.
27. Fedyukin, *The Enterprisers*, 211.
28. Sergeeva, *Teoriia i praktika chastnogo*, 95.
29. A. R. Vorontsov, *Zapiski*, in Petrov (ed.), *Naslednik*, 96–9.
30. R. M. Lotareva, *Gorod-zavody Rossii xviii-pervaia polivina xix veka* (Ekaterinburg: Sokrat, 2011), 93.
31. T. A. Shilina, *Evolutsiia zhenskogo obrazovaniia v Rossii: gosudarstvennaia politika obshchestvennaia initsiativa (konets xviii-nachala xx vv)* (Saratov: Amirit, 2015), 40–3.
32. James Cracraft, *The Petrine Revolution in Russian Culture* (Camgridge, MA: Harvard University Press, 2004), 221–2.

2 Roots of the System: Catherine the Great

1. Quoted in W. Bruce Lincoln, *The Romanovs: Autocrats of all the Russias* (New York: Dial Press, 1981), 218
2. J. L. Black, *Citizens for the Fatherland: Education, Educators, and Pedagogical Ideals in Eighteenth-Century Russia* (Boulder, CO: East Eurpoean Quarterly, 1979), 81–3; Isobel de Madariaga, *Russia in the Age of Catherine the Great* (London: Weidenfeld and Nicholson, 1981), 492–3; George K. Epp, *The Educational Policies of Catherine II: The Era of Enlightenment in Russia* (New York: Peter Lang, 1984), 44–7.
3. Black, *Citizens for the Fatherland*, 156–61; de Madariaga, *Russia in the Age of Catherine the Great*, 493; Epp, *The Educational Policies of Catherine II*, 50–3; T. A. Shilina, *Evolutsiia zhenskogo obrazovaniia v Rossii: gosudarstvennaia politika i obshchestvennaia initsiativa (konets xviii-nachala xx vv)* (Saratov: Amirit, 2015), 50–2.
4. Black, *Citizens for the Fatherland*, 114–15; Shilina, *Evolutsiia zhenskogo obrazovaniia v Rossii*, 46–7; Alexander Vucinich, *Science in Russian Culture: A History to 1860* (Stanford, CA: Stanford University Press, 1963), 82–8.
5. Epp, *The Educational Policies of Catherine II*, 52–3.
6. N. N. Avvrova, *Sistema voennogo obrazovaniia v Rossii: kadetskie korpusa vo vtoroi polovine xviii-pervoi polovne xix veka* (Moscow: Institut rossiiskoi istorii, 2003), 18–22.
7. Black, *Citizens of the Fatherland*, 87–9; Epp, *The Educational Policies of Catherine II*, 66–73; Nicholas A. Hans, *History of Russian Educational Policy (1701-1917)* (London: Russell and Russell, 1964), 20; E. K. Sysoeva, *Shkola v Rossii xviii-nachala xx vv: Vlast' i obshchestvo* (Moscow: Novyi khronograf, 2015), 56–61.

8. Patrick Alston, *Education and the State in Tsarist Russia* (Stanford, CA: Stanford University Press, 1969), 17; de Madariaga, *Russia in the Age of Catherine the Great*, 494.
9. Black, *Citizens of the Fatherland*, 133 and 143; de Madariaga, *Russia in the Age of Catherine the Great*, 496–9; Epp, *The Educational Policies of Catherine II*, 121; Jan Kusher, "Individual, Subject, and Empire: Towards a Discourse on Upbringing, Education, and Schooling in the Time of Catherine II," *Ab Imperio*, 2 (2008): 149–51; Sysoeva, *Shkola v Rossii xviii-nachala xx vv*, 68–72.
10. Sysoeva, *Shkola v Rossii xviii-nachala xx vv*, 64.
11. Robert L. Nichols, "Orthodoxy and Russia's Enlightenment, 1762–1825," in Robert L. Nichols and Theofanis George Stavrou (eds.), *Russian Orthodoxy under the Old Regime* (Minneapolis: University of Minnesota Press, 1978), 65–89.
12. Elise Kimerling Wirtschafter, "Religion and Enlightenment in Eighteenth-Century Russia: Father Platon at the Court of Catherine II," *The Slavonic and East European Review*, 88, nos. 1 and 2 (2010): 180–203.
13. Gregory L. Freeze, *The Russian Levites: Parish Clergy in the Eighteenth Century* (Cambridge, MA: Harvard University Press, 1979), 100–2.
14. Sysoeva, *Shkola v Rossii xviii-nachala xx vv*, 53; S. V. Sergeeva, *Teoriia i praktika chastnogo obrazovaniia v Rossii (poslednaia polovina xviii-pervaia polovina xix v)* (Moscow-Penza: MPGU, 2003), 98–101.
15. Epp, *The Educational Policies of Catherine II*, 78–9.
16. Sergeeva, *Teoriia i praktika chastnogo obrazovaniia*, 102–4.
17. Sysoeva, *Shkola v Rossii xviii-nachala xx vv*, 52; Epp, *The Educational Policies of Catherine II*, 130.
18. Epp, *The Educational Policies of Catherine II*, 132; Hans, *History of Russian Educational Policy (1701–1917)*, 24.
19. Alston, *Education and the State in Tsarist Russia*, 19.
20. De Madariaga, *Russia in the Age of Catherine the Great*, 503; Shilina, *Evolutsiia zhenskogo obrazovaniia v Rossii*, 53; M. P. Voitekhovskaia, *Politika reform i obshchestvennye initsiativy v razvitii ruskoi sistemy obshchego obrazovaniia v xix-nachale xx vv* (Tomsk: Izdatelstvo Tomskogo gosudarstvennogo pedagogicheskogo universiteta, 2012), 75.
21. John L. H. Keep, *Soldiers of the Tsar. Army and Society in Russia, 1462–1874* (Oxford: Clarendon Press, 1985), 243–4.
22. Olga Solodiankina, *Inostrannye guvernantki v Rossii (vtoraia polivina xviii-pervaia polivina xix vekov* (Moscow: Academiia, 2007), 49.

3 Refining the System: Alexander I and Nicholas I

1. Quoted in W. Bruce Lincoln, *The Romanovs: Autocrats of all the Russias* (New York: Dial Press, 1981), 410.
2. E. K. Sysoeva, *Shkola v Rossii xviii-nachala xx vv: Vlast' i obshchestvo* (Moscow: Novyi khronograf, 2015), 93.
3. James T. Flynn, *The University Reform of Tsar Alexander I, 1802–1825* (Washington, DC: Catholic University of America Press, 1988), 34.
4. Julia Disson, "Privileged Noble High Schools and the Formation of Russian National Elites in the First Part of the 19th Century," *Historical Social Research*, 23, no. 2 (January 2008): 174–89.

5. See Judith Cohen Zacek, "The Russian Bible Society and the Russian Orthodox Church," *Church History*, 35, no. 4 (December 1966): 411–37.
6. Quoted in Flynn, *The University Reform of Tsar Alexander I*, 112.
7. M. P. Voitekhovskaia, *Politika reform i obshchestvennye initiativy v razvitii ruskoi sistemy obshchego obrazovanniiav xix-nachala xx vv* (Tomsk: Izdatel'stvo Tomskogo gosudarstvennogo pedagogicheskogo universiteta, 2012), 106.
8. Alison K. Smith, *For the Common Good and Their Own Well-Being: Social Estates in Imperial Russia* (Oxford: Oxford University Press, 2014), 190.
9. Flynn, *The University Reform of Tsar Alexander I*, 203–4.
10. Quoted in ibid., 191.
11. Ibid., 205.
12. Quoted in Sysoeva, *Shkola v Rossii xviii-nachala xx vv*, 190.
13. Quoted in Flynn, *The University Reform of Tsar Alexander I*, 219.
14. Cynthia H. Whittaker, "The Ideology of Sergei Uvarov: Interpretive Essay," *The Russian Review*, 37, no. 2 (April 1978): 158–76.
15. Alain Besançon, *Éducation et société en Russie dans le second tiers du xixième siècle* (Paris: Mouton, 1974), 16.
16. Sysoeva, *Shkola v Rossii xviii-nachala xx vv*, 163.
17. Quoted in N. A. Mashkin, *Vyshaia voennaia shkola Rossiiskoi imperii xix-nachala xx veka* (Moscow: Academiia, 1947), 23.
18. N. N. Avrova, *Sistema voennogo obrazovaniia v Rossii: kadetskie korpusa vo vtoroi polovine xviii-pervoi polovne xix veka* (Moscow: Institut rossiiskoi istorii, 2003), 70.
19. Quoted in Mashkin, *Vyshaia voennaia shkola Rossiiskoi imperii*, 24.
20. Avrova, *Sistema voennogo obrazovaniia v Rossii*, 71.
21. Janet M. Hartley, *A Social History of the Russian Empire, 1650–1825* (London: Longman, 1999), 27.
22. Catherine Evtuhov, *Portrait of a Russian Province: Economy, Society, and Civilization in Nineteenth-Century Nizhnii Novgorod* (Pittsburgh, PA: Pittsburgh University Press, 2011), 202.
23. Ben Eklof, *Russian Peasant Schools: Officialdom, Village Culture, and Popular Pedagogy* (Berkeley: University of California Press, 1986), 29; Nicholas Hans, *Russian Educational Policy (1701–1917)* (London: King, 1931), 84.
24. Quoted in Besançon, *Éducation et société en Russie dans le second tiers du xixième siècle*, 32.
25. Gregory L. Freeze, *The Russian Levites. Parish Clergy in the Eighteenth Century* (Cambridge, MA: Harvard University Press, 1979), 152.
26. S. V. Sergeeva, *Teoriia i praktika chastnogo obrazovaniia v Rossii (poslednaia polovina xviii-pervaia polovina xix v* (Moscow-Penza: MPGU, 2003), 114.
27. Ibid., 125.
28. Olga Solodiankina, *Inostrannye guvernantki v Rossii (vtoraia polivina xviii-pervaia polivina xix vekov* (Moscow: Academiia, 2007), 55.
29. Ibid., 55–6.
30. Quoted in A. G. Cross, "Early Miss Emmies: English Nannies, Governesses, and Companions in Pre-Emancipation Russia," *New Zealand Slavonic Journal*, no. 1 (1981): 15.
31. Solodiankina, *Inostrannye guvernantki v Rossii*, 71.
32. Quoted in V. V. Ponomareva and L. B. Khoroshilova, *Mir russkoi zhenshchiny: vospitanie, obrazovanie, sud'ba xviii-nachala xx veka* (Moscow: Russkoe slovo, 2006), 139 and 150.

33. Hans, *Russian Educational Policy (1701–1917)*, 56.
34. Eklof, *Russian Peasant Schools*, 33.
35. Susan Smith-Peter, "Educating Peasant Girls for Motherhood: Religion and Primary Education in Mid-Nineteenth Century Russia," *The Russian Review*, 66, no. 3 (July 2007): 391–2.
36. V. M. Bokova and L. G. Sakharova, eds., *Institutki: Vospominaniia vospitanits institutov blagorodnykh devits* (Moscow: Novoe literaturnoe obozrenie, 2001), 11 and 17.
37. Sysoeva, *Shkola v Rossii xviii-nachala xx vv*, 147.
38. Quoted in Patrick L. Alston, *Education and the State in Tsarist Russia* (Stanford, CA: Stanford University Press, 1969), 43–4.
39. Quoted in Solodiankina, *Inostrannye guvernantki v Rossii*, 269 and 274.
40. Voitekhovskaia, *Politika reform i obshchestvennye initiativy*, 120.
41. Sysoeva, *Shkola v Rossii xviii-nachala xx vv*, 157.
42. Ibid., 163.

4 Engaging the Public: Alexander II

1. James C. McClelland, *Autocrats and Academics: Education, Culture, and Society in Tsarist Russia* (Chicago: University of Chicago Press, 1979), 5.
2. Quoted in F. F. Korolev, ed., *Ocherki istorii shkoly i pedagogicheskoi mysli narodov SSSR: Vtoraia polovinal xix v* (Moscow: Pedagogoika, 1976), 294.
3. L. N. Tolstoy, *Tolstoy on Education: Tolstoy's Educational Writings 1861–62*, ed. Alan Pinch and Michael Armstrong (Rutherford, NJ: Fairleigh Dickenson University Press, 1982), 83–4.
4. E. K. Sysoeva, *Shkola v Rossii xviii-nachala xx vv: Vlast' i obshchestvo* (Moscow: Novyi khronograf, 2015), 221.
5. Patrick L. Alston, *Education and the State in Tsarist Russia* (Stanford, CA: Stanford University Press, 1969), 86; Allen Sinel, *The Classroom and the Chancellery: Education and the State in Tsarist Russia* (Stanford, CA: Stanford University Press, 1969), 11.
6. Ben Eklof, *Russian Peasant Schools: Officialdom, Village Culture, and Popular Pedagogy* (Berkeley: University of California Press, 1986), 132; Sinel, *The Classroom and The Chancellory*, 236–7.
7. Sysoeva, *Shkola v Rossii xviii-nachala xx vv*, 241–2.
8. Ibid., 226.
9. Nicholas Hans, *History of Russian Educational Policy (1701–1917)* (London: King, 1931), 137.
10. Eklof, *Russian Peasant Schools*, 84.
11. Sysoeva, *Shkola v Rossii xviii-nachala xx vv*, 307–9.
12. Eklof, *Russian Peasant Schools*, 66–7; Sysoeva, *Shkola v Rossii xviii-nachala xx vv*, 310–11.
13. Quoted in Sysoeva, *Shkola v Rossii xviii-nachala xx vv*, 17.
14. N. A. Mashkin, *Vyshaia voennaia shkola Rossiiskoi imperii xix-nachala xx veka* (Moscow: Akademiia, 1997), 25–7 and 72.
15. Gregory L. Freeze, *The Russian Levites: Parish Clergy in the Eighteenth Century* (Cambridge, MA: Harvard University Press, 1979), 321–3 and 327–8.
16. Sysoeva, *Shkola v Rossii xviii-nachala xx vv*, 300.
17. Ibid., 302.

18. S. V. Sergeeva, *Teoriia i praktika chastnogo obrazovaniia v Rossii (poslednaia polovina xviii-pervaia polovina xix v)* (Moscow-Penza: MPGU, 2003), 126.
19. Sysoeva, *Shkola v Rossii xviii-nachala xx vv*, 155.
20. Quoted in A. N. Veselev, *Professional'no-tekhnicheskoe obrazovanie v SSSR: Ocherki po istorii srednego i nishego proftekhobrazovaniia* (Moscow: Proftekhizdat, 1961), 10.
21. Sysoeva, *Shkola v Rossii xviii-nachala xx vv*, 280.
22. McClelland, *Autocrats and Academics*, 36.
23. Quoted in Christine Johanson, *Women's Struggle for Higher Education in Russia, 1855-1900* (Montreal: McGill-Queen's University Press, 1987), 32.
24. Ibid., 31.
25. V. V. Ponomareva and L. B. Khoroshilova, *Mir russkoi zhenshchiny: vospitanie, obrazovanie, sud'ba, xviii-nachala xx veka* (Moscow: Russkoe slovo, 2006), 190-5.
26. Quoted in ibid., 266.
27. Quoted in S. N. Valk et al., eds., *Sankt-Peterburgskie vysshie zhenskie (Bestuzhevskie) Kursy 1878-1918. Sbornik Statei* (Leningrad: Izdatel'stvo Leningradskogo Universiteta, 1973), 11.
28. Johanson, *Women's Struggle for Higher Education in Russia*, 90-1.
29. Wayne Dowler, *Classroom and Empire: The Politics of Schooling Russia's Eastern Nationalities, 1860-1917* (Montreal: McGill-Queen's University Press, 2001), Introduction and Chapter 1.
30. Alain Besançon, *Éducation et société en Russie dans la second tiers du xix siècle* (Paris: Mouton, 1974), 45.

5 Reasserting Authority: Alexander III and Nicholas II

1. Quoted in W. Bruce Lincoln, *The Romanovs: Autocrats of all the Russias* (New York: Dial Press, 1981), 455, 602, and 605.
2. Richard S. Wortman, *Scenarios of Power: Myth and Ceremony in Russian Monarchy*, vol. 2 of *From Alexander II to the Abdication of Nicholas II* (Princeton, NJ: Princeton University Press, 2000), 343 and 443-8.
3. E. K. Sysoeva, *Shkola v Rossii xviii-nachala xx vv: Vlast' i obshchestvo* (Moscow: Novyi khronograf, 2015), 367.
4. Quoted in M. P. Voitekhovskaia, *Politika reform i obshchestvennye initiativy v razvitii russkoi sistemy obshchego obrazovanniiav xix-nachala xx vv* (Tomsk: Izdatel'stvo Tomskogo gosudarstvennogo pedagogicheskogo universiteta, 2012), 166.
5. Sysoeva, *Shkola v Rossii xviii-nachala xx vv*, 264.
6. Voitekhovskaia, *Politika reform i obshchestvennye*, 263.
7. Sysoeva, *Shkola v Rossii xviii-nachala xx vv*, 268.
8. Ibid., 268-9.
9. Quoted in ibid., 376.
10. Patrick L. Alston, *Education and the State in Tsarist Russia* (Stanford, CA: Stanford University Press, 1969), 142.
11. Quoted in Ben Eklof, *Russian Peasant Schools: Officialdom, Village Culture, and Popular Pedagogy, 1861-1914* (Berkeley: University of California Press, 1986), 279.
12. Jeffery Brooks, *When Russia Learned to Read: Literacy and Popular Culture, 1861-1914* (Princeton, NJ: Princeton University Press, 1985), xv-xvii; Eklof, *Russian Peasant Schools*, 257-62.

13. Eklof, *Russian Peasant Schools*, 332.
14. Quoted in Alston, *Education and the State in Tsarist Russia*, 132–3.
15. Ibid., 142.
16. Ibid., 160.
17. Samuel D. Kassow, *Students, Professors, and the State in Tsarist Russia* (Berkeley: University of California Press, 1989), 8.
18. Christine Johanson, *Women's Struggle for Higher Education in Russia, 1855–1900* (Montreal: McGill-Queen's University Press, 1987), 98–9.
19. V. V. Ponomareva and L. B. Khoroshilova, *Mir russkoi zhenshchiny: vospitanie, obrazovanie, sud'ba xviii-nachala xx veka* (Moscow: Russkoe slovo, 2006), 272.
20. E. I. Time, "Alma Mater," in S. N. Falk, N. G. Sladkevich, B. I. Smirnov, and M. L. Tronskaia (eds.), *Sankt-Peterburgskie vyshie zhenskie (Bestuzhevskie) Kursy, 1878–1918: Sbornik statei* (Leningrad: Lenigrad University Press, 1973), 228.
21. T. A. Shilina, *Evolutsiia zhenskogo obrazovaniia v Rossii: gosudarstvennaia politika i obshchestvennaia initsiativa (konets xviii-nachala xx vv)* (Saratov: Amirit, 2015), 164.
22. Ibid.
23. A. N. Veselev, *Professional'no-tekhnicheskoe obrazovanie v SSSR: Ocherki po istorii srednego i nishego proftekhobrazovaniia* (Moscow: Proftekhizdat, 1961), 20.
24. Voitekhovskaia, *Politika reform i obshchestvennye*, 260–1.
25. Veselev, *Professional'no-tekhnicheskoe obrazovanie v SSSR*, 44.
26. Voitekhovskaia, *Politika reform i obshchestvennye*, 260–1 and 290.
27. Gregory L. Freeze, *The Russian Levites: Parish Clergy in the Eighteenth Century* (Cambridge, MA: Harvard University Press, 1979), 438–9, 452–5; Kassow, *Students, Professors, and the State in Tsarist Russia*, Table A-3.
28. John Meyendorff, "Russian Bishops and Church Reform in 1905," in Robert L. Nichols and Theofanis George Stavrou (eds.), *Russian Orthodoxy under the Old Regime* (Minneapolis: University of Minnesota Press, 1978), 179.
29. Eklof, *Russian Peasant Schools*, 90; Nicholas Hans, *History of Russian Educational Policy (1701–1917)* (London: King, 1931), 187–8.
30. Sysoeva, *Shkola v Rossii xviii-nachala xx vv*, 271.
31. Ibid., 358–9.
32. Brooks, *When Russian Learned to Read*, 13–14.
33. Alston, *Education and the State in Tsarist Russia*, 130.
34. Eklof, *Russian Peasant Schools*, 468.
35. Sysoeva, *Shkola v Rossii xviii-nachala xx vv*, 273 and 277.
36. Ibid., 245; Eklof, *Russian Peasant Schools*, 332.
37. Sysoeva, *Shkola v Rossii xviii-nachala xx vv*, 296.
38. Harry D. Balzer, "The Engineering Profession in Tsarist Russia," in Harry D. Balzer (ed.), *Russia's Missing Middle Class: The Professions in Russian History* (Armonk: M.E.Sharpe, 1996), 59.
39. Sysoeva, *Shkola v Rossii xviii-nachala xx vv*, 302–4.
40. Ibid., 270–1.

6 From Revolution to Revolution: The Duma Period

1. Quoted in W. Bruce Lincoln, *The Romanovs: Autocrats of all the Russias* (New York: Dial Press, 1981), 665.

2. E. K. Sysoeva, *Shkola v Rossii xviii-nachala xx vv: Vlast' i obshchestvo* (Moscow: Novyi khronograf, 2015), 485.
3. M. P. Voitekhovskaia, *Politika reform i obshchestvennye initiativy v razvitii russkoi sistemy obshchego obrazovanniiav xix-nachala xx vv* (Tomsk: Izdatel'stvo Tomskogo gosudarstvennogo pedagogicheskogo universiteta, 2012), 380.
4. Ben Eklof, *Russian Peasant Schools: Officialdom, Village Culture, and Popular Pedagogy* (Berkeley: University of California Press, *1986*), 283–84; Sysoeva, *Shkola v Rossii xviii-nachala xx vv*, 370.
5. Sysoeva, *Shkola v Rossii xviii-nachala xx vv*, 379–80.
6. Voitekhovskaia, *Politika reform i obshchestvennye initiativy*, 380.
7. Sysoeva, *Shkola v Rossii xviii-nachala xx vv*, 383.
8. Voitekhovskaia, *Politika reform i obshchestvennye initiativy*, 424.
9. Patrick L. Alston, *Education and the State in Tsarist Russia* (Stanford, CA: Stanford University Press, 1969), 205.
10. A. N. Veselev, *Professional'no-tekhnicheskoe obrazovanie v SSSR. Ocherki po istorii srednego i nishego proftekhobrazovaniia* (Moscow: Proftekhizdat, 1961), 10–17, 45.
11. Samuel D. Kassow, *Students, Professors, and the State in Tsarist Russia* (Berkeley: University of California Press, 1989), 345.
12. Ibid., 357.
13. Christine Johanson, *Women's Struggle for Higher Education in Russia, 1855–1900* (Montreal: McGill-Queen's University Press, 1987), 100–1; Ruth A. Dudgeon, "The Forgotten Minority: Women Students in Imperial Russia, 1872–1917," *Russian History*, 9, no. 1 (1982): 2–4.
14. Robert W. Thurston, *Liberal City, Conservative State. Moscow and Russia's Urban Crisis, 1906–1914* (Oxford: Oxford University Press, 1987), 163–4; Kassow, *Students, Professors, and the State in Tsarist Russia*, 369.
15. Sysoeva, *Shkola v Rossii xviii-nachala xx vv*, 464–5.
16. Jeffery Brooks, *When Russia Learned to Read. Literacy and Popular Culture, 1861–1914* (Princeton, NJ: Princeton University Press, 1985), 347.
17. Christine Ruane, *Gender, Class, and the Professionalization of Russian City Teachers, 1860–1914* (Pittsburgh, PA: Pittsburgh University Press, 1994), 67.
18. Eklof, *Russian Peasant Schools*, 186.
19. Ibid., 33.
20. Ibid., 122.
21. Scott J. Seregny, *Russian Teachers and Peasant Revolution: The Politics of Education in 1905* (Bloomington: Indiana University Press, 1989), 197–9 and 205.
22. Sysoeva, *Shkola v Rossii xviii-nachala xx vv*, 452.
23. Eklof, *Russian Peasant Schools*, 218; Ruane, *Gender, Class, and the Professionalization of Russian City Teachers*, 59.
24. Eklof, *Russian Peasant Schools*, 306.
25. Sysoeva, *Shkola v Rossii xviii-nachala xx vv*, 456.
26. Ibid., 454–5.
27. Ibid., 434.
28. Ruane, *Gender, Class, and the Professionalization of Russian City Teachers*, 49.
29. Wayne Dowler, *Classroom and Empire: The Politics of Schooling Russia's Eastern Nationalities, 1860–1917* (Montreal: McGill-Queen's University Press, 2001), 221–2.
30. Alexander Dmitiev, "The Russian University System and the First World War," *Studies in East European Thought*, 66, nos. 1/2 (June 2014): 38.

31. Boris N. Mironov, "The Development of Literacy in Russia and the USSR from the Tenth to the Twentieth Centuries," *History of Education Quarterly*, 31, no. 2 (Summer 1991): 240 and 242.
32. Eklof, *Russian Peasant Schools*, 332–3.
33. Ibid., 402–7.
34. Ibid., 468–9.
35. Ibid., 457 (emphasis in the original).
36. Kendall E. Bayles, *Technology and Society under Lenin and Stalin. Origins of the Soviet Technological Intelligentsia, 1917–1941* (Princeton, NJ: Princeton University Press, 1978), 27.

7 Schooling for Socialism: Revolution to Cultural Revolution

1. Quoted in Laura Engelstein, *Russia in Flames: War, Revolution, Civil War, 1914–1921* (Oxford: Oxford University Press, 2018), 76.
2. Quoted in E. Thomas Ewing, *The Teachers of Stalinism: Policy, Practice, and Power in Soviet Schools of the 1930s* (New York: Peter Lang, 2000), 8.
3. Jaweed Ashraf, *Soviet Education: Theory and Practice* (New Delhi: Sterling, 1978), 78; and John Dunstan, "Coeducation and Revolution: Responses to Mixed Schooling in Early Twentieth-Century Russia," *History of Education*, 26, no. 4 (1997): 385.
4. Quoted in V. V. Gorshkova, "Russian Philosophers and Educators on the Pragmatism of John Dewey," *Russian Education and Society*, 57, no. 5 (May 2015): 324. Later Soviet and post-Soviet pedagogues have pointed to earlier distortions in the USSR of Dewey's thinking.
5. Catriona Kelly, *Children's World: Growing up in Russia, 1880–1991* (New Haven, CT: Yale University Press, 2007), 532. See also Sheila Fitzpatrick, *Education and Social Mobility in the Soviet Union, 1921–1934* (Cambridge: Cambridge University Press, 1979), 19–24; and Larry E. Holmes, *The Kremlin and the Schoolhouse: Reforming Education in Soviet Russia, 1917–1931* (Bloomington: Indiana University Press, 1991), 9–10.
6. John Dunstan, "Coeducation and Revolution: Responses to Mixed Schooling in Early Twentieth-Century Russia," *History of Education*, 26 (December 1997): 388–9.
7. J. J. Tomiak, *The Soviet Union: World Education Series* (Newton Abbot: David and Charles, 1972), 15.
8. Holmes, *The Kremlin and the Schoolhouse*, 18.
9. Ibid., 53–4.
10. Quoted in Orlando Figes, *The Whisperers: Private Life in Stalin's Russia* (New York: Picador, 2007), 25–7.
11. Fitzpatrick, *Education and Social Mobility*, 26–30.
12. Figes, *The Whisperers*, 294–5.
13. Holmes, *The Kremlin and the Schoolhouse*, 28–9.
14. Quoted in Kendall E. Bailes, *Technology and Society under Lenin and Stalin: Origins of the Soviet Technological Intelligentsia, 1917–1941* (Princeton, NJ: Princeton University Press, 1978), 49.
15. A. N. Veselev, *Professional'no-tekhnicheskoe obrazovanie v SSSR: Ocherki po istorii srednego i nishego proftekhobrazovaniia* (Moscow: Proftekhizdat, 1961), 185.

16. Ibid., 219.
17. Holmes, *The Kremlin and the Schoolhouse*, 86.
18. Veselev, *Professional'no-tekhnicheskoe obrazovanie v SSSR*, 189.
19. Ibid., 264.
20. Fitzpatrick, *Education and Social Mobility*, 501; and Gail Warshofsky-Lapidus, "Educational Strategies and Cultural Revolution: The Politics of Soviet Development," in Sheila Fitzpatrick (ed.), *Cultural Revolution in Russia, 1928-1931* (Bloomington: Indiana University Press, 1978), 83.
21. Fitzpatrick, *Education and Social Mobility*, 100.
22. Ibid., 82.
23. Ibid., 106-10.
24. Ibid., 184-7.
25. Ibid., 148.
26. Ibid., 192.
27. Elena Gorokhova, *A Mountain of Crumbs: A Memoir* (New York: Simon and Schuster, 2010), 85-6.
28. Holmes, 133-4.
29. Ibid., 130-1.
30. Ibid., 133.
31. Fitzpatrick, *Education and Social Mobility*, 195-6.
32. E. K. Sysoeva, *Shkola v Rossii xviii-nachala xx vv: Vlast' i obshchestvo* (Moscow: Novyi khronograf, 2015), 499.
33. Holmes, *The Kremlin and the Schoolhouse*, 133.
34. Ibid., 134-5.
35. Fitzpatrick, *Education and Social Mobility*, 198.
36. Veselev, *Professional'no-tekhnicheskoe obrazovanie v SSSR*, 190.
37. Fitzpatrick, *Education and Social Mobility*, 196.

8 Retrenchment: Stalin to Chernenko

1. Quoted in Larry E. Holmes, *The Kremlin and the Schoolhouse: Reforming Education in Soviet Russia, 1917-1931* (Bloomington: Indiana University Press, 1991), 137.
2. Catriona Kelly, *Children's World: Growing up in Russia, 1880-1991* (New Haven, CT: Yale University Press, 2007), 511, 516-17.
3. Quoted in E. Thomas Ewing, "Restoring Teachers to their Rights: Soviet Education and the 1936 Denunciation of Pedology," *History of Education Quarterly*, 41, no. 4 (Winter 2001): 487.
4. Quoted in Kelly, *Children's World*, 549.
5. E. Thomas Ewing, *The Teachers of Stalinism: Policy, Practice, and Power in Soviet Schools of the 1930s* (New York: Peter Lang, 2000), 7 and 69.
6. Ibid., 127.
7. Larry E. Holmes, "School and Schooling under Stalin, 1931-1953," in Ben Eklof, Larry E. Holmes, and Vera Kaplan (eds.), *Educational Reform in Post-Soviet Russia: Legacies and Prospect* (London: Frank Cass, 2005), 64 and 74.
8. Deborah Hoffman, "Memoirs of Childhood in the GULAG," *Toronto Slavic Quarterly* 34: *Academic Electronic Journal in Slavic Studies*: (http://www.sites.utoronto.ca./tsq).

9. Kendall E. Bailes, *Technology and Society under Lenin and Stalin: Origins of the Soviet Technological Intelligentsia, 1917–1941* (Princeton, NJ: Princeton University Press, 1978), 226.
10. Sheila Fitzpatrick, *Education and Social Mobility in the Soviet Union, 1921–1934* (Cambridge: Cambridge University Press, 1979), 220.
11. Ibid., 235.
12. John Dunstan, *Soviet Schooling in the Second World War* (New York: St. Martin's Press, 1997), 63–4.
13. A. N. Veselev, *Professional'no-tekhnicheskoe obrazovanie v SSSR: Ocherki po istorii srednego i nishego proftekhobrazovaniia* (Moscow: Proftekhizdat, 1961), 342–6.
14. Dunstan, *Soviet Schooling in the Second World War*, 86.
15. Quoted in ibid., 18.
16. Quoted in ibid., 172.
17. Quoted in ibid., 165–6.
18. Veselev, *Professional'no-tekhnicheskoe obrazovanie v SSSR*, 352–3.
19. Dunstan, *Soviet Schooling in the Second World War*, 179–82.
20. Quoted in Susan Jacoby, *Inside Soviet Schools* (New York: Hill and Wang, 1995), 13.
21. Theodore P. Gerber and Michael Hout, "Educational Stratification in Russia during the Soviet Period," *American Journal of Sociology*, 101, no. 3 (November 1995): 625.
22. T. Anthony Jones, "Modernization and Education in the USSR," *Social Forces*, 57, no. 2 (December 1978): 536.
23. Ibid., 541.
24. Mervyn Matthews, *Education in the Soviet Union: Policies and Institutions since Stalin* (London: George Allen and Unwin, 1982), 84–6.
25. Quoted in Nigel Grant, "Teacher Education in the USSR and Eastern Europe," *British Journal of Teacher* Education, 1, no. 3 (1975): 387.
26. Ibid., 150.
27. For a brief survey of higher military schooling in the USSR see Christina F. Shelton, "The Soviet Military Education System for Commissioning and Training Officers," Conference on Military and Political Affairs in the 1980s. United States Airforce (September 25–27, 1980).
28. Captain C. Ros, "Suvorovites, Nakhimovites, and Musicians," *RUSI Journal*, 128, no. 4 (December 1, 1983): 30–4.
29. David Hopkins, "The New Role of 'Social Science' in the Ideological Training of Students in the Post-Stalin Period" in George Avis (ed.), *Soviet Higher and Vocational Education: From Khrushchev to Gorbachev* (Bradford: Modern Language Centre, 1981), 6.
30. On the functions of these youth organizations, see Kelly, *Children's World*, 547–55.
31. Quoted in E. Thomas Ewing, "Ethnicity at School: Non-Russian' Education in the Soviet Union during the 1930s," *History of Education*, 35, nos. 4–5 (July–September 2006): 511.
32. Gerber and Hout, "Educational Stratification in Russia during the Soviet Period," 619–20.
33. Matthews, *Education in the Soviet Union*, 87; and Jones, "Modernization," 526.
34. Anthony Jones, "The Educational Legacy of the Soviet Period," in Anthony Jones (ed.), *Education and Society in the New Russia* (Armonk: M.E. Sharpe, 1994), 6.

9 Ends and Beginnings: Gorbachev to Putin

1. Quoted in Dilbert H. Long, Continuity and Change in Soviet Education under Gorbachev," *American Educational Research Journal*, 27, no. 3 (Fall 1990): 404.
2. Stephen T. Kerr, "Demographic Change and the Fate of Russia's Schools: The Impact of Population Shifts on Educational Practices and Policy," in Ben Eklof, Larry E. Holmes, and Vera Kaplan (eds.), *Educational Reform in Post-Soviet Russia: Legacies and Prospects* (London: Frank Cass, 2005), 158–9.
3. Elizaveta Potapova, "Education in the Russian Federation," *World Education News and Reviews*, June 6, 2017. Available online: https://wenr.wes.org/2017/06/education-in-the-russian-federation.
4. Bill Bowring, "Minority Language Rights in the Russian Federation: The End of a Long Tradition," in Gabrielle Hogan-Brun and Bernadette O'Rourke (eds.), *Handbook of Minority Languages and Communities* (London: Palgrave Macmillan, 2019), 8–9.
5. Stephen L. Webber, *School, Reform and Society in the New Russia* (London: Macmillan Press, 2000), 103.
6. Mary Canning, "New Directions for Vocational Training," in Th. J. Siskens and L. E. Beijlamit (eds.), *Crossroads in Russia: Experiences in Educational Cooperation* (Leuvens: ACCO, 2000), 58.
7. Quoted in Alexandra Blinkova and Paul Vermeer, "Religious Education in Russia: A Comparative and Critical Analysis," *British Journal of Religious Education*, 40, no. 2 (March 2018): 194–206.
8. Tatiana S. Komashinskaia and Grigorii P. Tsurkan, "The History and Revival of Sunday Schools in Russia," *Religious Education*, 114 (January 2019): 42–56.
9. T. V. Sklyarova, "Orthodox Christian Education in Modern Russia: Structure and Content," *Russian Education and Society*, 60, no. 3 (2018): 257–68.
10. Ben Eklof, "Russian Education: The Past in the Present," in Ben Eklof, Larry E. Holmes, and Vera Kaplan (eds.), *Educational Reform in Post-Soviet Russia: Legacies and Prospects* (London: Frank Cass, 2005), 15.
11. Isak D. Froumin, "Democratizing the Russian School. Achievements and Setbacks," in Ben Eklof, Larry E. Holmes, and Vera Kaplan (eds.), *Educational Reform in Post-Soviet Russia: Legacies and Prospects* (London: Frank Cass, 2005), 133–4.
12. Webber, *School, Reform and Society in the New Russia*, 97–8.
13. Vladimir Putin, "Welcome Remarks. Meeting of the Valdai International Discussion Club in Novgorod," *President of Russia*, September 19, 2013. Available online: http://en.kremlin.ru/events/president/news/19243.
14. Potapova, "Education in the Russian Federation."
15. Alexey Belaev, "The Structure of Public Spending and Economic Growth in Russia," *Journal of Economics*, 5, no. 2 (July 2019): 176.
16. T. L. Kliachko, "Main Tendencies of the Development of the System of Education of the Russian Federation in 2007," *Russian Education and Society*, 51, no. 7 (July 2009): 38, 43, and 54.
17. Marina Starodutseva and Irina Krivko, "The State Policy of Education in Modern Russia: Pro and Contra," *International Journal of Social Sciences and Humanities*, 5, no. 2 (February 2015): 209.
18. "Russia's Education System," European Parliamentary Research Service (http://www.europarl.europa.eu); European Parliament Think Tank (http://www.epthinktank.eu) (accessed January 25, 2017).

19. Potapova, "Education in the Russian Federation."
20. Ibid.
21. Ibid.
22. Ibid.
23. M. P. Gur'ianova, "Problems and Prospects of the Development of the Rural School in Russia," *Russian Education and Society*, 51, no. 7 (July 2009): 4–7.
24. A. Ia. Daniliuk, A. M. Kondakov, and V. A. Teshkov, "The Spiritual and Moral Education of Russian School Students," *Russian Education and Society*, 52, no. 2 (February 2010): 3–4 and 12.
25. Quoted in Vera Kaplan, "History Teaching in Post-Soviet Russia: Coping with antithetical traditions," in Ben Eklof, Larry E. Holmes, and Vera Kaplan (eds.), *Education Reform in Post-Soviet Russia: Legacies and Prospects* (London: Frank Cass, 2005), 262.
26. Quoted in Mark Edele, "Fighting Russia's History Wars: Vladimir Putin and the Codification of World War II," *History and Memory*, 29, no. 2 (Fall 2016/Winter 2017): 93.
27. Quoted in Dagmara Moskwa, "Rewriting Russian History," *Eurozine*, January 19, 2018. Available online: https://www.eurozine.com/rewriting-russian-history/.
28. Ibid.
29. Quoted in "Meet the Ministry of Enlightenment," *The Economist* (May 26, 2018), 49–50.
30. Anna Georgievna Sanina, "Patriotism and Patriotic Education in Contemporary Russia," *Russian Social Science Review*, 58, no. 5 (2018): unnumbered.
31. V. A. Teshkov, V. V. Stepanov, "Interethnic Relations and Ethnocultural Education in Russia," *Herald of the Russian Academy of Science*, 87, no. 5 (2017): 419.
32. Quoted in Bowring, "Minority Language Rights in the Russian Federation," 11.
33. Quoted in "Russia: Education cuts will erode minority rights," *Oxford Analytica Daily Briefing Service* (January 25, 2018): 1 (https//:dailybrief.oxan.com).
34. Sufia Zhmukhov and Sener Aktürk, "The Movement toward a Monolingual Nation in Russia: The Language Policy in Circassian Republics of the North Caucasus," *Journal of Caucasian Studies*, 1, no. 1 (September 2015): 51.
35. Potapova, "Education in the Russian Federation."
36. "Putin Proposes Constitutional Ban on Gay Marriage," *The Globe and Mail* (March 4, 2020) (http://www.theglobeandmail.com).

Bibliography

Alston, Patrick L. Education *and the State in Tsarist Russia*. Stanford, CA: Stanford University Press, 1969.
Anderson, Barbara A., Brian D. Silver, and Victoria A. Velkoff. "Education of the Handicapped in the USSR: Exploration of the Statistical Picture." *Soviet Studies* 39 (July 1987): 468–88.
Andreev, A. L. "On the Modernization of Education in Russia: A Historical Sociological Analysis." *Russian Social Science Review* 54 (September–October 2013): 4–21.
Ashraf, Jaweed. *Soviet Education: Theory and Practice*. New Delhi: Sterling, 1978.
Avis, George. "Aspirations for Higher Education and the Social Background of Soviet School Leavers: Changing Patterns in the 1960s." In *Soviet Higher and Vocational Education from Khrushchev to Gorbachev*, edited by George Avis, 29–64. Bradford: Modern Languages Centre, University of Bradford, 1987.
Avis, George. "Student Responses to Communist Upbringing in Soviet Higher Education." In *The Making of the Soviet Citizen: Character Formation and Civic Training in Soviet Education*, edited by George Avis, 212–35. London: Croom Helm, 1987.
Avrova, N. N. *Sistema voennogo obrazovaniia v Rossii: kadetskie korpusy vo vtoroi polovine xviii-pervoi polovine xix veka*. Moscow: Institut rossiiskoi istorii, 2003.
Bailes, Kendall E. *Technology and Society under Lenin and Stalin: Origins of the Soviet Technical Intelligentsia, 1917–1941*. Princeton, NJ: Princeton University Press, 1978.
Balaev, Alexey. "The Structure of Public Spending and Economic Growth in Russia." *Russian Journal of Economics* 5 (July 2019): 154–76.
Balzer, Harley D. "Plans to Reform Russian Higher Education." In *Education and Society in the New Russia*, edited by Anthony Jones, 27–46. Armonk: M.E. Sharpe, 1994.
Basil, John D. "Orthodoxy and Public Education in the Russian Federation: The First Fifteen Years." *Journal of Church and State* 49 (2007): 27–52.
Besançon, Alain. *Éducation et société en Russie dans le second tiers du xix siècle*. Paris: Mouton, 1974.
Black, J. L. *Citizens for the Fatherland. Education, Educators, and Pedagogical Ideals in Eighteenth-Century Russia*. Boulder, CO: East European Quarterly, 1979.
Blackwell, William L. *The Beginnings of Russian Industrialization, 1800–1860*. Princeton, NJ: Princeton University Press, 1968.
Blinkova, Alexandra, and Paul Vermeer. "Religious Education in Russia: A Comparative and Critical Analysis." *British Journal of Religious Education* 40 (March 2018): 194–206.
Boiter, Albert. "The Khrushchev School Reform." *Comparative Education Review* 2 (1959): 8–14.
Bokova, V. M., and L. G. Sakharova, eds. *Institutki: Vospominaniia vospitannits institutov blagorodnykh devits*. Moscow: Novoe literaturnoe obozrenie, 2001.
Bowring, Bill. "Minority Language Rights in the Russian Federation." In *Handbook of Minority Languages and Communities*, edited by Gabrielle Hogan-Brun and Bernadette O'Rourke, 2–25. London: Palgrave Macmillan, 2019.

Brooks, Jeffery. "The Zemstvo and the Education of the People." In *The Zemstvo in Russia: An Experiment in Local Self-Government*, edited by Terence Emmons and Wayne Vucinich, 244–73. Cambridge: Cambridge University Press, 1982.

Brooks, Jeffery. *When Russia Learned to Read: Literacy and Popular Culture, 1861–1914*. Princeton, NJ: Princeton University Press, 1985.

Bushkovitch, Paul. "Change and Culture in Early Modern Russia." *Kritika* 16, no. 2 (Spring 2015): 291–316.

Canning, Mary. "New Directions for Vocational Training." In *Crossroads in Russia's Experience in Educational Cooperation*, edited by Th. J. Siskens and L. E. Beijlamit, 57–86. Leuven: ACCO, 2000.

Chekhov, N. V. *Narodnoe obrazovanie v Rossii s 60kh godov xix veka*. Moscow: Pol'za, 1912.

Chevalier, Joan F. "Language Policy in the Russian Federation: Russian as the 'State' Language." *Ab Imperio* 1 (2005): 285–303.

Chrissidis, Nicholas A. *An Academy at the Court of the Tsars: Greek Scholars and Jesuit Education in Early Modern Russia*. DeKalb: Northern Illinois University Press, 2016.

Cracraft, James. *The Church Reform of Peter the Great*. London: Macmillan, 1971.

Cracraft, James. *The Petrine Revolution in Russian Culture*. Cambridge, MA: Harvard University Press, 2004.

Cross, A. G. "Early Miss Emmies: English Nannies, Governesses, and Companions in Pre-emancipation Russia." *New Zealand Slavonic Journal*, no. 1 (January 1981): 1–20.

Daniliuk, A. Ia., A. M. Kondakov, and V. A. Tishkov. "The Spiritual and Moral Education of Russia's School Students." *Russian Education and Society* 52 (February 2010): 3–18.

De Groof, J. "Higher Education: A matter of Joint Competence. A Brief Analysis of Federalism in Russia." In *Crossroads in Russia's Experience in Educational Cooperation*, edited by Th. J. Siskens and L. E. Beijlamit, 19–26. Leuven: ACCO, 2000.

De Madariaga, Isobel. *Russia in the Age of Catherine the Great*. London: Weidenfeld and Nicolson, 1981.

Disson, Julia. "Privileged Noble High Schools and the Formation of Russian National Elites in the First Part of the Nineteenth Century." *Historical Social Research* 33, no. 2 (January 2008): 174–89.

Dowler, Wayne. *Classroom and Empire: The Politics of Schooling Russia's Eastern Nationalities, 1860–1917*. Montreal: McGill-Queens University Press, 2001.

Dunstan, John. "Coeducation and Revolution: Responses to Mixed Schooling in Early Twentieth-Century Russia." *History of Education* 26 (December 1997): 375–93.

Dunstan, John. *Soviet Schooling in the Second World War*. New York: St. Martin's Press, 1997.

Dunstan, John. "Soviet Upbringing under Perestroika: From Atheism to Religious Education." In *Soviet Education under Perestroika*, edited by John Dunstan, 81–105. London: Routledge, 1992.

Dunstan, John, and Avril Suddaby. "The Progressive Tradition in Soviet Schooling to 1988." In *Soviet Education under Perestroika*, edited by John Dunstan, 1–13. London: Routledge, 1992.

Dudgeon, Ruth A. "The Forgotten Minority: Women Students in Imperial Russia, 1872–1917." *Russian History* 9, no. 1 (1982): 1–26.

Edele, Mark. "Fighting Russia's History Wars: Vladimir Putin and the Codification of World War II." *History and Memory* 29 (Fall 2016/Winter 2017): 90–124.

Education GPS. "Russian Federation. Overview of the Education System." OECD, 2019. Available online: https://gpseducation.oecd.org/CountryProfile?primaryCountry=RUS&treshold=10&topic=EO.

Eklof, Ben. "Russian Education: The Past in the Present." In *Educational Reform in Post-Soviet Russia: Legacies and Prospects*, edited by Ben Eklof, Larry Holmes, and Vera Kaplan, 1–20. London: Frank Cass, 2005.

Eklof, Ben. *Russian Peasant Schools: Officialdom, Village Culture, and Popular Pedagogy, 1864–1914*. Berkeley: University of California Press, 1986.

Eklof, Ben, and Scott Seregny. "Teachers in Russia. State, Community and Profession." In *Educational Reform in Post-Soviet Russia: Legacies and Prospects*, edited by Ben Eklof, Larry Holmes, and Vera Kaplan, 197–220. London: Frank Cass, 2005.

Epp, George K. *The Educational Policies of Catherine II: The Era of Enlightenment in Russia*. Frankfurt: Peter Lang, 1984.

Evtuhov, Catherine. *Portrait of a Russian Province. Economy, Society, and Civilization in Nineteenth-Century Nizhnii Novgorod*. Pittsburgh, PA: University of Pittsburgh Press, 2011.

Ewing, E. Thomas. "Ethnicity at School: Non-Russian Education in the Soviet Union during the 1930s." *History of Education* 35 (July–September 2006): 499–519.

Ewing, E. Thomas. "If the Teacher Were a Man: Masculinity and Power in Stalinist Schools." *Gender and History* 21 (March 2009): 107–29.

Ewing, E. Thomas. "The Repudiation of Single-Sex Education: Boys' Schools in the Soviet Union, 1943–1954." *American Educational Research Journal* 43 (Winter 2006): 621–50.

Ewing, E. Thomas. "Restoring Teachers to Their Rights: Soviet Education and the 1936 Denunciation of Pedology." *History of Education Quarterly* 41 (Winter 2001): 471–93.

Ewing, E. Thomas. *The Teachers of Stalinism: Policy, Practice, and Power in Soviet Schools of the 1930s*. New York: Peter Lang, 2002.

Fedyukin, Igor. *The Enterprisers: The Politics of School in Early Modern Russia*. Oxford: Oxford University Press, 2019.

Fedyukin, Igor. "Nobility and Schooling in Russia, 1700s–1760s: Choices in a Social Context." *Journal of Social History* 49, no. 3 (2016): 558–84.

Fedyukin, Igor, and Salavat Gabdrakhomanov. "Cultural Capital and Education in St. Petersburg: The Noble Cadets Corps, 1732–1762." *Journal of Interdisciplinary History* 46, no. 4 (Spring 2016): 485–511.

Figes, Orlando. *The Whisperers: Private Life in Stalin's Russia*. New York: Picador, 2007.

Fitzpatrick, Sheila. *The Commissariat of Enlightenment: Soviet Organization of Education and the Arts under Lunacharsky, October 1917–1921*. Cambridge: Cambridge University Press, 1970.

Fitzpatrick, Sheila. *Education and Social Mobility in the Soviet Union, 1921–1934*. Cambridge: Cambridge University Press, 1979.

Flynn, James T. *The University Reform of Tsar Alexander II, 1802–1825*. Washington, DC: Catholic University of America Press, 1988.

Freeze, Gregory L. "The Disintegration of Traditional Communities: The Parish in Eighteenth-Century Russia." *The Journal of Modern History* 48 (March 1976): 32–50.

Freeze, Gregory L. *The Parish Clergy in Nineteenth Century Russia: Crisis, Reform, Counter Reform*. Princeton, NJ: Princeton University Press, 1983.

Freeze, Gregory L. *The Russian Levites: Parish Clergy in the Eighteenth Century*. Cambridge, MA: Harvard University Press, 1979.

Froumin, Isak D. "Democratizing the Russian School. Achievements and Setbacks." In *Educational Reform in Post-Soviet Russia: Legacies and Prospects*, edited by Ben Eklof, Larry Holmes, and Vera Kaplan, 129–52. London: Frank Cass, 2005.

Gerber, Theodore, and Michael Hout. "Educational Stratification in Russia during the Soviet Period." *American Journal of Sociology* 101 (November 1995): 611–60.

Gindes, Boris. "Special Education in the Soviet Union: Problems and Perspectives." *Journal of Special Education* 20 (January 1986): 379–84.

Gorokhova, Elena. *A Mountain of Crumbs: A Memoir*. New York: Simon & Schuster, 2009.

Gorshkova, V. V. "Russian Philosophers and Educators on the Pragmatism of John Dewey." *Russian Education and Society* 57 (May 2015): 323–37.

Grant, Nigel, "Education in the Soviet Union: The Last Phase." *Compare* 22 (1992): 69–80.

Grant, Nigel. "Multicultural Education in the USSR." In *The Making of the Soviet Citizen: Character Formation and Civic Training in Soviet Education*, edited by George Avis, 184–211. London: Croom Helm, 1987.

Grant, Nigel. *Soviet Education*. Harmondsworth: Penguin Books, 1968, revised edition.

Grant, Nigel. "Teacher Education in the USSR and Eastern Europe." *British Journal of Teacher Education* 1 (1975): 383–400.

Grigor'ev, V. V. *Istoricheskii ocherk russkoi shkoly*. Moscow: T-vo Tipografii A.I. Mamontov, 1900.

Gur'ianova, M. P. "Problems and Prospects of the Development of the Rural School in Russia." *Russian Education and Society* 51 (July 2009): 3–12.

Hans, Nicholas A. *History of Russian Educational Policy*. London: King, 1931.

Hans, Nicholas A. *The Russian Tradition in Education*. New York: Routledge, 2012.

Hartley, Janet M. *A Social History of the Russian Empire*. London: Longman, 1999.

Heyneman, Stephen P. "A Comment on the Changes in Higher Education in the Former Soviet Union." *European Education* 42 (Spring 2010): 76–87.

Hoffman, Deborah. "Memoirs of Childhood in the GULAG." *Toronto Slavic Quarterly* 34: *Academic Electronic Journal in Slavic Studies*. Available online: http://www.sites.utoronto.ca./tsq.

Holmes, Larry E. "Magic into Hocus-Pocus: The Decline of Labor Education in Soviet Russia's Schools, 1931–1937." *Russian Review* 51 (October 1992): 545–65.

Holmes, Larry E. *The Kremlin and the Schoolhouse: Reforming Education in Soviet Russia, 1917–1931*. Bloomington: Indiana University Press, 1991.

Holmes, Larry E. "School and Schooling under Stalin, 1931–1953." In *Educational Reform in Post-Soviet Russia: Legacies and Prospects*, edited by Ben Eklof, Larry Holmes, and Vera Kaplan, 56–101. London: Frank Cass, 2005.

Hopkins, David. "The New Role of 'Social Science' in the Ideological Training of Students in the Post-Stalin Period." In *Soviet Higher and Vocational Education: From Khrushchev to Gorbachev*, edited by George Avis, 1–28. Bradford: Modern Language Centre, 1981.

Hughes, Lindsey. *Russia in the Age of Peter the Great*. New Haven, CT: Yale University Press, 1998.

Jacoby, Susan. *Inside Soviet Schools*. New York: Hill and Wang, 1975.

Johanson, Christine. *Women's Struggle for Higher Education in Russia, 1855–1900*. Kingston-Montreal: McGill-Queen's University Press, 1987.

Jones, Anthony. "The Educational Legacy of the Soviet Period." In *Education and Society in the New Russia*, edited by Anthony Jones, 3–25. Armonk: M.E. Sharpe, 1994.

Jones, Anthony. "Modernization and Education in the USSR." *Social Forces* 57 (December 1978): 522–46.

Jones, Anthony. "The Educational Legacy of the Soviet Period." In *Education and Society in the New Russia*, edited by Anthony Jones, 3–23. Armonk: M.E. Sharpe, 1994.

Jones, W. Gareth. "Russia's Eighteenth-Century Enlightenment." In *A History of Russian Thought*, edited by William Leatherbarrow and Derek Offord, 73–94. Cambridge: Cambridge University Press, 2010.

Kaplan, Vera. "History Teaching in Post-Soviet Russia: Coping with Antithetical Traditions." In *Educational Reform in Post-Soviet Russia: Legacies and Prospects*, edited by Ben Eklof, Larry Holmes, and Vera Kaplan, 247–71. London: Frank Cass, 2005.

Karp, Alexander. "We All Meandered through Our Schooling…: Note on Russian Mathematics Education in the Early Nineteenth Century." *BSHM Bulletin* 22 (2007): 104–19.

Karpov, Vyacheslav, and Elena Liskovskaia. "Educational Change in Time of Social Revolution: The Case of Post-Communist Russia in Comparative Perspective." In *Educational Reform in Post-Soviet Russia: Legacies and Prospects*, edited by Ben Eklof, Larry Holmes, and Bera Kaplan, 23–35. London: Frank Cass, 2005.

Kassow, Samuel D. *Students, Professors, and the State in Tsarist Russia*. Berkeley: University of California Press, 1989.

Keep, John L. H. *Soldiers of the Tsar: Army and Society in Russia, 1462–1874*. Oxford: Clarendon Press, 1985.

Kelly, Catriona. *Children's World: Growing Up in Russia, 1880–1991*. New Haven, CT: Yale University Press, 2007.

Kerr, Stephen T. "Debate and Controversy in Soviet Higher Education Reform: Reinventing a System." In *Soviet Education under Perestroika*, edited by John Dunstan, 146–63. London: Routledge, 1992.

Kerr, Stephen T. "Demographic Change and the Fate of Russia's Schools: The Impact of Population Shifts on Educational Practice and Policy." In *Educational Reform in Post-Soviet Russia: Legacies and Prospects*, edited by Ben Eklof, Larry Holmes, and Vera Kaplan, 153–75. London: Frank Cass, 2005.

Kerr, Stephen T. "Diversification in Russian Education." In *Education and Society in the New Russia*, edited by Anthony Jones, 47–74. Armonk: M.E. Sharpe, 1994.

Kerr, Stephen T. The Experimental Tradition in Russian Education." In *Educational Reform in Post-Soviet Russia: Legacies and Prospects*, edited by Ben Eklof, Larry Holmes, and Vera Kaplan, 102–28. London: Frank Cass, 2005.

Kimerling Wirtschafter, Elise. "Religion and Enlightenment in Eighteenth-Century Russia: Father Platon at the Court of Catherine II." *The Slavonic and East European Review* 88, nos. 1 and 2 (January–April 2010): 180–203.

Kingston-Manning, Esther. *In Search of the True West: Culture, Economics, and Problems of Russian Development*. Princeton, NJ: Princeton University Press, 1999.

Kliashko, T. L. "Main Tendencies of the Development of the System of Education and of the Russian Federation in 2007." *Russian Education and Society* 51 (July 2009): 35–57.

Komashinskaia, Tatiana, and Grigorii P. Tsurkin. "The History and Revival of Sunday Schools in Russia." *Religious Education* 114 (January 2019): 42–56.

Korkunov, Vladimir V., Alexander S. Nigayev, and Lynne Reynolds. "Special Education in Russia: History, Reality, and Prospects." *Journal of Learning Disabilities* 31 (March/April 1998): 186–92.

Korolev, F. F., ed. *Ocherki istorii shkoly i pedagogicheskoi mysly narodov SSSR*. Moscow: Pedagogika, 1973.

Kozyrev, Fedor. "Religious Education in Russian Schools." *East-West Church and Minority Report* 10 (Fall 2002): 1–7.

Kozyrin, Alexander, and Tatyana Troshikina. "The Law of Education of 2012 and the Development of Educational Law in Russia." *Law. Journal of the Higher School of Economics* 1 (March 10, 2017): 80–91.

Kreindler, Isabelle. "The Changing Status of Russian in the Soviet Union." *International Journal of the Sociology of Language* 33 (1982): 7–39.

Kuebart, Friedrich. "Reform in Soviet Vocational Education: The Interface of Economic, Labour and Educational Policies." In *Soviet Education under Perestroika*, edited by John Dunstan, 128–45. London: Routledge, 1992.

Kusher, Jan. "Individual, Subject, and Empire: Towards a Discourse on Upbringing, Education, and Schooling in the Time of Catherine II." *Ab Imperio* 2 (2008): 125–56.

Lenin, V. I. "On Polytechnical Education." In *Lenin Collected Works*, vol. 36: 532–4. Moscow: Progress Publishers, 1971.

Leprêtre, Marc. "Language Policy in the Russian Federation: Language, Diversity and National Identity." *Revista de Sociolinguistica* (Spring 2002). Available online: https://www.gencat/llengua/noves.

Long, Dilbert H. "Continuity and Change in Soviet Education under Gorbachev." *American Educational Research Journal* 27 (Fall 1990): 403–23.

Lotareva, R. M. *Gorod-zavody Rossii xviii-pervaia polovina xix veka*. Ekaterinburg: Sokrat, 2011.

Mashkin, N. A. *Vyshaia voennaia shkola Rossiiskoi Imperii xix-nachale xx veka*. Moscow: Academiia, 1997.

Matthews, Mervyn. *Education in the Soviet Union: Policies and Institutions since Stalin*. London: George Allen and Unwin, 1982.

McClelland, James C. *Autocrats and Academics. Education, Culture, and Society in Tsarist Russia*. Chicago: University of Chicago Press, 1979.

Meyendorff, John. "Russian Bishops and Church Reform in 1905." In *Russian Orthodoxy under the Old Regime*, edited by Robert L. Nichols and Theofanis George Stavrou, 170–82. Minneapolis: University of Minnesota Press, 1978.

Minter, Ian, Roza Valieva, and Aydar Kalimullin. "A Tale of Two Countries Forty Years On: Politics and Teacher Education in Russia and England." *European Journal of Teacher Education* 40 (October 2017): 616–29.

Mironov, Boris N. "The Development of Literacy in Russia and the USSR from the Tenth to the Twentieth Century." *History of Education Quarterly* 31, no. 2 (Summer 1991): 229–52.

Morrissey, Susan K. *Heralds of Revolution: Russian Students and the Mythologies of Radicalism*. New York: Oxford University Press, 1998.

Moskwa, Dagmara. "Rewriting Russian History." *Eurozine*, January 19, 2018. Available online: https://www.eurozine.com/rewriting-russian-history/.

Muckle, James. "The New Soviet Child: Moral Education in Soviet Schools." In *The Making of the Soviet Citizen: Character Formation and Civic Training in Soviet Education*, edited by George Avis, 1–22. London: Croom Helm, 1987.

Okenfuss, Max J. "From School Class to Social Caste: The Divisiveness of Early-Modern Russian Education." *Jahrbücher für Geschichte Osteuropas* 33 (1985): 321–44.

Pearson, Landon. *Children of Glasnost': Growing Up Soviet*. Toronto: Lester and Orpen Dennys, 1990.

Petrov, V., ed. *Naslednik vstal rano i za uroki sel–:Kak uchili i uchilis v xviii v*. Moscow: Lomonosov, 2010.

Pitcher, Harvey. *When Miss Emmie was in Russia: English Governesses before, during and after the October Revolution*. London: J. Murray, 1977.

Ponomarova, V. V., and L. B. Khoroshilova. *Mir russkoi zhenshchiny: vospitanie, obrazovania, sud'ba, xviii—nachalo xx veka*. Moscow: Russkoe slovo, 2006.
Potapova, Elizaveta. "Education in the Russian Federation." *World Education News and Reviews*, June 6, 2017. Available online: https://wenr.wes.org/2017/06/education-in-the-russian-federation.
Putin, Vladimir. "Welcome Remarks. Meeting of the Valdai International Discussion Club in Novgorod," *President of Russia*, September 19, 2013. Available online: http://en.kremlin.ru/events/president/news/19243.
"Putin Proposes Constitutional Ban on Gay Marriage," *The Globe and Mail* (March 4, 2020). Available online: http://www.theglobeandmail.com.
Raeff, Marc. *Origins of the Russian Intelligentsia: The Eighteenth-Century Nobility*. New York: Harcourt, Brace & World, 1966.
Rjéoutski, Vladislav, ed. *Quand le français gouvernait la Russie: L'éducation de la noblesse russe, 1750–1880*. Paris: L'Harmattan, 2016.
Rooney, Peter. "Soviet Schooling and the World of Work." In *Soviet Higher and Vocational Education from Khrushchev to Gorbachev*, edited by George Avis, 77–93. Bradford: Modern Languages Centre, University of Bradford, 1987.
Ropp, A. N. *Chto sdelala tret'i gosudarstvennaia Duma dlia narodnogo obrazovaniia?* St. Petersburg: Tip. T-va A.S. Suvorina, 1912.
Ros, Captain C. "Suvorites, Nakhimovites and Musicians." *RUSI Journal* 128 (December 1, 1983): 30–4.
Ruane, Christine. *Gender, Class, and the Professionalization of Russian City Teachers, 1860–1914*. Pittsburgh, PA: Pittsburgh University Press, 1994.
"Russia's Education Cuts Will Erode Minority Rights." *Oxford Analytica Daily Brief Service* 1 (January 25, 2018). Available online: http://www.dailybrief.oxan.com.
"Russia's Education System," European Parliamentary Research Service. Available online: http://www.europarl.europa.eu; European Parliament Think Tank: http://www.epthinktank.eu (accessed January 25, 2017).
Sams, John. "The Soviet Secondary PTU." In *Soviet Higher and Vocational Education from Khrushchev to Gorbachev*, edited by George Avis, 65–76. Bradford: Modern Languages Centre, University of Bradford. 1987.
Sanina, Anna Georgievna. "Patriotism and Patriotic Education in Contemporary Russia." *Russian Social Science Review* 59 (2018): 468–82.
Schlesenger, Ina. "Moral Education in the Soviet Union." *Phi Delta Kappa* 46 (October 1964): 72–5.
Seregny, Scott J. *Russian Teachers and Peasant Revolution: The Politics of Education in 1905*. Bloomington: Indiana University Press, 1989.
Sergeeva, S. V. *Teoriia i praktika chastnogo obrazovaniia v Rossii (poslednaia chetvert xviii–pervaia polovina xix v)*. Moscow-Penza: MPGU, 2003.
Shelton, Christian F. "The Soviet Military Education System for Commissioning and Training Officers." Conference on Military and Political Affairs in the 1980s. United States Airforce (September 25–27, 1980).
Shevchenko, P. V. "Srednie voenno-uchebnye zavedeniia Rossii pervoi poloviny XIX veka glazami ikh vospitannikov." *Vestnik PSTGU* 89 (2019): 83–96.
Shevyrev, Alexander. "Rewriting the National Past: New Images of Russia in History Textbooks of the 1990s." In *Educational Reform in Post-Soviet Russia: Legacies and Prospects*, edited by Ben Eklof, Larry Holmes, and Vera Kaplan, 272–90. London: Frank Cass, 2005.

Shilina, T. A. *Evoliutsiia zhenskogo obrazovaniia v Rossii: gosudarstvennaia politika i obshchestvennaia initsiativa (konets xviii-nachala xx vv)*. Saratov: Amirit, 2015.

Shturman, Dora. *The Soviet Secondary School*, translated by Philippe Shimrat. London: Routledge, 1988.

Sinel, Allen, *The Classroom and the Chancellery: State Educational Reform in Russia under Count Dmitry Tolstoi*. Cambridge, MA: Harvard University Press, 1973.

Sklyarova, T. V. "Orthodox Church Education in Modern Russia: Structure and Content." *Russian Education and Society* 60 (2018): 257–68.

Smith, Alison K. *For the Common Good and for Their Own Well-Being: Social Estates in Imperial Russia*. Oxford: Oxford University Press, 2014.

Starodutseva, Marina, and Irino Krivko. "The State Policy of Education in Modern Russia: Pro and Contra." *Journal of Social Sciences and Humanities* 5 (February 2015): 200–13.

Sukhova, N. Iu. *Vysshaia dukhovnaia shkola. Problemy i reform. Vtoraia polivina xix v.* Moscow: Izdatel'stvo PSTGU, 2012.

Sutherland, Jeanne. "Perestroika in the Soviet General School: From Innovation to Independence." In *Soviet Education under Perestroika*, edited by John Dunstan, 14–29. London: Routledge, 1992.

Sysoeva, E. K. *Shkola v Rossii xviii—nachala xx vv. Vlast' i obshchestvo*. Moscow: Novyi khronograf, 2015.

Szekely, Beatrice Black. "The New Soviet Education Reform." *Comparative Education Review* 30 (August 1986): 321–43.

Teshkov, V. A., and V. V. Stepanov. "Interethnc Relations and Ethnocultural Education in Russia." *Herald of the Russian Academy of Science* 87 (2017): 416–25.

Thurston, Robert W. *Liberal City, Conservative State: Moscow and Russia's Urban Crisis, 1906–1914*. Oxford: Oxford University Press, 1987.

Time, E. I. "Alma Mater." In *Sankt-Peterburgskie vyshie zhenskie (Bestuzhevskie) Kursy, 1878-1918: Sbornik statei*, edited by S.N. Valk, N. G. Sladkin, V. I. Smirnov, and M. L. Tronskaia, 227–32. Leningrad: Leningrad University Press, 1973.

Tolstoy, L. N. *Tolstoy on Education: Tolstoy's Educational Writings, 1861–62*. Edited by Alan Pinch and Michael Armstrong. Rutherford, NJ: Fairleigh Dickinson University Press, 1982.

Tomiak, J. J. *The Soviet Union: World Education Series*. Newton Abbot: David and Charles, 1972.

Troianovski, Anton, and Ellen Nakishima. "How Russia's School Children Are Recruited as Putin's Covert Muscle." *The Sydney Morning Herald*, December 30, 2018. Available online: https://www.smh.com.au/world/europe/how-russia-s-school-children-are-recruited-as-putin-s-covert-muscle-20181229-p50opd.html.

Troshkina, Tatyana N. "Reform of Russian Education and the New Law on Education of 2012." *Adam Mickewicz University Law Review* 3 (2014): 249–63.

Vaillant, Janet G. "Civic Education in a Changing Russia." In *Educational Reform in Post-Soviet Russia: Legacies and Prospects*, edited by Ben Eklof, Larry Holmes, and Vera Kaplan, 221–46. London: Frank Cass, 2005.

Valk, S. N., N. G. Sladkin, V. I. Smirnov, and M. L. Tronskaia, eds. *Sankt-Peterburgskie vyshie zhenskie (Bestuzhevskie) Kursy, 1878-1918: Sbornik Statei*. Leningrad: Leningrad University Press, 1973.

Veselov, A. N. *Professional'no-tekhnicheskoe obrazovanie v SSSR. Ocherki po istorii srednogo i nizshego protekhnobrazovanie*. Moscow: Proftekhizdat, 1961.

Vinogradov, D. V., and A. V. Zykov. "Military-Applied Means of Physical Education in Pre-University Educational Institutions of the Russian Ministry of Defense." *Obrazovanie I nauka* 21 (2019): 171–90.
Voitekhovskaia, M. P. *Politika reform i obshchestvennye initiativy v razvitii russkoi sistemy obshchego obrazovaniia v xix-nachala xx vv.* Tomsk: Tomsk gosudarstvennogo pedagogicheskogo universiteta, 2012.
Vucinich, Alexander. *Science in Russian Culture: A History to 1860.* Stanford, CA: Stanford University Press, 1963.
Vucinich, Alexander. *Science in Russian Culture: A History, 1861–1917.* Stanford, CA: Stanford University Press, 1970.
Warshofsky Lapidus, Gail. "Educational Strategies and Cultural Revolution: The Politics of Soviet Development." In *Cultural Revolution in Russia, 1928–31*, edited by Sheila Fitzpatrick, 78–104. Bloomington: Indiana University Press, 1978.
Wartenweiler, David. *Civil Society and Academic Debate in Russia, 1905–1914.* Oxford: Oxford University Press, 1999.
Webber, Stephen. *School, Reform and Society in the New Russia.* London: Macmillan Press Ltd., 2000.
Webber, Stephen, and Tatiana Webber. "Issues in Teacher Education." In *Education and Society in the New Russia*, edited by Anthony Jones, 231–59. Armonk: M.E. Sharpe, 1994.
Weiner, Douglas. "Struggle over the Soviet Future: Science Education versus Vocationalism during the 1920s." *Russian Review* 65 (January 2006): 72–97.
Whittaker, Cynthia H. "The Ideology of Sergei Uvarov: An Interpretive Essay." *The Russian Review* 37, no. 2 (April 1978): 158–76.
Whittaker, Cynthia H. *The Origins of Modern Russian Education: An Intellectual Biography of Count Sergei Uvarov, 1786–1855.* DeKalb: Northern Illinois University Press, 1984.
Wortman, Richard S. Scenarios of Power: Myth and Ceremony in Russian Monarchy, vol. 1 of *From Peter the Great to the Death of Nicholas I.* Princeton, NJ: Princeton University Press, 1995.
Wortman, Richard S. Scenarios of Power: Myth and Ceremony in Russian Monarchy, vol. 2 of *From Alexander II to the Abdication of Nicholas II.* Princeton, NJ: Princeton University Press, 2000.
Yusupova, Guzel. "Russia Is Cracking Down on Minority Languages—But a Resistance Movement Is Growing." *The Conversation*, September 11, 2018. Available online: https://theconversation.com/russia-is-cracking-down-on-minority-languages-but-a-resistance-movement-is-growing-101493.
Zacek, Judith Cohen, "The Russian Bible Society and the Russian Orthodox Church." *Church History* 35, no. 4 (December 1966): 411–37.
Zajda, Joseph I. *Education in the USSR.* Oxford: Pergamon Press, 1980.
Zamyatin, Konstantin. "The Education Reform in Russia and Its Impact on Teaching of the Minority Languages: An Effect of Nation-Building?" *Journal on Ethnopolitics and Minority Issues in Europe* 11 (2012): 17–47.
Zepper, John T. "N.K. Krupskaya on Complex Themes in Soviet Education." *Comparative Education Review* 9 (February 1965): 33–7.
Zhavoronkov, Sergey. "Two Lean Years: Russia's Budget for 2018–2020. The Russian File, Wilson Center, December 8, 2017. Available online: https://www.wilsoncenter.org/blog-post/two-lean-years-russias-budget-for-2018-2020.
Zhemukhov, Sufia, and Soiner Aktürk. "The Movement toward a Monolingual Nation in Russia: The Language Policy in Circassian Republics of the North Caucasus." *Journal of Caucasian Studies* 1 (September 2015): 33–52.

Index

Academy of Arts 13, 27
Academy of Pedagogical Sciences of the Russian Republic 160, 173–4
Academy of Sciences 10–11, 13–14, 27, 47
   foreign dominance in 11, 13
   gymnasium in 11, 14
adult education 66, 78, 110, 135, 139
Aepinus, Franz 30
Alexander I 2, 37–8, 42
   on education, 38–9
   on military education 50
   political views of 37–8
Alexander II 3, 63, 66, 85–6
Alexander III 3, 99
   political views 87
Alexis, Tsar 4
All-Russian Congress of School Construction 1929 151
All-Russian Society for Public Universities 109–10
All-Russian Union of Teachers and Education Activists 113
Anna, Empress 11–12
Artillery and Engineering Cadet Corps 28, 51
attestat 42, 101

Belorussia 35, 83, 116, 126, 132, 153, 155
Betskoi, Ivan 25–8
Bloody Sunday 102–3, 107, 112
boarding schools 28, 33, 156, 159
   girls 57, 78
   noble 34
   special education 163, 180
   Ukrainian 83
Boards of Welfare 29
   and school funding 31

Bolsheviks 3, 102, 124–5, 199
bourgeois specialists 125, 136–7, 144
Brezhnev, Leonid 158, 163, 165–6, 175
Bubnov, Andrei 137
Bushkovitch, Paul 6

cameralism 7, 10, 199
Catherine I 7, 11
Catherine II (the Great) 2, 200
   and Academy of Sciences 27
   on education 32
   and Enlightenment 23–4, 36
   as Minerva 23
certificate of maturity 93–4
Church Schism, 6
Church Slavonic 6, 15, 66, 68, 70, 88, 90
clergy 16–17, 28, 30, 32, 49, 66, 88, 99
   schooling daughters 79–80
coeducation 66, 90, 127–8, 141, 154, 156, 154, 156
collectivization 137, 140
Comenius, Johann 25
Commission of Ecclesiastical Schools 53
Commission on Public Schools 34
Committee on Higher Education 1932 150
Communist Youth League *See* Komsomol
completion rates 9, 60, 91, 100–1, 99, 118, 128–9, 135, 141, 150, 155, 159
complex method 127–8, 131, 137, 140–1
Conception of the Spiritual and Moral Upbringing of School Students 2016 191
Condillac, Etienne Bonnot de 25
Condorcet, Nicholas Marquis de 40
Constitutional Democratic Party (Kadets), 102–4
Corps of Pages 15, 50–1, 75
cultural revolution 135–40
   retreat from 143–4
curators of school districts 39, 43, 46, 66, 68–9, 76, 94, 117

Dalton Plan 128
Dashkova, Ekaterina 27
Decembrists 43–4, 50, 60
Declaration on the Unified Labor School 1918 126
defectology 145, 160
Delianov, Ivan 88, 93
  cooks' circular 91
  and higher women's courses 95
Democratic Congress of the Peoples of Russia 194
demography 35, 99, 155–6, 167, 171, 177–8, 185–6, 189
Department of the Empress Maria Feodorova 59, 78, 85, 96, 101
Department of Schools 145
Dewey, John 127
discipline 10, 26, 31–2, 40, 46, 145–6, 153–4, 173
  in church seminaries 17
duma 3, 48, 104–5, 114

Ecclesiastical Regulation, 16–17, 20
education 1, 34, 64–5, 85
  and cameralism 20
  limitations on 19–20
  and military conscription 75, 88–9
  purposes of 2, 201
  western influences on 6, 15–16, 18–19, 25, 64, 68, 127–8, 140
Eklof, Ben 119
Elizabeth, Empress 13, 23
Enlightenment 25, 32
  and Catherine II 23–4
estates 1–2, 47, 85, 100
  all-estate principle 35

faculty councils 45, 68, 94, 107, 117
Farquharson, Henry 8
Federal State Standards of General Education 2009 191
Fénelon, François 25
Feodor, Tsar 4
First World War 3, 120–3
Foreign Quarter 5
foreigners 5–6, 11–13
  and Russian education 6, 12, 15, 18–19, 60–1
foundling homes 25–6, 36, 56

Fourth Section of the Imperial Chancellery 59, 78, 81, 85

General Statute for the Education of Youth of Both Sexes 1764 28
General Statute on Military Educational Institutions 1830 50–1
girls 21, 29, 35–6, 44, 52, 57–9, 78, 90–1, 128, 158, 200
  communist support for 141, 151, 167
  pensions for 55
  schools for 78–9, 96
glasnost' 64, 172, 174, 176, 195
Golitsyn, Aleksandr 42–3
Golovnin, Aleksandr 66
Gorbachev, Mikhail 3, 144, 171, 176
  on education 173
  political views of 172
governesses 33–4, 36, 55–7, 58, 78, 101
Great Reforms 3, 64, 120
Grimm, Melchior 29–30

History 145, 165
  Putin on 192–3
higher technical institutes 98–9, 163–4
Holy Synod 16, 42, 52, 68, 76, 79–80, 87, 115
home schooling 13, 18–19, 33, 55–7, 179
  regulation of 19, 56
Honorable Mirror of Youth 7

Iagodin, Gennadi 174
Ignat'ev, Pavel 117
Il'minskii, Nicholas 84, 116–17, 166
Imperial Educational Institution and Hospital 1763 25–6
Imperial Medical-Surgical Academy 51, 81–2, 85
Imperial Russian Technological Society 78, 98, 107, 111
Inorodtsy See non-Russians
inspectors of schools 31–2, 34, 39, 46, 54, 69–70, 74, 77, 94–5, 105, 114–15, 130, 115, 183
Institutki 58, 61
Intelligentsia 3, 60
  on peasant reading 119–20

Jankovich de Mirjevo, Fedor 30-1
Jesuits 6, 18
Jews 94, 100

Kasso, Lev 108, 117
Katkov, Mikhaill 68, 74
Kazan Missionary Congress 1910 117
Khrushchev, Nikita 156-8, 166, 197
Kiev Latin Academy 6
Kirkpatrick, William Hearst 127
Komsomol 130-1, 132, 134, 141, 145-6, 164-5, 173-4, 182
  criticism of secondary school by 136
korenizatsiia 166, 169, 193
Korf, Nicholas 71
Krupskaia, Nadezhda 126-7, 131, 136-7, 144
kruzhok 94
Kurbatov, Aleksei 8
kuristy 96
Kutuzov, Mikhail 49

Lancaster system 51
Law of God 43, 49, 54-5, 58, 66, 68, 69-70, 77, 79, 89, 199
Law on Education 1992 178-80, 181, 195, 196
Law on Education 2012 187
Learned Guard 11
Legislative Commission 28
  and education 28-9
Lenin, Vladimir 69, 120, 124-5, 136
  on education 126,
  on language of study 165-7
  on technology 132
libraries 10-11, 53, 98, 105, 120, 129
Ligachev, Yegor 175
literacy 10, 90-1, 99-100, 118-20, 130, 139, 141, 151, 200
  committees of 110-11, 120
Locke, John 25
Lomonosov, Mikhail 11, 14, 15, 23
lubok 119
Lunacharskii, Anotoli 126, 135, 137

Magnitskii, Leonti 8
Magnitskii, Mikhail 43
Main Administration for Labor Reserves 152-3

Main Pedagogical Institute 41, 46, 72
Main School Administration 31, 39
Makarenko, Anton 128-9, 153-4
Mariia Feodorvna, Empress 58-9, 200
Marx, Karl 126-7, 136
Marxism-Leninism 135, 155, 157, 160, 165, 167-9
Medical Institute for Women 96, 108
Mensheviks, 102, 124
merchants 1, 5, 18, 23, 35, 55-6
  attitude to schooling of 9, 34, 48, 61, 101
  schools for 33-4, 44, 69, 78, 106
Mikhail, Tsar 88
Miliutin, Dmitrii 75
  and women's education 80-1
Ministry of Ecclesiastical Affairs and Public Instruction 42
Ministry of Finance 49, 94, 97-8, 112
Ministry of Higher Education 163
Ministry of National Enlightenment 2
  under Alexander I 38, 42-3
  under Alexander II 65, 67-8, 75, 79, 81, 83-4, 85
  under Alexander III 88, 94-5, 97-8
  under Nicholas I 46, 51, 52, 57, 61
  under Nicholas II 104-6, 112, 115-6, 117, 123
Ministry of State Properties 49
Ministry of Trade and Industry 108
Ministry of War 51, 80
moral upbringing See *vospitanie*
Moscow Society for the Dissemination of Technical Knowledge 78, 107
Münnich, Christian-Wilhelm, von 12

Narkompros 126-7, 129, 131-2, 134-8, 141, 144, 147-8, 153-4, 156
Naval Academy 8-9, 11, 15
Naval Cadet Corps 15, 51, 75
Naval School 75
New Economic Policy (NEP) 125, 129, 136, 140
Nicholas I 2, 37-8, 43, 63
  on education 44
  on military education 50-1
  political views of 38, 44
Nicholas II 3, 87, 89, 99, 103, 118, 120, 123
  on education 88
  political views of 88

nihilism 63–4
nobility 7, 23, 47
  attitudes to education 20, 27–8, 35, 41–2, 56, 71, 101
  boarding schools for 34
  education requirements of 12–13, 41–2
  language 56, 60–1
  pensions for 40–2, 47
Nobles Land Cadet Corps 12–13, 15, 20, 27–8, 35, 49–51, 75
Nobles Pension 42
Nobles Regiment 50
non-Russians 29, 35, 116, 165–7, 176, 179, 193–5
  and education 82–4, 194
  and nationalism 169, 195
  Il'minskii method 84, 116–17
  natural method 116–17
  in western regions 82–3, 116, 167
Norov, Avraam 65
Novodevichy Institute for Girls of the Third Estate 27, 36

Obrazovanie 2, 61
Obuchenie 2
Octobrist Children's Organization 146, 164–5, 173–4
Octobrist Party 102
Old Believers 6, 52, 90
On the Duties of Man and Citizens 30, 35, 40, 42
Orthodox Church 5–6, 33, 52, 181, 191, 196
  academies of 16, 32, 53, 99, 182
  and Russian Bible Society 42–3
  seminarians 17, 31, 33, 54, 76, 99, 101, 111
    alienation of 60–1, 63
    as teachers 20, 52, 111, 115
  seminaries of 16–17, 20–1, 52–3, 60, 61, 76, 101, 182
  funding of 53, 76
  reform of 99
  schools of 182
  Sunday schools of 181–2
  universities of 182

parents 12, 31, 37, 47, 55–6, 90, 101, 131, 148–9, 158, 168, 189
  attitudes to schooling 10, 17, 29, 54, 91, 98, 101, 105, 128, 132, 143–4, 147, 166, 171, 183, 191, 195, 200–1
  committees and councils 66, 93, 106, 112, 123, 157, 173–4, 179
  and daughters 29, 36, 118
  and language 194
  and teachers 74, 115, 128, 145, 148
  participation rates 35, 61, 91, 118–19, 128, 141, 158–9, 167, 196
Paul I, 37–8, 49
Peasant Union 113–14
peasants
  attitudes to education 21, 41, 49, 61, 74–5, 85, 90–1, 113, 128
  tastes in reading 119–20
  and teachers 110, 113
pedagogical councils 67–8, 69–70, 93, 106, 112, 179
pedagogy 31, 35–6, 40–1, 46, 65, 70–1, 77, 93, 200
  colleges of 160–1, 183
  courses in 72, 85, 115, 133, 155
  institutes of 41, 72, 115, 133, 140, 160–1, 183
  Soviet 127, 129, 137, 160
  training in 40, 46, 72, 79, 115, 161–2
Pedogogy of Cooperation 173, 195
pedology 125, 136, 145, 163
People's Commissariat for National Enlightenment *See* Narkompros
perestroika 172–3, 195
Permanent Council of Military Schools 50
Peter I (the Great) 2, 5, 9, 20, 47
  and cameralism 7
  on education 6–8
  and Orthodox Church, 16
  and schools for girls 21
Peter II 11
Peter III 23
Petrograd Soviet 124
Pirogov, Nicholas 65, 78, 126
Platon, Father 32
Pobedonostsev, Konstantin 87, 91, 99
  on education 88
poll tax 1–2, 41
popular culture 119–20
populism 64
Praktiki 138

Production Training Combine 172
Progressive Bloc 120
project method 127, 141
Prokopovich, Feofan 11, 16, 32
Protasov, Nikolai 53-4
Provisional Government 3, 123-4
Putin, Vladimir 3, 178, 184, 189-90, 201
  opposition to 196-7
  political views of 184-5, 196, 199

rabfaks 134-5, 137
Raeff, Marc 35
raznochintsy 21
rectors of universities 39, 45, 56, 68, 94-5, 117, 134, 164
Regulation on Church-Parish Schools 1884 88
Regulation on Elementary Schools 1864 66
Richilieu Lyceum 42
Rousseau, Jean Jacques 25
Runich, D. P. 43
Russian Bible Society 42-3
Russian Lyceum 42
Russian Social Democratic Party 102
Russification 116

Saint Hilaire, Joseph de 8-9
school boards 66-7, 69, 88
school conditions 41, 114, 129, 153, 167-8, 174, 182
school fees 29, 32, 41, 55, 64, 66, 70, 79, 81-2, 91, 94, 100, 70, 81, 94, 131, 180-1, 189
school funding 8, 29-30, 31, 40-1, 44, 47, 59-60, 70-2, 79, 89, 98, 100, 104-5, 131, 139, 174, 180, 182, 185-6, 195, 199-200
School of Mathematics and Navigation 8, 15
schools 61, 99-100, 118, 153, 155
  agricultural 97, 156
  appanage 49, 66
  boarding 180
    Tsarist 29, 34
    girls 57
    Soviet 156-7
  church-parish 52, 66, 88-90
  cipher 9
  commercial 29, 48, 93-4, 98

diocesan 9, 79-80
district 39-41, 44, 46, 48-9, 52, 54, 57, 61, 67, 69-70, 72-3
factory 19, 77, 140
factory-plant apprenticeship (FZU) 132-3, 137-8, 149, 152-3, 159
factory seven-year 132, 139
garrison 9, 13, 21, 29, 35, 51
gymnasiums 10, 14-15, 29, 39-40, 44 60, 66, 75, 85, 93, 100-1, 106, 117, 129, 187
  criticism of 91
  curriculum in 29, 44, 48-9, 94
  girls in 57, 78-9, 96, 101
  private 77, 101, 106
  real 67-8, 69-70, 85, 93
Islamic 84
land survey 29
literacy 65-6, 74-5, 88-9, 90
  legalization of 88
labor reserve 153, 155, 159
lyceum 50, 174, 179, 187-8
major 30-2, 35, 39
military 35, 50, 51, 75, 162-3
  academy 75
  gymnasiums 75
  military colony 51
  Military Music 162-3
  Nakhimov 162, 192
  Suvorov 162, 192
minor 30-1, 35-6, 39
mining 77, 19
model 70
municipal 70-1, 73, 98, 100, 114, 118
normal 31, 66
parish 28, 39-40, 41, 44, 48, 52, 55, 57, 61, 66-7, 70, 76, 78, 83, 88-91, 100, 104-5, 110, 117
peasant (collective farm) youth 133, 138-9
pensions 19, 33, 40-2, 47, 54-5, 56, 79, 109, 177
polytechnical 126, 144, 156
  incomplete secondary labor 157
private 17-20, 33-4, 55, 76-7, 101, 116, 179-80
  regulation of 19, 34 54-6, 76-7, 183
professional and technical (PTU) 159-60, 172, 175, 180

profile 179
real 69–70, 75, 97–8, 100, 117, 129
Realschule 48
Russian 10
secondary specialist (SSUZ) 160
special 145, 157, 163, 177, 180, 187
Stakhonovite 150
Sunday 66, 78, 101, 110, 181–2
technical, 48, 66, 78, 85, 97, 117, 120, 132–3
technicums 126, 132–3, 138–40, 141, 149–51, 157, 180, 188
women in 97, 133, 141
unified labor 125–6, 129
criticism of 131, 135–7
urban 28–9, 48, 98, 105, 114, 118, 133, 154
village 29, 49, 80
vocational 19–20, 77, 85, 97–8, 105, 107, 138, 144, 149, 168, 175, 180, 188
governance of 98
volost' 49, 52
School Production Mastery Workshops (UPMs) 155
Second World War 152–5, 168
Shishkov, Aleksandr 43
Shulgin, V. N. 136–8, 143–4
Sketes 52
Skhodka 94
Slavic-Greek-Latin Academy 6, 11, 15
Slavophiles 60
Smolnyi Institute for Noble Girls 26–7, 36
Socialist Revolutionary Party 102, 113, 124
Society of Women Educators and Teachers 111
Stalin, Josef 3, 125, 136, 144, 147, 155–6, 158, 167
on education of girls 154
on non-Russian education 166
Standard Rules for Students 1985 173
State Committee for National Education of the Soviet Union 174
State Committee for Professional and Technical Education 159
State Committee for Science and Higher Education 181

State Council 66, 104–6, 117
State Duma 3, 103–4, 105, 108, 120
education legislation by 104–5, 114–15, 117
of Russian Federation 178
Statute for the United Labor School 1923 130
Statute of the Schools of the Vilna School District 1803 39
Statute on Church Schools 1814 52
Statute on Church Schools 1902 89
Statute on Domestic Teachers and Tutors 1834 56
Statute on Elementary Education 1874 69
Statute on Gymnasiums 1871 69
Statute on Gymnasiums and Pro-gymnasiums 1864 67–8, 74
Statute on Municipal Schools 1872 70–1
Statute on Public Education 1786 30, 34–5
Statute on Real Schools 1872 69
Statute on Schools 1804 39–40
Statute on Schools 1828 44
Statute on the Education of Noble Girls 1764 26
Statute on Universities 1835 45
Statute on Universities 1863 68
Statute on Universities 1884 94
Stolypin, Piotr 103–4
Strategy on Development of Upbringing in the Russian Federation 191–2
studenchestvo 94, 107–8
students 151–2
aspirations of 168, 171, 189
protests by 63–4, 68, 94–5, 101–2, 107–8
social composition of 13, 20, 35, 41–2, 47–8, 50–1, 58, 64, 68, 73, 82, 85, 88, 100, 107–8, 111, 119, 133–4, 137, 141, 144, 148–9, 168
Supreme Soviet of the National Economy *See* Vesenkha
Sytin, Ivan 120

Table of Ranks 7, 12, 14, 20, 27, 41–2
and students 34, 45, 50, 67–8
and teachers 27, 31, 39
and women 96, 109
Tatishchev, Vasili 11, 19

teachers 6, 26, 30, 40, 70, 90, 93, 105–6, 110–16, 128, 137, 146, 147–9, 151, 160–2, 183–4, 186, 195, 200
   conditions of 31, 74, 93, 111, 114–16, 139–140, 148
   congresses 74, 85, 112
   and feminization of 110–1, 168, 187, 200
   institutes 41, 72, 106, 129
   manuals 31
   mutual aid 112
   and peasants 110, 113
   salaries 40, 44, 58, 66, 74, 79, 111, 114, 129, 162, 172, 184, 187
   seminaries 72–3, 85, 106, 115, 129
   shortages of 9, 31, 41, 72, 96, 106, 115, 129, 133, 147, 155, 166
   status of 46, 74–5, 111, 129, 162, 184
   on Table of Ranks 34
   tensions among 113–14
   training of 31, 41, 46, 56, 66, 72, 79, 85, 96, 101, 106, 115, 129–30, 140, 147–8, 160, 168, 173, 183, 186–7
   unions 112–13, 173
technical minimal circles 149–50
Third Element 73, 89
thousanders 137
Tolstoi, Dmitrii 68–9, 73, 88
   on Church reform 76
   and women's education 80–2
Tolstoi, Leo 65, 73, 120
trustees 67, 69, 74, 95, 106, 115
tutors 5, 18–19, 33–4, 54–6, 76, 96, 101, 111, 164
   regulation of 19, 34, 55–6

Ukraine 5–6, 28, 35, 82–3, 116, 126, 132, 136, 153, 167, 193–4
Uniate Church 6
Unified State Examination 188
Union of Zemstvos and Towns 120
United Nobility 104
universities 45, 60, 68, 94–5, 131, 133–5, 138, 150–1, 158, 163–4, 180–1, 188–9
   autonomy of 39, 45, 107–8, 134–5
   Kazan' 43
   Moscow, 35, 45
      founding of 14–15

   professors in 13, 39, 41, 43, 45, 134, 140
   training of 45, 135, 150–1, 155
   Shaniavskii Peoples' 108–9, 135
   St. Petersburg 45
   St. Vladimir 46
   Vilna 39, 45
Ushinskii, Konstantin 65, 70–1, 73, 116, 126
   on education of women 78
   on vocational education 77
Uvarov, Sergei 46–8
   and Academy of Sciences 47
   on education 47–8

Vannovskii, Piotr 93–4
Vesenkha 135, 137
volost' 64
vospitanie 2
   communist 148, 164–5, 173, 176, 199
   imperial 30, 35, 61, 66, 85
   Russian Federation 189–93, 196
vydvizhenie 134, 136
   and social mobility 141, 144

War Communism 125, 136
War Industries Committee 120
Westernizers 60
Wolff, Christian 10
women 2–3, 21, 26, 27, 61, 68, 78, 85, 96, 108–9, 167, 200
   campaign for higher education for 80–1
   doctors 82, 96
   faculties of law and medicine 108–9, 117
   higher courses 3, 81, 85, 95–6, 108–9, 135, 200
      Alarchinskie 81
      Bestushevskiie 81–2, 95–6, 108
      Guerrier 81
      Lubianskie 81
   as moral anchors 35–6, 57–8, 79
   occupational limits on 96, 101, 107, 111
Women's Pedagogical Institute 1903 96, 101
Wortman, Richard 7

Yeltsin, Boris 176–8
Young Army 192
Young Pioneers 130–1, 136, 146, 157, 164, 173–4, 182, 192

zemstvo 64, 85, 89, 100, 104–5, 110
   congresses 74
   inspectors 69
   schools of 70, 71–2
   teacher training of 73
   vocational schools 97

www.ingramcontent.com/pod-product-compliance
Lightning Source LLC
Chambersburg PA
CBHW041730300426
44115CB00021B/2967